THE SOCIAL THOUGHT OF SAINT BONAVENTURE
A Study in Social Philosophy

THE CATHOLIC UNIVERSITY OF AMERICA
PHILOSOPHICAL SERIES
VOLUME XCIII

THE SOCIAL THOUGHT OF SAINT BONAVENTURE

A STUDY IN SOCIAL PHILOSOPHY

BY

MATTHEW M. DE BENEDICTIS, O.F.M., M.A.
PRIEST OF THE IMMACULATE CONCEPTION PROVINCE

A DISSERTATION

SUBMITTED TO THE FACULTY OF THE SCHOOL OF PHILOSOPHY
OF THE CATHOLIC UNIVERSITY OF AMERICA IN PARTIAL
FULFILLMENT OF THE REQUIREMENTS FOR THE
DEGREE OF DOCTOR OF PHILOSOPHY

GREENWOOD PRESS, PUBLISHERS
WESTPORT, CONNECTICUT

DISCARD

E.K.C.C. LIBRARY

Library of Congress Cataloging in Publication Data

De Benedictis, Matthew M   1914-
   The social thought of Saint Bonaventure.

   Original ed., issued as v. 93 of the Catholic
University of America philosophical series.
   Originally presented as the author's thesis, Catholic
University of America, 1946.
   Bibliography: p.
   1. Bonaventura, Saint, Cardinal, 1221-1274.
2. Sociology, Christian (Catholic) 3. Social ethics.
I. Title. II. Series: Catholic University of
America. Philosophical studies, v. 93.
B765.B74D4 1972   189'.4   73-138108
ISBN 0-8371-5684-X

Imprimi Potest:
VIRGILIUS LIUCCI, O.F.M.
   Minister Provincialis.

Nihil Obstat:
IGNATIUS SMITH, O.P., Ph.D.,
   Censor Deputatus.

Imprimatur:
✠ MICHAEL J. CURLEY, D.D.,
   Archiepiscopus Baltimorensis et Washingtonensis.
Baltimorae, die 6 Aprilis, 1946.

Originally published in 1946 by The Catholic University
of America Press, Washington, D.C.

Reprinted with the permission of Matthew De Benedictis.

Reprinted in 1972 by Greenwood Press,
A division of Congressional Information Service, Inc.
88 Post Road West, Westport, Connecticut 06881

Library of Congress catalog card number 73-138108
ISBN 0-8371-5684-X

Printed in the United States of America

10 9 8 7 6 5 4 3

To
the Memory
of
My Mother

PREFACE

In this day of social upheavals, when the problems of social life affect men so vitally, it is most opportune that we return to the great systems of thought elaborated in the Middle Ages by the scholastic writers. In so doing, we do not presume to ask of these thinkers the precise solution to the problems peculiar to our own day and age. Instead we seek to ferret out from the writings of those great masters of the past the fundamental doctrines of social thought—those general principles necessary for all true, peaceful, and harmonious social life; those general principles which will enable the modern mind to face and solve the problems that beset our day. To those who would protest that a return to medieval philosophy is a·step backward, we need only to point out that Truth is eternal—that fundamental principles are immutable, timeless.

Mindful, therefore, of the paternal admonition of the Supreme Pontiff, Leo XIII, who in his letter *Quod Universa* places St. Thomas and St. Bonaventure side by side and urges the students of Thomistic Philosophy not to neglect the writings of the Seraphic Doctor, we intend to look into the doctrines of this great shining light of the Scholastic Era, St. Bonaventure, in order to bring to light the social thought of the Franciscan Saint, Doctor, and Cardinal.

This treatise is an endeavour to present a clear and concise statement of St. Bonaventure's teaching on the major questions of social philosophy. Our purpose is to examine the various writings of the saintly Doctor, to enter into the spirit that pervades all his work, and to set forth the principal details of his doctrine in the form of an objective exposition. It is not our intention, however, to institute a comparison between the Seraphic Doctor and any of his predecessors, contemporaries, or successors, but simply to try to determine and to state, as faithfully as we can, his social thought. The method employed is an objective study of the works of St. Bonaventure contained in the critical edition published by the Franciscan Fathers of the College of St. Bonaventure, Quaracchi, 1882–1902.

In the present study an effort has been made to place the social thought of the Franciscan Doctor in its proper setting. In other words, an attempt has been made not to isolate his social teaching from the general trend of his philosophical, theological, and mystical writings. In a work of this type it is imperative not to concentrate upon one section of an author's teaching to the exclusion of all others, for failure to take into account his doctrine in its entirety prevents one from grasping the author's genuine teaching. Besides, we propose to interpret Bonaventurean thought in the light of Bonaventure himself.

While we have a great deal of literature that rightfully seeks to discover to the modern mind the sublime treasures left to posterity by the Angelical Doctor, St. Thomas Aquinas, in his treatment of the various social questions, very little work has been done in this field with the doctrines of St. Bonaventure. The subject has been touched upon briefly by Drs. F. Imle,[1] and C. Nölkensmeier.[2] The most extensive treatise directly concerned with the social teaching of St. Bonaventure is: *Essai sur la Philosophie Sociale du Docteur Seraphique* by Dr. H. Legowicz.[3] This study by Legowicz is in most respects an excellent treatment of the subject, and we are gratefully cognizant of the extent of our debt to him for the constant and valuable assistance offered by his essay, of which we have made abundant use in our present study. Nevertheless, the otherwise scholarly writing of Legowicz leaves one with the impression that he has at times, by distorting the Bonaventurean text,[4] constrained the

---

[1] "Sozialuntersciede und Sozialausgleich nach dem hl. Bonaventura," *Franziskanische Studien*, XIX (1932), pp. 81–98, and "Die Gemeinschaftsidee in der Theologie des hl. Bonaventura," *Franziskanische Studien*, XVII (1930), pp. 325–341.

[2] "Ethische Grundfragen bei Bonaventura," *Forschungen zur Geschichte der Philosophie und der Pädagogik*, Band V, Heft 2, Leipzig, 1932.

[3] Published by Galley & Cie, Fribourg (Suisse), 1936.

[4] Although Legowicz, *op. cit.*, p. 11, claims that it is necessary, because Bonaventure has not left us an *ex-professo* treatise on social philosophy, to take the text out of the context, and confesses to the danger that is joined

Seraphic Doctor to affirm things he had no intention of affirming and that, consequently, he has departed from true Bonaventurean thought.

Finally, in a work of this kind, dedicated to so broad and comprehensive a subject, it is plainly impossible to do more than lay down the general trends. Needless to say, then, this study does not pretend to exhaust the potentialities of our topic. It is not our intention to delve into any single question, but simply to examine the more important phases in the social thought of St. Bonaventure, and to enunciate them clearly and concisely.

The publication of this dissertation affords the author the opportunity to express his sincerest gratitude to all those who have made possible and have encouraged his graduate studies. A special word of appreciation is extended to his Very Reverend

---

to this manner of proceeding, nevertheless it is our opinion that he has overdone it. Witness, for instance, ft. 679, p. 193, where he distorts the Bonaventurean text to read as follows: "... homo ex prima sua conditione ordinatus est ad ... operationem," whereas the actual text of St. Bonaventure is the following: "Quod ergo objicitur, quod homo ex prima sua conditione ordinatus est ad istam operationem; dicendum, quod nullus homo debet esse sine labore in hac vita, ne forte dicatur quod de reprobis dicitur in Psalmo: in labore hominum non sunt et cum hominibus non flagellabuntur; sed ex hoc non sequitur, quod oportet occupari circa laborem manuum et maxime lucrativum." *Q. D. De Perf. Evan.*, q. 2, a. 3, ad 1, 2, V, p. 162. Surely this mode of procedure is not conducive to an exposition of Bonaventure's actual teaching.

Furthermore, in the same footnote we meet with still another and more serious defect—namely, that of using Bonaventure's objections as his actual teaching. Compare this footnote with *Q. D. De Perf. Evan.*, q. 2, a. 3, ob. 1, V, p. 156.

Yet another point which leads one to discredit Legowicz's work, even though fundamentally it is a good exposition of Bonaventure's teaching, is the fact that he attributes to Bonaventure words that Bonaventure never wrote. Thus, e.g., in his chapter on Marriage, *op. cit.*, pp. 161–183, we find at least ten places in which he refers the text of Peter of Lombard as the text of the Seraphic Doctor. Compare ft. 566, p. 166, with IV (of Quaracchi edition), p. 728; ft. 596, p. 173, with IV, p. 672; ft. 603, pp. 174–175, with IV, p. 687; ft. 608, p. 176, with IV, p. 706; ft. 612, p. 177, with IV, p. 713; ft. 613, p. 177, with IV, p. 713; ft. 613, p. 177, with IV, p. 714; ft. 614, p. 177, with IV, p. 713; ft. 615, p. 178, with IV, p. 714; ft. 617, p. 178, with IV, p. 713; and ft. 631, p. 181, with IV, p. 744.

Superiors for the valued opportunity to attend the Catholic University of America. To Very Reverend Doctor Ignatius Smith, O.P., Dean of the School of Philosophy, under whose supervision this work was written, he offers special thanks for constant inspiration and valuable suggestions. To Right Reverend Monsignor Fulton J. Sheen and the Reverend Doctors William J. McDonald and Robert J. Slavin, O.P., he is indebted for their careful reading of the manuscript and their helpful criticisms. He likewise desires to acknowledge his gratitude to his confrere, Reverend Luke M. Ciampi, O.F.M., for his many suggestions to make this work more readable. Finally, abiding appreciation is hereby expressed to the many other confreres and friends for their countless kindnesses and continual encouragement.

TABLE OF CONTENTS

xi

CHAPTER I

THE SOURCES AND NATURE OF ST. BONAVEN-
TURE'S SOCIAL THOUGHT

In order to arrive at a true understanding of an author and his doctrine, it is necessary to examine the various forces that have exerted influence upon his character and mind, for no thinker can be entirely unaffected by that which has preceded him or that which is contemporaneous. It is obvious, therefore, that we cannot hope to appreciate the social thought of the Seraphic Doctor unless we know the sources from which he has acquired his doctrine. Moreover, in considering a definite or particular phase of an author's teaching we cannot neglect his doctrine in general, especially the purpose of his various studies and writings. For this reason it would seem imperative that we have some idea of the nature of St. Bonaventure's doctrine in general before setting out to explain his thoughts on the social order in particular. Accordingly, the purpose of this chapter is to present, as succinctly as possible, (1) the sources used by St. Bonaventure, (2) the nature of his doctrine in general, and (3) the main theme of his social thought.

ARTICLE I. THE SOURCES

The Seraphic Doctor has assigned four groups of books as the sources of knowledge. In the use of these books, he has established a precise order to be observed always—and so has manifested the importance he ascribes to each group. Before all others he places the inspired books of the Bible; second in order of importance are those which he classifies as the *originalia Sanctorum*—namely, the writings of the Fathers; next are the *Commentaries on the Sentences* and the *Theological Summas;* and in the last and least important place appear the writings of secular authors, or the works of the philosophers.[1] Following

---

[1] "Sunt ergo quatuor genera scripturarum, circa quae oportet ordinate

1

this outline, we can distinguish five main sources in the writings of the Seraphic Doctor. They are:—first, the inspired books of both the Old and the New Testaments; second, St. Augustine and, together with him, the various Neo-Platonic writers; third, the writings of the Fathers and, through them, the various authors of Graeco-Roman philosophy; fourth, the scholastics; and last, but not least, the Seraphic Father, St. Francis of Assisi. These, then, are the main sources from which St. Bonaventure derived his doctrines and, consequently, also his social thought. It will be our duty to investigate each of these and attempt to determine how important a role each has played in influencing his social doctrine.

SECTION 1.   SACRED SCRIPTURE

It is in the inspired books of Sacred Scripture that St. Bonaventure places the highest authority. The use of the Bible throughout his different writings is indeed great. To verify this fact, we need only refer to the work of the Editors of Quaracchi, who have faithfully recorded and indexed the numerous passages quoted by the Seraphic Doctor.[2]   The knowledge of the Scriptures is for Bonaventure the only delectable knowledge.[3] His reverence for Holy Writ is so penetrating that it translates itself into the sublimest notions we have on the subject.[4]

As regards his social thought, the Sacred Scriptures have influenced his mind concerning the creation, the order that exists in the universe, and his hierarchical teaching (i.e., that man is ordained for God, and all inferior creatures for man). This scriptural influence is felt once again in his considerations on the dignity, the liberty, and the end of man. Perhaps the greatest

---

exerceri. Primi libri sunt sacrae Scripturae. . . . Secundi libri sunt originalia Sanctorum; tertii, Sententiae magistrorum; quarti, doctrinarum mundalium sive philosophorum." *In Hex.,* coll. 19, n. 6, V, p. 421.

The writings of St. Bonaventure will always be quoted according to the critical edition published by the Franciscan Fathers of the College of St. Bonaventure, Quaracchi, 1882–1902.

[2] *Opera Omnia,* X, pp. 181ss.

[3] *In Hex.,* coll. 17, n. 7, V, p. 410.

[4] *Brev.,* prologus, V, pp. 201–208. Cf. L. Wegemer, O.F.M., " St. Bonaventure, the Seraphic Doctor," *Franciscan Studies,* II (1924), pp. 13–15.

influence has been exerted by the doctrine of the Mystical Body and the command of Christ-like charity. Indeed, it is upon the doctrine of the Mystical Body that he bases his organic and hierarchical conception of society; and it is the command of charity that he makes the crowning point of all his social considerations. Therefore, we may rightly and truthfully affirm that the authority of the Holy Bible is so preeminent in the opinion of St. Bonaventure that its influence on his mind cannot be exaggerated.

SECTION 2. ST. AUGUSTINE AND NEO-PLATONISTS

A. St. Augustine

After the inspired books our Saint attaches the greatest moment to the writings of the Bishop of Hippo. Regarding the influence of St. Augustine on the writings of the Seraphic Doctor there is no doubt, for almost all are agreed as to the Augustinian character of his writings.[5] It is necessary to emphasize that Bonaventure understood, admired, and made his own the doctrinal legacy of St. Augustine; that he fashioned this into a system deserving of the greatest praise. His quotations from St. Augustine are very numerous, next in number to his quotations from Holy Writ.[6] What attracted St. Bonaventure was not simply that Augustine was one of the Fathers of the Church, but that in him Bonaventure saw the synthesis of science and wisdom. In this connection let us recall the words that he uses in his sermon, *Christus unus omnium Magister:*

> "And therefore it seems that, amongst the philosophers, the gift of wisdom was given to Plato, to Aristotle, however, the gift of science. . . . Both gifts, however, i.e.,

---

[5] Tinivella, "De Impossibili Sapientiae Adeptione in Philosophia Pagana juxta Collationes in Hexaemeron S. Bonaventurae," *Antonianum*, XI (1936), Rome, p. 31, ft. 1, and p. 283, ft. 3. For Bonaventure's own testimony of his Augustinianism we refer the reader to the article of Fr. Ludger Meier, O.F.M., "Bonaventuras Selbstzeugnis über seinem Augustinismus," *Franziskanische Studien*, XVII (1930), Münster, pp. 342–355.

[6] *Opera Omnia*, X, pp. 267–269.

of wisdom and of science, were given to Augustine by the Holy Ghost." [7]

We find in these two thinkers a oneness of thought, the origin of which is to be sought in the depths of their love of God and of creatures. It was St. Augustine's *De Civitate Dei* that found an echo in St. Bonaventure's social doctrine. It was this work which led him to the consideration of the eternal and the temporal, of the spiritual and the material elements in the universal terrestrial hierarchy. It was this work, too, that gave him his concept of order. Accordingly, we may say that the *City of God* is the one source which, after Sacred Scripture, imparted most to Bonaventurean social thought.

B. Neo-Platonists

Moreover, from the Bishop of Hippo the Seraphic Doctor received his respect for Plato, since St. Augustine shows a distinct preference for Plato over Aristotle. [8] As we shall point out, St. Bonaventure was, besides, a conservative and a follower of the old scholasticism, which was Neo-Platonic in tendency and character. Plato, however, we must remember, was introduced to the Middle Ages—and, therefore, also to St. Bonaventure— more through the instrumentality of St. Augustine and the Neo-Platonists than through his own Dialogues. [9] What St. Bonaventure actually knew of Plato was almost entirely taken from the writings of St. Augustine and others. Indeed, the thirteenth century scholastics had only a fragment of the *Timaeus* in the translation of Cicero and Chalcidius and a few copies of the *Phaedo* and the *Meno* translated by Henricus Aristippus. Besides,

---

[7] " Et ideo videtur, quod inter philosophos datus sit Platoni sermo sapientiae, Aristoteli vero sermo scientiae. . . . Uterque autem sermo, scilicet sapientiae et scientiae, per Spiritum Sanctum datus est Augustino. . . ." nn. 18–19, V, p. 572.

[8] *De Civitate Dei*, 1. VIII, c. 12, *P.L.*, 41, 236–237.

[9] M. De Wulf, *History of Mediaeval Philosophy* (Third English edition based on sixth French edition, translated by Ernest C. Messenger, London, Longmans, 1935, 1938), I, p. 15.

the *Timaeus,* obscure in itself, was rendered still more ambiguous by the commentaries of Chalcidius.[10]

With regard to the Neo-Platonists who helped to mold the social doctrines of St. Bonaventure, there are four especially to be recorded. They are Plotinus, Macrobius, Cicero, and the Pseudo-Dionysius. While St. Bonaventure makes ample mention of Plotinus as one of his sources, he could not have used the latter as a *direct* source, because the *Enneads* of Plotinus were unknown in the Middle Ages. As a matter of fact, though the Scholastics in general refer to the various tenets of Plotinus, they do not quote directly from him, but from the writings of Macrobius.[11] It must also be remembered that Macrobius, though substantially retaining the thought of Plotinus, altered it a bit, by adding to it both from Porphyry and from his own teaching.[12] The scholastics, unaware of this fact, thought that in quoting from Macrobius they were using genuine Plotinian teaching.[13] An example of this point appears in that section' of the *Collationes in Hexaemeron* where, after a long citation from the *Somnium Scipionis* of Macrobius on the Plotinian division of the virtues, Bonaventure concludes, "Hucusque Plotinus."[14] Therefore, we must contend that it is from Plotinus *indirectly* and from Macrobius *directly* that he acquires this division of the virtues which appears in various other sections of his writings.[15]

That Cicero is another source of Neo-Platonic teaching is apparent from the way the Seraphic Doctor praises his exemplar ideas and adopts his definitions of the cardinal virtues.[16] Pseudo-Dionysius, the Areopagite (as the supposed disciple of the Apostle), likewise wielded considerable force in molding the

---

[10] *Ibid.,* p. 64. Cf. Tinivella, *op. cit.,* p. 287.

[11] M. De Wulf, *op. cit.,* I, p. 15, ft. 1; Van Lieshout, *La Theorie Plotinienne de la Vertu,* Fribourg, 1926, pp. 125–127, 137–180, especially p. 125, where he states: "les oeuvres de Plotin étant inconnues."

[12] Van Lieshout, *op. cit.,* pp. 117–121.

[13] *Ibid.,* pp. 125–127. Cf. Tinivella, *op. cit.,* pp. 289–290.

[14] *In Hex.,* coll. 6, nn. 29–32, V, p. 364.

[15] *Ibid.,* coll. 1, n. 33, pp. 334–335; *Liber III S.,* d. 33, a. 1, q. 6, f. 4, III, p. 726; *S. de Sanctis, In Festo Omnium Sanctorum,* s. ii, IX, p. 604.

[16] *In Hex.,* coll. 6, nn. 15–18, V, p. 363. Cf. footnotes of the Editors of Quaracchi.

social doctrine of our Saint with his treatises on the *Divine Name*, the *Mystical Theology*, the *Celestial Hierarchy*, and the *Ecclesiastical Hierarchy*.[17]

There are, then, two Neo-Platonic fountain-heads from which St. Bonaventure drew. The first is St. Augustine; the second, Macrobius, Cicero, and Pseudo-Dionysius. From Macrobius he took the Plotinian division of virtues, from Cicero the definitions of the cardinal virtues, and from Pseudo-Dionysius the doctrine of hierarchy that played such an important role in all his social writings.

SECTION 3.   THE FATHERS AND GRECO-ROMAN PHILOSOPHERS

A. The Fathers

The Seraphic Doctor's acquaintance with the Fathers of the Church was very broad and extensive. In fact, almost all of the Fathers, or at least all the more noted ones, are quoted in his works.[18] What is more, certain of his writings contain page upon page of passages and explanations taken from patristic sources. A classic example of this is his *Apologia Pauperum*.[19] In relation to Bonaventure's social doctrine, special notice should be made of St. Gregory the Great and his well-known *Moralia*, of which our Saint made much use in his ethical and moral teachings. Nor should we disregard St. Isidore of Seville and his *Etymologies*, which served as a sort of encyclopedia and made itself felt in St. Bonaventure's doctrine concerning the divine origin of authority as well as in his teaching on the natural law.

B. The Greco-Roman Philosophers

Through the medium of the Fathers also, the Seraphic Doctor drew from the writings of the Greco-Roman philosophers.

---

[17] That the works of the Pseudo-Dionysius were available in the West in our saint's time is an established fact. De Wulf, *op. cit.*, I, p. 68, sets the date of their entrance into the West between 828 and 835.

[18] Cf. the index in the tenth volume of the *Opera Omnia*, wherein the Editors of Quaracchi have set down the various quotations of which St. Bonaventure has made use.

[19] *Opera Omnia*, VIII, pp. 233–330.

Among these Aristotle, the great thinker of pagan antiquity, deserves special mention. The impression made by Aristotle upon the Seraphic Doctor is very pronounced. However, it is an exaggeration of this effect to state that Bonaventure is a peripatetic like St. Thomas and that the only difference between the two doctors is purely accidental—as though that which prevented Bonaventure from reaching the height of Aristotelianism attained by St. Thomas was the lack of Aristotelian resources.[20] This latter notion is not true, for in following the traditional doctrine of the past and particularly the principles laid down by St. Augustine, the Seraphic Doctor had not set out upon the road which would have led him to Christian Aristotelianism.

It was neither through ignorance nor through mere chronological chance that he did not become an Aristotelian. In point of fact, when St. Bonaventure studied at Paris, not only Aristotle's *Organon*, but also his *Physics* and *Metaphysics* were being taught. Furthermore, while there, he must have heard of the teaching of St. Albert the Great. Whether or not the Seraphic Doctor was present at any of the lectures, it scarcely seems likely that he could have failed to become acquainted with the daring enterprise of St. Albert's Aristotelian reform.[21] That this did not affect him shows his mind was made up to follow the common and accepted doctrine. Those words in which he presents himself as the simple continuator of Alexander of Hales are rightly interpreted as a proof of his great modesty, but they also prove, and this no less clearly, that his mind was firmly set.[22]

However, St. Bonaventure knew Aristotle's teachings, quoted him constantly, and even adopted a large part of his technical vocabulary. He admired the pagan philosopher sincerely and regarded him as the man of science *par excellence*.[23] He speaks of Aristotle simply and unequivocally as the *Philosophus* and quotes from him more often than from any other author, St.

---

[20] Etienne Gilson, *La Philosophie de S. Bonaventure*, Paris, Vrin, 1924, pp. 11–12.

[21] *Ibid.*, p. 13.

[22] *Liber II S.*, praelocutio, II, p. 1.

[23] *Christus unus Om. Magister*, n. 18, V, p. 572.

Augustine alone excepted.[24]   Nevertheless, despite the fact that our author has taken a great deal from Aristotle and continually appeals to his authority, we are convinced that he is not a peripatetic.[25]   For, in our opinion, it is not the acceptance of certain teachings or certain terminologies, numerous though they be, that establishes the writer as a member of this or that school of thought, but the acceptance of the school's spirit, its outlook, and its final goal.

The Augustinian spirit that thoroughly permeates his teaching is especially seen in the fact that Bonaventure seeks the Divine everywhere and always.   Looking upon this world as a mirror of the Eternal, as a stepping-stone by means of which we are to reach the world beyond, our Saint never separates the earth from heaven.   In opposition to a philosophy which considers all things from the viewpoint of the things in themselves, our author, in following the path traced out by the Bishop of Hippo, strives to build a system in which all things are related to God and find their place as works of God.   We have two ways of looking at created reality, the Seraphic Doctor tells us.   We can regard creatures as they are or conceive of them as signs.[26]   Accordingly, we can in our study of the creatures become engrossed in them and enslaved by their apparent beauty; or we can, on the other hand, recognize their incompleteness and insufficiency and mount beyond them to their Maker.   This second method is, for the holy Doctor, the only true manner of procedure.[27]   In fact, a creature, St. Bonaventure tells us, is known truly only when it is known in relation to that according to which it was made—viz., the exemplary ideas.[28]

Naturally, this brings us to the question of exemplarism and Bonaventure's condemnation of Aristotle for the latter's denial thereof.   Exemplarism, both intellectual and moral, we must

---

[24] *Opera Omnia*, X, p. 266.

[25] Gilson, *op. cit.,* pp. 11–17, 29–41, 89–118; Tinivella, *op. cit.,* p. 31, ft. 1 and p. 283, ft. 3.

[26] *Liber I S.,* d. 3, p. 1, a. 1, q. 3, ad 2, I, p. 75.

[27] *Ibid.,* q. 2, ad 1, p. 72.

[28] *In Hex.,* coll. 1, n. 10, V, p. 331. ". . . ad notitiam creaturae pervenire non potest nisi per id per quod facta est. . . ."

recall, plays a very important role in the philosophy of the Seraphic Doctor. Indeed, it lies at the very heart and core of his metaphysics.[29] Since, therefore, the rejection of exemplarism would destroy, in his opinion, the very foundation of metaphysics and render impossible the true interpretation of created reality, it is only natural that Bonaventure would have nothing to do with the philosophical system that denies the very core of all metaphysics, but would, on the other hand, praise that school of thought which affirms the existence of exemplary ideas.[30]

Bearing this in mind, then, we can appreciate the full import of Bonaventure's condemnation of Aristotle contained in his *Collationes in Hexaemeron.*[31] It is a condemnation not simply of Aristotle's rejection of exemplary ideas, but of his whole philosophical system.[32] In his *Collationes De Septem Donis Spiritus Sancti* the Seraphic Doctor considers the Averroistic errors, condemns them, and against them sets up Christ as the Cause of Being, the Ground of knowledge, and the Order of life.[33] Then in his *Collationes in Hexaemeron,* he maintains that the fault for these errors dates back to Aristotle and his denial of exemplarism.[34]

If we accept this condemnation for what it actually seems to be—a condemnation of the system which, denying exemplarism, destroys the very core of metaphysics—it should be clear that Bonaventure, despite his apparent acceptance of the Philosopher's teaching, is by no means a peripatetic.

SECTION 4.   THE SCHOLASTICS

Among the Scholastics who have helped to fashion the social thought of St. Bonaventure particular mention should be made of Friar Alexander of Hales and of Peter of Lombardy. The former was his master at Paris and, needless to say, influenced

---

[29] Tinivella, *op. cit.,* pp. 282–286; Gilson, *op. cit.,* pp. 99–102.

[30] *In Hex.,* coll. 6, nn. 2–6, V, pp. 360–361.

[31] *Ibidem.* Gilson, *op. cit.,* pp. 99–102.

[32] Tinivella, *op. cit.,* pp. 282–286.

[33] Coll. 8, nn. 16–20, V, pp. 497–498. This is also found in *Decem praeceptis,* coll. 2, n. 25, V, p. 514.

[34] Coll. 6, nn. 2–6, V, pp. 360–361. Gilson, *l. c.;* Tinievella, *l. c.*

him greatly. We need only to point out that Bonaventure proclaims himself to be the simple continuator of Alexander, and ever speaks of the *Doctor Irrefutabilis* in a tender and reverent manner.[35] Peter Lombard, on the other hand, was his guide, for it was on Peter's renowned book of the *Sentences* that he wrote his celebrated *Commentaries.*

Besides Alexander of Hales, St. Bonaventure had other teachers, two of whom merit special mention, namely: the Franciscan John of Rochelle and the Dominican Hugh of Saint-Cher.[36] In addition, a privileged place of authority in Bonaventurean doctrine is enjoyed by St. Bernard of Clairvaux, mainly on account of his *De Consideratione,* and by the two Victorines, Hugh and Richard. The high esteem in which our author held Hugh of St. Victor appears from his writings. Thus, in his *De Reductione Artium ad Theologiam* Bonaventure praises him as one in whom is found a happy balance of intellectual and devotional piety, one of the foremost characteristics of his own writings.[37]

SECTION 5.   THE SERAPHIC FATHER

We cannot terminate our consideration of the sources employed by the Seraphic Doctor without referring to the great influence exercised on him by the Seraphic Father, St. Francis of Assisi.[38] No one of the Poverello's followers, in the role of writer, has

---

[35] *Liber II S.,* praelocutio, II, p. 1; *Ibid.,* d. 23, a. 2, q. 3, ad 7, p. 547.

[36] As regards the influence of Hugh of Saint-Cher confer P. C. V. P. Borne, "De Fontibus Commentarii S. Bonaventurae in Ecclesiastem," *Archivum Franciscanum Historicum,* X (1917), Quaracchi, pp. 257–270.

[37] N. 5, V, p. 321. Cf. Healy, *Saint Bonaventure's De Reductione Artium ad Theologiam,* St. Bonaventure College, St. Bonaventure, N. Y., 1939, pp. 27–31 where the writer shows how the *De Reductione* of St. Bonaventure and the *Expositio in Hierarchiam Caelestem S. Dionysii Areopagitae* as well as the *Eruditio Didascalica* of Hugh of St. Victor are closely related.

[38] With regard to the influence of St. Francis, cf. Léonard Carvalho e Castro, *Saint Bonaventure Le Docteur Franciscain, L'Idéal de S. Francois e l'Œuvre de S. Bonaventure à l'égard de la Science,* Beauchesne, Paris, 1923; P. Ephraem Longprè, O.F.M., "La Theologie Mystique de S. Bonaventure," *Archivum Franciscanum Historicum,* XIV (1921), Quaracchi, pp. 36–108; Gilson, *op. cit.,* pp. 69–88; Tinivella, *op. cit.,* p. 31, ft. 2.

kept closer than St. Bonaventure to the genuine spirit of the Poor Man of Assisi.[39] As a true and faithful son of the Holy Founder of the Franciscan Order, the Seraphic Doctor penetrated so deeply into the mind of the Seraph of Assisi that "his own mind was like a philosophical and theological reflection of that of the Saint."[40] The influence of St. Francis upon St. Bonaventure was not simply moral; it penetrated to the very depths of his intellect. Thus, the disdain of the Seraphic Father for presumptuous, useless knowledge and his wholesome respect for the Sacred Scriptures emerged in the Seraphic Doctor as the exaltation of Theology—as can be seen from his *De Reductione Artium ad Theologiam.*[41] In fact, it was from St. Francis ultimately that Bonaventure absorbed the lesson of complete abandonment to God which he was to make the general theme of all his writings.[42] Again, it was the Seraph of Assisi who introduced St. Bonaventure into the mysteries of love and the all-embracing law of charity which was to occupy so prominent a place in his social teachings. St. Bonaventure was not the man to forget the lessons taught him by the Seraphic Father, and, consequently, we can affirm with certainty that his whole system of thought is, in no small way, conditioned by Franciscan spirituality.[43]

ARTICLE II. THE NATURE OF HIS DOCTRINES IN GENERAL

SECTION 1. THE GOAL OF HIS INTELLECTUAL ENDEAVOURS

St. Bonaventure, we have already pointed out, is a conservative. He regards himself merely as one continuing and furthering the traditional doctrine.[44] Nevertheless, despite his determination to

[39] Agostino Gemelli, O.F.M., *The Franciscan Message to the World* (translation by H. L. Hughes, London, Burns, Oates & Washbourne, 1934), p. 56.

[40] *Ibid.,* p. 55.

[41] *Opera Omnia,* V, pp. 319–325.

[42] Gilson, *op. cit.,* p. 67.

[43] *Ibid.,* p. 75. Cf. *Itin.,* especially the prologue, V, pp. 295–296, and c. 7, pp. 312–313. This will be considered in the following article.

[44] "Non enim intendo novas opiniones adversare, sed communes et approbatas retexere. Nec quisquam aestimet, quod novi scripti velim esse

follow the common opinions held by the Fathers and Scholastics before him rather than to set forth something new, the Seraphic Doctor does not in any way allow the respect he bears them to prejudice what he believes to be the truth. He, therefore, points out not only the various errors of the pagan philosophers,[45] but also those of the Masters of Christianity.[46] For it is true knowledge that St. Bonaventure seeks, even though in his great humility he professes himself to be a simple compiler. The knowledge that our saintly Doctor pursues is not sought for itself. For him learning has a role to play—to lead man to an end more perfect and profound than learning itself, the knowledge and the love of God.

In order to understand the true nature of Bonaventure's doctrine we must seek to determine the goal towards which all his intellectual searchings are leading him and us, his readers. We can do no less, for to enter into the thought of an author, we must grasp the end that he has in mind, since this end will determine the means to be used and the path to be followed. Now, it is true that all the great philosophers knew and stated but one goal, namely, *Wisdom;* but not all understood it in the same manner. This truth is remarkably shown in the two foremost leaders in philosophy, Plato and Aristotle. Both sought wisdom—but it was not the same wisdom.

In considering these two leading thinkers of antiquity, St. Bonaventure tells us that Aristotle is great—nay, more, the greatest—but only in the realm of the things of earth. A profound scientist, Aristotle confined himself to this temporal world, which he could see, touch, and study, and cared not overmuch about the more real world beyond all sensible things. His aim, hence, is mere science and the delight that comes from knowledge as knowledge. Such a goal the Seraphic Doctor rejects,

---

fabricator; hoc enim sentio et fateor, quod sum pauper et tenuis compilator." *Liber II S.,* praelocutio, II, p. 1.

[45] *In Hex.,* coll. 6, nn. 2–6, V, pp. 360–361; coll. 7, nn. 3–12, pp. 365–367.

[46] Witness, for example, what he relates concerning Peter Lombard: ". . . nec credo, in omnibus his eum esse sustinendum, ne amore hominis veritati fiat praejudicium. . . ." *Liber II S.,* d. 44, dub. 3, II, p. 1016.

looking instead to the highest delight that comes from knowing and loving the eternal Goodness.[47]

Plato, on the other hand, had his gaze fixed on the higher things in a higher world. In his concentration upon the eternal world, however, he despised this world which we see and touch, and in so doing destroyed the way of science. Thus, both Aristotle and Plato were one-sided, and, consequently, neither reached the fullness of wisdom. It was St. Augustine, the master of Christian Wisdom, who brought about the happy synthesis between Aristotle and Plato, between wisdom and science—that synthesis wherein all things are related to God and creatures find their place as works of God.[48] Bonaventure, in turn, following in the footsteps of Augustine, makes wisdom in its comprehensive sense the ideal in his search for knowledge.

What is the wisdom that the Seraphic Doctor holds to be the end of his intellectual investigations? In answer to this question we must recall that our author speaks of a fourfold wisdom. First is what is *commonly* understood by the term wisdom, i.e., a knowledge of human and divine things, identified with philosophy.[49] Second, there is that which is *less commonly* referred

---

[47] " Philosophus dicit, quod magna delectatio est scire, quod diameter sit asymeter costae; haec delectatio sit sua; modo comedat illam." *In Hex.,* coll. 17, n. 7, V, p. 410. Our exposition in this chapter is, to a large extent, based on Gilson, *op. cit.,* pp. 89–118, 452–473; Healy, *op. cit.,* pp. 149–156; Tinivella, *op. cit.,* passim.

[48] " Unde quia Plato totam cognitionem certitudinalem convertit ad mundum intelligibilem sive idealem, ideo merito reprehensus fuit ab Aristotele; non quia male diceret, ideas esse et aeternas rationes, cum eum in hoc laudet Augustinus; sed quia, despecto mundo sensibili, totam certitudinem cognitionis reducere voluit ad illas ideas; et hoc ponendo, licet videretur stabilire viam sapientiae, quae procedit secundum rationes aeternas, destruebat tamen viam scientiae, quae procedit secundum rationes creatas; quam viam Aristoteles e contrario stabiliebat, illa superiore neglecta. Et ideo videtur, quod inter philosophos datus sit Platoni sermo sapientiae, Aristoteli vero sermo scientiae. Ille enim principaliter aspiciebat ad superiora, hic vero principaliter ad inferiora. Uterque autem sermo, scilicet sapientiae et scientiae, per Spiritum sanctum datus est Augustino, tanquam praecipuo expositori totius Scripturae, satis excellenter, sicut ex scriptis ejus apparet." *Christus unus om. Magister,* nn. 18–19, V, p. 572.

[49] ". . . sapientia quadrupliciter accipi consuevit tam a philosophis quam

to as wisdom—a higher knowledge, i.e., the knowledge of things eternal as distinguished from science, which is the knowledge of created things.[50] *Properly speaking,* though, wisdom is the knowledge of God *secundum pietatem,* which consists in divine worship through faith, hope, and charity.[51] Even this, however, is not wisdom in its truest sense, since *more properly* wisdom is an experimental knowledge of God, whose act consists in savouring the divine sweetness. It is that mystical union with God which begins in intellection and is consummated in affection.[52] This—the experimental knowledge of God, the *savouring* of the eternal Goodness, and the *peace* that results therefrom—is the goal of all Bonaventure's intellectual striving.[53]

We can better understand this reasoning when we realize that the acquisition of blessedness, as St. Augustine tells us, is the end of all philosophizing.[54] The highest blessedness that can be acquired on this earth is to be found in wisdom considered as

---

a Sanctis, videlicet communiter et minus communiter et proprie et magis proprie.—Communiter accipiendo sapientiam, sic sapientia dicit cognitionem rerum generalem, secundum quod eam definit Augustinus et Philosophus, quod ' sapientia est cognitio rerum divinarum et humanarum '; et Philosophus in Prima Philosophia dicit, quod ' sapiens est qui omnia novit, secundum quod convenit.' " *Liber III S.,* d. 35, a. 1, q. 1, conc., III, p. 774.

[50] " Alio modo dicitur sapientia minus communiter; et sic sapientia dicit cognitionem non quamcumque, sed cognitionem sublimen, videlicet cognitionem rerum aeternarum." *Ibidem.*

[51] " Tertio modo accipitur sapientia proprie; et sic nominat cognitionem Dei secundum pietatem; et haec quidem cognitio est quae attenditur in cultu latriae, quem exhibemus Deo per fidem, spem et caritatem. . . ." *Ibidem.*

[52] " Quarto modo dicitur sapientiae magis proprie, et sic nominat cognitionem Dei experimentalem . . . cujus actus consistit in degustando divinam suavitatem . . . actus doni sapientiae partim est cognitivus, et partim est affectivus; ita quod in cognitione inchoatur et in affectione consummatur, secundum quod ipse gustus vel saporatio est experimentalis boni et dulcis cognitio." *Ibidem.*

[53] " Unde haec scientia sapientia est, quia secum habet junctum saporem; et per hanc illuminatur intellectus, et stabilitur affectus. . . . Et haec est cognitio excellentissima, quam docet Dionysius, quae quidem est in ecstaico amore et elevat supra cognitionem fidei secundum statum communem." *Ibid.,* d. 25, dub. 4, p. 531.

[54] " Nulla est homini causa philosophandi, nisi ut beatus sit." *De Civitate Dei,* l. XIX, c. 1, *P. L.* 41, 623.

the experimental knowledge of the Eternal. Indeed, man naturally desires knowledge, happiness, and peace—knowledge, since we see him curiously investigating the sources of things; happiness, since all his actions are directed to the procuring of good and the avoidance of evil; and peace, since it is the perfection and complement of the other two, because it exists only when these desires—of knowledge and happiness—are appeased by the attainment of their end. This love of peace is so profoundly innate in the human soul that even the damned long for it in the midst of their despair.[55]

Now, this threefold desire, innate in the soul of man, must lead us to God, as nothing finite can truly satisfy it. Accordingly, since we are capable of knowing *all* that is knowable, we are never satisfied with the knowledge of a determined object and always tend beyond each thing finite towards that something which, being known, would enable us to know all other things.[56] The same is true of our ability to love good. Capable of enjoying *all* that is good, we are satisfied with no one particular good, but our desire continually tends beyond each finite good to that *absolute* good which is the source and end of all the others.[57] Consequently, it is obvious that no finite good can give us that peace which flows from the complete satisfaction and appeasement of all our desires. This thought, that nothing finite can satisfy perfectly our desire of knowledge, happiness, and

---

[55] "... insertus est mentibus hominum appetitus sapientiae, quia dicit Philosophus: 'Omnes homines natura scire desiderant'; sed sapientia maxime appetibilis est sapientia aeterna ... appetitus beatitudinis adeo est nobis insertus, ut nullus possit dubitare de altero, utrum velit esse beatus, ... sed beatitudo consistit in summo bono, quod Deus est ... insertus est ipsi animae appetitus pacis, et adeo insertus, ut quaeratur per suum contrarium, nec etiam ipse appetitus auferri potest ab ipsis damnatis et daemonibus ..." *De Mys. Trinitatis,* q. 1, a. 1, ff. 6, 7, 8, V, p. 46.

[56] "Cognitio enim animae naturalis est cognitio non arctata; unde nata est quodam modo omnia cognoscere, unde non impletur cognitio ejus aliquo cognoscibili, nisi quod habet in se omnia cognoscibilia et quo cognito omnia cognoscuntur." *Liber I S.,* d. 1, a. 3, q. 2, conc., 1, p. 40.

[57] "Similiter affectio ejus nata est diligere omne bonum; ergo nullo bono sufficienter finitur affectus, nisi quod est bonum omni bono et quod est omnia in omnibus. ... Hoc autem est summum bonum. ..." *Ibid.,* pp. 40–41.

peace, brings us to one of the central doctrines in the teaching of the Seraphic Doctor, namely, that the human soul is born to perceive the infinite good, to enjoy Him, and to repose in Him.[58] If this is the case, then, does it not follow that the end of all intellectual endeavour, of all human striving, is the highest possible knowledge, happiness, and peace that man can attain on this earth, the *experimental knowledge of the Eternal?*

The orientation of Bonaventure's thought, therefore, must be apparent—he seeks *peace*, the result of true and perfect wisdom. In this respect, doubtlessly, he was swayed by the teachings of the various Fathers and Masters of Holy Mother Church. Nevertheless, the main influence seems to have been the life of the Seraphic Father, St. Francis of Assisi, for we must admit that Franciscan spirituality has played a commanding role in conditioning the thought of our holy Doctor.[59] In both the life of the Seraph of Assisi and the Rule of his Order, Bonaventure finds a threefold desire and purpose: (a) total imitation of Christ through the practice of virtue; (b) total adherence to God by the savor of contemplation; (c) the conversion and salvation of souls.[60] Of these, the enjoyment of the Divine Goodness in contemplation, together with resultant peace, seems to be the most important. This influence becomes more apparent when we recall that the peace which Christ came to bring to the world, which the Poverello preached unto all men, desired for all men, and experienced on Mt. Alvernia is the ideal that the Seraphic Doctor seeks in his *Itinerarium Mentis in Deum.*[61]

Thus, the saintly son has taken as his own the goal of his Seraphic Father. However, while both look for ecstatic peace, the consequent of true wisdom, their methods of procedure are nevertheless quite different. The saint of Assisi is a mystic, pure and simple. He goes straight to the goal of ecstatic union, love, and peace, seeking it in total abandonment to the love of God, hurriedly dismissing all science, all methodical thinking, all the

---

[58] ". . . nata est anima ad percipiendum bonum infinitum, quod Deus est, ideo in eo solo debet quiescere et eo frui." *Ibid.*, p. 41.

[59] Cf. above, pp. 10–11.

[60] *Determinationes Quaestionum*, p. 1, q. 1, VIII, p. 338,

[61] Prologus, nn. 1, 2, V, p. 295,

detours of reasoning. Bonaventure, on the other hand, is by vocation an intellectual person. He arrives at the same goal through the medium of learning. His is an intelligence dedicated to the service of devotion, which translates learning into love. His aim is to converge all knowledge towards the attainment of this unique peace of love—to reorganize the whole of learning into an all-embracing system of holy knowledge.[62]

This attempt of our saintly author—to set up a system of learning which will lead to that ecstasy of love and peace exemplified by St. Francis on Mt. Alvernia—is what Gilson terms the *personal problem* of St. Bonaventure.[63] No title, consequently, could have described him more completely than that of *Seraphic Doctor*, for "the spirit that breathes in his writings seems to reflect that of the celestial beings who stand nearest to the Throne, and the title of *Seraphic Doctor* is a beautiful tribute to his all-absorbing love.[64]

For him all learning must enter into the service of love. To this idea, so often recurrent in his writings and so predominant in all his works, he devoted a special treatise, *De Reductione Artium ad Theologiam.* In this treatise he begins with scientific skill in its lowest representative, the seven mechanical arts, and continues on through empirical knowledge and the philosophical sciences to establish the connection between each branch of learning and theology—and between each and the mystical union, through theology. Hence his conclusion:

> "And this is the advantage of all sciences, that in all faith is strengthened, God is honored, character is formed, and consolation is derived from union of the spouse with her beloved, a union which takes place through charity, to the attainment of which the whole purpose of Sacred Scripture, and, consequently, every illumination descending from above, is directed . . ."[65]

---

[62] *De Reductione,* n. 26, V, p. 325.
[63] *Op. cit.,* pp. 69–88.
[64] Healy, *op. cit.,* p. 23.
[65] "Et hic est fructus omnium scientiarum, ut in omnibus aedificetur fides, honorificetur Deus, componantur mores, hauriantur consolationes, quae sunt in unione speciei et sponsae, quae quidem fit per caritatem, ad quem ter-

SECTION 2. FAITH AND REASON

It is clear from the foregoing that the only purpose philosophy can have in the system of St. Bonaventure is to lead us to a loving knowledge of our First Beginning and Last End. Indeed, as Gilson notes, philosophy for our saintly Doctor cannot begin without Christ, for He is its object, and it cannot attain completion without Christ, for He is its end.[66] This Deo- and Christo-centric theme predominates in the writings of the saint. God—better, Christ—is the center of all, and we must start from this Center if we wish to attain Christian Wisdom.[67] At the same time creatures are truly known only when they are known in relation to God—only when we know how they originated, to what end they tend, and in what manner they manifest God.[68]

Accordingly, his whole metaphysics consists of: Emanationism, which treats of the universe as created by God; Exemplarism, which considers God as the Exemplar of all creation; and Consummation or Reduction (Return), which is concerned with God as the goal of created beings, who, illumined by His light, return to Him.[69] Therefore, any discussion on a particular problem is merely a digression from the one topic, God. In coming to God, however—to the God of Christianity, since the Seraphic Doctor cannot be satisfied with the God of pure philosophy[70]— faith is our starting point. We start from faith—not to end

minatur tota intentio sacrae Scripturae, et per consequens omnia illuminatio desursum descendens . . ." n. 26, V, p. 325.

[66] "Elle ne commencerait pas sans le Christ, car c'est lui qui en est l'objet; et elle ne s'achèverait pas sans le Christ, car c'est lui qui en est la fin." *Op. cit.,* p. 456.

[67] ". . . incipiendum est a medio, quod est Christus. . . . Unde ab illo incipiendum necessario, si quis vult venire ad sapientiam christianam . . ." *In Hex.,* coll. 1, n. 10, V, p. 330. Cf. *Ibid.,* nn. 10–38, pp. 330–335; Gilson, *op. cit.,* pp. 453–460; Healy, *op. cit.,* p. 157.

[68] "Nisi enim quis possit considerare de rebus, qualiter originantur, qualiter in finem reducuntur, et qualiter in eis refulget Deus; intelligentiam habere non potest." *In Hex.,* coll. 3, n. 2, V, p. 343.

[69] ". . . et haec est tota nostra metaphysica: de emanatione, de exemplaritate, de consummatione, scilicet illuminari per radios spirituales et reduci ad summum." *Ibid.,* coll. 1, n. 17, V, p. 332.

[70] *De Donis,* coll. 4, n. 12, V, pp. 475–476.

there, but to proceed to understanding and to arrive finally at a mystical knowledge.[71]

In order to understand Bonaventure's teaching we should bear in mind that faith contains in itself a factor that calls for speculation, i.e., love. The believer is firmly grounded in revealed truth only because he has placed the act of faith out of love.[72] Faith, however, is the imperfect state of the wayfarer, whereas the goal of man is to behold God, to see the Truth.[73] Since, therefore, faith of itself is imperfect, love postulates a deeper, a more complete understanding of the truths in which it has faith, for, as Bonaventure states, truly delightful is the state of the soul that understands what it believes.[74] As a result, philosophy would appear to be born out of the believer's desire to enjoy more fully the object of his faith.

This teaching does not imply any confusion of philosophy and theology by our author, who in numerous passages draws a sharp line of distinction between these two orders of knowledge. They are distinct, he tells us, and it would be absurd to expect the one to fulfill what is the proper function of the other. The formal object of the one is reason; of the other, faith.[75] Philosophy, properly so called, is for him, as for every one of the

---

71 "Ordo enim est, ut, inchoetur a stabilitate fidei, et procedatur per serenitatem rationis, ut perveniatur ad suavitatem contemplationis . . ." *Christus unus om. Magister*, n. 15, V, p. 571.

72 *Liber III S.*, d. 23, a. 1, q. 2, conc., III, pp. 476–477. Cf. *Liber I S.*, prooemium, q. 2, conc., I, p. 11.

73 *Liber III S.*, d. 31, a. 2, q. 1, ad 1, III, p. 681.

74 "Miro enim modo anima delectatur in intelligendo quod perfecta fide credit." *Liber I S.*, proemium, q. 2, conc., I, p. 11. Cf. the whole question. ". . . quando fides non assentit propter rationem, sed propter amorem ejus cui assentit, desiderat habere rationes; tunc non evacuat ratio humana meritum, sed auget solatium." *Ibid.*, ad 6, p. 11.

75 ". . . scientiae quadruplex est differentia. Quaedam est, quae consistit in intellectu pure speculativo; et haec est fundata super principia rationis, et haec est scientia acquisita de quacumque creatura, sicut scientia humanae philosophiae.—Quaedam autem est, quae consistit in intellectu inclinato ab affectu; et haec est fundata super principia fidei, quae quidem sunt articuli, et nihilominus acquisita; et haec est scientia Sacrae Scripturae . . ." *Liber III S.*, d. 35, a. 1, q. 2, conc., III, p. 776. Cf. *Breviloquium*, prologus, n. 3, V, p. 205; *De Donis*, coll. 4, n. 2, V, p. 474.

Scholastics, the knowledge of things that man can acquire by means of reason alone.

> " Philosophy treats of things as they are in nature, or in the soul according to an acquired knowledge or one naturally inherent in it; but theology, a science founded on faith and revealed by the Holy Ghost, treats of those things which concern grace and glory and also eternal Wisdom." [76]

The distinctive character of philosophy lies in the certitude it gives rise to, which, unlike the certitude that faith inspires, is founded on the clear perception of truth by reason alone.[77]

Nevertheless, although our saintly author differentiates between these two spheres of learning, although he declares philosophy to be the highest degree of human intellectual activity and clearly indicates the content and division of philosophy, he is openly opposed to any practical separation of the two.[78] According to the Seraphic Doctor, then, philosophy and theology, while distinct from each other, cannot be estranged from each other, for the former must aid the latter, and the latter the former. And this is to the very best interests of philosophy itself.

Natural reason, upon which philosophy is founded, we must recall, must be radically good, since it is a light from on High, supernatural in its origin as are the light of faith and the gifts of the Holy Spirit, which are to elevate and perfect it.[79] Clearly

[76] " . . . philosophia quidem agit de rebus, ut sunt in natura, seu in anima secundum notitiam naturaliter insitam, vel etiam acquisitam; sed theológia, tanquam scientia supra fidem fundata et per Spiritum Sanctum revelata, agit et de eis quae spectant ad gratiam et gloriam et etiam ad Sapientiam aeternam." *Breviloquium,* prologus, n. 3, V, p. 205.

[77] Cf. above, ft. 75.

[78] " Tertium lumen, quod illuminat ad veritates intelligibiles perscrutandas, est lumen cognitionis philosophiae, quod ideo interius dicitur, quia interiores causas et latentes inquirit, et hoc per principia disciplinarum et veritatis naturalis, quae homini naturaliter sunt inserta." *De Reductione,* n. 4, V, p. 320. The division of philosophy will be considered in the next article. For Bonaventure's opposition to the practical separation of philosophy and theology, cf. Gilson, *op. cit.,* pp. 463–464, especially ft. 1, p. 463.

[79] *De Donis,* coll. 4, n. 4, V, p. 474. Cf. the whole of this *collatio; In Hex.,* coll. 4, n. 1, V, p. 349. The same thought is found in his *De Reductione,* V, pp. 319ss.

then, if reason is a light of divine origin, it cannot of itself lead us to error. However, a further question arises: are we capable of using this light, infallible in itself, infallibly? In his *Collationes in Hexaemeron* the Seraphic Doctor takes into consideration the great philosophers of the past and shows their teachings to be proof that mere human reason, beclouded by the sin of the first man and subjected to countless influences of pride and other passions, can and does go astray.[80] Aristotle, Bonaventure points out, was guilty of three errors: ignorance of exemplarism, of Divine Providence, and of the purpose of the world. This triple error involved, in turn, a triple blindness: belief in the eternity of the world, belief in the unicity of the active intellect, and denial of reward and punishment after death.[81] Plato and the Neo-Platonists, on the other hand, though able to avoid these errors, achieved but a stunted and deformed truth. Their basic defect seems to have been ignorance of original sin—ignorance of the disease with which man was afflicted coupled with the inability to apply the necessary remedy. All this, because they did not have the light of faith.[82]

We must bear in mind that the intention of our author is to show the insufficiency of these two philosophical systems. Both the system of Aristotle and that of Plato and the Neo-Platonists are insufficient, not only because of the errors into which they have fallen, but also because of their failure to keep their promise. They had sworn to satisfy the human longing for blessedness and peace by giving their followers a tenth science,

---

[80] *In Hex.*, coll. 7, nn. 3–12, V, pp. 365–367; coll. 6, nn. 2–6, pp. 360–361. ". . . instatu innocentiae videbatur mediante speculo claro sine aliqua obscuritate, eo quod nulla erat in anima peccati nebula, sed omnimoda puritas; et nulla rebellio carnis et virium inferiorum ad spiritum, sed omnimoda subjectio . . ." *S. de Temp., Dom. XII, p. Pent.*, s. 1, IX, p. 399. ". . . secundum ea quae percipit a sensibus, vel etiam secundum lumen sibi datum et innatum, potest deficere et errare, maxime in statu naturae lapsae." *Liber II S.*, d. 24, p. 2, a. 1, q. 1, conc., II, p. 575. Cf. *Ibid.*, prooemium, pp. 3–6; d. 23, a. 2, q. 3, conc., pp. 544–545; d. 30, a. 1, q. 1, conc., p. 716.

[81] *In Hex.*, coll. 6, nn. 2–6, pp. 360–361. Cf. Tinivella, *op. cit.*, pp. 282–285.

[82] *In Hex.*, coll. 7, nn. 3–12, V, pp. 365–367. Cf. Tinivella, *op. cit.*, pp. 303–310.

that of wisdom and contemplation. This goal they were unable to achieve.[83]

Reason, we concede, has no need of faith in order to grasp the first principles, to recognize the details of beings, and to understand their nature considered *in se*. Yet, if God is, in truth, the proper object of philosophy—and this seems to be the case in Bonaventure's system of thought—our reason cannot attain its goal without the aid of faith, since reason must halt when it reaches the limits of its natural powers. However, for reason to stop and to rest in itself is erroneous, since philosophy is but a way to the sciences above itself and he who rests therein is plunged into darkness.[84] Consequently, all philosophy not enlightened by faith must, according to the mind of our author, fall into error, for the philosophers of pure reason are like ostriches who have wings, but do not fly, only run.[85]

SECTION 3.   THE ORGANISM OF LEARNING

If philosophy is to remain free from error and to lead to true wisdom, it must, in being subjected to faith, receive therefrom a more sublime irradiation. Conducted by that light, then, reason enters on the right path, and philosophy becomes for man a stage in his return to God—a part of the great organism of learning. For philosophy, Bonaventure tells us, lies midway between faith

---

[83] " Philosophi dederunt novem scientias et polliciti sunt dare decimam, scilicet contemplationem.   Sed multi philosophi, dum se voluerunt dividere a tenebris erroris, magnis erroribus se immiscuerunt; dicentes enim, se esse sapientes, stulti facti sunt; superbientes de sua scientia, luciferiani facti." *In Hex.*, coll. 4, n. 1, V, p. 349. Cf. *Ibid.*, coll. 5, n. 22, p. 357; Tinivella, *op. cit.*, passim.   The whole of this dissertation is an attempt to show that the acquisition of true wisdom, according to the teaching as set forth in his *Hexaemeron* by St. Bonaventure, is impossible in a purely pagan philosophy.

[84] " Philosophica scientia via est ad alias scientias; sed qui ibi vult stare cadit in tenebris." *De Donis,* coll. 4, n. 12, V, p. 476.

[85] " Isti philosophi habuerunt pennas struthionum, quia affectus non erant sanati nec ordinati nec rectificati ; quod non fit nisi per fidem." *In Hex.*, coll. 7, n. 12, V, p. 367. Cf. footnote 5 of Editors of Quaracchi; *Ibid.*, coll. 5, n. 27, p. 357; *De Donis,* coll. 4, n. 12, V, p. 475. ". . . omnis sapientia de Deo in via absque fide magis est stultitia quam vera scientia." *Liber III S.*, d. 24, a. 2, q. 3, ad 4, III, p. 524.

and theology, just as theology is but a passage between philosophy and the gift of knowledge, and the gift of knowledge a step between theology and the light of glory.[86]

Only this last stage brings man to the fullness of his desire and capacity for knowledge. The other steps direct the whole of their activity to reaching the point at which the higher stage begins. All forms of knowledge, then, whether philosophical, theological, or gratuitous, are, in the system of the holy author, just but so many milestones in the soul's pilgrimage to God. They are not to be separated one from the other, but each is to aid, perfect, and complement the other until finally the light of glory has been received.[87]

Indeed, since the light of faith, of philosophical sciences, and of theological science, as well as the gift of knowledge all spring from the same divine source, there is no reason why they cannot be blended into an organic unity. This is precisely what Bonaventure has accomplished. He has developed a vast structure in which the mind rises from the humblest operations upon material objects to the highest inpourings of grace without the faintest breach in the continuity of its movement.[88] And may we not say that he was justified in doing this? When we remember the goal of all his intellectual endeavours, when we recall that blessedness and peace, the results of true wisdom, constitute the common desire of all men, when we realize that we are unable to attain this wisdom without the assistance of faith and grace, is it not just to ask why faith and grace must be excluded from our system of thought—our philosophy?

---

[86] " Hic notandum est, quod est claritas scientiae philosophicae, scientiae theologicae, scientiae gratuitae, et claritas scientiae gloriosae. Claritas scientiae philosophicae est magna secundum opinionem hominum mundalium, parva tamen est in comparatione ad claritatem scientiae christianae. Claritas vero scientiae theologicae prava videtur secundum opinionem hominum mundialium, sed secundum veritatem magna est. Claritas scientiae gratuitae est major, sed claritas scientiae gloriosae maxima; ibi est status." *De Donis,* coll. 4, n. 3, V, p. 474. Cf. remainder of this *collatio.* The same thought runs throughout his work *De Reductione,* V, pp. 319ss.

[87] *Christus unus om. Magister,* n. 15, V, p. 571; *De Reductione,* n. 26, V, p. 325; *De Donis,* coll. 4, nn. 3, 4, V, p. 474.

[88] Cf. Gilson, *op. cit.,* p. 470.

Perhaps one may object that this is not *pure* philosophy. If such be the case, then we must conclude that there is no pure philosophy in the teachings of St. Bonaventure, since, according to his way of thinking, either philosophy must accept the guiding light of faith and lead us on to the higher stages of knowledge, or it has not performed its purpose. It has plunged us into darkness instead of leading us onward to the attainment of perfect and true wisdom.[89]

In the light of these considerations, then, it is apparent that no work of the Seraphic Doctor can be strictly and exclusively philosophical. Theology finds its way into each and every one of his writings, and it is a theology permeated with mysticism. This threefold nature of the holy Franciscan's works must be kept in mind if we wish to arrive at a true understanding of his teachings. He is a philosopher, a theologian, and a mystic. The three roles are so intimately and continuously interwoven that we cannot separate one from the other without running the risk of misinterpreting his thought. Hence the words of Fr. Gemelli: " With St. Bonaventure one never knows where philosophy ends and where mysticism begins, so mystical is his philosophy and so philosophical is his mysticism." [90]

Article III. The Main Theme of His Social Thought

From the very start, we feel impelled to point out that St. Bonaventure does not treat of social philosophy as such. In no section of his writings does he give us a systematic and detailed exposition of his social doctrines. Not a single one of his works, not even a notable part of one, is given over expressly to this subject. Instead, his social thought is to be found scattered about in the midst of his other thoughts on other subjects. And yet these scattered thoughts are not so much isolated principles of social philosophy as they are part and parcel of the one overall theme—the return of all things to the Source whence they came, God.

It will, therefore, be our duty to examine his various writings,

---

[89] Gilson, *op. cit.*, pp. 462–463.
[90] *Ob. cit.*, p. 304.

to seek out and gather together into a unified whole his doctrine on the more important social questions. For this reason, we must not expect to uncover a complete social and political system, but only the general rules and principles he lays down for governing the moral social order.[91]

Carefully dividing philosophy into three branches—rational, natural, and moral—the Seraphic Doctor teaches that this division owes its origin to the Uncreated Truth and, therefore, is not an arbitrary act of the philosophers. In his *Collationes in Hexaemeron* he tells us that this division corresponds to the triple ray of truth—*rerum, sermonum* and *morum*—proceeding from the Eternal Truth Itself, the Source of all truth, and deduces therefrom that it was not brought into being by the philosophers, since they did not place truth in things, words, and morals. Rather, recognizing the truth shining forth in these three, they accepted philosophy as being threefold—viz., natural, rational, and moral.[92] Furthermore, this triple ray of light leads us to the First Truth, Who is the *Cause of being, the Principle of knowing, and the Order of living.*[93] This principle—namely, that

---

[91] We may point out that the works which contain the greatest part of his social thought are the following: *Commentaria in Quatuor Libros Sententiarum Magistri Petri Lombardi,* (I–IV); *Collationes in Hexaemeron,* V, pp. 327–454; *Collationes De Decem Praeceptis,* V, pp. 505–532; *Q. D. De Perfectione Evangelica,* V, pp. 117–198.

[92] "Emittit autem haec lux tres radios primos. . . . Est enim veritas rerum, veritas signorum seu vocum et veritas morum. Veritas rerum est indivisio entis et esse, veritas sermonum est adaequatio vocis et intellectus, veritas morum est rectitudo vivendi. Et istae sunt tres partes philosophiae, quas philosophi non invenerunt, ut essent: sed quia, jam secundum veritatem essent, in anima adverterunt, secundum Augustinum." *In Hex.,* coll. 4, n. 2, V, p. 349.

The influence here is Augustine. Cf. his *De Civitate Dei,* l. XI, c. 25, *P.L.* 41, 338–339.

[93] "Ergo veritas indicat, quod mens nostra fertur naturali inclinatione ad Veritatem, secundum quod est 'causa essendi, ratio intelligendi et ordo vivendi'; secundum causam essendi, veritas rerum; secundum rationem intelligendi, veritas vocum; secundum ordinem vivendi, veritas morum." *In Hex.,* coll. 4, n. 3, V, p. 349.

This principle, which plays such an important role in the thought of our author was taken from St. Augustine (*De Civitate Dei,* l. VIII, c. 4, *P.L.* 41, 228–229), who attributes it to Plato. Tinivella (*op. cit.,* p. 139, ft. 2)

God is the Cause of being, the Principle of knowing, and the Order of living—as Tinivella remarks, must be accepted as the ultimate foundation upon which Bonaventure rests the threefold division of Philosophy.[94]

Thus, according to the mind of the Seraphic Doctor, we have *natural philosophy*, concerned with the *truth of things*, and, in turn, subdivided into *metaphysics, mathematics,* and *physics; rational philosophy,* concerned with the *truth of speech,* and divided into *grammar, logic,* and *rhetoric;* and *moral philosophy,* concerned with the *truth of morals,* and further divided into *individual ethics, economics,* and *politics.*[95]

Since moral philosophy has as its object the *veritas morum,* it deals in general with the right order that should prevail in man and in man's actions—i.e., it deals with the right order of liv-

---

has sought and found evidence for the Platonic origin of this teaching in the *Republic* of Plato.

[94] *Op. cit.,* p. 139. Bonaventure himself asserts the same when he writes: "Dico, quod potest esse verbum Dei. Ipse enim describit scientiam philosophicam tripliciter, id est secundum triplicem rationem describit eam, ut naturalem, ut rationalem et ut moralem, scilicet in quantum est 'causa essendi, ratio intelligendi et ordo vivendi.' In quantum est causa essendi, designat scientiam naturalem; in quantum est ratio intelligendi, significat scientiam rationalem; in quantum est ordo vivendi, describit scientiam moralem." *De Donis,* coll. 4, n. 6, V, p. 474.

[95] Bonaventure's division of philosophy is found in: *In Hex.,* coll. 4, nn. 2–5, V, p. 349; *De Reductione,* n. 4, V, pp. 320–321; *Itin.,* c. 3, n. 6, V, p. 305; *De Donis,* coll. 4, n. 6, V, pp. 474–475; *S. de Temp., Epiphania,* s. 3, IX, p. 159.

The Bonaventurian division of philosophy into natural, rational, and moral seems to date back to St. Augustine, and through St. Augustine, to Plato, since the Seraphic Doctor bases this division upon the famous principle: God is the Cause of being, the Principle of knowing, and the Order of living. The source of his subdivisions, however, seems to be Aristotle, although Bonaventure need not have taken these divisions directly from him. He could have borrowed them from Hugh of St. Victor, who is connected with Aristotle through the medium of Boetius. This question is examined by Tinivella (*op. cit.,* pp. 141–142), whose conclusions we have accepted.

As is his wont, Bonaventure sees in the three branches of philosophy, as well as their subdivisions, representations of the Blessed Trinity. Cf. *Itin.,* c. 3, n. 6, V, p. 305.

ing.[96] In particular, then, *ethics* treats of right order in man's actions as an individual; *economics* governs his actions as a member of the domestic society; and *politics* regulates his actions as a member of the city or of the civil society.[97]

By means of this latter division we arrive at the very heart of our subject, for it is the *philosophia-moralis-politica* which claims our attention. In his exposition of this section of philosophical learning—and we have been able to discover but one place where the Seraphic Doctor treats of it explicitly [98]—our author sets forth what he terms the *justitiae morales*, or moral justices. They are four in number: *ritus colendi, forma convivendi, norma praesidendi,* and *censura judicandi.*

Here St. Bonaventure proposes the rules for right government—not as a theologian or a jurist, but as a philosopher.[99] These *justices,* which form the basis of all political laws, dovetail so mutually and intimately, he reasons, that the fourth moral justice cannot exist without the third, not the third without the second, nor the second without the first.[100] In other words,

---

[96] "... veritas morum est rectitudo vivendi." *In Hex.,* coll. 4, n. 2, V, p. 349. "Veritas morum est rectitudo, secundum quam homo bene vivit intus et extra secundum dictamen juris, quia jus est regula rectitudinis ..." *De Donis,* coll. 4, n. 7, V, p. 475.

[97] Although this subdivision dates back to Aristotle (cf. the *Nich. Ethics,* vi, 8, 1141b; *Eud. Ethics,* i, 8, 1218b, and the first two chapters of the *Politics*), nevertheless, Bonaventure need not have taken it directly from Aristotle since it is also found in Hugh of St. Victor, *Eruditio Didascalica,* 20, *P.L.* 176, 759.

For further details concerning the moral philosophy of St. Bonaventure, the reader is referred to the work of Christ Nölkensmeier, O.F.M., "Ethische Grundfragen bei Bonaventura," *Forschungen zur Geschichte der Philosophie und der Pädagogik,* Band 5, Heft 2, Leipzig, 1932.

In his *In Hex.,* coll. 5, nn. 1–21, V, pp. 353–357, the Seraphic Doctor divides moral philosophy according to the various types of virtues.

[98] *In Hex.,* coll. 5, nn. 14–20, V, pp. 356–357.

[99] "Hic non debeo loqui sicut theologus nec sicut jurista, sed sicut philosophus loquitur." *Ibid.,* n. 14, p. 356.

[100] "Ad censuram judicandi non pervenitur nisi per normam praesidendi; nec ad normam praesidendi nisi per formam convivendi; nec ad istam nisi per primam." *Ibidem.*

St. Bonaventure also asserts that these four justices are not found in any one philosopher, although they, or something similar to them, can be arfor a truly harmonious political life, man must be rightly ordered: first, with regard to God; second, with regard to his fellowman; third, with reference to the social organism; and fourth, relative to his norm of judgment. In these four moral justices, moreover, are contained, in the form of conclusions, all that modern authors include in their tracts on *Special Ethics*, excepting the duties of man towards himself.[101]

The *ritus colendi* is the moral justice which concerns the worship due to God. That God must be worshipped is clearly known not only from faith, but also from reason. Indeed, the divine cult of sacrifice and praise is a dictate of nature itself.[102] Furthermore, not only is the individual held to worship God, but civil authority as well is obliged to enforce the fulfillment of this duty and to punish those who do not render homage to the Deity.[103] The orientation of Bonaventure's thought is seen right from the start. Civil authority and civil law, in order to be right, must not only refrain from infringing upon the rights due to God, but must even foster divine homage—nay, more, command it and punish those who are negligent in this matter.

The *forma convivendi* is the moral justice which dictates that inter-individual relations should be regulated in accordance with that command inscribed in the heart of man—namely, " Do not unto another what you do not wish another to do unto you." [104] From this basic natural law, Bonaventure affirms, proceed the

---

rived at from examining the works of the different philosophers. " Nullus autem philosophorum dedit hanc, sed si fuerit collecta ex multis, aliquid proveniat." *Ibidem.*

[101] This is also the opinion of Tinivella, *op. cit.,* p. 181.

[102] " Sacrificium autem laudis in corde naturale judicatorium dictat, et est de dictamine naturae; et in hoc consenserunt omnes veri philosophi." *Ibid.,* n. 17, pp. 356–357. " Cultus autem Dei consistit in laude et sacrificio." *Ibid.,* n. 15, p. 356.

[103] " Unde dicit ille, quod 'quid dubitat, utrum parentes honorandi sunt, et Deus venerandus, poena dignus est.' " *Ibidem.*

[104] " Secundus modus est forma convivendi, ut: 'Quod tibi non vis fieri, ne facias alteri.' Hoc in corde scriptum est per legem aeternam." *Ibid.,* n. 18, p. 357.

other laws and canons which make for harmonious living among human beings.[105]

The *norma praesidendi* refers to the relations that should exist between the ruler and the people on the one hand, and between the people and the ruler on the other. This norm, likewise a prescription of the natural law, sets forth the rules governing the conduct of the citizens (i.e., that they are to be zealous for the observance of law and aid the ruler in punishing and warring) as well as the rules regulating the conduct of those constituted in authority (namely, that they are to seek, at all times, the common good of the commonwealth and not their own private utility). In other words, the same rule—seek the common good—is to govern the activities of both the ruled and the rulers.[106]

The *censura judicandi* relates to the correct judgment which

---

[105] "Ex hac naturali lege emanant leges et canones, pullulationes pulcriae." *Ibidem.*

In answer to the objection: "You do not wish to be hanged, and yet you hang the thief?" the Seraphic Doctor advances the teaching that the good of the whole social organism must be set above the convenience of the individual. "Sed quid? Tu non vis suspendi, et latronem suspendis? Dicendum, quod latro prius debet suspendi, quam ut respublica laedatur . . ." *Ibidem.*

[106] "Tertia est norma praesidendi, id est qualiter princeps ad populum debet se habere, et e converso. Et haec emanat a veritate prima: quia populus debet assistere punienti et vindicanti; princeps non debet suam utilitatem quaerere, sed respublicae." *Ibid.*, n. 19, p. 357. Further teaching on the norma praesidendi is contained in *Liber II S.*, d. 44, aa. 2, 3, II, pp. 1005ss; d. 9, a. 1, q. 6, conc., p. 252; d. 6, a. 3, q. 2, pp. 168–169. Moreover, cf. Tinivella, *op. cit.*, p. 183.

In his consideration of this moral justice, St. Bonaventure presents what he considers to be the best form of government—the constitutional monarchy. He demands that the rulers be elected, since those societies that are ruled by leaders elected by the people are generally better governed than those societies which are regulated by rulers designated through heredity. To show his point he appeals to the history of the Romans and reminds his readers that the Roman state was well-governed when the people elected their rulers, whereas such was not the case when their rulers succeeded by heredity. *In Hex.*, coll. 5, n. 19, V, p. 357.

man must exercise with reference to persons, things, and the method of acting.[107]

These four moral justices, therefore, are the main principles that govern the whole of man's social life. They are the bases upon which the whole structure of St. Bonaventure's social doctrine can be erected. Nevertheless, as we approach the precise matter of our discussion, we must not lose sight of what has already been said concerning the Seraphic Doctor's teachings in general, for behind and beneath all his writings there lies one main, one general theme—the ordering of all things towards the central Being, God. This underlying motive—ever present, ever principal in all of Bonaventure's works—must not and cannot be overlooked in the consideration of his social thought.

From this focal point of his teachings, then, and from the fact that, for him, faith must be joined to reason, it follows that any consideration of man, whether as an individual person or as a social entity, cannot, without proving unfaithful to the thought of our saintly author, overlook the various phases of man's history and nature which are known through the medium of revelation. We must, therefore, concern ourselves with the real and the entire man. We must consider him not solely as an animal raised to the heights of rationality, not simply as one possessing human nature, but as a creature of God, fallen from the state of innocence, redeemed by Christ, elevated to supernatural life, destined to a supernatural end.

That pure, unaided reason cannot acquaint us with these facts we know to be true, and hence we agree with our saintly author that reason is not to be separated from faith. If, therefore, we intend to study the social thought of the Seraphic Doctor and desire to grasp his true teaching, we must study Bonaventure in the light of Bonaventure, not in the light of our own strict separation of philosophy from theology. To act differently is to act erroneously; it is to acquire a deformed notion of his teachings, to accept a half-truth. That is why our title reads: *The*

---

[107] "Ultima est censura judicandi, ut homo sciat, quid de quacumque re sit judicandum, quod spectat ad personas, ad res, ad modum agendi. Haec omnia manant a veritate prima." *In Hex.*, coll. 5, n. 20, V, p. 357.

Social Thought of St. Bonaventure and not the *Social Philosophy*.

We must note, too, that the Seraphic Doctor will not accept a stunted and deformed view of man. Is not that view, after all, a stunted and deformed one from which are excluded the facts of man's fall, his redemption, his elevation to the state of grace, and his supernatural destiny? Pure rational philosophy cannot, it is true, arrive at these truths. Are we, then, to change our man to suit our learning, or are we not to change the standards of our learning and accept the higher light of faith, in order to attain to a true knowledge of man? Is not the purely rational man merely a myth? Then, if our science has this man of myth as its object, can our science itself be anything more than mythical?

With St. Bonaventure there is no question of what is to be done. Faith must supply for the deficiency of reason. Consequently, the Seraphic Doctor is concerned with man as he actually is—with the true man—and his social considerations are necessarily influenced by this concern. Thus, for instance, man's goal of supernatural blessedness, since it conditions his mode of behaviour and dictates the means that are to be used, plays an important role in the orientation of Bonaventure's social thought. Indeed, our author derives the very end of social life itself from the final goal of man. For we, our saintly doctor writes, must so regulate our life, be it as a private individual or as a member of society, that "this earthly exile may become a true outpost of the heavenly kingdom in such a wise that we may every day savour in advance something of the eternal beatitude." [108]

---

[108] "Revera aestimo, o anima, si haec caelestia gaudia jugiter in mente teneres, *de hoc exilio quoddam suburbium caelestis regni construeres, in quo illam aeternam dulcedinem quotidie spiritualiter praelibando degustares.*" *Soliloquium*, c. 4, pp. 1, n. 4, VIII, p. 57.

CHAPTER II

MAN AND THE UNIVERSE

Before we can examine the trend of an author's social thought, it is of prime importance that we have at least a general conspectus of his teaching concerning the nature of man, since social philosophy is nothing more than a certain aspect in the study of man—man considered as a social entity. In order to acquire a true picture of St. Bonaventure's social thought, therefore, we should be acquainted with his teaching on man— what man is, whence he comes, why he comes, where he goes. Accordingly, the purpose of the present chapter is to discuss in three articles his ideas on: (1) the Universe and Man's Place Therein, (2) the Nature and Dignity of Man, and (3) the Present Condition of Man.

ARTICLE I. THE UNIVERSE AND MAN'S PLACE THEREIN

SECTION 1. CREATION AND ITS THREEFOLD RELATION TO GOD

As we approach St. Bonaventure's doctrine concerning creation, we meet with the general content of his philosophy, which, as we have seen, consists of Emanationism, Exemplarism, and Return. In his mind, the creature is related to God by means of a triple causal relation—it is produced by the Efficient Cause, in conformity to the Exemplar Cause, and ordered to Him as to its Final End, since the First and Most Perfect Principle, from which the perfection of all other things flows, must act of itself, according to itself, and for itself.[1] When, therefore, we study God as the efficient cause of creation, we encounter Bonaventure's *Emanationism;* when, again, we consider God as the exemplar cause of creation, we enter into the second section of his philosophy, i.e., *Exemplarism;* and, finally, when we are con-

---

[1] *Breviloquium,* p. 2, c. 1, V, p. 219.

cerned with God as the final cause, we come to his third and final stage in philosophy, namely, the *Return*.

The Seraphic Doctor's teaching regarding God as the efficient cause of creation can be summarized thus:—all creatures have been created out of nothing, in time, and immediately, by a unique and sole principle, God.[2] However, since the First Principle is an intelligent agent and since He is of another nature than the things produced, God brings things into being not in the manner of nature, but by the way of art.[3] At this point arises, then, the question of exemplary ideas, according to which the *exemplata* are produced.

According to our author, there is a *ratio* in the Divine Mind corresponding to everything which God knows or does.[4] These prototypal forms, fixed and unchanging principles existing in the mind of God from all eternity, we call *ideas*.[5] Since these ideas are in reality the truth of God, they are identical with the essence of the Divine, and, consequently, there is no real distinction among the different ideas.[6] On the other hand, although the knowing subject is one, the things known are many; and hence, while all the ideas are actually one in God, still they are many because of the relationship to the things they connote.[7]

---

[2] " Circa quam haec tenenda sunt in summa: videlicet quod universitas machinae mundialis producta est in esse ex tempore et de nihilo ab uno principio primo, solo et summo . . ." *Ibidem.* For a detailed report and study of creation, cf. *Liber II S.,* d. 1, II, pp. 13–52.

[3] For Bonaventure, an agent in the manner of nature produces through forms which are true natures; thus man produces man, and an ass produces another ass. An agent in manner of intellect, on the other hand, produces through forms which are not something of the thing, but ideas in the mind, as the idea a carpenter has in his mind when making a box. There is no third way. *Liber II S.,* d. 1, p. 1, a. 1, q. 1, ad 3, II, p. 17; *In Hex.,* coll. 12, n. 3, V, p. 385.

[4] ". . . similitudo rei, per quam res cognoscitur et producitur, est idea . . ." *Liber I. S.,* d. 35, a. 1, q. 1, f. 2, I, p. 600.

[5] *Ibid.,* conc., pp. 600–601.

[6] ". . . ideae sunt unum secundum rem. Et hoc patet sic: idea in Deo dicit similitudinem, quae est ratio cognoscendi; illa autem secundum rem est ipsa divina veritas . . . et quia illa est una, patet, quod secundum rem omnes ideae unum sunt." *Ibid.,* q. 2, conc., pp. 605–606. Cf. *Ibid.,* q. 1, conc., p. 601.

[7] " Et quoniam cognoscens est unum, et cognita sunt multa; ideo omnes

The Seraphic Doctor not only places the ideas in the essence of God, but also connects the production of exemplar ideas with the generation of the Word. Indeed, in his teaching, the act by which the Father thinks Himself, knows Himself, and expresses Himself, would not be an integral image of Himself if it failed to represent not only the Infinite Being of God, but also all the possibilities which are virtually contained in Him. So, the Word is both the representation of God and the Model, the Exemplar of all things as well.[8]

Furthermore, God is the Supreme Good, and, since it is the nature of good to diffuse itself, this must be true of God to a supreme and eminent degree.[9] In fact, the better the good in question, the more it tends to communicate itself; and the more it diffuses itself, the greater the number of beings to which it tends to communicate itself.[10] In this manner, then, the creation of the world in time is explained as a manifestation of the diffusion of Divine Goodness. However, not only does good tend of its nature to diffuse itself, but it is also the end to which everything else is ordered. Therefore, we can conclude that God must, since He is the Supreme Good, be also the Supreme and Final End of all things.

With these preliminary thoughts in mind we can readily perceive that the purpose of creation is the manifestation of the

---

ideae in Deo sunt unum secundum rem, sed tamen plures secundum rationem intelligendi sive dicendi." *Ibid.,* q. 3, conc., p. 608.

[8] *In Hex.,* coll. 1, n. 13, V, p. 331. For a fuller understanding of Bonaventure's teaching in this regard, cf.: *Liber I. S.,* d. 35, I, pp. 600–613; *In Hex.,* coll. 3, nn. 4–5, V, pp. 343–344; coll. 20, n. 5, p. 426. Reference can also be had to Gilson, *op. cit.,* c. 4, pp. 141–159.

[9] "Nam bonum dicitur diffusivum, et bonum est propter quod omnia." *Liber I. S.,* d. 45, a. 2, q. 1, conc., I, p. 804.

We may remark, at this point, that we cannot, from the above-stated principle, conclude that the creation was in any way necessary. For, although it is of the nature of good to diffuse itself, the necessary productivity of the Eternal Good is seen in the Blessed Trinity, for the Trinity of the Divine Persons expresses at the outset this infinite power of the internal expansion in the engendering of the Son and the procession of the Holy Spirit from the Son and the Father. Cf. *Itin.,* c. 6, n. 2, V, pp. 310–311.

[10] *Liber II S.,* d. 1, p. 2, a. 1, q. 1, ff. 1–3, conc., and ad 4, II, pp. 39–40.

Glory of God. At the same time, though, we must understand that the Perfection and Goodness of the Eternal is in no way increased by the production of created beings, since creatures, which are but the images of the Eternal Perfection and participations of the Infinite Goodness, do not increase but only manifest the Eternal Glory. It is this manifestation of Eternal Glory, precisely, that constitutes the immediate end of creation and that becomes, in turn, the end of the creatures themselves, since each and every thing created, no matter what degree of creation is considered, exists solely to manifest the Glory of God and, as a result, finds its usefulness, glory, and happiness only in glorifying God and reflecting His Beatitude.[11]

Since the end of creation is the manifestation of God's Glory, it follows that the realm of creation must bear the stamp of the Power, Wisdom, and Goodness of the Divine. The power of an agent, St. Bonaventure tells us, is measured by his ability to produce objects that are vastly distinct from one another and to institute a certain communication and harmony among these distant and different beings. There is a vast distance and difference between corporeal and spiritual substances and, consequently, the power of the Eternal was made manifest when He united these two vastly distant and separated spheres of creation by producing man, a substance, at once, both spiritual and corporeal.[12]

The wisdom of the agent, on the other hand, is known from the perfection of order which exists in his work. Order, however, supposes a superior, an inferior, and a middle degree. The wisdom of the Divine, therefore, is manifested in the universe, for here we have a superior, an inferior, and a middle degree—in the lowest degree of creation we find the purely corporeal natures; in the highest, the purely spiritual; and in the central position, a nature composed of both the spiritual and the corporeal creation—man.[13]

Finally, the goodness of the agent appears from the manner in which his own goodness is diffused in others. God, in order

---

[11] *Ibid.*, a. 2, q. 1, conc., p. 44. Cf. *Ibid.*, ad 3, pp. 44–45.

[12] *Ibid.*, a. 1, q. 2, f. 1, p. 41.

[13] *Ibid.*, f. 2, p. 41.

to diffuse Himself in the most intimate manner, had to give to creatures not only the most noble perfections, such as being, life, and intelligence, but also the very power of communication. Here, then, is the reason why man has been created and placed midway between the purely spiritual natures endowed with life and intelligence and the purely corporeal natures which can be perfected only through intelligence and life. Being a substance composed of both the spiritual and corporeal creation, man not only possesses, through the medium of his soul, the most noble perfections of life and intelligence proper to the spiritual creation, but also enjoys, because of his substantial unity, the power of communicating these noble perfections to the corporeal sphere of creation represented in his body.[14]

SECTION 2.   THE UNIVERSE AS THE MIRROR OF GOD

At this point we begin to gain a keener insight into Bonaventure's outlook concerning the universe. Having seen that God, in creating the world, intended to manifest His Power, Wisdom, and Goodness, we can conclude that the universe must, in its entirety, be a vast mirror reflecting the Eternal Glory. Thus we come to one of the most refreshing and inspiring sections of St. Bonaventure's thought—the section which Gilson refers to as the *Universal Analogy,* but which we prefer to term *The Universe as the Mirror of God.*[15] The basis of this doctrine is found in the Exemplarism of the Seraphic Doctor. For, he tells us, corresponding to the active element on the part of God, Who is the type, pattern, and model of all things, there is on the part of creatures—once the Divine Power has given them

---

[14] *Ibid.,* f. 3, pp. 41–42.

[15] This is not our invention. Gilson, himself, makes use of the same terminology. Cf. *op. cit.,* p. 221. Nor have we any argument with Gilson, for although Gilson's manner of expressing it may be more scientific, since ultimately it is an analogy-relation between the model and the copy with which St. Bonaventure is concerned, nevertheless, we prefer the above-mentioned terminology as being, in our opinion, more expressive of the thought of the Seraphic Doctor.

For a deeper insight into Bonaventure's teachings we refer the reader to Gilson, *op. cit.,* pp. 196–227; Bissen, Jean Marie, O.F.M., *L'Exemplarisme Divin Selon S. Bonaventure.*

existence—a passive character which reflects their Divine origin in proportion to their respective powers of representation. The study of exemplarism, then, invites a twofold approach—namely, the study of God as the Exemplar of all things and the study of created beings as copies or likenesses of their Exemplar and Creator.[16] From this consideration of the creature as the copy of the Divine Model we come to Bonaventure's true evaluation of the universe, which he holds to be a vast society of diverse beings, each showing forth, in its own manner, the greatness of God— the whole together manifesting that perfection which none of the individual beings taken separately could hope to express adequately.[17] Since each and every creature bears the imprint of the Divine Fashioner, having been created *secundum Deum,* it follows that all things created proclaim the perfection of the Creative Goodness.[18]

The Seraphic Doctor finds various types of resemblance and degrees of imprint in creatures. For this reason, he speaks of: (a) the *umbra* or *shadow,* which is a distant and confused representation of God; (b) the *vestigium* or *vestige,* a distant

---

[16] *Liber I S.,* d. 31, p. 2, a. 1, q. 1, conc., I, p. 540.

In this regard, Father Bissen claims that the term *exemplarism,* in the strict sense of the word, excludes the outstanding element of Bonaventure's doctrine, namely, the consideration of the creature as the expression of God, and, consequently, he remarks that the doctrine should be called *expressionism.* He then attempts to formulate a definition which would cover both aspects of the problem, i.e., "La doctrine des relations d'expression qui existent entre Dieu e la creature." *Op. cit.,* p. 4.

St. Bonaventure himself makes constant use of the term *expressio.* Cf. *Liber I S.,* d. 35, a. 1, q. 1, I, pp. 600–602; *De Scientia Xti.,* q. 2, ad 5, V, p. 9; *In Hex.,* coll. 11, nn. 13–25, V, pp. 382–384.

[17] ". . . creatura, quae est bonitatis finitae; ideo quod non potuit capere creatura in se, accepit quodam modo in sibi socia, ut sic ex multis una perficeretur mundialis machina." *Liber II S.,* d. 1, p. 2, a. 1, q. 1, ad 4, II, p. 40. Cf. *Ibid.,* ff. 1, 2, 3, p. 39.

[18] Bonaventure tells us that a certain type of analogy—that whereby one imitates the other or is the similitude of the other—is found in the relation of *exemplaritas* between the universe and God. *Liber I S.,* d. 1, a. 3, q. 1, ad 1, I, pp. 38–39; *Ibid.,* d. 3, p. 1, a. 1, q. 2, ad 3, p. 72; *Liber II S.,* d. 16, a. 1, q. 1, ad 2, II, p. 395.

but distinct representation; and (c) the *imago* or *image*, a representation that is both distinct and close.[19]   All creatures without exception, according to the teaching of the Saint, are both shadows and vestiges of the Eternal.   Rational creatures, and only they, since they alone are related to God as to their object and are capable of Him through cognition and love, are also the images of God.[20]

Having posited the various degrees of divine imprint established by the Seraphic Doctor, we must go further and recall that, according to his mind, the fact of representation found in the creation is not something accidental.   Creatures are *naturally*, and hence *necessarily*, the imitations and analogies of God.   Indeed, as our saintly author tells us, it is in the very nature of the creature to be an image and reflection of the Creator, for the property of divine likeness is a substantial property of each and every created being.[21]   Therefore, Bonaventure views creation as a sort of representation—a picture or statue—of Divine

----

[19] *Liber I S.*, d. 3, p. 1, a. 1, q. 2, ad 4, I, pp. 72–73.

Besides these three imprints of the Divine—shadow, vestige, and image— St. Bonaventure makes mention of a fourth degree of representation, i.e., the *similitudo* or divine grace.   Our author terms this the *imago recreationis* to distinguish it from the Divine reflection—*imago creationis*—which every rational creature naturally bears.   Designating a supreme participation in the Divine, the *similitudo*—a quality of the Divine Essence, created and yet Godlike—renders man deiform, acceptable to God, and worthy of eternal life.   More, it enables him to enter into the society of the Divine, for, by means of the similitude of grace, the soul becomes the temple of the Holy Spirit, the spouse of the Incarnate Son, and the daughter of the Eternal Father. *Breviloquium*, p. 2, c. 12, V, p. 230; *Ibid.*, p. 5, c. 1, pp. 252–253; *Liber II S.*, d. 16, a. 2, q. 3, conc., II, p. 405.

[20] ". . . ideo omnis creatura est umbra vel vestigium.   Sed quoniam sola rationalis creatura comparatur ad Deum ut objectum, quia sola est capax Dei per cognitionem et amorem: ideo sola est imago." *Liber I S.*, d. 3, p. 1, a. 1, q. 2, ad 4, I, p. 73.

[21] " Omnis enim creatura ex natura est illius aeternae sapientiae quaedam effigies et similitudo . . ." *Itin.*, c. 2, n. 12, V, p. 303.

". . . esse imaginem Dei non est homini accidens, sed potius substantiale, sicut esse vestigium nulli accidit creaturae." *Liber II S.*, d. 16, a. 1, q. 2, f. 4, II, p. 397.

Wisdom.[22] The universe is a book in which the creative Trinity resplends, is represented, and is to be read.[23]

If the created world is a book that is to be read, does it not follow, then, that there should exist a creature capable of reading it? Indeed, as Supreme Power and Majesty, God made all things for His glory; as Supreme Light, He created all things to manifest Himself; as Supreme Goodness, He produced all things to communicate Himself.[24] However, there can be no perfect glory, unless there is a being to admire and approve the traces of this supreme power and majesty; no perfect manifestation, unless there is a creature capable of understanding the reflected brilliance of the Eternal Light; no perfect communication of goodness, unless there is a beneficiary to whom the reflected goods have been communicated and who is free to use them and delight in them.[25] Therefore, there must exist a creature endowed with rational life, who can celebrate this Glory, grasp this manifestation of truth, and have power over these communicated goods—who is ordered immediately towards God. That creature is man.[26]

---

[22] ". . . creatura non est nisi quoddam simulacrum sapientiae Dei et quoddam sculptile." *In Hex.,* coll. 12, n. 14, V, p. 386.

[23] ". . . creatura mundi est quasi quidam liber, in quo relucet, repraesentatur et legitur Trinitas fabricatrix. . . ." *Breviloquium,* p. 2, c. 12, V, p. 230.

[24] "Deus enim universa propter semetipsum operatus est, ita quod, cum sit summa potestas et majestas, fecit omnia ad sui laudem; cum sit summa lux, fecit omnia ad sui manifestationem; cum sit summa bonitas, fecit omnia ad sui communicationem." *Liber II S.,* d. 16, a. 1, q. 1, conc., II, p. 394.

[25] "Non est autem perfecta laus, nisi adsit qui approbet; nec est perfecta manifestatio, nisi adsit qui intelligat; non perfecta communicatio bonorum, nisi adsit qui eis uti valeat." *Ibidem.*

[26] "Et quoniam laudem approbare, veritatem scire, dona in usum assumere non est nisi solummodo rationalis creaturae; ideo non habent ipsae creaturae irrationales immediate ad Deum ordinari, sed mediante creatura rationali. Ipsa autem creatura rationalis, quia de se nata est et laudare et nosse et res alias in facultatem voluntatis assumere, nata est ordinari in Deum immediate." *Ibidem.*

Bonaventure's teaching on the image can be found in *Liber I S.,* d. 10, p. 2, a. 1, q. 1, conc., I, p. 540; *Ibid.,* d. 3, p. 2, a. 1, q. 2, conc., p. 83 and ad 5, p. 84; *Liber II S.,* d. 16, II, pp. 394ss.

SECTION 3. MAN'S ROLE IN THE UNIVERSE

We have seen that all creatures, since they were brought into existence to show forth the Glory of the Eternal Maker, are, of their very nature, reflections of the Divine. We have also noted that only the rational creatures are immediately ordered towards God. Since all things have been made by God, according to God, and for God, there now arises the question: in what manner are the *irrational* creatures ordered towards the Eternal? If not immediately, then, surely, in an indirect and mediate manner.[27]

As there is but one Efficient Cause from which all things proceed, so there is but one Ultimate End towards which all things, rational or irrational, tend—God. At the same time, however, irrational creatures have been assigned a secondary and subordinate end, i.e., man. All irrational creatures are ordered towards man as to their proximate end, and through this ordination to man, whose ultimate end is God, they are, in turn, ultimately ordered to God (i.e., led to their ultimate end).[28] We can better understand such proximate and remote ordination when we recall that though all things created are to participate in the Eternal Goodness, nevertheless, as Bonaventure notes, there is a twofold manner of participation. Certain creatures, those of a spiritual nature, are born to participate in the Eternal Glory *immediately;* others, the irrational, participate *indirectly,* i.e., by being of service to those who participate therein directly.[29] Brought into existence for the sake of man, these creatures must, therefore, minister to man and be at his disposal.[30] Also, from the fact that man is the proximate end of the purely corporeal creation, our author derives the corollary that man's superior perfection and dignity required that he be created after all the

---

[27] *Liber II S.,* d. 16, a. 1, q. 1, conc., II, p. 394. Cf. footnote 26.

[28] *Liber II S.,* d. 15, a. 2, q. 1, conc., II, pp. 382–383. Cf. *Ibid.,* d. 19, a. 1, q. 1, conc., p. 463.

[29] *Ibid.,* d. 1, p. 2, a. 1, q. 2, ad 1, p. 42.

[30] " Vide jam, anima mea, et diligenter considera, quod Creator tuus, rex tuus, sponsus et amicus, totam machinam mundialem ad tuum ordinavit ministerium." *Soliloquium,* c. 1, n. 7, VIII, pp. 31–32. Cf. the whole of this number; *Breviloquium,* p. 2, c. 4, V, p. 222.

other creatures, in a world fully prepared to receive him, since the end crowns the work.[31]

This thought brings with it another question: why was the irrational creation subjected to man? Surely, to provide for the needs of his body and to offer delight to his senses.[32] However, as Bonaventure asserts, creation, besides administering to man's body, must first and foremost be of service to man's soul.[33] It must offer him the means whereby he can rise to praise and love the Eternal. This acquaints us with man's role in the universe—to order the unconscious creation to God, by referring the world to Him of Whom it speaks.[34]

With these considerations before us, we begin to grasp the reason why the mind of the Seraphic Doctor was totally and solely directed to God. Since the whole world was created to manifest and communicate the Divine Goodness, since it is in the essence of every creature to be a representation of the Eternal, our saintly author could not remain satisfied with mere imitations and representations. Consequently, he sought to soar beyond this world of copies in order to seek out the Exemplar, the Model of all things. His aim was wisdom. He could not allow his mind to lower itself and waste itself in the contemplation of the mere corporeal natures.[35]

As a true Franciscan, Bonaventure could not really despise the world, nor sense-knowledge, nor the pleasure derived from sense-

---

[31] " Quia enim homo sua dignitate et complemento finis est omnium corporalium; ideo post omnia erat producenda, ut sua productione finiret et compleret omnia praecidentia, tanquam, finis complet quod ad ipsum ordinari habet." *Liber II S.,* d. 15, a. 2, a. 2, conc., II, p. 385.

[32] *S. de Temp., Dom. XVII p. Pent.,* s. 1, IX, p. 420; *Soliloquium,* c. 1, n. 7, VIII, p. 32.

[33] " Notandum autem, quod mundus, etsi servit homini quantum ad corpus, potissime tamen quantum ad animam, etsi servit quantum ad vitam, potissime quantum ad sapientiam." *In Hex.,* coll. 13, n. 12, V, pp. 389–390.

[34] ". . . primum principium fecit mundum istum sensibilem ad declarandum se ipsum, videlicet ad hoc, quod per illum tanquam per speculum et vestigium reduceretur homo in Deum artificem amandum et laudandum." *Breviloquium,* p. 2, c. 11, V, p. 229. Cf. *Ibid.,* p. 2, c. 4, p. 222; *Liber II S.,* d. 1, p. 2, a. 1, q. 2, ad 1, II, p. 42.

[35] *In Hex.,* coll. 2, n. 21, V, p. 340.

knowledge. Nor could he, on the other hand, be fully content with this world, be attached to it, or seek his delight in it. Following in the footsteps of the Seraph of Assisi, he embraced and loved all things because each told him something of the Eternal Father and lifted his heart to the love of the Divine and because each creature was a rung in the ladder whereby he could ascend to the attainment of Him, Who is all that can be desired.[36]

To grasp the philosophy behind this attitude of our author, we must recall that, according to his teaching, creatures may be considered either as things or as symbols.[37] Thus, there are two ways of viewing the universe: (a) that of the natural philosopher, who is interested in the nature of things; and (b) that of the contemplative, who looks upon all creatures as symbols of something higher and more real. The path followed by St. Bonaventure is clear. For him, it is wrong to allow the mind to be captivated by the beauty of the creature, since the creature is offered to the mind as a way to higher things, as a sign inviting man to mount to the One Whose beauty it merely reflects and of Whose goodness it partakes.[38]

The creatures do exist; they have a certain entity, truth, beauty, and goodness. Still, to ignore the *vestige character* natural to each creature and concentrate exclusively upon the mere *nature* of the creature is, in the mind of our author, to follow in the footsteps of the blind philosophers of nature, who, having neglected the fact that creatures are essentially signs of the Divine, have lost that which makes creation intelligible. For them, creation is a mere conglomeration of things.[39]

---

[36] *Legenda Sti. Francisci,* c. 9, n. 1, VIII, p. 530.

[37] ". . . aliae creaturae possunt considerari ut res, vel ut signa. Primo modo sunt inferiores homine, secundo modo sunt media in deveniendo, sive in via, non in termino, quia illae non perveniunt, sed per illas pervenit homo ad Deum, illis post se relictis." *Liber I S.,* d. 3, p. 1, a. 1, q. 3, ad 2, I, p. 75.

[38] ". . . aut sistitur in pulchritudine creaturae, aut per illam tenditur in aliud. Si primo modo, tunc est via deviationis. . . . Si secundo modo, prout est via in aliud, sic est ratio cognoscendi per superexcellentiam, quia omnia proprietas nobilis in creatura Deo est attribuenda in summo . . ." *Ibid.,* q. 2, ad 1, p. 72.

[39] *In Hex.,* coll. 12, n. 14, V, p. 386; *Ibid.,* coll. 1, n. 10, p. 331.

The true thinker, on the contrary, must rise above the mere nature of things and seek the Eternal Model according to which these *natures* have been brought into being. The reason is that created realities can be most fully known only when we know them in their Eternal Exemplars, which express these realities more fully and more perfectly than they express themselves.[40] To see God in every creature, therefore, is the highest degree of knowledge—the domain reserved to the metaphysician. Then, only, St. Bonaventure believes, does the philosopher walk on ground that is exclusively his; then, only, is he a true metaphysician—when he rises to the consideration of God as the exemplary cause of all things.[41] Exemplarism, therefore, for the Seraphic Doctor, is the very heart of metaphysics. From it flows all light; without it there is total darkness.[42]

Hence, the role man is to play in this universe is rendered clear—to read the analogies below him and to refer them to their invisible source in the Word. When he does this, then is man truly wise.[43] When he does this, then is the universe through man's agency ordered towards its Maker.

In the dawn of time man found the fulfilling of this role a simple task. With the Fall, however, the book of creation became unintelligible and closed to man—a veritable Babel of unknown tongues. Another book was required, a code book that would unscramble the confusion and aid man in arriving at an understanding of the universe—a book of revealed truth.[44] When man's understanding is enlightened by faith, the

---

[40] ". . . illa enim similitudo exemplaris perfectius exprimit rem, quam ipsa res causata exprimit se ipsam." *De Scientia Xti*, q. 2, ad 9, V, p. 10. Cf. remainder of this section.

[41] "Sed ut considerat illud esse in ratione omnia exemplantis, cum nullo communicat et verus est metaphysicus." *In Hex.*, coll. 1, n. 13, V, p. 331. Cf. the whole of this *collatio*.

[42] *In Hex.*, coll. 6, nn. 2–6, V, pp. 360–361. In this section Bonaventure condemns Aristotle for his denial of exemplarism.

[43] ". . . ut sic sapiens esset, cum universas res videret in se, videret in proprio genere, videret etiam in arte, secundum quod res tripliciter habent esse, scilicet in materia vel propria, in intelligentia creata et in arte aeterna . . ." *Breviloquium*, p. 2, c. 12, V, p. 230.

[44] *In Hex.*, coll. 2, n. 20, V, p. 340; coll. 13, n. 12, pp. 389–390.

book of nature is again intelligible, and the world becomes a radiant constellation showing forth the glory of the Divine.[45]

From this brief study of Bonaventure's doctrine concerning the universe, we have seen that all things were produced by God, according to God, and for God, since He is the efficient, the exemplary, and final Cause of all. We have been told that all creatures were produced from nothing, in time, and immediately, by a sole, unique Principle; that they were brought into being *per artem et voluntatem;* and that they were given existence in order to exhibit the Eternal Glory. Therefrom we received the concept of a hierarchically constituted universe—God is the central point; in the sphere closest to Him is the purely spiritual creation; in the sphere furthest removed from Him is the purely material and corporeal; and in the intermediate sphere exists the union of the corporeal and spiritual in the creature man. At the same time, the universe was represented to us as the Mirror of God—with each and every creature reflecting God, its Maker, its Exemplar, and its End, since the universe is a book in which the creative Trinity resplends, is reflected, and can be read. Here, too, we caught a glimpse of hierarchical constitution, for at one extreme we have the shadow and the vestige; at the other extreme, the similitude of grace; and in between, the image.

Finally, as we sought to pierce the mystery of the universe in its relation to man, we discovered that the whole of irrational creation tends towards a proximate and subordinate end—man. In fact, man, who was brought into being only when the earthly abode was fully prepared to receive him, is the king of the inferior creation. To man, its king, the world ministers by providing for his bodily needs and by speaking to him of their mutual Author, God. It is then man's duty to direct this world of inferior creation, subject to him, towards its First Beginning and its Last End. Thus, having been placed in a world pregnant with the divine imprint, man has been assigned the role of leading the world back to its Author by seeing Him, praising Him, and loving Him in all things.

---

[45] *Ibid.,* coll. 2, n. 27, p. 340.

ARTICLE II. THE NATURE AND DIGNITY OF MAN

In considering the various beings produced by the Creator, we discovered that midway between the purely spiritual and the purely material creation there exists a being both spiritual and material in nature—man. Before we can touch on that section of Bonaventure's thought which may be strictly termed as social, we must establish his teaching concerning the nature and the status of man. For, without a true understanding of human nature, we would attempt in vain to set up a system of social thought. Hence, our aim in the present article is to bring the following points under brief consideration: (a) man, the composite; (b) the rational powers of man—cognitive and affective; (c) the human personality; (d) man's final end; and (e) the equality of men.

SECTION 1. MAN, THE COMPOSITE

Few writers have given us a more beautiful and more complete description of man than has the Seraphic Doctor. Man, he declares, partakes of the mineral world inasmuch as his body contains the various elements and is at the same time most delicate and most complete in composition.[46] Besides, he enjoys all the powers and virtues that are predicated of the animal kingdom.[47] Finally, and above all, he is of the spiritual world, for he possesses the faculties of intellect and will by means of which he is able to make use of the material creation, to surpass it and govern it, and through it to tend directly to God, his ultimate end.[48]

For this reason, according to Bonaventurian doctrine, neither the body nor the soul can be called man, for man is a composite —the *" forma totius."* [49] In order to demonstrate His Power,

---

[46] *Liber II S.,* d. 15, a. 2, q. 2, conc., II, p. 385.

[47] ". . . omnes virtutes, quae sunt in animalibus dispersae, in homine colliguntur, sicut arma omnium animalium in manu hominum . . ." *Liber IV S.,* d. 33, a. 1, q. 1, conc., IV, p. 748.

[48] *Liber II S.,* d. 16, a. 1, q. 1, conc., II, p. 394; *Breviloquium,* p. 2, c. 4, V, p. 222; *Ibid.,* p. 7, c. 4, pp. 284–285.

[49] " Nihil enim facit hominem esse actu, nisi actualis conjunctio animae cum carne." *Liber III S.,* d. 22, a. 1, q. 1, conc., III, p. 451. ". . . quod

God made man a composite of two substances that are most distant from one another—the material and the spiritual—joining these in one nature and one person.[50] Thus, we cannot speak of a perfect man unless we mean a body with all its members and a soul with all its faculties.[51] Man is composed of rational soul and organized flesh, which are united after the manner of matter and form—the organized flesh is the material and the rational soul the formal element of man.[52]

As regards the human body itself, the Seraphic Doctor teaches that it is the most complex of all bodies. In fact, because this body is destined to be united to a most perfect form, the rational soul, it must enjoy a nobility greater than that of other bodies. In it must be found a harmony of parts far exceeding the harmony found in other corporeal entities.[53] It must have a natural disposition and inclination for the rational soul, so much so that when it is united to the soul all its appetites are so fully sated that it cannot aspire to, or desire, another form.[54] Nevertheless, this body, or better, this organized flesh, despite its nobility and harmony of parts, possesses no movement or power except through the presence of the soul, which is the life-giving prin-

---

aliquis sit homo, necessario praeexigitur et coexigitur unio animae ad carnem, cum homo dicat formam totius sive consequentem totum compositum." *Ibid.*, p. 452.

[50] *Breviloquium,* p. 2, c. 10, V, p. 228.

[51] ". . . perfectus homo non est, nisi habeat corpus cum omnibus membris et animam cum omnibus potentiis . . ." *Liber III S.,* d. 2, a. 2, q. 2, conc., III, p. 47.

[52] "Quoniam igitur Deus assumsit carnem et animam humanam, et caro est principium hominis materiale, anima vero formale; hinc est, quod vere non solum humanam naturam, sed etiam totam humanam naturam dicitur assumsisse." *Ibid.,* d. 5, a. 2, q. 1, conc., p. 131. Cf. *Ibid.,* d. 22, a. 1, q. 1, pp. 450ss.

[53] ". . . et inter omnia potissime reperitur in homine, quia nobilior debet esse in ejus corpore proportio et harmonia miscibilium, secundum quod disp. nditur ad nobiliorem formam." *Liber II S.,* d. 17, a. 2, q. 3, conc., II, p. 425. Cf. *Ibid.,* q. 2, ad 6, p. 423; *Ibid.,* d. 1, p. 2, a. 3, q. 2, conc., p. 50.

[54] ". . . materia, quae huic formae (animae) unitur, tanto appetitu ei conjungitur, et ita ejus appetitus in ipsa terminatur, quod nullatenus queat aliam formam appetere . . ." *Ibid.,* d. 19, a. 1, q. 1, conc., p. 460.

ciple of the human body.[55]   It is the soul that makes the body a living thing, and this "*per modum informantis.*" [56]

In considering the human soul, we must, if we wish to acquire a fair understanding of Bonaventure's thought, distinguish, together with him, the soul considered as spirit from the soul considered as the form of the body.[57]   There are, in particular, two doctrines of his referring to the soul, considered in itself, that attract our attention: namely, (a) that the rational soul is composed of matter and form; and (b) that the soul is a "*hoc aliquid,*" a subsistent individual of a determinate genus.

Since the soul is a being that is of another, our author argues, it is not its own life.   Consequently, besides the principle that gives life there must also be present in the soul the principle that receives life, matter.[58]   Again, since the soul is endowed not only with faculties which put matter external to itself at its disposal (e.g. the faculty of giving life to the body), but also with faculties that perform internally (e.g. memory, intellect, and will), it must, then, also possess an internal matter so as to be capable of development.   In short, the soul is subject to potency and act; it can act and be acted upon; it moves and is moved.   Hence, there must be in the soul a principle that is subject to these accidental changes, a material principle.[59]

---

[55] "Corpus humanum, quando non habet spiritum, non habet virtutem, etiam si esset corpus giganteum . . ." *De Donis,* coll. V, n. 7, V, p. 480.

[56] *Liber II S.,* d. 8, p. 1, a. 1, q. 1, ad 5, II, p. 211.

[57] O'Leary, C. J., *The Substantial Composition of Man According to Saint Bonaventure,* C. U. Dissertation (Philosophical Studies, volume XXII), Washington, 1931, p. 87.

[58] ". . . ergo ponere in anima, secundum se considerata, aliquid quod det vitam, et aliquid quod recipiat.   Et si hoc, ergo est composita ex materia et forma." *Liber II S.,* d. 17, a. 1, q. 2, f. 6, II, p. 414.

[59] *Liber II S.,* d. 17, a. 1, q. 2, conc., II, pp. 414–415.   Cf. *Ibid.,* d. 3, p. 1, a. 1, q. 1, pp. 89–92.

Needless to say, the matter here referred to is a spiritual matter, a matter without extension.   The Seraphic Doctor uses the word "*matter*" in its most general sense, i.e., as expressive of an absolutely indeterminate potentiality.   To understand his teaching in this regard, we should bear in mind the distinction he places between matter considered in the abstract (*materia in se considerata,* or *materia secundum essentiam*) and the actually existent matter (*materia secundum esse vel substantiam*).   Matter, taken in

This composition of matter and form in the soul explains its substantiality and guarantees its ability to subsist separately. Indeed, the soul, in the teaching of our saintly author, is a substance properly so called, a *" hoc aliquid "* capable of subsisting in the full sense of the word.[60] As a subsistent individual, the soul is endowed with the faculties proper to a purely spiritual substance—it exists, lives, knows, and is blessed with liberty.[61]

Although he teaches that the soul is a complete substance, a " hoc aliquid," and that the flesh must be organized, St. Bonaventure insists upon the substantial union of body and soul in the human composite. The objection that a substance already composed of matter and form constitutes a complete being which cannot co-operate to constitute a third complete substance, our author maintains to be an improper generalization holding true only in certain cases. It holds true, he says, only when the matter completely satisfies the appetites of the form and the form fully actualizes all the possibilities of the matter. The case is quite different, he points out, when the form possesses certain powers that the matter of which it has possessed itself does not enable it to develop, or when the already organized matter contains an inclination and disposition for a still higher and nobler form. Here we have two appetites that have not been satisfied. Such, indeed, according to the Seraphic Doctor, is the case with both the human soul and the human body.

The soul, considered in itself, has already informed its spiritual matter and thereby constitutes a true substance. Nevertheless, its capacity has not been wholly satisfied by this original matter. Consequently, a hunger, consubstantial with its very essence,

the abstract and metaphysical sense, is indifferent to any form, spiritual or corporeal. It is the principle of receptivity. However, matter, considered *" secundum esse,"* is not the same in spiritual and corporeal creatures. It is the form, whether corporeal or spiritual, that differentiates one from the other. Thus, spiritual matter is simply the foundation of variation and potentiality; it is in no way extended. It is only when matter, considered as abstract, has been informed by a corporeal form that it becomes extended. On this score, see *Liber II S.,* d. 17, a. 1, q. 2, II, p. 413ss; *Ibid.,* d. 3, p. 1, a. 1, qq. 2, 3, pp. 94ss.

[60] *Liber II S.,* d. 17, a. 1, q. 2, f. 5, II, p. 414; *Ibid.,* conc., pp. 414–415.
[61] *Breviloquium,* p. 2, c. 9, V, p. 226.

draws it to a matter suitably organized for the development of all its faculties—draws it to inform organized flesh that is to become the human body. On the other hand, while the flesh is organized and contains its own matter and form, still it desires to be informed by the rational soul. It is thus that the human composite, man, comes into being.[62]

This union of body and soul, Bonaventure repeatedly assures us, is a natural and substantial union.[63] The body and soul, he tells us, are joined together as matter and form.[64] Again, the body is not the prison of the soul, but its companion and friend.[65] Moreover, body and soul have a natural aptitude and inclination for each other, and are mutually dependent. For although the soul can exist separated from the body, nevertheless, because of the inclination that it has to its body, it depends upon that body as the form depends upon its matter.[66] Indeed, so strong

---

[62] " Ad illud quod objicitur, quod compositum ex materia et forma est ens completum, et ita non venit ad constitutionem tertii; dicendum, quod hoc non est verum generaliter, sed tunc, quando materia terminat omnem appetitum formae, et forma omnem appetitum materiae; tunc non est appetitus ad aliquid extra, et ita nec possibilitas ad compositionem, quae praeexigit in componentibus appetitum et inclinationem. Licet autem anima rationalis compositionem habeat ex materia et forma, appetitum tamen habet ad perficiendam corporalem naturam; sicut corpus organicum ex materia et forma compositum est, et tamen habet appetitum ad suscipiendam animam." *Liber II S.*, d. 17, a. 1, q. 2, ad 6, II, pp. 415-416.

[63] ". . . animum uniri corpori humano sive vivificare corpus humanum, non dicit actum accidentalem nec dicit actum ignobilem: non accidentalem, quia ratione illius est anima forma substantialis; non ignobilem, quia ratione illius est anima nobilissima formarum omnium, et in anima stat appetitus totius naturae." *Ibid.*, d. 1, p. 2, a. 3, q. 2, conc., p. 50.

[64] ". . . homo constet simul ex corpore et anima tanquam ex materia et forma, quae mutuum habent appetitum et inclinationem mutuam . . ." *Breviloquium*, p. 7, c. 5, V, p. 286.

[65] " Contra rationem et sensibilem experientiam est, quia videmus, animam, quantumcumque bonam, nolle a corpore separari . . . quod mirum esset si ad corpus naturalem aptitudinem et inclinationem non haberet sicut ad suum sodalem, non sicut ad carceram." *Liber II S.*, d. 18, a. 2, q. 2, conc., II, p. 449.

[66] ". . . etsi (anima) non dependeat a corpore tanquam indigens eo ad sui conservationem, dependet tamen per appetitus sui inclinationem, quem habet ad ipsum, sicut forma ad materiam propriam . . ." *Ibid.*, d. 17, a. 1, q. 3, ad 4, p. 418. Cf. *Ibid.*, ad 5.

is this inclination of the soul for its body that the blessed souls long for a reunion with their respective bodies; they cannot be perfectly happy unless the bodies they once informed be restored to them.[67]

SECTION 2.   MAN'S RATIONAL POWERS—COGNITIVE AND AFFECTIVE

Having considered the human composite as a natural and substantial unity of body and soul, we now turn our attention to a consideration of man's activities. The first thing that strikes us in this regard is the fact that his activities are many and diversified—man not only exists, but also lives, senses, and rationalizes. These activities—bodily growth, sensitive perception, and conscious thought—all proceed from the one common principle, the soul. It is the soul, St. Bonaventure affirms, that gives life, sensation and intellection; consequently, the soul must possess vegetative, sensitive, and intellective powers.[68]

In this connection we must note that although St. Bonaventure differentiates the powers of the soul in various ways, i.e., according to the various functions they perform, according to the various objects to which they are turned, according to the various manners in which they act, etc., nevertheless it does not follow that all these denote specifically distinct faculties. Thus, when he speaks of the "*ratio inferior*" and the "*ratio superior*"; when he differentiates between the "*intellectus speculativus*" and the

---

[67] *Breviloquium,* p. 7, c. 7, V, p. 289; *Soliloquium,* c. 4, n. 21, VIII, p. 64.

[68] "Et quoniam ipsa non tantum dat esse, verum etiam vivere et sentire et intelligere; ideo potentiam habet vegetativam, sensitivam et intellectivam . . ." *Breviloquium,* p. 2, c. 9, V, p. 227.
We may here recall that, in the teaching of the Seraphic Doctor, the faculties of the soul are actually consubstantial with the soul. They are not, on the one hand, identical with the substance of the soul; nor are they, on the other hand, so different and distinct from the soul as to be grouped under another genus, e.g., accidents. They are reduced to the category of the soul, being something that arises from it, something that is neither the soul nor other than the soul. Strictly speaking they have no other essence than the substance of the soul itself and thus they cannot differ from one another or from the substance of the soul as do distinct essences. Moreover, as different faculties, they are distinct; yet, as faculties of the same soul, they are one. Cf. *Liber II S.,* d. 24, p. 1, a. 2, q. 1, II, pp. 558–563; Gilson, *op. cit.,* pp. 326–334; Healy, *op. cit.,* pp. 89–91.

" *intellectus practicus* "; when he refers to the " *ratio,*" the " *intellectus* " and the " *intelligentia* " our author is referring to one and the same cognitive faculty of the rational soul, which is termed differently only according as its function, content, or outlook is changed. In fact, the Seraphic Doctor actually speaks of but three specifically distinct faculties: the vegetative, the sensitive, and the rational—the latter being again subdivided into cognitive and affective. These alone are the faculties truly so understood; the others are simply different outlooks of the same faculties, of the same soul.[69]

At this point it is not our purpose to investigate the various powers of the soul—vegetative, sensitive, and rational—as explained by the Seraphic Doctor, for this would entail too lengthy a treatise. Rather, we intend to make a brief mention of man's rational nature, since it is here that we discover man's true dignity. We are desirous of showing that man is blessed with a rational life, that he is endowed with both cognitive and affective powers and can, therefore, know things with certainty and will things freely.

A. Cognitive

With reference to man's cognitive activity, St. Bonaventure speaks of a threefold knowledge in man corresponding to the threefold mode of being, i.e., that existing in the external and created reality outside of the mind, that existing in our minds, and that existing in the Eternal Word, namely the Exemplar Ideas.[70] Hence, we will consider, very briefly, the threefold knowledge that our author ascribes to man: (a) knowledge of things extrinsic to himself and existing in the sensible creation, or knowledge derived from the senses; (b) knowledge of things intrinsic to man, or the knowledge of his own mind and what is innate therein; (c) knowledge of the things that are above man, i.e., of the Divine Exemplars, or Divine Illumination.

Let us, turning our attention to man's threefold knowledge, begin with the lowest form—the knowledge of things external

---

[69] *Liber II S.*, d. 24, p. 1, a. 2, q. 3, conc., II, p. 566.
[70] *Itinerarium,* c. 1, nn. 3, 4, V, p. 297.

and inferior to the mind. It is by this type of knowing that man comes into contact with the created universe, i.e., through the medium of his senses. The mind is truly a " *tabula rasa* " in this respect; our intellect presupposes sensation and operates on the materials supplied by the sentient powers.[71] Consequent to the operation of the senses and the formation of the sensible species, we have the operation of the intellect as such and the formation of the intelligible species, for the image of the external objects received into the intellect must be transformed into something spiritual. This, then, is the function of the intellect— to apprehend the universal and intelligible form embodied in the concrete physical reality.[72]

Through this first knowledge, i.e., of things outside the mind and rooted in matter, man arrives at the acquisition of first prin-

---

[71] *Liber II S.,* d. 3, p. 2, a. 2, q. 1, f. 5, II, p. 118; *Ibid.,* ad 4, pp. 120–121.

Although we are here concerned solely with the intellectual knowledge that is based on sense-perception and not with sense-perception as such, it would be advisable to recall that the Seraphic Doctor speaks of both external and internal senses. The external senses are five. Since the macrocosmos is composed of five corporeal substances, i.e., the four elements and light, the fifth element, man is endowed with five external senses, through which, as through so many doors, he may come into contact with the material and sensible world. Cf. *Itinerarium,* c. 2, n. 3, V, p. 300.

Besides the external senses our author posits certain internal senses. Thus, he speaks of the " *sensus communis,*" in which all the external senses are united as in one trunk. Cf. *Liber IV S.,* d. 50, p. 2, a. 1, q. 1, conc., IV, pp. 1045–6; *Ibid.,* d. 12, p. 1, dub. 1, p. 286; *Liber II S.,* d. 24, p. 2, dub. 3, II, pp. 587–588.

Moreover, he refers to the sense-memory and the imagination, or " *phantasia.*" Cf. *Liber I S.,* d. 16, a. 1, q. 2, ad 4, I, p. 282; *Liber II S.,* d. 7, p. 2, a. 1, q. 2, conc., II, p. 193; *Ibid.,* d. 7, p. 2, a. 1, q. 2, conc., and ad 3, p. 193; *Breviloquium,* p. 2, c. 9, V, p. 227.

Finally mention seems to be made of a sense-appetite. Cf. footnote 6 of the Editors of Quaracchi, V, p. 300.

For further development on this and the process of sensation, see Gilson, *op. cit.,* pp. 327–346; Healy, *op. cit.,* pp. 89–106; Dady, M. R., *The Theory of Knowledge of St. Bonaventure,* C. U. Dissertation (Philosophical Studies, volume LII), Washington, 1939, pp. 21–25.

[72] *Itinerarium,* c. 2, n. 6, V, p. 301. In reference to Bonaventure's doctrine concerning the passive and active intellect, cf. Gilson, *op. cit.,* pp. 346–353; Dady, *op. cit.,* pp. 13–17.

ciples. These first principles, whether intellectual or moral, are in a certain sense innate and in another sense acquired. They are *acquired,* since the intellect could never arrive at the knowledge thereof unless sense experience had supplied the mind with the terms of the principles. Thus, for example, the mind must have some knowledge of a " whole " and a " part " in order to come to the conclusion that the whole is greater than any of its parts. On the other hand, they are *innate* because of the innate natural light in the soul, the *" judicatorium naturale."* The principles, themselves known in the terms, do not come from the terms as such; they are not abstractions from sense-knowledge, but, rather, are formulated on the occasion of sense-knowledge through the help of the light that is innate in us.[73]* Therefore, as Gilson remarks: ". . . it is not their content that is innate, either clearly or confusedly, but the instrument that enables them to acquire it . . . innateness of intellect, acquisition of principles . . ." [74]

Besides the knowledge of things external to the mind and immersed in matter, our author speaks of an intrinsic and innate knowledge. In answer to the question whether all our knowledge comes from the senses, Bonaventure replies negatively.[75] He teaches a form of " innatism," and this in reference to all things that pertain to the soul and God. Man, he tells us, is able to know himself, his rational soul, and the content of his soul immediately without the aid of an image or a " representa-

---

[73] *Liber II S.,* d. 39, a. 1, q. 2, conc., II, p. 903.

[74] ". . . ce n'est pas leur contentu qui est inné, ni clairement ni confusément, mais l'instrument qui permet de les acquérir . . . innéité de l'intellect, acquisition des principes . . ." *Op. cit.,* p. 357.

[75] ". . . utrum omnis cognitio sit a sensu, Dicendum est, quod non. Necessario enim oportet ponere, quod anima novit Deum et se ipsam et quae sunt in se ipsa, sine adminiculo sensuum exteriorum. Unde si aliquando dicit Philosophus, quod 'nihil est in intellectu, quod prius non fuerit in sensu' et quod 'omnis cognitio habet ortum a sensu'; intelligendum est de illis quae quidem habent esse in anima per similitudinem abstractam; et illa dicuntur esse in anima ad modum scripturae. Et propterea valde notabiliter dicit Philosophus, quod in anima nihil scriptum est, non quia nulla sit in ea notitia, sed quia nulla est in ea pictura vel similitudo abstracta." *Liber II S.,* d. 39, a. 1, q. 2, conc., II, p. 904.

tive" species, i.e., an intelligible species abstracted from the sensile representation.[76]

To comprehend the teaching of the Seraphic Doctor on this score, we must remember that besides the "representative species" he speaks of a twofold infused or innate species—species here being understood as all that is a means of knowing. He first makes note of that infused species which is the similitude of a thing, e.g., the species of a stone. The soul, he affirms, is created entirely devoid of this type of innate species. On the other hand, we have a second type of infused species, which is an impression on the soul—a means of knowing without being a means of imagining—as, e.g., the knowledge of our faculty of desiring implies the knowledge of the inclination of our desire towards the good.[77] Through the "impressions on the soul" man enjoys, according to the teaching of our author, an innate knowledge of the virtues and of God.

Such, then, is the form of innatism that is found in the writings of St. Bonaventure. We call it "innatism," because to know, e.g., the virtues and God, man needs no new resources from the external and sensible world. The soul knows by a mere reflection upon itself, its faculties, and content.[78]

Over and above these forms of knowledge, and penetrating through them, we have Bonaventure's theory of divine illumination. We shall not attempt an adequate explanation of his teaching in this regard, but shall simply cite it. We find the key to our author's teaching in his insistence that God is not only the cause of being, but also the reason of knowing. Just as God is the cause of being in such a manner that nothing can be effected by any cause unless God and His eternal power move the agent performing this act, so, too, nothing can be known unless He directly enlightens the knower by His Eternal Truth.[79] If truth

---

[76] *Ibidem.* Cf. *De Mysterio Trinitatis,* q. 1, a. 1, ff. 6–10, V, p. 46.

[77] *Liber I S.,* d. 17, p. 1, a. 1, q. 4, conc., I, p. 301. Cf. Scholion, pp. 302ss.

[78] *Ibidem; De Mysterio Trinitatis,* q. 1, a. 1, V, pp. 45ss; *Liber II S.,* d. 39, a. 1, q. 2, conc., II, p. 904. For further development of this doctrine, see Gilson, *op. cit.,* pp. 356–362.

[79] "Item, sicut Deus est causa essendi, ita est ratio intelligendi et ordo

is the "*adequatio intellectus et rei,*" then truth diminishes as it lacks either being on which it is based or the concept by which it is expressed. Consequently, in order to arrive at certain, necessary, and immutable truth we must come into contact with the ultimate ground of all truth, God. Or, better still, because certainty of knowledge requires on the part of the object known an immutability which cannot be found in the created and contingent being, and on the part of the knower an infallibility which is not found in the contingent mind, we must have recourse to the Supreme Source as the truth which gives immutability to the thing known and the light which gives infallibility to the knower.[80]

In answer to the question, how the knowing mind comes into contact with God, the Seraphic Doctor maintains that this takes place by an immediate and direct action of the "*rationes aeternae*" on our mind. This action is such that it concurs with our own action of knowledge. In other words, the Divine Exemplars are not the sole "*ratio intelligendi*"; they are not a substitute for the abstractive activity of the soul. Besides the divine illumination, both the natural light of reason and the species of things abstracted from the phantasms are needed in order to know.[81]

However, our author insists that the uncreated Light in which all things are known is not itself the object of our knowledge. Although it is more intimate to the soul than the soul is to itself, this Light remains inaccessible to the intellect.[82] This fact we

vivendi; sed Deus sic est causa essendi, quod nihil potest ab aliqua causa effici, quin ipse se ipso et sua aeterna virtute moveat operantem: ergo nihil potest intelligi, quin ipse sua aeterna veritate immediate illustret intelligentem." *De Scientia Christi,* q. 4, f. 24, V, p. 19.

[80] *Ibid.,* conc., p. 23; *Breviloquium,* p. 6, c. 8, V, p. 273.

[81] ". . . quia non omnino distincte videmus illas rationes in se, ideo non sunt tota ratio cognoscendi; sed requiritur cum illis lumen creatum principiorum et similitudines rerum cognitarum, ex quibus propria ratio cognoscendi habetur respectu cujuslibet cogniti." *De Scientia Christi,* q. 4, ad 15, V, p. 25. Cf. *Ibid.,* ad 4, p. 24; ad 7, 8, 9, p. 25; ad 18, p. 26.

[82] "Haec lux est inaccessibilis, et tamen proxima animae, etiam plus quam ipsa sibi." *In Hex.,* coll. XII, n. 11, V, p. 386. Cf. *Liber IV S.,* d. 48, a. 1, q. 2, f. 2, IV, p. 985.

must continuously bear in mind. Though the External Exemplars are that by means of which the mind knows with certainty, they are not the object of knowledge; they are never
perceived, never known directly and immediately, but rather by
" *contuition,*" in virtue of which one recognizes in a perceived
effect a cause which cannot be directly known.[83]   The object
of our knowledge remains the contingent beings, but these can
be seen absolutely; and it is this necessity of the truth of contingent facts that is referred to an immediate contact with God.[84]

From the foregoing considerations we can conclude that man
is truly capable of knowing—of knowing with certainty, without
the fear of error.   At the same time, however, man is not endowed alone with the capacity to know; he also possesses the
power of willing—of willing freely.   Hence, we come to a consideration of man's free will.

B.   *Affective*

St. Bonaventure approaches the subject by insisting that free-
will is found only in rational substances.   He proves his point
by showing that both the element of freedom and the element
of choice required for free-will are proper only to beings blessed
with rationality.[85]

Taking the element of freedom in consideration, he states that
only that faculty is free which possesses full dominion over its
object and its act.[86]   It is free with respect to its object when
it is born to desire all that can be desired and to spurn all that

---

[83] *De Scientia Christi,* q. 4, conc., V, p. 23; *Ibid.,* ad 16, p. 25.   Cf. *In
Hex.,* coll. II, n. 9, V, p. 338; *Christus unus Omn. Magister,* n. 17, V,
p. 571.

[84] For a deeper study of St. Bonaventure's doctrine of Divine Illumination, see: Gilson, *op. cit.,* pp. 362–387; Healy, *op. cit.,* pp. 130–133; Dady,
op. cit., pp. 31–51.

[85] " Respondeo: Dicendum, quod absque dubio liberum arbitrium reperitur
in solis substantiis rationalibus.—Et ratio hujus sumitur tum ex parte
libertatis, tum ex parte arbitrationis." *Liber II S.,* d. 25, p. 1, a. 1, q. 1,
conc., II, p. 593.

[86] " Ex parte libertatis: libertas enim opponitur servituti.   Unde, illa sola
potentia dicitur esse libera, quae dominium habet plenum tum respectu objecti, quam respectu actus proprii." *Ibidem.*

should be shunned. After showing that there are three types of desirable objects—the useful good (*bonum conferens*), the agreeable good (*bonum delectabile*), and the good desirable in itself and of itself (*bonum honestum*)—the Seraphic Doctor affirms that while the first two " *bona* " can be desired by both rational and irrational beings, the last good (*bonum honestum*) is accessible only to a being endowed with reason. Thus, since only the rational being is not determined to a certain type of desirable object, since only the rational being enjoys the ability to aspire after all that it is possible to desire, only the rational being enjoys freedom of will.[87]

Moreover, only that faculty enjoys complete freedom over its act which possesses complete mastery not only over its external acts (e.g., the moving or restraining of hand or foot) but also over itself, as, for instance, the ability of detesting what it previously loved and loving what it previously detested. This complete mastery is not to be found in the irrational animals. Indeed, as Bonaventure argues, although the brutes may possess some sort of mastery over their external actions, they have none over their internal actions, over their appetitive nature. For instance, what an irrational animal loves, it cannot help but love.[88]

---

[87] " Illa autem potentia dominium habet ex libertate respectu objecti, quae non est arctata ad aliquid genus appetibilis, sed nata est omnia appetibilia appetere et omne fugibile respuere. Tria autem sunt, quae sunt in appetitibus, et quorum opposita sunt in fugis, videlicet bonum, conferens, et delectabile; et nomine boni ibi intelligitur honestum. Cum autem bonum conferens et delectabile nata sint appeti ab irrationalibus, bonum honestum a solis rationalibus potest appeti; et ideo in eis solum reperitur virtus, quae non est ad aliquid genus appetibilis arctata, ac per hoc habens libertatem respectu objecti." *Ibidem.*

[88] " Nam voluntas in rationalibus non solum compescit manum exteriorem vel pedem, sed etiam compescit se ipsam et refrenat, incipiens odire frequenter quod prius diligebat; et hoc ex sui ipsius imperio et dominio. In brutis autem animalibus, etsi aliquo modo sit reperire dominium respectu actus exterioris, quia bene refrenant aliquando, sicut patet in animalibus domesticis; respectu tamen actus proprii interioris, videlicet appetitus, dominium non est. Unde si aliquid amant, non possunt illud non amare, licet a prosecutione alicujus rei amatae arceantur timore alicujus passionis inflictivae." *Ibidem.*

When we weigh the second element necessary for free-will, choice, it appears still clearer that the power of freedom is proper to the rational substances alone. Indeed, the being that chooses must be capable of discerning what is just and unjust, of selecting between one's own and another's.[89] No faculty, however, can come to the knowledge of what is just and unjust except that faculty which is capable of knowing the Supreme Justice from which every other rule of justice flows—that faculty which is made to the image of God, the rational substance.[90]

Furthermore, no being can distinguish between what is his own and what is another's, unless it knows both itself and its proper activity. To know both itself and its proper activity, it must be able to reflect upon itself. This function is proper only to that faculty which is not bound up with matter, nor depends on it for its exercise. Since this condition is true only of the rational substances, only the rational substances are, consequently, free.[91]

From the conditions required for freedom we can conclude that free-will is a privilege belonging only to beings endowed with reason; that free-will is proper to man because he is a rational being. Man, therefore, is not only capable of knowing, but he is also blessed with the ability to choose between the

---

[89] " Sumitur etiam ratio ex parte arbitrationis. Arbitrium enim idem est quod judicium, ad cujus nutum ceterae virtutes moventur et obediunt. Judicare autem illius est secundum rationem completam, cujus est discernere inter justum et injustum, et inter proprium et alienum." *Ibidem*.

[90] " Nulla autem potentia novit, quid justum et quid injustum, nisi illa sola, quae est particeps rationis et nata est cognoscere summam justitiam, a qua est regula omnis juris. Haec autem solum est in ea substantia, quae est ad imaginem Dei; qualis est tantum potentia rationalis." *Ibidem*.

[91] " Nulla enim substantia discernit, quid proprium et quid alienum, nisi cognoscat et ipsum et actum suum proprium. Sed nunquam aliqua potentia se ipsam cognoscit, vel super se ipsam reflectitur, quae sit alligata materiae. Si igitur omnes potentiae sunt alligatae materiae et substantiae corporali praeter solam rationalem, sola illa est, quae potest se super se ipsam reflectere; et ideo ipsa sola est, in qua est plenum judicium et arbitrium in discernendo, quid justum et quid injustum, quid proprium et quid alienum. —Tam igitur ratione libertatis, quam ratione arbitrationis liberum arbitrium in solis substantiis rationalibus reperitur." *Ibidem*.

just and the unjust; to desire all that is desirable; to exercise complete mastery over himself.[92]

This power of willing freely is intimately rooted in the soul to such an extent that it cannot be taken away from man. In fact, since the cognitive and the affective powers of man are, according to our author, faculties consubstantial with the soul, it follows that free-will—the faculty of these faculties—based as it is upon the inseparability of these two faculties from each other and from the soul, is itself inseparable from the rational soul. So essential is free-will to man that it is impossible even for God to constrain man's freedom without destroying man's nature.[93]

---

[92] As for the nature of the free-will, Bonaventure asserts it is not a supplementary faculty—a really distinct and separate faculty—added to our reason and will. Nor is it, on the other hand, either our will or our intellect, but both these faculties functioning as one. It is reduced to a certain definite mode in which these two faculties collaborate—a collaboration of both reason and will, a "consensus rationis et voluntatis." Both faculties are necessary for it. If the soul possessed reason alone, it would be capable of reflecting upon itself and its acts, but it would not be capable of setting itself in motion or deciding its course of activity. If, on the other hand, it possessed only desire without reason, it would be able to set itself in motion, but would be incapable of reflecting upon its own acts and judging them and would also be incapable of self-restraint—and, consequently, would not possess self-mastery. Thus, free-will is born of a collaboration of reason and will; it is "*inchoative*" in the reason and "*consummative*" in the will. Cf. *Ibid.*, qq. 2, 3, 4, 5, 6, pp. 596ss.

As to the essence of free-will, Bonaventure teaches it consists in self-mastery. The will is free not so much because it wills a thing in such a way that it could will its opposite, not so much because it is not determined, but because whatever it wills, it does so according to its own command. Cf. *Ibid.*, p. 2, a. 1, q. 2, conc., p. 612.

[93] *Ibid.*, q. 5, conc., p. 612.

However, it must be noted that the exercise of free-will seems, at times, to be beyond man's power. To explain this (how free-will, so essential to man, is at times impeded in its exercise), Bonaventure distinguishes between free-will considered in its total act (i.e., including the collaboration of the intellect in the discernment of objects and that of the body in carrying out the decision arrived at) and free-will considered solely as the faculty of willing. In the first case, the free-will of man, though free from all constraint with regard to its essence, remains, nonetheless, subject to all divine and created influences which incline it without actual compulsion. On the

SECTION 3.   THE HUMAN PERSONALITY

All created beings, our author tells us, are individuals in virtue of both matter and form, for individuality is effected by the union of these two constitutive elements. Matter is, in point of fact, a "*conditio sine qua non,*" but individuation results neither from the form alone, nor from the matter alone, but from the union of the two, in which union each principle becomes possessed of the other and appropriates it to itself.[94] Thus, the individual, says St. Bonaventure, is a "*hoc aliquid*"— "this something." It is a "*hoc,*" i.e., a particular being to which a determined place in time and space has been assigned by virtue of its matter. It is an "*aliquid,*" i.e., a being of a definite essence specifically distinct from other essences, through the medium of its form.[95]

However, though all created beings are individuals, only the beings of a rational nature are endowed with the dignity of personality, in virtue of which they occupy the first place among all created natures and are ordered immediately to God, as to their sole end.[96] Personality, therefore, is something more than

---

other hand, when we speak of free-will as the faculty of willing, it presents itself as something inviolable, something that God Himself cannot constrain without destroying. Cf. *Ibid.,* qq. 4, 5, 6, pp. 615–624.

[94] "Ideo est tertia positio satis planior, quod individuatio consurgit ex actuali conjunctione materiae cum forma, ex qua conjunctione unum sibi appropriat alterum; sicut patet, cum impressio vel expressio sit multorum sigillorum in cera, quae prius erat una, nec sigilla plurificari possunt sine cera, nec cera numeratur, nisi quia fiunt in ea diversa signilla." *Ibid.,* d. 3, p. 1, a. 2, q. 3, conc., p. 109.

[95] "Si tamen quaeras, a quo veniat principaliter; dicendum, quod individuum est hoc aliquid. Quod sit hoc, principalius habet ex materia, ratione cujus forma habet positionem in loco et tempore. Quod sit aliquid, habet a forma. Individuum enim habet esse, habet etiam existere. Existere dat materia formae, sed essendi actum dat forma materiae." *Ibid.,* pp. 109–110.

[96] "Et sic individualis discretio dicit aliquid accidentale, et aliquid substantiale; personalis autem addit supra hanc dignitatem personalitatis. Dignitas autem illa duo dicit, scilicet nobilitatem rationalis naturae, quae est, quod natura rationalis tenet principatum inter naturas creatas; unde non est ordinabilis ad perfectiorem formam. Et haec nobilitas, etsi per modum qualitatis habeat intelligi, tamen essentialis est naturae rationali.—

mere individuality; it adds something to individuality.⁹⁷ Consequently, it cannot be sufficiently explained by the union of matter with any form whatsoever. The form, in this case, must enjoy a certain eminence and dignity.⁹⁸ Hence, personality is not something negative. It is fundamentally a "*positio*," a positive perfection.⁹⁹

This dignity and eminence, our author avers, is not something accidental, but, rather, an essential property of the rational natures.¹⁰⁰ In man personality appears at the precise moment when the rational soul informs its matter. Thus, the "*persona*" is neither the soul in itself nor the body itself, but the composite of body and soul—man.¹⁰¹ Needless to say, St. Bonaventure has the greatest respect for the eminent dignity of the human person. He declares "*persona*" to be "*quasi per se sonare.*" ¹⁰²

Dicit etiam illa nobilitas actualem eminentiam, ita quod in supposito nulla sit alia natura ita principalis, ut natura rationalis, ut quasi per se sonans." *Ibid.,* q. 2, conc., p. 106.

⁹⁷ " Discretio personalis addit supra discretionem individualem . . ." *Ibidem.*

⁹⁸ " Personalis autem discretio dicit singularitatem et dignitatem. In quantum dicit singularitatem, hoc dicit ex ipsa conjunctione principiorum, ex quibus resultat ipsum quod est. Sed dignitatem dicit principaliter ratione formae; et sic patet, unde sit personalis discretio originaliter, in creaturis loquendo, sive in hominibus, sive in Angelis." *Ibid.,* q. 3, conc., p. 110. Cf. *Liber III S.,* d. 5, a. 2, q. 2, ad 1, III, p. 133; *Liber I S.,* d. 23, a. 1, q. 1, conc., I, pp. 405–406.

⁹⁹ ". . . privatio illa in persona magis est positio quam privatio." *Liber I S.,* d. 25, a. 2, q. 1, conc., I, p. 443.

It should be noted that in Bonaventurean teaching three things are involved in the notion of personality: ". . . individium in notificatione personae triplicem importat distinctionem, videlicet singularitatis, incommunicabilitatis et supereminentis dignitatis." *Liber III S.,* d. 5, a. 2, q. 2, ad 1, III, p. 133. Cf. *Ibid.,* q. 3, conc., p. 136.

¹⁰⁰ " Similiter proprietas personalis non dicit ultra hoc nisi dignitatem sive nobilitatem naturae rationalis, quae nobilitas non est ei accidentalis, immo simpliciter et omnino essentialis." *Liber II S.,* d. 3, p. 1, a. 2, q. 2, ad 1, II, p. 107.

¹⁰¹ ". . . intentio personalitatis consequitur animam unitam corpori, ita tamen quod nec anima nec corpus est persona, sed totum compositum." *Liber III S.,* d. 5, a. 2, q. 3, ad 6, III, p. 137.

¹⁰² " Dicit etiam illa nobilitas actualem eminentiam, ita quod in supposito

His words clearly mean that man can pronounce himself on that which regards his individual life; he possesses a certain self-determination.[103]   Indeed, he tells us that nothing in the whole-expanse of nature is more noble than the person.   Here, then, we find man's true grandeur—that man occupies, together with other rational creatures, the first place among created natures; that man is ordered immediately to God, as to his sole end.[104]

However, we have not, as yet, completed our picture of man's dignity and greatness, for, thanks to his rational nature, man is not only a person, but also the image of God.   Since we have already given consideration to this essential property of the rational soul, it will be sufficient to recall that man, because of the image-character printed upon the very essence of his being, is capable of attaining God and participating in His Eternal Glory.[105]   This fact now brings us to our next section, which treats of man's final end, his natural desire for blessedness, and the nature of " *beatitudo.*"

SECTION 4.   MAN'S FINAL END

" *Beatitude* " or happiness, the Seraphic Doctor teaches, is the ultimate end of man's every action—the goal towards which the rational creatures naturally aspire.[106]   Any consideration of man will show that he has, from his very nature, an aptitude for happiness; that his will necessarily desires happiness; that this desire is innate to such an extent that man cannot bring himself to doubt it.[107]   Thus, the end of man's desire is happiness—that

nulla sit alia natura ita principalis, ut natura rationalis, ut quasi sit per se sonans." *Liber II S.,* d. 3, p. 1, a. 2, q. 2, conc., II, p. 106.

Bonaventure's source in this regard, as the Editors of Quaracchi assert (II, p. 106, ft. 6), is Boethius (*De Duabus Naturis et Una Persona,* c. 3).

[103] *Liber I S.,* d. 23, a. 1, q. 1, conc., I, p. 405.

[104] *Liber II S.,* d. 3, p. 1, a. 2, q. 2, conc., II, p. 106.

[105] Cf. above, pp. 37–38.

[106] ". . . finis ultimus omnis operationis rationalis est beatitudo perfecta . . . omnis anima rationalis naturaliter appetit beatitudinem . . ." *Liber II S.,* d. 19, a. 1, q. 1, ff. 5–6, II, p. 459.

[107] ". . . homo enim a natura sua habet aptitudinem ad beatitudinem. *Ibid.,* a. 3, q. 1, conc., p. 469. Cf. *Ibid.,* d. 24, p. 1, a. 2, q. 3, ad 2, p. 566. ". . . appetitus beatitudinis adeo est nobis insertus, ut nullus possit dubitare

state in which all desires are perfectly quieted by the possession of all good.[108]

What happiness, then, does man naturally desire? St. Bonaventure states clearly that man naturally desires true happiness.[109]   He seems to assert that man has a natural desire for God as the source of true happiness, and this, first of all, because of the ontological inclination of his nature.   In fact, he tells us, two things are necessary for a natural desire: aptitude (*convenientia*) and indigence (*indigentia*).   Both are present in the human soul: (a) *aptitude,* because the soul was created according to the image of God and was made capable of participating in the Supreme Good; (b) *indigence,* because the soul, vain and deficient in itself, cannot find within itself that with which to satisfy completely its desire for happiness.   Therefore, he concludes, the soul naturally desires true happiness.[110]

Besides this ontological inclination of the rational nature towards God as the source of its happiness, our author speaks of a natural desire of the will, considered as "*naturalis,*" for true happiness, viewed in its general aspect,—a desire which follows upon a general, natural, and innate consciousness of this ontological inclination.[111]   It is our opinion that man, in the mind

---

de altero, utrum velit esse beatus . . ." *De Mysterio Trinitatis,* q. 1, a. 1, f. 7, V, p. 46.

[108] "Finem namque desideriorum omnium constat esse beatitudinem, quae est status omnium bonorum congregatione perfectus." *Op. 3, Lignum Vitae,* n. 48, VIII, p. 85.   "Beatitudo est quies omnium desideriorum . . ." *Liber IV, S.,* d. 43, a. 1, q. 1, f. 4, IV, p. 883. Cf. *Liber II S.,* d. 19, a. 1, q. 1, ff. 5–6, II, p. 459.

[109] *Liber IV S.,* d. 49, p. 1, a. 1, q. 2, conc., IV, p. 1003.

[110] ". . . duo sunt, quae faciunt appetitum, scilicet convenientia et indigentia.   Quoniam igitur anima rationalis creata est ad Dei imaginem et similitudinem et facta est capax boni sufficientissimi; et ipsa sibi non sufficit cum sit vana et deficiens: ideo dico, quod veram beatitudinem appetit naturaliter." *Ibidem.*

[111] "Omnes ergo habent appetitum beatitudinis verae in generali et habent cognitionem in generali. . . . Si quaeras: quomodo cognovit in generali? dico, quod innata est illa cognitio. Si quaeras: per quid? dico, quod sufficientiam cognoscit per indigentiam.—Si opponas, quod privatio non est via cognoscendi habitum; dicendum, quod est quaedam indigentia omnino

of our saintly author, has an innate desire for the supernatural end, which desire proceeds from both the ontological inclination of his nature and the innate consciousness of this inclination.[112] Our conclusion in this regard is strengthened by Bonaventure's insistence upon the fact that the soul is born to perceive God, the Infinite Good, and consequently cannot find perfect quietude and fruition except in God.[113] It is further strengthened by the fact that from this innate desire for happiness our author argues to our knowledge of the existence of God. How then, we may ask, can he otherwise conclude from man's innate desire for happiness to a knowledge of God's existence, unless this be an innate desire for God, as the source of our happiness?[114]

We are at this point faced with the following difficulty: how

---

privans, quaedam disponens et inclinans; et haec est ratio cognoscendi . . ." *Ibid.,* ad 1, 2, pp. 1003–1004.

[112] Cf. P. Victorinus Doucet, O.F.M., "De Naturali Dei Innato Supernaturalis Beatitudinis Desiderio," *Antonianum,* IV (1929), pp. 180–182.

[113] ". . . nata est anima ad percipiendum bonum infinitum, quod Deus est, ideo in eo solo debet quiescere et eo frui." *Liber I S.,* d. 1, a. 3, q. 2, conc., I, p. 40.

[114] *De Mysterio Trinitatis,* q. 1, a. 1, f. 7, V, p. 46.
There are, it is true, certain texts in the writings of the Seraphic Doctor which seem to imply otherwise, but these can be explained in such a manner as to enable us to hold fast to our conclusion. Thus Bonaventure writes: ". . . cognitio beatitudinis duplex est, videlicet in universali et in particulari. Cognito beatitudinis in universali omnibus est innata; cognitia vero in particulari, videlicet ubi beatitudo ponenda, habetur a nobis per habitum fidei aliquo modo, et aliquo modo exspectatur habenda per deiformitatem gloriae. Nunc autem cognoscimus quasi speculando et a remotis et semiplene; tunc autem cognoscemus experiendo perfecte." *Liber II S.,* d. 38, dub. I, II, p. 894. Here our author is referring to the nature of the Beatific Vision and not simply to the fact that man naturally desires true happiness in general and is conscious of this inclination to God, as the source of his happiness. Again he writes: "Ad illud vero quod objicitur, quod inserta est nobis veri boni cupiditas; dicendum, quod verum est in generali; ut autem cognoscatur in speciali, quid sit illud bonum, et desideretur et requiratur, hoc non est absque Dei dono." *Ibid.,* d. 28, a. 2, q. 1, ad 2, p. 683. But here, as we see, the saint is concerned with *"bonum in speciali"* which concerns the will as *"deliberativa"* and not as *"naturalis."* Again, he is speaking here of grace.

is it that all men, though they naturally desire true happiness, do not strive thereafter? In order to solve this difficulty we must, together with the Seraphic Doctor, distinguish between the natural rational appetite (voluntas naturalis) and the will considered as deliberative or elective (voluntas electiva, seu deliberata). Man's desire for true happiness, considered in its general aspect, is the appetite of man's will considered as "*naturalis*" and is based, as we have seen, on man's ontological inclination and his natural, innate knowledge thereof. In this regard man cannot err; all men, because of this inborn appetite, naturally seek true happiness. Man's attempt, on the other hand, to find happiness in this or that specific object is the result of his will considered as deliberate and is based on man's deliberate knowledge, or reasoning, which can err. Now, since the deliberate reasoning can err and since our deliberate will is based on deliberate reasoning, it follows that, although all men naturally desire true happiness, nevertheless, some men refuse to accept the Beatific Vision as the true source of their happiness. Thus it is that some men, while naturally desiring true happiness, still seek it where it cannot be found, e.g., in riches, honors, and the like.[115]

God alone, however, can make man truly happy. The Seraphic Doctor proves this point in various ways, but for our purpose it is sufficient to note that no finite good, nor any multiplication of finite goods, can fully satisfy man's soul, since both the cognitive and affective powers of man tend beyond each and every thing finite to the possession of the Infinite. The soul was born to perceive God; it was made capable of attaining Him, and, accordingly, it cannot rest and delight except in Him.[116]

---

[115] *Liber IV S.*, d. 49, p. 1, a. 1, q. 2, ad 1–3, IV, pp. 1003–1004. This fact, according to St. Bonaventure, is due to the perversity of the will, which, in turn, is based on the error of our deliberate reasoning. As he avers, the will as "*naturalis*" must tend to true happiness, but as "*electiva*" it can seek its happiness in diversified objects. For, the will of man is both determined and non-determined—as "*naturalis*," it is determined to seek true happiness; as "*electiva*," it is non-determined as regards the object in which it chooses to seek it. *Liber II S.*, d. 22, dub. III, II, p. 528; *Ibid.*, d. 24, p. 1, a. 2, q. 3, ad 2, p. 566.

[116] "... quia nata est anima ad percipiendum bonum infinitum, quod Deus

It is in the Uncreated Good alone that man will find his complete and permanent satisfaction—in the possession of Him, Who is the source of all good, both natural and gratuitous; corporeal and spiritual; temporal and eternal.[117]   Without a doubt, only God is Happiness of His very Essence. We, on the other hand, can possess happiness in a participated manner, i.e., by participating in God, the source of all beatitude.[118]   This, therefore, is man's final end—participation in the Divine Blessedness, the Beatific Vision.

If, then, we were asked what " *beatitudo* " is, we would answer in the words of our author: " Beatitude, considered as the beatifying object, is the Uncreated Good; considered, however, as the form informing the human soul, it is a created good." [119]   God, therefore, is the object contemplated, possessed, and enjoyed. He is not, however, the form perfecting the souls that have attained to the state of eternal happiness, since every perfection of a creature must itself be created, and God cannot be the perfective form of anything " *ad extra.* " [120]   The perfective form of the blessed is that certain " influence of God in the soul, by means of which the soul is rendered deiform and fully sated." [121]

---

est, ideo in eo solo debet quiescere et eo frui." *Liber I S.*, d. 1, a. 3, q. 2, conc., I, p. 41. Cf. *Com. In Ecc.*, prooemium, nn. 4–5, VI, p. 4; *Ibid.*, c. 3, q. 2, f. 2, p. 36; *Sermones de Temp., Dom. II p. Pent.*, s. 1, IX, p. 359.

[117] " Finem namque desideriorum omnium constat esse beatitudinem, quae est 'status omnium bonorum congregatione perfectus.' Ad quem quidem statum nullus pervenit nisi per ultimam resolutionem in eum qui est fons et origo bonorum tam naturalium quam gratuitorum, tam corporalium quam spiritualium, tam temporalium quam aeternorum." *Op. 3, Lignum Vitae*, n. 48, VIII, p. 85.

[118] " Illi ergo soli inest beatitudo et potentia per essentiam, beatitudo autem nostra est per participationem; secundum quod est per participationem, ortum habet ab illo quod est per essentiam; ergo beati sumus participantes fontem beatitudinis, qui est Deus." *Com. In Ecc.*, prooemium, n. 2, VI, p. 3.

[119] " Beatitudo sumta pro objecto beatificante est bonum increatum, sumta vero pro forma animam informante est bonum creatum." *Liber IV S.*, d. 49, p. 1, a. 1, q. 1, conc., IV, p. 1000.

[120] " Quia beatitudo est perfectio Beati; sed omnis perfectio creaturae est creata, quia Deus nullius est forma perfectiva: ergo beatitudo est bonum creatum." *Ibid.*, f. 1, p. 1000.

[121] " Satians autem sicut informans est ipsa influentia Dei in animam, quae est ipsa deiformitas et satietas." *Ibid.*, conc., p. 1001.

Therefore, God is both the object and the principal cause of our true happiness.[122]

In this state of eternal happiness all the appetites and powers of the soul, our author remarks, are fully sated. Thus, the rational powers, which now believe through the medium of faith, will see God clearly and perfectly; the concupiscible, whose act is love, will love Him perfectly; the irascible, which elevate the soul and enable it to remain steadfast through the medium of hope, will possess the Eternal Goodness permanently, without fear of loss. The blessed, endowed with perfect vision, possession, and love of the Eternal, will, therefore, experience perfect joy.[123]

In seeking to determine the ultimate constituent of eternal happiness, we wish to remark that all joy, in Bonaventure's opinion, belongs essentially to the will. The happiness of the blessed, to be sure, is based upon their knowledge of the Supreme Good and made possible by it, since joy and vision are inseparable.[124] However, the Seraphic Doctor insists, to enjoy is to take delight in an object and to adhere to it in an act of love.

---

[122] Although we have a natural desire for this supernatural end, nevertheless, faith alone can assure us that this end will actually be attained. Cf. *Com. In Ecc.*, c. 3, q. 2, conc., VI, p. 37. Moreover, although the soul has an aptitude for true happiness, Bonaventure hastens to affirm that the soul has not the sufficient disposition necessary for the actual attainment of this supernatural end. Divine Grace, the aid of the Most High, is needed in order that man may be sufficiently disposed for the state of glory; nature cannot suffice. Cf. *Liber II S.*, d. 19, a. 3, q. 1, conc., II, p. 469; *Ibid.*, d. 29, a. 1, q. 2, conc., p. 698; *Liber I S.*, d. 8, p. 1, a. 2, q. 2, ad 7–8, I, p. 161.

[123] "Unde rationalis, cujus est modo credere per fidem, tunc videbit aperte; concupiscibilis, cujus est amare, diliget tunc perfecte; irascibilis, cujus est erigi et inniti per spem, tunc tenebit continue et certe. Unde secundum hoc tres actus distinguuntur tres dotes, scilicet visio, dilectio, comprehensio sive tentio sive fruitio per appropriationem; nam fruitio ista tria complecitur." *Liber IV S.*, d. 49, p. 1, a. 1, q. 5, conc., IV, p. 1009.

[124] "Ad illud: Visio est tota. merces; dicendum, quod illud non dicitur proprie, sed per concomitantiam, quia visio et complacentia, in qua est perfecta ratio fruitionis, inseparabiliter se habent." *Liber I S.*, d. 1, a. 2, q. 1, ad 3, I, p. 37. Cf. Scholion of the Editors of Quaracchi, p. 37; *Liber IV S.*, d. 49, p. 1, a. 1, q. 5, ad 1–3, IV, p. 1009.

Hence it seems that ultimately it is the will that plays the greater role in " *beatitudo.*" [125]

SECTION 5.   THE EQUALITY OF MEN

Another point of interest in the study of man, a point of importance in social studies, is the equality or inequality of men. There are, in this regard, three questions which arouse our interest: (1) why did God create so many men? (2) are all men equal? and (3) whence come the inequalities that we find amongst the various human entities?

To answer the first question, we need only recall what has been said in reference to the purpose of creation—namely, that God created all things for the manifestation of His Eternal Perfection.   Thus, the principal reason for the multiplication of human individuals is the manifestation of God's Goodness, for the more souls to which the gifts of His Infinite Bounty can be distributed, the more clearly is His Goodness revealed.[126]

Are all men equal?   From what has already been stated with

---

[125] " Ad illud quod objicitur, quod amans non fruitur, nisi videat vel habeat; dicendum, quod videre et habere requiruntur ad frui, similiter et amare.   Nam si quis videt aliquid et habet, nunquam delectatur, nisi amet; aliter tamen requiritur visio quam amor.   Nam visio disponit, similiter et tentio, sed amor delicias suggerit.   Unde est quasi acumen penetrans, et ideo ei maxime convenit unire et per consequens delectare et quietare: ideo essentialiter, non dispositive, est fruitio.   Propter quod est intelligendum, quod actus voluntatis potest dupliciter considerari, scilicet per modum appetitus et complacentiae.   Primo moto antecedere potest ipsam visionem; secundo vero consequitur, et *in hoc est perfecta ratio ipsius fruitionis,* scilicet in complacentia rei visae et habitae." *Liber I S.,* d. 1, a. 2, q. 1, ad 2, I, p. 37.   Cf. *Liber II S.,* d. 38, a. 1, q. 3, ad 4, II, p. 885; Gilson, *op. cit.,* pp. 448–451; Tinivella, *op. cit.,* pp. 158–159.

[126] ". . . principalis ratio est manifestationem bonitatis divinae; et haec praecipue est in animabus, quae multae sunt, ut eis distribuatur gratiarum Dei multiformitas, et compleatur illius supernae civitatis integritas et numerositas." *Liber II S.,* d. 18, a. 2, q. 1, ad 3, II, p. 447.

Another reason is deduced from the virtue of charity, the love that men should have for one another.   Indeed, this love is such that it demands a multitude of souls joined together in one " good " society.   The greater the number of souls in this society, the more is the charitable soul gladdened. *Ibid.,* d. 3, a. 1, q. 2, ad 2, p. 104.

reference to the nature of man, we can conclude that all men are equal in so far as they are men. In other words, as it is the very essence of man to be a composite of corporeal and spiritual natures, all men are composed of material body and rational soul; all men are endowed with vegetative, sensitive, and rational powers; all men are rational animals, capable of knowing and of willing freely. In addition, since it is the nature of a rational creature to be not simply an individual but also a person, it follows that all men are, to an equal degree, persons, and, consequently, are ordered not to any other creature, no matter how noble, but directly and immediately to God, as to their sole end. Furthermore, since all rational souls are immediately created by God, all men are equal as regards their origin. And, finally, because rational creatures are destined to a supernatural end, all men are equal in regard to their final supernatural end, i.e., union with God.

However, there are, as daily experience reveals, inequalities among the various human entities. Bonaventure was quick to take notice of this fact. In men he sees various grades of perfection not only in bodily and intellectual powers, but also in the gratuitous gifts of the soul. Not all men are suited for the same things; different men are diversely and unequally disposed.[127]

Hence, we may conclude that men are both equal and unequal. They are equal in that which concerns their origin, nature, and end; unequal in their perfections and gifts, both natural and supernatural. They are, therefore, essentially equal, accidentally unequal.

---

[127] In seeking to determine the reason for this diversity and inequality among men the Seraphic Doctor informs us that a twofold answer may be offered. As natural philosophers, we might explain this diversity by the varied disposition and organization of the body. This answer contains some truth, but it does not satisfy fully, since it does not assign the ultimate cause. Consequently, the Seraphic Doctor accepts, as being more reasonable, the answer of the theologian who teaches that this diversity and inequality in the distribution of gifts is due to God, from Whom proceed all gifts, both gratuitous and natural. Cf. *Ibid.*, d. 32, dub. VI, II, pp. 777–778.

ARTICLE III. THE PRESENT CONDITION OF MAN

From the foregoing considerations on the nature of man we must have come to the conclusion that man is, indeed, an extraordinary creature. When we recall that man possesses a rational and immortal soul made according to the image of the Eternal and is capable of attaining to God and participating in His Eternal Perfection; that man is a person immediately ordered to God; that man was made for an eternity of supreme happiness in union with Happiness Itself—we must conclude that nothing in the whole expanse of nature is nobler than man. On the other hand, daily experience insistently reminds us that all is not right, for the creature man, ennobled by so exalted a nature, now finds himself in a state of real wretchedness. This fact cannot help but raise the question: was man created in this state of dire distress? was this the condition of man when he first came from the hands of his Creator?

Here the philosopher enlightened by faith has a marked advantage over the philosopher who limits himself to the unaided light of reason. Never can reason discover, when left to itself, the Fall of man; revelation alone can inform us of it. The natural philosopher, relying upon his own reasoning power, cannot come to the knowledge of the Fall because it is the nature of fallen knowledge, when it reasons as fallen, to be unaware of the fact that it is fallen knowledge. The thinker, however, who is enlightened by faith as to the fact of the fall, can show how absurd it is to suppose that a perfect God created man in the state of wretchedness in which he now finds himself. To suppose that man's present condition corresponds with his original condition would be revolting injustice, irreconcilable with the idea of creation by God.[128] If it is certain that the First Principle is most just and most clement, we must, after all, conclude that man, in his original condition, was without fault or defect, and that this present sad state of affairs is an accidental disorder, a punishment for sin.[129]

Man, therefore, has fallen and no longer is what he ought to

---

[128] *Liber II S.,* d. 30, a. 1, q. 1, conc., II, p. 716.
[129] *Brev.,* p. 3, c. 5, V, p. 234; *Liber II S.,* d. 30, a. 1, q. 1, f. 2, II, p. 714.

be. This fact necessarily exerts a great influence upon the thought of our author. Indeed, at the very moment when he comes to consider the various problems that concern man, St. Bonaventure makes use of the words of *Ecclesiastes:* " Only this I have found, that God made man right, and he hath entangled himself with an infinity of questions." [130] Two things, our author tells us, are contained in this quotation from Sacred Scripture: (a) the fact that man's rightness proceeds from God, and (b) the corresponding fact that man's miserable obliqueness (obliquatio) comes from himself. From this appears what ought to be man's mode of life. Knowing the Source of all good, man should seek this Source of goodness, strive to attain it, and rest in it; knowing, moreover, the principle and origin of evil, man should seek to avoid it.[131]

Man must, therefore, turn to God in order to be right, since all good and rightness proceed from God. In considering man's ideal state (recta conditio) the Seraphic Doctor assures us not only that God made man capable of rectitude by imprinting the image of Himself within man; but, by turning man to Himself, He also made him right. This, then, was the original state of man—he (his intellect, will, and power) was just and upright, because he was wholly and completely turned to God. Besides, by being turned to God, he gained for himself the position due him—the central position below God and above other creatures.[132]

---

[130] C. 7, v. 30; *Liber II S.*, prooemium, II, p. 3.

[131] " In quo verbo duo clauduntur, scilicet quod hominis recta formatio et rectitudo est a Deo. . . . Aliud est, quod hominis misera obliquatio est a se ipso. . . . In his autem duobus clauditur terminus totius humanae comprehensionis, ut cognoscat originem boni et cognoscendo requirat et ad illam perveniat et ibi requiescat; et ut cognoscat originem et principium mali, et illud vitet et caveat." *Ibid.*, pp. 3–4.

[132] ". . . Deus non tantum fecit hominem possibilem ad rectitudinem, suam ei imaginem conferendo, sed etiam fecit hominem rectum, ipsum ad se convertendo. Tunc enim homo rectus est . . . quando homo ad Deum convertitur ex se toto." *Ibid.*, p. 4. " Homo enim in medio constitutus, dum factus est ad Deum conversus et subjectus, cetera sunt ei subjecta, ita quod Deus omnem veritatem creatam subjecerat ejus intellectui ad dijudicandum, omnem bonitatem ejus affectui ad utendum, omnem veritatem ejus potestati ad gubernandum." *Ibid.*, p. 5.

This ideal state, present in the First Man, did not remain long. First of all, man's free-will was not an absolute good. Being a creature, created from nothing, man and, of course, his will, were defective and could, therefore, turn to evil.[133] Moreover, even in the ideal state, man, as the Seraphic Doctor notes, was not permitted to see God face to face. Hence, his will was not established in Divine love to such an extent that he could not turn away from it.[134] Finally, endowed with an intermediate nature—with senses and reason—man was capable of reading both the interior book of the divine exemplars and the exterior book of the universe of sense. He could, on the one hand, contemplate the world of exemplars through the medium of divine illumination and refer the divine vestiges perceived in things to their eternal Source; or he could, on the other hand, limit himself to the universe of sense, the mere created natures.[135] This, then, was man's status: permitted to read both books, he found himself between two objects—one higher, the other lower —both of which solicited him. His was to choose between the two objects—to turn to God or to the creatures.[136]

Turned to God by God in the beginning, man was made right. In turning away from God towards the created natures, which were incapable of fully satisfying either his thought or his desires, man lost his rightness. Such was the Fall—an act of curiosity and pride whereby man turned away from the Eternal to the temporal and limited himself to the domain of the accidental and non-being.[137] However, in falling, man lost, as our author points out, his rightness, but not his aptitude and appetite for rightness. He still desired and sought it. Since nothing created could compensate for the infinite good that he has lost, man sought in vain—his desire, his search is continuous; nowhere does he find rest.[138]

---

[133] *Liber II S.*, d. 25, p. 2, a. 1, q. 3, conc., II, p. 614.

[134] *Ibid.*, d. 23, a. 2, q. 3, conc., pp. 544–545.

[135] *Brev.*, p. 2, c. 11, V, p. 229.

[136] *Ibid.*, p. 3, c. 3, pp. 232–233.

[137] *In Hex.*, coll. XIX, n. 4, V, p. 420; *Ibid.*, coll. I, n. 17, p. 332.

[138] " Sic enim cecidit a rectitudine, ut perderet ipsam rectitudinem, non rectitudinis aptitudinem, perderet habitum, non appetitum. . . . Quoniam

Separated from the Highest Truth, man's intelligence lost the real measure of truth, and became entangled in an infinity of questions. Now man's inquiries are interminable; one question follows another; his doubts are multiplied, because he cannot find that which will fully satisfy his desire to know.[139] In like manner, by refusing to conform itself to the Supreme Good in loving, the will became poor and was afflicted with concupiscence and cupidity, which, like burning fires, are never sated. Retaining its desire for infinity, but having forsaken God, the will now seeks to satisfy this desire in an indefinite number of delights. This deformed love—deformed since it has turned from the source of all rightness—has brought about the most abominable vices.[140] Finally, by turning away from the Supreme Power, man's power lost its center of stability and became weak, restless, and fickle—like dust whirled about by the wind.[141] And this is the present and real status of man. His will is enslaved by cupidity; his mind is besieged by a multitude of questions, and his power is afflicted with instability and fickleness.[142]

---

igitur remansit appetitus sine habitu, ideo factus est homo quaerendo sollicitus. Et quia nihil creatum recompensare potest bonum amissum, cum sit infinitum, ideo appetit, quaerit et nunquam quiescit; et ideo declinando a rectitudine infinitis quaestionibus se immiscuit." *Liber II S.*, prooemium, II, p. 5.

[139] " Unde intelligentia, avertendo se a summa veritate ignara effecta, infinitis quaestionibus se immiscuit per curiositatem. . . . Est homo, qui diebus et noctibus somnum non capit oculis, et intellexi, quod omnium operum Dei nullam possit homo invenire rationem, supple, quae finiat appetitum sive inquisitionem; immo generat aliam quaestionem, et parit novam contentionem, et immiscet inextricabilem dubitationem." *Ibidem.*

[140] " Voluntas, discordando a summa bonitate egena effecta, immiscuit se infinitis quaestionibus per concupiscentiam et cupiditatem: quia . . . ignis numquam dicit: sufficit. Unde et avarus non implebitur pecunia. . . . Ideo semper quaerit et mendicat. Similiter concupiscentia nunquam satiatur, immo infinitis voluptatum quaestionibus implicatur . . ." *Ibid.*, pp. 5–6.

[141] " Virtus autem, discontinuando se a summa potestate facta infirma, immiscuit se infinitis quaestionibus per instabilitatem, unde semper quaerit quietem et non invenit. . . . Iste est spiritus instabilitatis, pro eo quod nihil potest stabilire. Unde homo peccator est sicut pulvis, quem projicit ventus a facie terrae." *Ibid.*, p. 6.

[142] " Immiscuit igitur se homo infinitis quaestionibus per curiositatem, dum

Moreover, because of man's Fall the whole universe became separated from God. After all, a world which exists for the purpose of manifesting the Divine Majesty to the mind of man achieves its end only if man's mind sees God in it. In the ideal and original state man regarded creatures as so many vestiges and representations of God and was led by them to the praise, adoration, and love of the Eternal. The universe was in this manner enabled to reach its end. When man, however, in his Fall, turned away from God, he became interested in the creature itself and sought to discover for the world a meaning intrinsic to the world itself. Thereby the universe was no longer ordered to the end assigned to it by the Creator. The universe did continue to speak of God, but man, interested in the creature as a mere nature and not as a divine vestige, refused to listen to its canticle of praise and to join therein.[143]

Finally, in rejecting the Eternal Good in order to embrace the mutable good, man became unworthy of both.[144] While all things were fully subjected to man when he was wholly and completely turned to God, when man rebelled against the Eternal the lower creation, in turn, rebelled against man.[145] Witness, for instance, the relation of body and soul, of the inferior and superior powers in man. God so created man that the soul would preside over the body and the body would be submissive to the soul as long as the latter remained subject to the Uncreated. However, once the soul refused her allegiance to God, then the body rebelled

---

cecidit a veritate in ignorantiam; per cupiditatem, dum cecidit a bonitate in malitiam; per instabilitatem, dum cecidit a potestate in impotentiam." *Ibidem.*

[143] *In Hex.,* coll. XIII, n. 12, V, pp. 389–390.

[144] "Rursus, quia deserens bonum incommutabile propter bonum commutabile efficitur indignus utroque: hinc est, quod ratione carentiae originalis justitiae perdit anima quietem temporalem in corpore per multiplicem corrumptionem et mortem, et tandem separatur a visione lucis aeternae, amittendo felicitatem gloriae tam in anima quam in corpore." *Brev.,* p. 3, c. 5, V, p. 234.

[145] "Quoniam ergo uterque parens, superbiendo in mente et gustando in carne, inobediens fuit suo superiori, justo Dei juidicio factum est, ut sibi fieret inobediens suum inferius . . ." *Ibid.,* c. 4, p. 235.

against the soul, and the inferior powers refused to remain subject and submissive to the superior powers of man.[146]

Accordingly, although created just and upright, man has, in
virtue of his Fall, heaped misery upon himself. Is man, then,
to despair? Is he hopelessly lost, forever banished from the
One Who alone can fully satisfy the longings of his heart? Of
himself man is powerless to recover what he has been justly
deprived of, yet whose lack presses on him so cruelly—powerless to satisfy his innate desire of a supernatural end. Cast into
ignorance, he needs a Teacher; weakened in power, he needs
Solace; his will marred by sin, he needs an Advocate.[147] Only
one thing is at the disposal of man—prayer, which, however,
while it is the first and necessary condition for his return, is not
of itself sufficiently efficacious.[148] Since there is a question of
reaching above himself on the part of man, he must be helped
by supernatural strength and be lifted up by a higher power that
stoops to raise him.[149] Indeed, man, who turned away from
God by a free act, cannot, on the other hand, return to God and
be reunited with Him of his own power. Aid must be obtained
from on High—the aid of revelation and grace. This aid has
been granted to man. Thus our author writes:

> " In his primitive constitution man was created by God
> capable of untroubled contemplation, and for that reason
> was placed by God in ' a garden of delight.' But, turning
> his back on the true light in order to pursue the mutable
> good, he found himself, through his own fault, dimin-
> ished and removed from his pristine stature. With him
> the whole human race, through original sin, was afflicted
> in a twofold manner: the human mind by ignorance and

---

[146] ". . . sic condidit Deus hominem, ut spiritus corpori praeesset, et corpus
subesset spiritui creato, quamdiu ille obediret Spiritui increato; et econtra,
si spiritus non obediret Deo, justo Dei judicio corpus suum inciperet sibi
rebellere; quod et factum est, cum Adam peccavit." *Ibid.,* c. 6, p. 235.

In reference to the various other punishments following upon the fall
confer *Ibid.,* cc. 4–6, pp. 233–235.

[147] *In Joannem,* c. 14, coll. LIII, n. 1, VI, p. 602.

[148] *Itinerarium,* c. 1, n. 1, V, pp. 296–297.

[149] " Sed supra nos levari non possumus nisi per virtutem superiorem nos
elevantem." *Ibid.,* p. 296.

the human body by concupiscence. As a result man, blinded and bent down, sits in darkness and sees not the light of heaven, unless he is strengthened against concupiscence by grace with justice, and against ignorance by knowledge with wisdom. All this is done by Jesus Christ, ' who of God is made unto us wisdom and justice and sanctification and redemption.' " [150]

With this, our picture of man nears completion. This rational creature, so exalted in nature and dignity, who, unfortunately, had chosen to depart from the Eternal and was, consequently, cast into a state of misery and want—a state of ignorance, cupidity, and instability—has been redeemed. His sin has been atoned for, and to him have been offered special supernatural aids—revelation and the manifold ramifications of grace—necessary for a return to God and a reunion with the sole Good that can fully satisfy the yearnings of his soul.

---

[150] " Secundum enim primam naturae institutionem creatus fuit homo habilis ad contemplationis quietem, et ideo posuit eum Deus in paradiso deliciarum. Sed avertens se a vero lumine ad commutabile bonum, incurvatus est ipse per culpam propriam, et totum genus suum per originale peccatum, quod dupliciter infecit humanam naturam, scilicet ignorantia mentem et concupiscentia carnem; ita quod excaecatus homo et incurvatus in tenebris sedet et caeli lumen non videt, nisi succurrat gratia cum justitia contra concupiscentiam, et scientia cum sapientia contra ignorantiam. Quod totum fit per Jesum Christum, qui factus est nobis a Deo Sapientia et justitia et sanctificatio et redemptio." *Ibid.*, n. 7, pp. 297–298.

For a fuller development of this thought we refer the reader to St. Bonaventure's *Itinerarium Mentis* (V, pp. 295–313) in which the author outlines the various steps to be followed in man's return to God. The reader is also referred to Gilson, *op. cit.*, pp. 421–451.

CHAPTER III

SOCIAL ORDER AND THE MAIN SOCIAL PRECEPTS

The moral and social doctrine of St. Bonaventure is a body of conclusions argued from two fundamental premises—the existence of order in the universe and the necessity of order in the life of man, whether we consider him as a private individual or as a social entity. These two notions and their consequences constitute the basis and foundation of all the Seraphic Doctor's social teachings. It is imperative, then, that from the very beginning we have an exact notion regarding Bonaventure's concept of order and of the manner in which this order affects man's personal and social life.

It is the scope of the present chapter to submit to scrutiny this Bonaventurian concept, together with its application to creation in general and to man in particular, that from it we may determine the more general principles which apply to man's social nature. The chapter will be divided into five articles: the first, treating of the concept of order in general; the second, of eternal order; the third, of moral order; the fourth, of man as a social being; and the fifth, of the main social precepts.

ARTICLE I. THE CONCEPT OF ORDER

Man's idea of order proceeds from the sensible world, i.e., from a consideration of the universe inasmuch as it reflects the power, wisdom, and goodness of the First Cause, Who has regulated all things in the very perfection of harmony. For the world, mirroring God's perfections, proclaims the power of God producing all things from nothing, the wisdom of God clearly arranging and distinguishing all things, and the goodness of God generously adorning all things.[1] This selfsame universe,

---

[1] ". . . totus enim mundus est quasi liber quidam, in quo Creator potest cognosci per ejus potentiam, sapientiam, bonitatem, reluctans in creaturis . . ."

moreover, manifests the immensity of that power, art, and goodness which, indeed, is to all things the cause of their being, the ground of their understanding, and the ultimate reason of their harmony.[2]

Furthermore, an examination of the universe acquaints us with the fact that it is hierarchically constituted. In it we find some things that have only being, others that have being and life, and still others that are blessed with being, life, and intelligence.[3]   Again, the inquiring mind discovers that certain creatures are purely corporeal, that others are composed of both corporeal and spiritual substances, and that still others are of a purely spiritual nature.[4] This gradation is also found in the various degrees in which the creatures represent the divine; for some are mere shadows and vestiges, others are images, and still others possess the similitude of grace.[5] From this hierarchical constitution of the universe we must come to the conclusion that not all things have been endowed with equal power and perfection—that there is a certain order of progression in the universe.[6]

The concept of order becomes more apparent when the mind discovers that all things have been produced in a certain measure, number, and weight—measure, by which they are limited; number, by which they are distinguished; and weight, which marks the point towards which each thing tends.[7]   In this manner we

---

Com. in Sap., c. 13, v. 5, VI, p. 193. Cf. *S. de Temp., Dom. IV Adventus,* s. viii, IX, p. 83; *In Hex.*, coll. II, n. 27, V, p. 340.

[2] *Itin.*, c. 1, n. 14, V, p. 299.

[3] " Tertio modo aspectus ratiocinabiliter investigantis videt, quaedam tantum esse, quaedam autem esse et vivere, quaedam vero esse, vivere et discernere . . ." *Ibid.*, n. 13, p. 298.

[4] " Videt iterum, quaedam esse tantum corporalia, quaedam partim corporalia, partim spiritualia; ex quo advertit, aliqua esse mere spiritualia . . ." *Ibidem.*

[5] Cf. above, p. 37–38.

[6] ". . . dicendum, quod Deus non dat unicuique quod simpliciter melius, quia tunc non faceret res ordinatas, sed aequaliter perfectas: et hoc repugnaret perfectioni, ' quia, si essent aequalia, non essent omnia,' ut dicit Augustinus." *Liber II S.*, d. 1, p. 2, a. 1, q. 2, ad 5, II, p. 43. Cf. *Ibid.*, p. 1, a. 1, q. 1, ad 2, p. 17.

[7] " Primo modo aspectus contemplantis, res in se ipsis considerans, videt in eis pondus, numerum et mensuram: pondus quoad situm, ubi inclinantur,

arrive at the heart of the problem, for there is no doubt that Bonaventure's concept of order was inspired by the sacred text: ". . . thou hast ordered all things in measure and number and weight." [8] Number and measure do not constitute order as such; they are presupposed by order. For, as our author points out, order presupposes number and number presupposes measure, for things are not ordered to one another unless they are numbered, nor are they numbered unless they are limited and measured. [9] The main, the formal constituent of order, hence,

---

numerum, quo distinguuntur, et mensuram, qua limitantur." *Itin.,* c. 1, n. 11, V, p. 298.

[8] *Book of Wisdom,* c. xi, v. 21.

[9] ". . . ordo praesupponit numerum, et numerus praesupponit mensuram, quia non ordinantur ad aliud nisi numerata, et non numerantur nisi limitata . . ." *Liber I S.,* d. 43, a. 1, q. 3, conc., I, p. 772.

We may mention that measure, number, and weight are but three of the nine properties of being contained in Bonaventurian thought. It is not our purpose to examine this teaching of our author; however, it would be well to recall that since each creature is created by God, according to God, and for God, it is, therefore, related to God as to its efficient, exemplar, and final cause. Each creature, inasmuch as it is constituted in being by God, its efficient cause, possesses unity, mode, and measure; inasmuch as it is conformed to God, its exemplar cause, it possesses truth, species, and number; inasmuch as it is ordered to God, its final cause, it possesses goodness, order, and weight. Considered in itself, the creature is measured, numbered, and possessive of a certain tendency. Referred to God, the creature is stamped with a certain mode of being, conferred to its proper species, and assigned to its proper and determined order. Referred to God and likened to Him, each creature is one, true, and good. Needless to say, the teaching of the Seraphic Doctor on this point is quite complicated. For further study, confer *Brev.,* p. 2, c. 1, V, p. 219; *Liber I S.,* d. 3, p. 1, dub. 3, I, p. 79; *Com. in Sap.,* c. 11, v. 21, VI, p. 182; *S. de Temp., S. de Trinitate,* IX, p. 353.

Legowicz, *op. cit.,* pp. 33–49, in attempting to determine the essence of order in the teaching of St. Bonaventure, gives an explanation of these nine properties of being. However, we fear that he has not fully understood Bonaventure on this score. Bonaventure's thought, it must be remembered, is never to be separated from God. He would not consider the creature except in so far as it refers to the Creator, and this relationship of the creature to the Creator as its efficient, exemplar, and final cause is at the basis of any explanation of Bonaventure's nine properties of being. Legowicz seems to overlook this fact and considers these properties from

is the "*pondus,*" since order, as Bonaventure tells us, is the same as " pondus," and " ' pondus ' is an ordering inclination." [10]

Following in the footsteps of St. Augustine, the Seraphic Doctor identifies order with what he terms " the property of a thing that establishes it in its rightful place." [11]   On this account, the saintly author seems to conceive order as more dynamic than static.   In fact, for him order is an inclination, a tendency, a movement towards a certain end.   That end is the place due each thing in the total disposition of the universe.   Thus we are brought to his definition of order, namely: " Order is that which disposes all things, equal and unequal, giving unto each its proper place." [12]

Accordingly, order seems to demand: (a) a *distinction* of objects, since order presupposes number and measure; (b) some *relation* between these objects, because that which is ordered must have an inclination to that to which it is to be ordered, i.e., its proper place; and (c) a *purpose or goal,* namely: the attainment of the rightful place due that which is ordered.

ARTICLE II—ETERNAL ORDER

SECTION 1.   THE NATURE OF ETERNAL ORDER

Since all things come from the one Source and have been produced in perfect harmony with the Eternal Ideas of the Divine Wisdom and the inscrutable designs of the Divine Will, it stands to reason that of necessity there must be but one Supreme

---

the viewpoint of the creature alone, which, in our mode of thinking, is not conducive to a true understanding of Bonaventure's teaching.

[10] ". . . ordo idem, quod pondus." *Com. in Sap.,* c. 11, v. 21, VI, p. 182. ". . . est enim pondus inclinatio ordinativa." *Brev.,* p. 2, c. 1, V, p. 219.

[11] ". . . proprietas rei stabiliens eam in loco suo." *S. de Temp., S. de Trinitate,* IX, p. 353.

The origin of St. Bonaventure's teaching is to be sought in St. Augustine, especially in his *Enarrationes in Psalmos,* Ps. xxix, enarrat. 2, n. 10, *P.L.,* 36, 222.

[12] ". . . ordo est parium dispariumque sua loca cuique tribuens dispositio . . ." *De Perf. Evan.,* q. 4, a. 1, f. 4, V, p. 179.

The Seraphic Doctor has taken this definition from St. Augustine. Cf. *De Civitate Dei,* 1, xix, c. 13, *P.L.,* 41, 640.

Director of all things and one Supreme Order.[13] Our saintly author, therefore, states in no uncertain terms that all that is ordered proceeds, as such, from God Who is the Source of all order.[14] In fact, since God alone is Goodness itself and all other beings are good in so far as they participate in this Highest Good, it follows that all creatures must be ordered to Him, to Whom and by Whom all things are ordered, and Who is above all order.[15] Accordingly, it behooved the Creator to fix upon all His works a certain law, beyond which they cannot.[16]

This order, proceeding as it does from the Creator, can never be destroyed, for the economy of all things in the universe is immutably determined by the eternal law, which can be considered as an expression of the divine Wisdom, an unchanging providence so governing the world that nothing in the totality of the created universe can function outside the sphere of this primordial rule.[17] The never-failing character of the eternal order is better understood when we bear in mind the threefold order which, according to the Seraphic Doctor, plays its role in the creation, namely: the order ascribed to Divine Wisdom, the

---

[13] ". . . unus est omnium ordinator . . ." *Com. in Ecc.*, c. v, vv. 7, 8, VI, p. 44. Cf. *Liber I S.*, d. 3, p. 1, dub. 4, I, p. 80.

[14] ". . . omne ordinatum, ut tale est, procedit a Deo, a quo est omnis ordo . . ." *Liber II S.*, d. 36, a. 3, q. 2, conc., II, p. 855.

[15] *Com. in Ecc.*, c. v, vv. 7-8, VI, p. 44; *Liber I S.*, d. 43, a. 1, q. 3, conc., I, p. 772; *Liber III S.*, d. 1, a. 2, q. 2, conc., III, p. 25.

[16] " Decet Conditorem cunctis operibus suis legem certam et limitem praefigere, ultra quam non debeant progredi; sicut patet, quia omnes creaturae reguntur secundum leges sibi a Creatore impositas . . ." *Ibid.*, d. 37, a. 1, q. 1, f. 1, p. 813. Cf. the whole question.

[17] ". . . lex autem aeterna est illa, qua incommutabili permanente, cetera ordinantur." *De Perf. Evan.*, q. 4, a. 1, conc., V, p. 181.

" Nihil enim fit visibiliter et sensibiliter in ista totius creaturae amplissima quadam immensaque respublica, quod non de interiore invisibili atque intelligibili aula summi Imperatoris aut jubeatur, aut permittatur, secundum ineffabilem justitiam . . ." *Brev.*, p. 1, c. 9, V, p. 217.

". . . nihil potest hunc ordinem deordinare . . ." *Liber I S.*, d. 44, a. 1, q. 3, conc., I, p. 786. Cf. *Liber II S.*, d. 14, p. 2, a. 2, q. 3, ad 5, II, p. 365.

The Seraphic Doctor describes the eternal laws as: " immutabiles, infallibiles, indubitabiles, injudicabiles, incommutabiles, incoarctabiles and interminabiles." Cf. *In Hex.*, coll. II, nn. 9-10, V, p. 338.

order assigned to Divine Goodness, and finally, the order reserved to Divine Justice.[18]

The order ascribed to wisdom refers to the disposition of all things in the universe—i.e., the order of parts, which seems to be twofold, namely: *intra-individual,* or of the parts to the whole; and *inter-individual,* or of the things among themselves and with reference to the universal order.[19]

In the order of goodness is included the ordering of creatures to their end. This direction, as we have seen, can be twofold: viz., (a) to a created and proximate end, as is the case with the irrational creation; and (b) to the final and ultimate end—God.[20]

---

[18] "Differt enim triplex ordo in creaturis, quia per justitiam fit ordinatio remunerationum et meritorum, per sapientiam vero ordinatio partium ad se invicem, per bonitatem vero ordinatio rerum in suum finem." *Liber II S.,* d. 30, a. 1, q. 1, II, p. 714.

[19] ". . . dicendum, quod est ordo duplex: unus, dispositio rerum in universo, et hic appropriatur scientiae; alius, directio in finem, et hic appropriatur bonitati sive voluntati . . ." *Liber I S.,* d. 40, a. 1, q. 2, ad 1, I, p. 705.

". . . ordo partium est duplex, scilicet partium in toto, et rerum in universo. Et sicut creatura non potest produci a Deo deordinata a fine ultimo, ita quod illam deordinationem habeat a Deo; sic nec ab ordinatione, quae est in universo; et quamvis deforme corpus sit deordinatum in se, est tamen ordinatum in mundo." *Liber IV S.,* d. 44, p. 1, a. 3, q. 2, ad 4, IV, p. 917.

In this regard we may recall that although each creature must possess what essentially pertains to its degree of being, it may, nevertheless, be deprived of some power proper to it, as, for example, in the case of a blind man. However, although a particular creature may, when considered in itself, be somewhat deformed, it is, nonetheless, ordered with reference to the universal order, which is manifestive of Divine Wisdom and remains at all times intact; for the beauty and order present in the universe is so firmly established that it cannot, even for a moment, be rendered deformed. Cf. *Liber II S.,* d. 18, a. 1, q. 2, ad 5, II, pp. 437–438; *Ibid.,* d. 36, a. 2, q. 1, conc., p. 848.

[20] ". . . ordo creaturae quantum ad finem est dupliciter: vel quantum ad finem creatum, vel quantum ad finem ultimum, qui Deus est, qui est finis universalis." *Liber IV S.,* d. 44, p. 1, a. 3, q. 2, ad 4, IV, p. 917. Cf. above, c. 2, a. 1, s. 3.

Here we again encounter the unfailing character of the divine order, since no creature can be produced by the Eternal unless it is somehow ordered to Him as to its ultimate end. Cf. *Liber I S.,* d. 43, a. 1, q. 3, conc., I, p. 772; *Liber IV S.,* d. 44, p. 1, a. 3, q. 2, ad 4, IV, p. 917.

Finally, the order of justice is concerned with remunerations— merits and punishments. Naturally, this order refers to creatures that are free—creatures who, since they are creatures and, consequently, defective, can depart from the correct mode of behaviour and can thus disrupt, to a certain extent, the Divine plan. However, when a creature does depart from the particular order assigned to it, it must, our author affirms, necessarily fall under the rule and sway of another order, the order of justice.[21] The reason for this is clear. God, Who is supremely just, Who is, indeed, Justice itself, cannot permit evil to go unpunished or good unrewarded.[22] Accordingly, we may conclude that God so orders everything that nothing in the whole sphere of creation remains unordered.[23]

SECTION 2.   THE SUBJECTION OF CREATURES TO THE ETERNAL
ORDER

From the fact that each creature has, in accordance with the Divine Plan, been disposed to a certain mode of action, it follows that God so rules the works of His hand that the creatures act in conformity with the demands of their nature.[24] Consequently, while all creatures are subject to the law of the Eternal,

---

[21] "Ad illud autem quod objicitur, quod malum est privatio ordinis; dicendum, quod verum est, particularis naturae, sed non est verum, prout ordo dicit dispositionem universalis providentiae . . . si quis ab assignata sibi ordinis ratione discesserit, necesse sit, ut in alteram differentiam relabatur." *Liber I S.,* d. 46, a. 1, q. 5, ad 1, I, p. 831.

[22] ". . . cum primum principium, eo ipso quod primum, sit optimum et perfectissimum, et eo ipso quod optimum, sit summe amativum boni et summe detestativum mali; sicut summa bonitas non patitur, quod bonum remaneat irremuneratum, sic etiam pati non debet, quod halum remaneat impunitum." *Brev.,* p. 7, c. 2, V, p. 282. Cf. *Liber II S.,* d. 28, a. 1, q. 1, f. 5, II, p. 675; *Com. in Ecc.,* c. v, q. 3, f. 3, VI, p. 45.

[23] "Pater omnia disposuit ab aeterno, per quam fecit et saecula factaque gubernat et ordinat ad gloriam suam, partim per naturam, partim per gratiam, partim per justatiam, partim per misericordiam, ut nihil in hoc mundo inordinatum relinquat." *Op. III, Lignum Vitae,* n. 1, VIII, p. 71.

[24] ". . . nullam rem gubernat nec regit (Deus) aliter, quam natura ejus sive justitia naturalis exigat." *Liber I S.,* d. 43, a. 1, q. 4, conc., I, p. 775. Cf. *Liber II S.,* d. 1, p. 1, a. 1, q. 1, ad 2, II, p. 17; *Ibid.,* d. 16, a. 2, q. 1, conc. nn. 400–402.

nevertheless, a certain differentiation must be observed in the application of this law to the world of creation.

On the one hand, we have irrational creatures, who, having no freedom of choice and no power of self-determination, cannot help following the dictates of the instincts and appetites implanted in them from without.[25] These creatures, in fact, are not agents, in the true sense of the word. Rather than act of themselves, they are, in reality, acted upon from without.[26] Here, we meet with the order of nature, the " *ordo factus,*" which is a static and determined order.[27]

On the other hand, we have rational creation, which is endowed with liberty and is capable of self-government. Man, as we have seen, can, because of his rational powers, govern himself and direct his activity according to the dictates of his own reason and will.[28] As a matter of fact, when confronted with a " bonum," man has the power to reflect on it, to judge as to its convenience or inconvenience, and to weigh it in relation to the " beatitudo " which he naturally seeks. Accordingly, he is competent to act or to suspend the actuation of his faculties; he is truly a free agent.[29]

However, as a creature, man was produced by God, according to God, and for God—he was given a certain mode of exist-

---

[25] " . . . providentia quaedam provenit ex actu deliberationis et praecognitionis, quaedam provenit ex instinctu naturali. Prima est libertatis arbitrariae et reperitur in solis rationalibus; secunda vero est naturalis sagacitatis et industriae; natura enim prudentissima est; et haec reperitur in brutis animalibus, et talis non ponit liberum arbitrium." *Ibid.,* d. 25, p. 1, a. 1, q. 1, ad 5, p. 594. Cf. the whole question.

[26] " Et ideo dicit Damascenus, quod ' magis agantur quam agant '; ac per hoc, cum non possint actum proprium reprimere, respectu actus proprii non habent libertatem, nec etiam respectu objecti; et ideo, deficiente in eis libertate, liberum arbitrium non possunt participare." *Ibid.,* conc., p. 593.

[27] " . . . est limitatio potentiae agentis ad talem et talem effectum secundum dispositionem Dei et primariam ordinationem causarum." *Ibid.,* d. 7, p. 2, a. 2, q. 2, conc., p. 202.

" Et quia voluntas est instrumentum seipsum movens, natura vero minime; hinc est quod ordo justitiae est ordo non tantum factus, sed etiam factivus; ordo vero naturae est ordo factus." *Brev.,* p. 3, c. 10, V, p. 239.

[28] *Liber II S.,* d. 25, p. 1, a. 1, q. 1, II, pp. 592–594.

[29] Cf. above, pp. 56ss.

ence; he was produced according to a certain species or exemplar idea; he was created for a certain determined end. To man, therefore, was given a certain, determined nature; his intellect is determined towards knowing the true, his will towards loving the good; and the end of all his activity and striving must be "*beatitudo.*" As a consequence, man, besides being an agent, is also acted upon from without; besides being free, he is also, in a certain sense, determined.[30] This determination on the one hand and dynamism on the other brings us to the dual order that the Seraphic Doctor finds in man—the "*ordo naturae*" and the "*ordo justitiae.*" [31]

ARTICLE III. THE MORAL ORDER IN MAN

SECTION 1. THE ORDER OF NATURE AND THE ORDER OF JUSTICE

Bonaventure distinguishes a twofold goodness in man's deliberate action: the "*bonitas naturae,*" in the sense that this act results from some faculty natural to man; and the "*bonitas moris,*" in the sense that it is a deliberate act of the human person.[32] Because all of man's actions are the natural effects of powers proper to him, no action of man can be deprived of natural goodness, a goodness which coincides with being itself— the metaphysical good.[33] Corresponding to this natural goodness is the order of nature, which is a determined order, since

---

[30] As our author notes, only God is purely and simply an agent; the irrational creatures, on the contrary, are entirely acted upon; whereas the rational creatures are both agents in their own right and acted upon. Cf. *Sermo II, De Regno Dei Descripto in Parabolis Evangelicis,* n. 43, V, p. 551.

[31] *Brev.*, p. 3, c. 10, V, p. 239; *Liber II S.*, d. 7, p. 2, a. 2, q. 2, conc., II, p. 202.

[32] "... est notandum, quod actio deliberativa nata est habere duplicem bonitatem: et bonitatem naturae, in quantum est actio procedens ab aliqua virtute, et bonitatem moris, in quantum est procedens a libero arbitrio sive a voluntate." *Ibid.*, d. 41, a. 1, q. 1, conc., p. 937.

[33] "Cum ergo quaeritur, utrum bonitas et malitia circa actionem habeant repugnantiam, ita quod ipsam dividant tanquam membra opposita; dicendum, quod hoc non est verum de bono, prout dicitur a bonitate essentiali vel naturali; sic enim bonum non est differentia actionis, immo convertitur cum ente et reperitur in omni actione." *Ibidem.* Cf. *Ibid.*, d. 37, a. 2, q. 3, conc., p. 874.

nature, unlike the will, is an instrument moving itself not according to its own pleasure, but according to the form given it by the Creator.[34] For this reason, the Seraphic Doctor calls it the "*ordo factus*," i.e., the order established and determined by the Primary Cause.

Furthermore, the human act, since it is a deliberate act of the human person, should also possess a certain moral goodness. For, besides being of a certain, determined nature, the rational will is, in addition, a free agent. Consequently, just as the will, *considered as a nature,* must be referred to God via the three-fold causal relation and thereby possess its proper mode, species, and order, i.e., the natural good, in which it communicates with every type of creature; so also must the will, *considered as free,* be referred to God as to its efficient, exemplar, and final cause and thereby attain to its proper mode, species, and order, i.e., its moral good.[35] In other words, the human will should possess both the goodness that essentially belongs to it as a nature—natural goodness—and the goodness that is expected of it as a free agent—moral goodness. Unlike the natural goodness, however, the moral goodness is accidental and capable of being lost.[36] Moreover, it does not extend to all the actions of man.[37]

---

[34] "Ordo autem est duplex, scilicet ordo naturae et ordo justitiae. Ordo naturae est in bono naturali, ordo justitiae in bono morali; et quia bonum naturale est in omni natura, bonùm morale in voluntate habet consistere: ideo ordo naturae est in omni natura, ordo vero justitiae in voluntate electiva consistit. Et quia voluntas est instrumentum seipsum movens, natura vero minime; hinc est quod ordo justitiae est ordo non tantum factus, sed etiam factivus; ordo vero naturae est ordo factus." *Brev.,* p. 3, c. 10, V, p. 239. Cf. *Liber II S.,* d. 7, p. 2, a. 2, q. 2, conc., II, p. 202.

[35] ". . . attendendum est, quod creatura rationalis et est natura quaedam, et est ulterius praeter alias creaturas, operans per voluntatem. Et utroque modo habet comparari ad Deum; et utroque modo habet reperiri in ea modus, species et ordo . . ." *Ibid.,* d. 35, a. 2, q. 1, conc., p. 829.

"Voluntas autem, cum habet modum, speciem et ordinem, sicut debet, bona est." *Ibid.,* pp. 829–830. Cf. the whole question.

[36] ". . . in actione duplex consideratur bonitas: una naturae, altera moris, et una est essentialis, et altera accidentalis . . ." *Ibid.,* d. 37, a 2, q. 3, conc., p. 874.

[37] Bonaventure is explicit on this point, stating that although there is no medium between being and non-being, and hence all that exists must possess

Allied to the moral good is the order of justice. Since the human act is neither the result of reason, as such, which acts in a set manner, nor the result of the will, inasmuch as it is a natural appetite, but rather the effect of reason and will united in a deliberate act of the human person, the order of justice has reference to man's elective capacity or power of self-determina-tion.[38]   Accordingly, the Seraphic Doctor terms it the " *ordo factivus* "—an order of becoming, a dynamic order.[39]   However, although man is endowed with a free will and can, as a result, dominate his activity, nevertheless, because he is a creature, he is subject to laws imposed from above.[40]   Consequently, it ap-pears that the order of justice is not only " *factivus*," but also " *factus*." [41]   It is a determined order—" *ordo factus* "—because man is obliged to act in a certain manner, namely: " a Deo, secundum Deum, et propter Deum." [42]   It is a dynamic order— " *ordo factivus* "—because man, being free, is the master of his acts, capable of accepting the rectitude of justice or of deserting it.

Needless to say, it is with this order of justice that we are concerned—the order that has reference to man's freely direct-

---

natural or metaphysical goodness; nevertheless, there is a medium between what is morally good and morally evil, namely: indifferent acts. For further development of this thought, see *Liber II S.*, d. 41, a. 1, q. 3, II, pp. 942–946. In the " Scholion " following this question (pp. 946–947), the editors of Quaracchi have affirmed, and rightly so, that Bonaventure considers this question in a practical manner and is concerned with meritorious acts, whereas St. Thomas considers the same question under a speculative aspect and is concerned with the morality of actions in the natural order. How-ever, although the Seraphic Doctor is .chiefly and directly concerned with the meritoriousness of human acts, his manner of reasoning, especially that contained in his " ad 5, 6," sufficiently manifests that he also teaches the indifference of human acts with regard to morality in the natural order.

[38] " . . . ex concursu rationis et voluntatis resultat quaedam libertas sive quoddam dominium ad aliquid faciendum et disponendum." *Liber II S.*, d. 25, p. 1, a. 1, q. 3, conc., II, p. 599. Cf. the whole question.

[39] *Brev.*, p. 3, c. 10, V, p. 239. Cf. above, footnote 34.

[40] " Item, liberum arbitrium creatum, hoc ipso quod liberum est, dominatur actui suo; hoc ipso quod creatum est, factum est debens aliquid suo Crea-tori . . ." *Liber II S.*, d. 24, p. 1, a. 1, q. 1, f. 3, II, p. 555.

[41] Cf. above, footnote 34.

[42] *Brev.*, p. 3, c. 1, V, p. 231.

ing his actions and rightly ordering his life, whether as a private individual or as a social entity. Accordingly, we enter into the social moral order, where man, endowed with a social nature, must order aright not only his private personal life, but also his relations with his fellowmen, with whom he is to live in harmony. Before we come to a consideration of the social nature of man and the main social precepts, however, it seems advisable to discuss briefly the moral good, the moral law, and the natural faculties given to man to help him regulate his life.

SECTION 2. THE MORAL GOOD [43]

According to Bonaventurian teaching, the human act possesses moral goodness only when it enjoys proper mode, species, and order, i.e., only when God is the principle, the exemplar, and the

---

[43] The natural good, which, as we have seen, is an essential good, is, according to the thought of the Seraphic Doctor, the "*inchoatio*," the beginning or basis, as it were, of the moral good, since we must have an action before we can determine whether or not this action is morally good. Thus the "bonum naturale" is said to be in material potency with regard to moral goodness.

The human act, when reference is made to the moral good, is either a "*bonum in genere*" or a "*bonum perfectum*." It is said to be "bonum in genere" when it is concerned with a proper and due object—"*materia debita.*" This type of goodness is likened by St. Bonaventure to "genus" in the order of being. As genus is in potency to complete being and is completed by the advent of the specific difference, so, too, the "bonum in genere" is in potency to the "bonum perfectum" and is, in turn, specified, perfected, and completed by the advent of circumstances, which make the "bonum in genere" either a good or an evil. In opposition to the "bonum naturae," the "bonum in genere" is not in material (passive) but active potency with regard to perfect moral goodness, as it is concerned not solely with the effecting principle but also with proper and due matter. Moreover, it is, in a certain sense, an actual moral goodness, since genus, even though it is as matter in reference to the specific difference, is, nonetheless, a form, and, consequently, something actual. The "bonum perfectum," therefore, appears only when man's action deals not only with a proper object, but also with a congruous end—when it is invested with all the required conditions and circumstances. For, as Bonaventure asserts, a thing is good only "*ex integra causa*" and evil "*ex quocumque dectu.*" *Liber II S.,* d. 36, dub. V, II, pp. 858–859; *Ibid.,* d. 40, a. 1, q. 1, ad 4, p. 922.

end of man's activity.[44]   Man's action, Bonaventure tells us, is good when the will producing it is good.   However, the will is good only when it operates as a " *continuatio* " of the divine power (a Deo) ; when it is conformed to God as the directing principle (secundum Deum) ; and, finally, when it is united to God as the quieting end (propter Deum).[45]

This thought brings us, once again, to that well-known and widely used principle of the Seraphic Doctor, namely: that God is the Cause of being, the Principle of knowledge, and the Order of living.   In our present consideration God appears as the order and rectitude of life.   As God alone is Being and all others are participated beings, as God alone is truth and all others are but participated truths—likewise God alone is Goodness, and all others are good by participation in the Eternal Good, the Source of all Goodness.   Once this relation to the Eternal ceases, whether it is the relation to Him as efficient, exemplar, or final cause, goodness ceases and evil enters.[46]

---

[44] " Creatura enim rationalis . . . si agit a Deo et secundum Deum et propter Deum, ut constituat Deum suae actionis principium, exemplar et finem ; tunc ejus actio bona est, habens modum, speciem et ordinem." *Sermo II, De Regno Dei Descripto in Parabolis Evangelicis*, n. 43, V, pp. 551–552. Cf. *Brev.*, p. 3, c. 1, V, p. 231.

[45] " Tunc autem voluntas nostra bona est, quando in movendo sive operando continuatur divinae virtuti ut principio moventi, et conformatur ei ut regulae dirigenti, et unitur ei ut fini quietanti ; et in primo attenditur modus, in secundo species, in tertio ordo secundum comparationem in triplici genere causae." *Liber II S.*, d. 35, a: 2, q. 1, conc., II, p. 830.

[46] At the root of moral evil, St. Bonaventure teaches, are the natural defectibility of the created will, due to which man can depart from the order of justice, and the freedom of the will, which decides to depart from the correct mode of behaviour, namely: to act " a se, secundum se, and propter se," instead of acting " a Deo, secundum Deum, and propter Deum." In this case man's action is deprived of the mode, species, and order it should possess ; it becomes deranged, morally evil, sinful. For Bonaventure sin is the privation of rectitude, the deranging of the order of justice, the upsetting of the order whereby the rational creatures, images of the Eternal, should be immediately ordered to their Maker. It is the " aversio a Deo " and the " conversio ad creaturam."

For the teaching of the Seraphic Doctor, confer : *Liber II S.*, d. 41, a. 2, II, pp. 947ss ; *Ibid.*, dd. 34, 35, 36, pp. 802ss ; *Ibid.*, d. 24, p. 2, pp. 573ss ;

In reference to the morality of the human act, the Seraphic Doctor explicitly affirms that the quality of the intention determines the quality of the act. Proper distinction, however, must be made if we are to grasp the true teaching of our author. Thus, while the evil intention always renders the act evil, it does not follow that the good intention must, in turn, necessarily render the act good.[47] Indeed, the saintly Franciscan Doctor tells us, four conditions are required that the will may be rightly ordered: two, with regard to the object intended, i.e., "*ex parte objecti*"; and two, with regard to the movement towards the end, i.e., "*ex parte ordinationis.*"

"*Ex parte objecti*," he demands that the end be both a "*bonum in se*" and a "*bonum sub ratione finiendi.*" In other words, the end intended must, first of all, be a good in itself. This goodness resides primarily in the intrinsic perfection of the object intended, so that the higher its dignity in the order of being, the more eminent and ultimate it is in the order of end. Moreover, the end must be good "*sub ratione finiendi*," i.e., in its aptitude to be treated as an end. Not all that is good in itself must necessarily also be good as an end, since, for example, a lesser good cannot be a good end for a being higher than it in the scale of goodness. Furthermore, in order that the will may be good, there must be "*ex parte ordinationis*": (a) on the part of that which is ordered an aptitude to be ordered to the end intended; and (b) an actual conversion of the will to the end intended, i.e., an effective act by which the will wills this end and makes it its own.

Only when these four conditions are present—(a) that the end is good in itself; (b) that it is good in its aptitude to be treated as an end by the agent; (c) that the act which is directed to this end is objectively good in itself and in its aptitude to be ordered to the end intended; and (d) that the will actually wills this end and makes it its own—can we conclude that the goodness of the will and, consequently, of its act is judged by

---

Brev., p. 3, V, pp. 231ss; *Ibid.*, p. 7, c. 2, p. 282; *Sermo II, De Regno Dei Descripto in Parabolis Evangelicis*, n. 43, V, pp. 551–552.

[47] *Liber II S.*, d. 40, a. 1, q. 1, conc., II, p. 921; ad 6, p. 922.

the goodness of the end. Thus, as must be clear, both the perfection of the end intended and the rectitude of the intention cooperate to constitute the proper value of any given act.[48]

SECTION 3. "SECUNDUM DEUM" OR THE NATURAL LAW

As we have seen, the will, in order to be good, must operate as a "*continuato*" of the divine power; it must be conformed to God as the directing principle; and, finally, it must be united to God as the quieting end.[49] Accordingly, man must act "*secundum Deum,*" i.e., in conformity with the dictates of the Divine: for, although man is endowed with free will and can, as a result, dominate his actions, nevertheless, because he is a creature, he is subject to God.[50]

God, Justice itself, has obligated man to the rule of justice, not because He needs man's obedience, but because man must, in order to be rightly ordered and to possess justice, obey the Eternal as His Lord and Master.[51] This subjection of man to the law of the Eternal does not, in any way, destroy man's freedom. In considering this point the Seraphic Doctor distinguishes between liberty which is opposed to the servitude of force, and

---

[48] "Dicendum, quod cum dicitur voluntas esse bona ex bonitate finis, hoc est dicere, quod voluntas est bona ex ordinatione ad bonum finem.—Ad hoc autem, quod sit recta ordinatio ad bonum finem, requiritur, quod finis sit bonus duobus modis, videlicet secundum id quod est et sub ratione finiendi. Aliquid enim est bonum in se, quod tamen non recte ordinatur ad alterum in ratione finis; sicut minus bonum, quamvis sit bonum, non tamen est bonus finis majoris boni, pro eo quod 'finis melior debet esse his quae sunt ad finem.'—Similiter ex parte ordinationis duo requiruntur, videlicet idoneitas ex parte ordinabilis, et actualis conversio ex parte voluntatis ordinantis.—Et cum ista concurrunt, tunc absque dubio voluntas bona ex fine bono judicatur. Cum autem horum aliquid deficit, bonitas finis non sufficit ad bonitatem voluntatis . . ." *Liber II S.,* d. 38, a. 1, q. 1, conc., II, p. 882.
As appears, we have given but a brief and very sketchy view of Bonaventure's teaching along these lines. For further details, confer *Ibid.,* d. 38, pp. 881ss; d. 40, pp. 920ss; Gilson, *op. cit.,* pp. 395–405; Nölkensmeier, *op. cit.,* passim.
[49] *Liber II S.,* d. 35, a. 2, q. 1, conc., II, p. 830.
[50] *Ibid.,* d. 24, p. 1, a. 1, q. 1, f. 3, p. 555.
[51] *Brev.,* p. 5, c. 9, V, p. 262; *Liber I S.,* d. 35, a. 1, q. 1, ad 4, I, p. 602; *Liber III S.,* d. 20, a 1, q. 2, ad 2, III, p. 421.

liberty which is opposed to the servitude of subjection. The first type of liberty (that opposed to constraint) is essential to free will; it must be found complete and undiminished in all beings who have been blessed with freedom. The second type of liberty, however, is not essential to free will; the being endowed with freedom remains free even when he is subjected to another, e.g., to God.[52] Our author further stresses this point by asserting that to be subject to God and to serve Him is the greatest freedom, for to serve the Divine is to rule.[53]

If man is bound to observe the command of the Eternal, this law must, in some manner, be known by the human soul, for no one can be bound to observe the dictates of a law of which he is not conscious.[54] How, then, is this rule known to man? Our author replies that it is known as the natural law, and in an immediate manner. He defines the natural law as an impression made upon the soul by the eternal law.[55] Therefore, the

---

[52] ". . . cum quaeritur de diminutione dominii libertatis arbitrii, distinguendum est in dominio. Quoddam enim est dominium quod opponitur coactioni; quoddam, quod opponitur subjectioni. Si autem loquamur de dominio libertatis, quod opponitur servituti coactionis . . . hoc dominium est essentiale libero arbitrio, et ideo non minuitur nec augetur. . . . Si autem dicatur dominium, quod opponitur servituti subjectionis, sic recipit magis et minus nec inest aequaliter omnibus. Nam in miseris est subjectum miseriae, in beatis liberum; . . . in creaturis subjectum mandatis, in Deo vero supra omne mandatum." *Liber II S.,* d. 7, p. 1, a. 2, q. 3, conc., II, p. 188.

[53] "Sicut maxima servitus est servire diabolo, ita maxima libertas est servire Deo; quia ei 'servire est regnare.'" *S. de Temp., Dom. XXI p. Pent.,* s. 2, IX, p. 440.

For him, our subjection to God, far from destroying our freedom, actually enhances it. This thought is again expressed when he affirms that the fact of man's obligation towards good does not oppose liberty as such but only the freedom to sin—which, in turn, is neither liberty nor a part of liberty. Confer, *Liber III S.,* d. 37, a. 1, q. 1, ad 3, III, p. 814.

[54] ". . . jus naturale naturaliter ligat voluntatem; sed ligamen voluntatis necessario praecedit actus cognitionis—affectum enim praecedit intellectus—ergo si voluntas naturaliter ad illud jus ligatur, videtur, quod illud jus naturaliter ab anima cognoscatur." *Liber II S.,* d. 39, a. 1, q. 2, f. 6, II, p. 901. Cf. *Brev.,* p. 1, c. 9, V, p. 218.

[55] ". . . lex naturalis est impressio facta in anima a lege aeterna . . ." *De Perf. Evan.,* q. 4, a. 1, conc., V, p. 181. Bonaventure takes this from St. Augustine, *De Diversis Quaestionibus LXXXIII,* q. 53, n. 2, *P.L.,* 40, 36.

natural law, according to which man must regulate his actions, is something innate, something impressed upon us to such an extent that we cannot be ignorant of it.[56] Indeed, St. Bonaventure is so insistent on this point that he teaches God will punish all men who do not live in accordance with the Divine Decree, because, while some men may be ignorant of the written law, all men have a natural knowledge of the natural law imprinted in them by their Maker.[57]

The Seraphic Doctor, we should recall, speaks of a threefold natural law.[58] First we have what he calls natural law in the *more proper sense*, i.e., that which nature has impressed upon all animals.[59] Such a natural law is common to both men and brutes. Consequently, it is not, as we interpret the thought of our saintly author, the chief norm by which man is to regulate his life. Indeed, this law seems to coincide with the instincts

---

[56] "Et primo modo est de consideratione philosophorum, illorum maxime, qui versati sunt circa mores componendos, quorum liberum arbitrium est principium secundum regulam et dictamen juris naturalis, quod est unicuique impressum." *Liber II S.,* d. 25, p. 1, dub. 1, II, p. 607.

[57] "Punit autem Dominus illos etiam, quibus Legem non dedit, a quibus requirit justitiam, quia, etsi non habent legem scriptam, habent tamen legem naturae interius impressam . . ." *Com. in Ev. Lucae.,* c. 19, n. 34, VII, p. 484.

[58] "Respondeo: Dicendum, quod jus naturale tripliciter dicitur, scilicet communiter, proprie, et magis proprie . . ." *Liber IV S.,* d. 33, a. 1, q. 1, conc., IV, pp. 747–748.

Besides this threefold natural law, St. Bonaventure speaks of two types of precepts arising from the natural law. The first are the *absolute* precepts of nature, remaining immutably valid in all the states of human existence. The second are the *relative* precepts, which refer only to a certain state of human existence. Confer, *Ibid.,* d. 26, a. 1, q. 3, conc., p. 665; *Liber II S.,* d. 44, a. 2, q. 2, ad 4, II, p. 1009; *De Pref. Evan.,* q. 4, a. 1, conc., V, p. 81.

The doctrine of the Seraphic Doctor in reference to the natural law is somewhat complicated; a complete and thorough exposition of his teaching in this regard is not our purpose, since this would require a far deeper study than that which we have been able to give to it.

[59] "Tertio modo dicitur jus naturale propriisime, quod 'natura docuit omnia animalia' . . ." *Liber IV S.,* d. 33, a. 1, q. 1, conc., IV, p. 748. ". . . dicatur jus naturale quod natura impressit animalibus . . ." *Ibid.,* q. 2, conc., p. 750.

The basis of this teaching is the *Digest of Justinian* (1, 1), 1, 3.

placed in each animal, rational as well as irrational, according to which each operates and conducts his activity.[60]

In the second place we have what our author calls the natural law in the *proper sense,* namely, that which is dictated by right reason and is common to all nations and peoples.[61]   This, we gather, is that part of the natural law which is proper to man

---

[60] " Alio modo dicatur natura proprie vis insita rebus, secundum quam res naturales peragunt cursus suos et motus solitos . . ." *Liber II S.,* d. 18, a. 1, q. 2, ad 5, II, p. 437.

[61] " Secundo modo dicitur proprie, et sic definitur in principio Decretorum: ' Jus naturale est quod est commune omnium nationum '; et hoc jus est, quod dictat recta ratio." *Liber IV S.,* d. 33, a. 1, q. 1, conc., IV, p. 748.

Bonaventure quotes Gratian (*Decretum,* p. 1, d. 1, c. 7, *P.L.,* 187, 31) as his source, but this is actually the teaching of St. Isidore of Seville (*Etymologiarum Lib. XIII,* 1, v, c. 4, nn. 1–2, *P.L.,* 82, 199), from whom Gratian quotes.

At this point it may be noted that the natural law in the *proper sense* seems, to a certain extent, to coincide with the *jus gentium.*   The same thought can be found in St. Thomas, who, in his *Commentary on the Nichomachean Ethics,* V, 7, defines " jus gentium " as that part of the natural law which is proper to man, excluding what is common to men and animals.

However, it is our humble opinion that they are not to be identified. St. Bonaventure, it must be recalled, describes the " jus gentium " as the law which proceeds both from reason and the instinct of nature.   This description of the Seraphic Doctor, as we see it, expresses the thought that the body of laws included under the " jus gentium " is *deduced by reason* from the natural instinct in man.   Here, we appeal to the Editors of Quaracchi (V, p. 181, ft. 4), who have sought to explain the " jus gentium " as *that which natural reason has established* amongst all men and which is observed amongst all peoples and at all times.

Here, again, we find a point of agreement between the Seraphic and the Angelical Doctors, for St. Thomas (*S. Th.* I–II, q. 94, a. 4, c) seems to identify the " jus gentium " with the body of proximate and easy conclusions *derived* from natural principles, which natural principles are dictates of the natural law strictly so called.

Accordingly, we seem to find the following points included in the concept of " jus gentium ": (a) the fact that the body of laws included in the " jus gentium " is based on the natural law, (b) the fact that these laws are common to all men and nations; (c) the fact that they are conclusions arrived at through reasoning, and (d) the fact that these conclusions are proximate and apparent.

St. Bonaventure's teaching concerning the " jus gentium " is found in his *De Perf. Evan.,* q. 4, a. 1, conc., V, p. 181.

and which is to guide man in regulating his life. The reason for our conclusion is based on the fact that the natural law in the *more proper sense* is concerned with nature as common to both rational and irrational animals, while the natural law in the *proper sense* is concerned solely with rational nature—i.e., with the dictates of right reason.[62] For this, indeed, is the law which demands that man act in accordance with right reason.[63] From this natural law proceed such precepts as: God must be honored, loved, and feared;[64] parents must be respected and revered;[65] order, hierarchical order, must be observed;[66] peace must be maintained;[67] to each must be given his due;[68] " do not unto others what you do not want others to do unto you; and, do unto others what you want others to do unto you." [69]

Finally, we have what the Seraphic Doctor terms the natural law in the *commonly accepted sense,* i.e., that which is contained in the Law and Gospel.[70] St. Bonaventure looks upon the Decalogue and the Gospel precepts as further determinations and elaborations of the natural law. We can best arrive at his thought by remembering that all governance and legislation of the Eternal is pious, true, and holy. From this threefold character of divine governance he concludes to a threefold law— the law of piety, which is the law of nature and attributed to the Father; the law of truth, which is the written law and attributed to the Son; and the law of sanctity, which is the law of grace and attributed to the Holy Spirit.

Now, all moral law, he affirms, is contained in each of these,

---

[62] ". . . jus naturale dicitur quod ratio recta dictat . . ." *Liber IV S.,* d. 33, a. 1, q. 2, conc., IV, p. 750.

[63] ". . . de dictamine juris naturalis est, quod homo totus obediat rationi rectae in se . . ." *De Perf. Evan.,* q. 4, a. 1, q. 10, V, p. 180.

[64] *Liber II S.,* d. 39, a. 1, q. 2, conc., II, p. 904.

[65] *De Perf. Evan.,* q. 4, a. 1, f. 1, V, p. 179.

[66] *Ibid.,* f. 4, p. 179; f. 7, p. 180.

[67] *Ibid.,* f. 5, p. 179.

[68] *Ibid.,* f. 8, p. 180.

[69] *Liber IV S.,* d. 33, a. 1, q. 1, f. 6, IV, p. 747.

[70] "Uno modo sic: 'Jus naturale est quod in Lege et Evangelio continetur' . . ." *Ibid.,* conc., p. 748. The source of this is Gratian, *Decretum,* p. 1, d. 1, introduction, *P.L.,* 187, 29.

but in different ways. In the law of nature, it is neither explicit nor distinct. In the written law, it is more explicit, but lacks perfection. In the law of grace, it is both more explicit and more perfect.[71] From this it appears that both the Law (the written law) and the Gospel (the law of grace) are nothing more than further determinations of the natural law, since the moral law is embodied in the law of nature—even though it is contained only in a general and indeterminate manner. The need for further determination was brought about by man's Fall, because of which the light of reason was obscured and man's will rendered corrupt.[72]

SECTION 4. CONSCIENCE AND SYNDERESIS

Having seen that the natural law has been imprinted upon man's soul, our next step is to consider the natural faculties given to man whereby he may regulate his life rightly. In creating man, God blessed him with an intellect, which is both speculative and practical. He gave him a natural light—" *judicatorium naturale* "—which enables him to know not only what is true but also what is good, and which directs the mind in coming to the " operabilia " as well as the " cognoscibilia." The speculative and practical intellects are, in the thought of our author, two different phases or functions of the one intellect. For, in his wording, ". . . the speculative intellect becomes the practical, since the self-same faculty which directs in contemplating afterwards regulates in operating." [73] Just as the intellect, as specula-

---

[71] " Secunda appropriatio est soli aeterno, secundum quod est medium cuncta gubernans; et secundum hoc sunt tria appropriata, scilicet pietas, veritas, sanctitas: quia omnis gubernatio et omnis legislatio est pia, vera, sancta. . . . —Ab his enim tribus manant tres leges, nec possunt esse plures, scilicet naturae, legis scriptae et gratiae. Lex naturae appropriatur Patri, lex scripta Verbo, lex gratiae Spiritui sancto.—Lex naturae est lex pietatis. . . . Lex Scripta est lex veritatis. . . . Lex sanctitatis est lex gratiae. . . . Omnis enim moralis lex est secundum haec tria, sive secundum has tres; sed in lege naturae sunt minus distinctae et explicitae; in lege scripta, magis explicitae et minus perfectae; in lege gratiae, magis explicitae et perfectae . . ." *In Hex.,* coll. XXI, nn. 6–7, V, p. 432.

[72] *Liber III S.,* d. 37, a. 1, q. 3, conc., III, pp. 819–820.

[73] ". . . bene dicit, intellectum speculativum fieri practicum, quia ille idem

tive, consists of an innate natural light which engenders the habit of the principles of knowledge, so the same intellect, as practical, by virtue of the same natural light, engenders the habit of the principles of action.

This habit is called conscience, for conscience, the Seraphic Doctor states, is a habit of the practical intellect (in the order of action) corresponding exactly to science, a habit of the speculative intellect (in the order of knowledge). Accordingly, it is a habit perfecting our intellect in so far as it is practical, or, a habit which enables the intellect to decide upon the principles to which our actions should conform—the habit which dictates the rule according to which we are to regulate our lives.[74]

This habit, St. Bonaventure tells us, is both innate and acquired: *innate*, with reference to the natural directive light (judicatorium naturale); *acquired*, with respect to the species. Hence, man is gifted with a natural light, which suffices of itself to acquaint him with the fact that parents must be honored, that neighbors are not to be injured, etc. In order to come to these conclusions, however, man must, first of all, acquire the species of parents and of neighbors. Once the species are presented to the mind, however, the intellect, through the medium of the natural light, immediately concludes to the honor due to parents, to the fact that man's neighbours are not to be injured, etc.

Moreover, this habit is said to be innate, with reference to the

---

intellectus et illa eadem potentia, quae dirigit in considerando, postmodum regulat in operando." *Liber II S.,* d. 24, p. 1, a. 2, q. 1, ad 2, II, p. 561. Cf. *Liber I S.,* prooemium, q. 3, conc., I, p. 13.

[74] ". . . usitatiori tamen modo nomen conscientiae pro habitu accipitur sicut et nomen scientiae a quo componitur . . . est habitus potentiae cognitivae, aliter tamen, quam sit ipsa speculativa scientia: quia scientia speculativa est perfectio intellectus nostri, in quantum est speculativus; conscientia vero est habitus perficiens intellectum nostrum, in quantum est practicus, sive in quantum dirigit in opere. . . . Et propterea talis habitus non simpliciter nominatur scientia, sed conscientia, ut in hoc significetur, quod habitus iste non perficit ipsam potentiam speculativam in se, sed prout est quodam modo juncta affectioni et operationi. Propter quod nos non dicimus, quod dictamen conscientiae sit ad hoc principium: omne totum est majus sua parte, et ad consimilia; sed bene dicimus, quod conscientia dictat, Deum esse honorandum et consimilia principia, quae sint sicut regulae agendorum." *Liber II S.,* d. 39, a. 1, q. 1, conc., II, p. 899.

first dictates of nature; and acquired, with regard to the particular conclusions.[75]   Certain principles as, e.g., " do not unto others what you do not want others to do unto you," are most evident.   In such cases they are said to be innate, because the natural light, having been presented with the necessary species, suffices of itself for a knowledge of these without any further persuasion.   Others, on the contrary, especially the particular conclusions, are not so evident.   Accordingly, they are said to be acquired, because in order to gain knowledge of them, further investigation and instruction are needed.[76]

Enabling man to decide upon the moral principles regulating his actions, conscience appears as the law of our intellect.[77]   As a law, however, it is based on the natural law, for natural law is the object of conscience as " dictantis "—i.e., conscience dictates the precepts that are contained in the natural law.[78]

The rule of action dictated by conscience may be either in con-

---

[75] " Quoniam igitur conscientia nominat habitum directivum nostri judicii respectu operabilium, hinc est, quod quodam modo habitum nominat innatum, et quodam modo nominat acquisitum.   Habitum, inquam, innatum nominat respectu eorum quae sunt de primo dictamine naturae; habitum vero acquisitum respectu eorum quae sunt institutionis superaddiate.   Habitum etiam innatum dicit respectu luminis directivi; habitum nihilominus acquisitum respectu speciei ipsius cognoscibilis.   Naturale enim habeo lumen, quod sufficit ad cognoscendum, quod parentes sunt honorandi, et quod proximi non sunt laedendi; non tamen habeo naturaliter mihi impressum speciem patris, vel speciem proximi." *Ibid.*, q. 2, conc., p. 903.

[76] " . . . in operabilibus quaedam sunt maxime evidentia, utpote illud: ' quod tibi non vis fieri, alii ne feceris,' et quod Deo obtemperandum est, et consimilia . . . primorum principiorum moralium cognitio nobis innata est, pro eo quod judicatorium illud sufficit ad illa cognoscenda.   Rursus, quemadmodum cognitio particularium conclusionum scientiarum acquisita est, pro eo quod lumen nobis innatum non plene sufficit ad illa cognoscenda, sed indiget aliqua persuasione et habilitatione nova: sic etiam intelligendum est ex parte operabilium, quod quaedam sunt agenda, ad quae tenemur, quae non cognoscimus nisi per instructionem superadditam." *Ibidem.*
Furthermore, some of the moral principles are wholly innate, as, e.g., God must be loved and feared.   In this case, no species from the exterior is needed, as the soul comes to a knowledge of God, love, and fear from an examination of itself. *Ibid.*, p. 904.

[77] *Ibid.*, q. 3, ad 2–3, p. 907.
[78] *Ibid.*, a. 2, q. 1, conc., p. 911.

formity with the Will of God, indifferent to it, or contrary to it. This is so because conscience is not always right. Whenever conscience refers to the universal (the first dictates of nature) and acts as a natural, innate habit, it is always right. When, on the other hand, it descends to particular conclusions and is considered as an acquired habit, it is prone to error, especially because it is mingled with deliberate reasoning.[79] Accordingly, when the rule of action dictated by conscience is in conformity with the Eternal Will, then man is universally and absolutely obligated, since he is bound by God's law and conscience merely shows him that he is so bound. When it is indifferent to the Will of God, then man remains obligated so long as conscience continues to dictate. This obligation is not perpetual, for investigation will bring to light the fact that there is no real obligation simply because God's law contains no such obligation. In the third case, i.e., when the rule of action dictated by conscience is contrary to the eternal law, man is obliged not to act upon the dictates of conscience, but to reform it.[80]

From what has been said it appears that the law of conscience obliges not on its own account, but on account of its agreement with the eternal law. In point of fact, the law of conscience, St. Bonaventure points out, obliges only so long as it does not dictate anything contrary to a superior law—the law of the Divine.[81] Thus, the obligatory force of the law of conscience

---

[79] " Et ideo, licet conscientia, prout stat in universali et movetur aspectu simplici, sit semper recta; prout autem descendit ad particularia et confert, potest fieri erronea, propter hoc quod intermiscet se actus rationis deliberativae." *Ibid.,* q. 3, ad 4, p. 915.

[80] ". . . conscientia aliquando dictat aliquid, quod est secundum legem Dei, aliquando aliquid, quod est praeter legem Dei, aliquando aliquid, quod est contra legem Dei. . . . In primis quidem conscientia simpliciter ligat et universaliter, pro eo quod homo ad illa ligatus est per legem divinam, et conscientia, quae illi concordat, ligatum ostendit. In secundis vero conscientia ligat, quamdiu manet; unde vel tenetur homo conscientiam deponere, vel tenetur illud quod dictat conscientia adimplere. . . . In tertiis vero conscientia non ligat ad faciendum, vel non faciendum, sed ligat ad se deponendum . . ." *Ibid.,* a. 1, q. 3, conc., p. 906. Cf. the whole question.

[81] " Ad illud quod objicitur, quod conscientia est lex intellectus nostri: dicendum, quod verum est, quod lex est, sed non est lex suprema; supra ipsam enim est lex alia, scilicet lex divina. Cum autem dicitur, quod lex

rests ultimately upon the Eternal law—the supreme norm of morality.

As the intellect has been blessed with an innate light which directs intellectual activity, whether purely speculative or practical, likewise, there has been implanted in the affective part of the soul a " *pondus*," a natural weight, directing and inclining man towards good. This weight which stimulates the will to what is good, just as the natural light stimulates the intellect towards what is true, is called " *synderesis*." [82] It is an habitual faculty of the will—a natural faculty which acts spontaneously. However, synderesis is the cause not of every movement or inclination of our will in general, but only of the inclinations which bear the will towards the good that is desired for itself (the " bonum honestum "), independently of the advantage or profit that accrues to it.[83]

The activity of the synderesis, according to the teaching of our author, comprises three acts: (1) it inclines and stimulates the will towards good—" bonum honestum "; (2) it causes the will to shrink from evil—evil being understood as the opposite of " bonum honestum "; and (3) it cries out in remorse against the evil that has been committed.[84]

Synderesis, being a natural faculty that acts spontaneously, does not come under the command of man's deliberate free will

---

ligat ad faciendum omne illud, quod dictat, dicendum quod verum est, quando lex inferior non dictat contrarium legi superiori; hoc autem saepe facit conscientia." *Ibid.*, ad 2–3, p. 907. Cf. *In Hex.*, coll. *XII*, nn. 7–8, V, p. 385.

[82] ". . . sicut intellectus indiget lumine ad judicandum, ita affectus indiget calore quodam et pondere spirituali ad recte amandum: ergo sicut in parte animae cognivitae est quodam naturale judicatorium, quod quidem est conscientia, ita in parte animae affectiva erit pondus ad bonum dirigens et inclinans; hoc autem non est nisi synderesis . . ." *Liber II S.*, a. 2, q. 1, f. 4, II, p. 908. Cf. *Ibid.*, conc., p. 910.

[83] ". . . dicendum, quod est potentia proprie, attamen non nominat potentiam voluntatis generaliter, sed solum voluntatem, in quantum movetur naturaliter; nec adhuc universaliter, sed solummodo respectu boni honesti, vel ejus oppositi." *Ibid.*, ad 4, p. 910.

[84] ". . . synderesis triplex est actus: unus, qui est instigare ad bonum . . . secundus, qui est retrahere a malo faciendo . . . tertius, qui est remurmuratio contra malum factum . . ." *Liber IV S.*, d. 50, p. 2, a. 2, q. 2, ad 4, IV, p. 1052.

and cannot, therefore, be abused.[85]   Indeed, our author notes, the voice of synderesis (calling man to do good and to avoid evil, crying out in remorse against the evil done) is always right.[86]

Though infallible in itself, it can nevertheless be overthrown. This appears so when we recall that its task is to rule and direct the other faculties of man, to preside over them and influence them.   However, the power of precedence depends on both the rectitude of the one presiding and the obedience of the one subject.   Accordingly, although the recitude of the one presiding (synderesis) always remains, nevertheless, both reason, because of the blindness of error, and will, because of the obstinacy of impiety, can and frequently do oppose synderesis, impeding it from exerting its influence.[87]

Still, while the voice of synderesis may be choked off for a time, it cannot be entirely taken from us.   To illustrate this, the Seraphic Doctor proposes the example of the " lost " souls, who have been confirmed in their state of sin and evil.   In their case the activity of synderesis has been impeded not only for a time but forever with regard to both the stimulus towards good and the aversion from evil.   Nonetheless, there remains a further activity of synderesis—its cry and pang of remorse against perpetrated evil, a cry which can never be completely stilled.[88]

---

[85] ". . . synderesis autem, cum sit potentia naturalis et naturaliter moveatur, non subest imperio liberi arbitrii; et ideo non sequitur, quod liberum arbitrium possit ea abuti." *Liber II S.,* d. 39, a. 2, q. 3, ad 5, II, p. 915.

[86] *Ibid.,* conc., p. 914; *Ibid.,* ad 4, p. 915.

[87] " Quia tamen ipsa habet alias regere et dirigere et dominium regendi potest perdere; hinc est, quod contingit, eam per culpam praecipitari. Praesidentia enim dominii a duobus pendet, videlicet a rectitudine praesidentis, et ab obtemperantia famulantis; et quamvis synderesis, quantum est de se, semper sit recta, quia tamen ratio et voluntas frequentur ei obviant—ratio per erroris excaecationem, et voluntas per impietatis obstinationem—hinc est, quod synderesis praecipitari dicitur, pro eo quod effectus ejus et praesidentia in vires alias deliberativas propter earum repugnantiam repellitur et cassatur." *Ibid.,* conc., p. 914.

[88] " Respondeo: Dicendum, quod synderesis quantum ad actum impediri potest, sed exstingui non potest.   Ideo autem non potest exstingui, quia, cum dicat quid naturale, non potest a nobis omnino auferri . . . potest tamen ad tempus impediri, sive propter tenebram abcaecationis, sive propter lasciviam delectationis, sive propter duritiam obstinationis . . . impeditur

From these considerations we have seen that God not only implanted the natural law in the very heart of man, but He also provided him with a natural light by which he can arrive at the first moral principles and apply them to his own personal life. Furthermore, the Eternal has supplied man with a natural weight that inclines him towards good, draws him away from evil, and cries out in remorse against whatsoever evil he may have committed. Accordingly, not only is the law of the Eternal, which regulates our life, known naturally to us, but our intellect has been blessed with an innate light and our will with a natural weight in order to keep us on the straight path of rightness and orderly living.

ARTICLE IV. THE SOCIAL NATURE OF MAN

Before we present what St. Bonaventure considers the governing principles of the social order, it is expedient to show that the Seraphic Doctor leaves no doubt in our minds concerning man's social character. He tells us expressly that man is by nature a social animal.[89] Of his very nature man enjoys an " *affectus socialis,*" because of which he desires the companionship of his fellows.[90] This character appears still clearer when we find that Bonaventure terms the "*amor socialis*" as that

---

etiam synderesis, ne ad bonum stimulet, sicut in damnatis, qui adeo sunt in malo confirmati, ut nunquam possint ad bonum inclinari. Et ideo synderesis, quantum ad instigationem ad bonum, sempiternum habet impedimentum; et propterea quantum ad istum actum, potest dici exstincta; non tamen est exstincta simpliciter, quia habet alium usum, videlicet remurmurationis. Secundum enim illum usum, secundum quem synderesis habet pungere et remurmurare contra malum, maxime vigebit in damnatis . . ." *Ibid.,* q. 2, conc., p. 912.

[89] " ' Homo est animal socialis naturae ' et ' animal mansuetum.' " *S. de Temp., Feria Sexta in Parasceve,* s. 1, IX, p. 262.

Confer footnote 2 of the Editors of Quaracchi, who show that the teaching concerning the social nature of man dates back to Aristotle, whereas the teaching that man is a gentle animal dates back to Plato.

"Et sunt (virtutes) politicae hominis, quia sociale animal est." *In Hex.,* coll. VI, n. 28, V, p. 364. Cf. Legowicz, *op. cit.,* pp. 212-217.

[90] " . . . affectus socialis est hominis ad hominem per naturam." *S. de Sanctis, De S. P. N. Francisco,* s. v, IX, p. 594.

virtue which enables men to live together in harmony. He makes explicit mention of this and stresses its necessity for a harmonious life in common when he treats of the conjugal life of man and woman.[91]

Furthermore, the Seraphic Doctor illustrates that man is not self-sufficient, but has need of his neighbor in order to fulfill the purpose of his creation and to satisfy his natural desires. This he shows to be the case especially with regard to marriage. In treating of the marital state he alludes clearly to the co-operation of husband and wife as absolutely necessary for the procreation of offspring.[92] Such "*mutuum auxilium*," he further declares, is also essential to the effective governing of the family.[93] In fact, he stresses the need of this mutual assistance in all forms of society, affirming that two things above all are requisite in a society—namely, oneness of purpose and reciprocal help.[94]

Man's social nature appears again in the fact that he is to share with his fellows the gifts with which he has been blessed. St. Bonaventure is most insistent upon this point. According to his teaching, knowledge must be communicated; it is not to be solely and totally reserved for the advantage and advancement of the one who has gained some education. His wording leaves no room for doubt: " It is a sin to know and to refuse to teach others." [95] Again: " Although it is a great sin for the wealthy person to refuse alms to the needy, it is *a still greater sin* for the learned not to communicate his learning " [96] especially with regard to moral education. Therefore, he demands, the

---

[91] " Nam (sponsus et sponsa) diligunt se amore sociali ad convivendum . . ." *Liber I S.,* d. 10, a. 2, q. 1, conc., I, p. 201.

[92] *Liber II S.,* d. 20, a. 1, q. 1, conc., II, p. 478.

[93] *Ibid.,* d. 25, p. 1, a. 1, q. 3, conc., p. 599.

[94] " In societate autem considerantur duo, scilicet mutuum auxilium et conformitas voluntatis." *Liber I S.,* d. 37, p. 1, dub. i, I, p. 650.

[95] " . . . peccatum est scire et proximum non docere . . ." *S. de Sanctis, S. de S. Marco Evangelista,* s. ii, IX, p. 525. Cf. *S. de B. V. M., De Assumptione B. V. M.,* s. iv, *Ibid.,* p. 697.

[96] " Sicut ergo est magnum peccatum, cum indigenti dives non dat eleesmosynam; sic majus est, cum sciens non communicat doctrinam . . ." *Com. in Ev. Lucae,* c. ix, n. 108, VII, p. 251.

treasury of divine wisdom that one may have received is not to be kept concealed, but to be used for the instruction and edification of the neighbor. Indeed, unless one who has been given the opportunity faithfully teaches others, he will not only be reprimanded, but will in addition be blamed and held accountable for the faults of others.[97]

Every gift with which man has been blessed seems to carry with it this social characteristic and obligation of being communicated to others. Man has not received them for his own personal use and advantage alone. " Whatever good man has received . . . must be extended (poured forth) to others." [98] The same thought is expressed in Bonaventure's teaching that God in judging " will demand not only the gift He gave man, but also the fruit He expected from it." [99]

Accordingly, he maintains, we must come to the aid of our fellows, to supply for the deficiency of others along economical, educational, and moral lines. Witness for instance his words: " As good dispensers of divine gifts, each one is bound to administer to others according to what he has received. This is done by aiding the needy, by teaching the ignorant, by correcting the delinquents, by bearing with the malicious, by comforting the afflicted, by elevating the fallen, by having compassion on all unfortunates, by showing peace and love to all men." [100] Coin-

---

[97] " . . . sic nec homo, qui habet thesaurum sapientiae divinae, debet illum abscondere, sed proferre ad aedificationem proximorum et doctrinam. Nisi enim fideliter doceat, argueretur et reprehendetur." *S. de Sanctis, S. de S. Nicolao,* IX, p. 478.

" Qui ergo neglexit alios docere, quos potuit, illorum negligentiae sibi imputabuntur." *Com. in Ev. Lucae.,* c. xix, n. 36, VII, p. 485.

[98] " Quidquid igitur habes datum, sive sit fecundia, sive aliquod bonum, semper debes in alium refundere." *S. de Sanctis, De S. Stephano M.,* s. 1, IX, p. 480.

[99] " Unde et Dominus, veniens ad judicium, non requirit solum donum, quod dedit, verum etiam fructum, quem ex dono exspectavit." *Com. in Ev. Lucae,* c. xix, n. 36, VII, p. 485.

[100] " . . . unusquisque gratiam, secundum quod accepit, in alterutrum debet administrare sicut boni dispensatores multiformis gratiae Dei. . . . Et hoc idem fit, cum indigentibus exhibetur subventio, ignorantibus eruditio, deliquentibus correptio, malignantibus supportatio, afflictis confortatio, cadenti-

cident with this thought is his teaching on the Mystical Body: as all the members of a living body depend upon one another and mutually aid one another in the common purpose of vital development, so, too, should the various members of the One Mystical Body aid one another.[101] Bonaventure's idea is further borne out by his doctrine concerning the unity of mankind and the brotherhood of all men.[102] Therefore, we can rightly assert that man, according to the teaching of St. Bonaventure, was created not for a life of solitude, but for a life in society which answers to his physical, intellectual, and moral needs.[103]

The Seraphic Doctor places additional emphasis on man's social nature when he discusses the "*political virtues,*" which have to do with the various relations existing among men living in society and enable them to live together in harmony.[104]

Man's social nature can also be deduced from the fact that St. Bonaventure demands order, a hierarchical order at that—and from the fact that he teaches a definite gradation among humans, which presupposes social inequality, authority, and subordination to authority. All these requirements of themselves postulate that man be a social animal by nature. Besides, the Seraphic Doctor affirms that this social characteristic does not apply to man in his present state alone; he speaks of a certain inequality and subordination even in the state of original justice, as, for ex-

---

bus elevatio, ceteris miseris et cunctis hominibus pax et dilectio . . ." *S. De Diversis, De Modo Vivendi,* IX, p. 724.

[101] "Nonne videtis, quod sicut unum membrum compatitur alteri membro, sic et nos debemus nobis invicem compati? Omnes sumus membra unius corporis, uno cibo cibamur, ad eodem utero producimur, ad eamdem haeraditatem tendimus. . . . Sumus unus corpus, pie debemus affici ad invicem." *De Donis,* coll. III, n. 13, V, p. 471.

[102] *Com. in Ev. Lucae,* c. x, n. 49, VII, p. 268; *In Joannem,* c. xvii, coll. LXI, nn. 4–5, VI, p. 609.

[103] St. Bonaventure tells us that the life of solitude is praiseworthy in one instance alone, i.e., "Est et alia solitudo per quietem contemplationis, et haec laudabilis et honesta." *Com. in Ecc.,* c. iv, vv. 9–12, q. 1, conc., VI, p. 40.

[104] *In Hex.,* coll. VI, n. 28, V, p. 364; *Liber III S.,* d. 33, dub. v, III, p. 730.

ample, the authority of husband over wife and of parents over their children.[105]

Likewise, reference is made to man as a social being in that section of the *Collatio V* of the *Hexaemeron* in which St. Bonaventure advances the four moral justices: the "*ritus colendi*," the "*forma convivendi*," the "*norma praesidendi*," and the "*censura judicandi*"—all of which are commanded by the natural law.[106] If these four justices are obligatory on man by reason of the natural law, it follows, then, that man, of his nature, constitutes a social entity. From these moral justices—especially the "*forma convivendi*," which regulates our conduct towards our fellowmen through the precept indelibly inscribed on the human heart ("Do not unto another what you do not wish another to do unto you"); and the "*norma praesidendi*," which regulates the actions of the citizens and rulers respectively—we can conclude that the Seraphic Doctor had no doubt whatsoever regarding man's social nature.

Article V. The Main Social Precepts

Having established our point that according to Bonaventurian thought man is necessarily a social entity, we shall now attempt to examine those rules which the Seraphic Doctor advances as the guiding principles of the social order—i.e., that part of the moral order which is concerned with the voluntary and free acts of man, the social animal. These precepts can be included under two headings: viz., (1) the necessity of order, together with the precepts derived therefrom; and (2) the precepts governing man's relations as a social being.

Section 1. Order, Social Inequality, and Submission to Authority

Since society is the union of rational individuals abiding together in peaceful and harmonious relationship, observing the same laws, and tending towards the same end,[107] the necessity

---

[105] *De Perf. Evan.*, q. 4, a. 1, conc., V, p. 181; *Liber II S.*, d. 44, a. 2, q. 2, conc., II, p. 1008.

[106] *In Hex.*, coll. V, nn. 14–21, V, pp. 356–357.

[107] Confer article 1 of the following chapter.

of order for the existence of society must be patent. Indeed, right-living, peaceful relations, harmony, and oneness of purpose are impossible without order.[108] Accordingly, Bonaventure's first demand is order—that disposition whereby each being occupies its proper place. Order, he tells us, is postulated by the natural law.[109] In fact, the law of nature requires an hierarchically constituted order.[110]

Proceeding from this general rule of nature that each being is to be located in its proper place, our saintly author arrives at the precepts that concern social order as such. They are two— social gradation and inequality, and the need of subjection to legitimate authority, both of which proceed from the natural law.

In the corporeal life St. Bonaventure notices a certain unity and a definite and perfect gradation of faculties and acts which contribute to the conservation and perfection of the entire organism.[111] Comparing the social order to a living body, then, the Seraphic Doctor requires in the former positive grades of social function. As the living organism, so, too, the social order cannot rightly function without some gradation of powers, offices, and dignities. If such progression did not exist, there would be a perfect equality of powers, aptitudes, and merits; and if there

---

[108] *Liber IV S.*, d. 24, p. 1, a. 2, q. 1, conc., and ad 1–3, IV, pp. 614–615; *Ibid.*, d. 19, a. 3, q. 1, conc. and ad 6, pp. 508–509; *Liber I S.*, d. 20, a. 2, q. 1, f. 5, I, p. 372.

[109] ". . . jus naturae dictat ordinem . . ." *De Perf. Evan.*, q. 4, a. 1, f. 4, V, p. 179.

[110] ". . . jus naturae dictat ordinem hierarchicum . . ." *Ibid.*, f. 7, p. 180.

[111] ". . . sicut in corpore nostro est considerare naturam, per quam est unitas et convenientia, et naturam, secundum quam est distinctio sive differentia—prima est complexio, secunda est organizatio—sic in corpore quod est Ecclesia. Per naturam enim caritatis omnes unimur, sed per dona alia gratiarum . . . distinguimur et ordinamur." *Liber IV S.*, d. 24, p. 1, a. 2, q. 1, ad 1, IV, p. 615.

". . . sicut ad perfectionem corporis vivi requiritur aequalitas complexionis, in qua omnia membra conformantur, et multiformitas organizationis, in qua membra distinguuntur et ordinantur et secundum variam influentiam alia aliis praeponuntur; sic intelligendum est circa corpus Christi mysticum." *De Perf. Evan.*, q. 4, a. 1, ad 6, V, p. 182.

Although Bonaventure is speaking of the Mystical Body of Christ, his teaching, nevertheless, can be extended to all types of society.

were such a perfect distribution, there could, naturally, be no order among them.[112]

St. Bonaventure's insistence on the different grades of being, powers, and the like we already touched upon when we witnessed to his conception of an hierarchically constituted universe.[113] We meet such gradation once more in the microcosmos, man, in whom there is one principal corporeal member which influences the others and one principal power of the soul that is regulative of all the powers of the soul and of the entire man.[114] The angelic choirs are another example of this progression of powers and perfections—a gradation that exists not only among the different orders but also among the various angels of the same order.[115] Finally, as we have already seen, there is also a certain accidental inequality among men, stemming from the different grades of perfection and excellence in both their natural and praeternatural powers.[116]

The fact of social inequality necessarily leads to the fact of submission to authority, the subjection of the inferior to the superior. This requirement is in perfect accord with man's rational nature. As right reason demands the subordination of the lower faculties to the higher in the individual man, it must likewise ordain the subordination of the inferiors to the superiors in the social life.[117] Accordingly, St. Bonaventure maintains that the command of submission and obedience to lawfully constituted authority proceeds from natural law itself.

Natural law demands order, as we have seen. Order is the

---

[112] ". . . jus naturae dictat, gradum esse servandum, 'quia si essent omnia aequalia, non essent omnia' . . ." *Ibid.*, f. 6, p. 180.

[113] Confer above, p. 35, and pp. 78ss.

[114] " Naturalis etiam justitia in minori mundo requirit, quod unum sit membrum principale, a quo cetera recipiant influentiam secundum veritatem, ut cor, secundum evidentiam, ut caput; quod una etiam sit virtus principaliter omnium virium animae et totius hominis regitiva, scilicet liberum arbitrium." *De Perf. Evan.*, q. 4, a. 3, conc., V, p. 194. Cf. *Ibid.*, f. 20, p. 192.

[115] *Liber II S.*, d. 9, a. 1, q. 8, conc., II, pp. 255–256; *Ibid.*, q. 9, conc., p. 257.

[116] Confer above, pp. 68–69.

[117] Confer above, ft. 114.

disposition whereby each thing occupies its proper place. Consequently, if it is in the nature of the superior to preside and of the inferior to be submissive and obedient, then the natural law which commands order likewise demands the obedient submission of the inferior to the superior.[118] The same conclusion is drawn by the Seraphic Doctor from the natural injunction placed upon man, viz., that he live in peace and harmony. This provision, however, cannot be observed without submission to authority, since peace is the ordered harmony of command and obedience. Accordingly, the natural law, in calling for peace and harmony, demands the observance of the law of submission to authority.[119]

Moreover, the law of nature requires that honor, respect, and obedience be rendered to parents.[120] However, as St. Bonaventure points out in his *" Collationes De Decem Praeceptis,"* all persons vested with authority bear the title of parent.[121] Therefore, this injunction of the natural law is to be extended also to the obedience and reverence due to all lawfully constituted superiors. Furthermore, in Bonaventure's mind, the rulers of society serve as directive agents for their subjects, who, in general, are considered incapable of conceiving and judging the common good of the whole social organism.[122] Hence again the subjection of lower to higher.

---

[118] ". . . jus naturae dictat ordinem; sed ' ordo est parium dispariumque sua loca cuique tribuens dispositio ' . . . si ergo ordo est, quod unus subdatur alteri, et jus naturae dictat ordinem; dictat ergo, quod unus alteri debeat subjici." *De Perf. Evan.,* q. 4, a. 1, f. 4, V, p. 179.

" Si ergo superioris est praeesse, et inferioris subesse, lex naturalis, quae manat a lege aeterna, naturaliter dictat, quod inferior superiori obediendo subjaceat . . ." *Ibid.,* conc., p. 181.

[119] ". . . jus naturae dictat pacem inter domesticos; sed pax in domo est ' ordinata imperandi obediendique concordia ': ergo juri naturae competit imperare et obedire." *Ibid.,* f. 5, pp. 179–180. Cf. *Ibid.,* a. 2, conc., p. 185.

[120] " Pietas enim naturalis dictat, parentes esse honorandos; sed honor parentum est in exhibitione reverentiae, exhibitio autem reverentiae est obtemperando et obediendo . . ." *Ibid.,* a. 1, f. 1, p. 179.

[121] Coll. V, nn. 11–13, V, p. 524.

[122] *S. de Sanctis, De S. Mathia Ap.,* s. ii, IX, pp. 517–519; *In Hex.,* coll. XXII, n. 18, V, p. 440. ". . . superiora nata sunt influere in inferiora . . ." *Liber II S.,* d. 8, p. 2, a. 1, q. 3, conc., II, p. 228.

From the above arguments we must conclude that, according to Bonaventurian thought, the obedient submission of the inferior to the superior is commanded—more, demanded—by natural law.

SECTION 2.   THE PRECEPTS GOVERNING MAN'S RELATIONS AS A
SOCIAL BEING

A. Justice

The basic law of social order, in St. Bonaventure's opinion, is justice, for justice is the only one of the cardinal virtues which concerns man's actions *ad extra*. The others concern man's actions *ad intra*, i.e., with reference to his own person or being.[123]

The Seraphic Doctor, it would be well to note here, distinguishes between general and special justice. As a *general virtue*, justice is nothing else but rectitude or righteousness— rectitude of the will, of the whole soul, of human life.[124] It commands the performance of good and the avoidance of evil. Its object is the promotion of right order.[125] *Special justice*, or the cardinal virtue of justice, on the other hand, is not simply the rectitude of the will, but the rectitude of the will with reference to *another*.[126] It consists in rendering to everyone his due— e.g., adoring God because He has a right to be adored; cherishing my neighbor and respecting his possessions because he has a right to these; etc.[127]

The primary fundamental law of justice, regulating our actions towards God and comprising the first three precepts of the

---

[123] *Liber III S.,* d. 33, a. 1, q. 4, conc., III, p. 720.

[124] *In Hex.,* coll. XVIII, n. 18, V, p. 417; *Brev.,* p. 5, c. 4, V, p. 256; *In Sapientiam,* c. 8, v. 7, VI, p. 161. Cf. infra, pp. 273ss.

[125] *Liber III S.,* d. 33, dub. I, III, p. 728; *Ibid.,* a. 1, q. 2, ad 4, p. 715; *Ibid.,* d. 35, dub. I, p. 787; *Ibid.,* d. 37, a. 2, q. 1, conc., p. 822; *De Perf. Evan.,* q. 1, conc., V, p. 121; *Liber IV S.,* d. 31, a. 2, q. 1, conc., IV, p. 722; *S. de Temp., Dom. XIV p. Pent.,* s. 1, IX, pp. 409–410.

[126] "Justitia vero specialis non est simpliciter rectitudo voluntatis, sed rectitudo voluntatis ordinans ad alterum . . ." *Liber III S.,* d. 33, a. 1, q. 2, ad 4, III, p. 715.

[127] *Brev.,* p. 5, c. 4, V, p. 256; *S. de Temp., Sabbato Sancto,* s. ii, IX, pp. 270–271; *Ibid., In Ascensione Domini,* s. viii, p. 325; *S. de Diversis, De Modo Vivendi,* pp. 724–725; *Op. VII, De Regimine Animae,* n. 9, VIII, p. 130.

Decalogue, is identifiable with the first moral justice, the "*ritus colendi,*" which concerns the worship due to God commanded by the natural law.[128] Because there can be no rightly ordered social life unless God be given His due, the Seraphic Doctor concludes that the divine cult and honor are at the very foundation of the whole edifice of justice.[129] We find the same thought expressed when he insists that it is impossible to observe the other moral justices unless this first moral justice be put into operation.[130] Accordingly, the first precept governing all social relations—in fact, the very basis of all order—is the dictate of the natural law, viz., God must be worshiped, honored, praised, and obeyed.

The second fundamental law of justice, regulating our relations to our neighbor and comprising the last seven of the Ten Commandments, is actually the command of special or cardinal justice, which, in turn, is identified with the command of the natural law, viz., render to each his due.[131] From this dictate of nature the Seraphic Doctor deduces two other precepts of the natural law which govern our relationship with our neighbor. They are: the *law of innocence,* viz., "Do not unto others what you do not wish others to do unto you"; and the *law of beneficence,* viz., "do unto others what you wish others to do unto you."[132] St. Bonaventure identifies the law of beneficence with

---

128 *In Hex.,* coll. V, nn. 15–17, V, pp. 356–357.

129 ". . . initium totius justitiae est cultus et honor divinus . . ." *De Perf. Evan.,* q. 1, conc., V, p. 121.

130 "Ad censuram judicandi non pervenitur nisi per normam praesidendi; nec ad normam praesidendi nisi per formam convivendi; nec ad istam nisi per primam." *In Hex.,* coll. V, n. 14, V, p. 356.

131 *De Perf. Evan.,* q. 4, a. 1, f. 8, V, p. 180.

132 "In secunda tabula continentur septem mandata ordinantia nos ad proximum, quae significantur per duo praecepta legis naturae, scilicet: hoc facias alii, quod tibi vis fieri; non facias alii, quod tibi non vis fieri.—Et secundum haec duo praecepta legis naturae accipitur duplex justitiae, quarum una est innocentiae, altera beneficentiae; et secundum istam duplicem justitiam duplex est mandatum: primum beneficentiae, alterum innocentiae." *Decem Praeceptis,* coll, I, n. 23, V, p. 510. Cf. *Liber III S.,* d. 37, a. 1, q. 3, conc., III, pp. 819–820; *Ibid.,* a. 2, q. 2, conc., p. 826; *Com. in Ev. Lucae,* c. vi, n. 76, VII, p. 156; *Ibid.,* c. xviii, n. 39, p. 462; *S. de Sanctis, De S. Andrea Ap.,* s. ii, IX, p. 471.

the fourth Commandment, inasmuch as it commands beneficence not only to parents and those in need, but to all men.[133] The law of innocence, on the other hand, forbidding injury to the neighbor, comprises the last six precepts of the Decalogue.[134]

This second fundamental law of justice, as must be apparent, coincides with the second moral justice, the "*forma convivendi,*" which concerns inter-individual relations, and demands that they be regulated in accordance with that command inscribed by the eternal law in the heart of man—namely: "Do not unto another what you do not wish another to do unto you." [135] The importance of this second moral justice in the social order cannot be exaggerated. Requiring that each be rendered his due, it seeks to preserve and defend the rights most intimate and sacred to man. Consequently, it is necessary not only for the perfection of society, but also for its very existence. As the Seraphic Doctor points out, the "norma praesidendi," regulating the respective duties of citizens and rulers, cannot begin to operate until the rights of each individual person have been taken into account.[136] Accordingly, the second precept, governing social relations, is the "*forma convivendi,*" which is, in turn, reduced to that dictate of right reason which demands that each be given his due and to the two subordinate precepts of the natural law—the *law of innocence* and the *law of beneficence.*

The third fundamental law of justice advanced by our saintly author is the "*norma praesidendi,*" which is likewise a prescription of the natural law. It sets forth the rules governing the

---

[133] *Decem Praeceptis,* coll. I, n. 23, V, p. 510; *Ibid.,* coll. V, nn. 14–15, p. 524.

The fourth Commandment, as we have understood the thought of the Seraphic Doctor, contains two sections. In one case, inasmuch as it commands beneficence to all men, it agrees with the law of beneficence. In the second case, inasmuch as it is concerned with the relations that should exist between superior and inferior, and vice versa, it coincides with the third moral justice, the "norma praesidendi" (*Ibid.,* nn. 11–15, p. 524). Legowicz (*op. cit.,* pp. 137–138) seems to grasp only the second aspect of this Commandment—the one that has reference to the duties of those who are in authority and those who are subjects.

[134] *Decem Praeceptis,* coll. I, n. 24, V, p. 510.

[135] *In Hex.,* coll. V, n. 18, V, p. 357.

[136] *Ibid.,* n. 14, p. 356.

conduct of the ruled and the ruler. Establishing the duties of the subjects, it commands that they be submissive to the laws established for the common good and aid the rulers in seeing to it that these rules are observed. On the other hand, concerned with the duties of the governing body, it demands that they seek not their own private interests, but the common good. Consequently, the " norma praesidendi " postulates that the same rule, viz., seek the common good, is to govern the activities of both the ruling and the ruled.[137] The importance of this norm for the existence and harmonious development of society is so patent that we need make no comment.

Finally, Bonaventure's fourth moral justice, the " *censura judicandi,*" which is concerned with the correct norm of judgment that must be used in reference to persons, things, and the method of acting, appears as his fourth precept regulating social relations.[138]

B. Charity

Our author does not fail to realize the insufficiency of justice alone to rule the social order. Protecting the rights of the individuals by commanding that each be given his just due, rightly ordering the external relations of the various human individuals so that each member of the social whole occupies that place which justly belongs to him, justice effects a certain unity and orderliness. Nevertheless, this unity is neither lasting nor perfect. Something more than justice is called for, because, as St. Bonaventure notes, justice left to itself will deteriorate. Its observance becomes difficult, in fact quite impossible, unless justice is perfected by the virtue of charity.[139] In commenting upon the words of the Apostle St. Paul: " For he that loveth his neighbor, hath fulfilled the law," the Seraphic Doctor stresses the need for love by affirming: " In the payment of the debt of love all debts are paid, especially when we love the neighbor not only in word or tongue, but also in deed and truth." [140] There-

---

[137] *Ibid.*, n. 19, p. 357.

[138] *Ibid.*, n. 20, p. 357.

[139] " Nisi enim quis proximum suum diligat, non est facile, ut jus debitum sibi reddat." *Liber III S.*, d. 33, a. 1, q. 5, ad 3, III, p. 721.

[140] *Epistle to the Romans*, c. xiii, v. 8. " In hujus enim debiti solutione

fore, not justice alone, but justice, aided, abetted, and elevated by charity, is, according to Bonaventurian thought, the perfect rule governing social relations.

The role that charity plays in the social life is, indeed, very great. In the first place, it fosters and protects right order, since charity, as St. Bonaventure writes, is more than simply a tie which binds; it is also a " *pondus* " (weight) effecting perfect order.[141] Secondly, it is charity which promotes the practice of virtue and the observance of law, because it is the guardian of law and, therefore, the protector of social order.[142] Again, the influence of charity in the social order enables the different members to aid one another, to sacrifice the " *bonum proprium,*" and to join forces in promoting the common good.[143] Above all, it produces among the various members of society a true and perfect harmony—the end of all social living.[144]

cuncta debita solvuntur, maxime cum proximos diligimus non tantum verbo vel lingua, sed etiam opere et veritate . . ." *S. de Diversis, De Modo Vivendi,* IX, p. 724.

[141] " Nec tantum est caritas vinculum ligans, sed etiam pondus inclinans. . . . Quoniam igitur unumquodque per suum pondus habet ordinari, et caritas pondus est et aequa ponderatrix; hinc est quod ipsi caritati maxime competit ratio ordinis." *Liber III S.,* d. 29, a. 1, q. 1, conc., III, p. 639.

[142] " Cura ergo disciplinae est dilectio. Si enim habes disciplinae dilectionem, eris amator virtutis in te et in aliis et in suo fonte. . . . Dilectio autem custodia legum est. Si enim diligis bonum, observas legem, quia finis praecepti est caritas de corde puro." *In Hex.,* coll. II, n. 4, V, p. 337. Cf. *In Sapientiam,* c. iv, v. 19, VI, p. 149.

[143] ". . . caritas non quaerit quae sua sunt . . . suum idem est quod proprium. Proprium autem quaerere hoc est dupliciter: uno modo, prout propriam dicitur cum praecisione; et sic excludit bonum commune, et isto modo sonat in vitium, et secundum istam acceptionem consuevit dici, quod libido est amor boni proprii; et quantum ad hunc modum dicit Apostolus, quod caritas non quaerit quae sua sunt." *Liber III S.,* d. 29, a. 1, q. 3, ad 1, III, p. 644.

". . . lex caritatis facit in membris corporalibus et concivibus civitatis, quod unum membrum supplet indigentiam alterius—ut patet, quia oculus videt viam sibi et pedi, et pes fert se ipsum et oculum, et in civibus terrenae civitatis similiter contingit." *Liber II S.,* d. 1, p. 2, a. 2, q. 2, conc., II, p. 46.

[144] ". . . totius hierarchiae finis et consummatio est unitiva dilectio." *Expositio super Regulam Fratrum Minorum,* introductio, n. 2, VIII, p. 392. ". . . caritas inter virtutes theologicas est maxime unitiva . . ." *Liber III S.,* d. 27, a. 2, q. 1, ad 6, III, p. 604.

CHAPTER IV

SOCIETY, ITS NATURE AND KINDS

The present chapter, devoted to examining the Seraphic Doctor's teaching on the nature and kinds of society, can properly be divided into four articles. The first will treat of society in general; the second will deal with marriage, or the conjugal society; the third will consider the family, or the domestic society; and the fourth will touch upon the State, or the civil society.

ARTICLE I. THE NATURE OF SOCIETY

SECTION 1. THE CONCEPT OF SOCIETY

Just as our notion of order proceeds from the sensible world about us, so, too, our concept of society derives from the various institutions found in man's social life. We can best gather St. Bonaventure's idea of society from his definition of the Church. For him the Church is a body of rational beings living together in harmony and uniformity. Their common purpose—to render praise to God—is arrived at by living together in peace through the uniform and harmonious observance of the divine law.[1] These three characteristics, the Seraphic Doctor adds, are so intimately connected that we cannot neglect the one without actually destroying the whole. In a word, we cannot attain the purpose, the praise of the Almighty, unless there be peace among the different members; and we cannot have this peace, unless the laws established by the Divine Lawgiver be observed by all.[2] From this consideration we may conclude that a society,

---

[1] ". . . unio rationalium concorditer et uniformiter viventium per concordem et uniformem observantiam divinae legis, per concordem et uniformem cohaerentiam divinae pacis, per concordem et uniformem consonantiam divinae laudis." *In Hex.*, coll. I, n. 2, V, p. 329.

[2] "Haec autem ordinata sunt: quia laus esse non potest, ubi non est pax, nec divina pax, ubi non est observantia divinae legis." *Ibidem.*

in the mind of St. Bonaventure, is a union of rational individuals abiding together in peace and harmony, observing the same laws and tending towards the same end.

SECTION 2.   THE CAUSES OF SOCIETY

A. The Material Cause

The material cause, or the *materia* of a society, therefore, is a plurality of social entities.   These beings must be rational in nature, for only such are capable of striving towards the same end through harmonious and uniform activity.   St. Bonaventure openly affirms this.   First of all, as we have seen, he tells us that the Church is a "*unio rationalium.*"   Then, in treating of hierarchy, he tells us that a hierarchy is possible only among "*intellectual substances.*" [3]   The expression he employs, "*substantia intellectualis*" is in accord with the definition given by Boethius and denotes "*persona.*" [4]   Hence, the person is the constituent element of society.   This need not signify a human person alone, since our author speaks of the hierarchy among the Divine Persons of the Blessed Trinity and the hierarchy among the Angels, as well as the human hierarchy.[5]   In view of the foregoing, it becomes quite evident that St. Bonaventure would hardly look upon animal groupings and the like as societies.   According to his thought, society is peculiar and proper to rational beings.

B. The Formal Cause

Since society is a union of rational beings, united for the purpose of bending their common efforts towards the same end, it follows that a society must be a stable, moral union, arising not simply from coexistence in the same place nor from the mere

---

[3] ". . . hierarchia non est nisi in substantia intellectuali . . ." *Liber II S.*, d. 9, praenotata, II, p. 240.

[4] ". . . naturae rationalis individua substantia." *Liber de Persona et Duabus Naturis Contra Eutychen et Nestorium,* c. 3, *P.L.,* 64, 1343.

[5] "Quoniam enim hierarchia non est nisi in substantia intellectuali, haec autem triplex est, scilicet divina, angelica, et humana; ideo triplex distinguitur hierarchica; et divina dicitur supercaelestis, angelica caelestis, humana autem subcaelestis." *Liber II S.,* d. 9, praenotata, II, p. 240.

identity of purpose, but from pursuit of a common end, attainable only by the cooperative activity of those who conjointly will it and work for it. Accordingly, the rational social entities must be united into a harmonious whole. In fact, the Seraphic Doctor demands a perfect and true unity, stating explicitly that such a union cannot exist unless there is a threefold uniformity—of nature, of purpose or will, and of operation.[6]

The *uniformity of nature* needs no further clarification, as it stands to reason there can be no true unity if the constituent elements are of diverse natures.[7] The *uniformity of purpose* appears quite clear in the writings of the Seraphic Doctor. In a society, he asserts, two things are of prime importance—"mutual aid and conformity of will."[8] Moreover, he does not hesitate to declare that the conformity of will is more important for the continued existence and good of society than oneness of feature or of external appearance.[9] Indeed, without such common ground, Bonaventure tells us, there could not be any true unity.[10]

In addition to uniformity of nature and of purpose, there must be a *oneness of operation,* which naturally follows from the conformity of will. Here we may consider two points: uniformity of morals and mutual aid. The uniformity of morals, or method of behaviour, can readily be deduced from St. Bonaventure's definition of the Church, in which he maintains that ecclesiastical unity is achieved through the "harmonious observance of the

---

[6] "Ad plenam autem conformitatem requiritur triplex conformitas, scilicet in natura, in voluntate et in operatione; et quando illa tria concurrunt ad aliqua duo, tunc illa duo dicuntur unum . . ." *Liber I S.,* d. 31, p. 2, a. 2, q. 2, conc., I, p. 547.

[7] Bonaventure is here concerned with the fact that all members of the society should be rational beings. Confer *Liber II S.,* d. 9, a. 1, q. 5, ad 1, II, p. 251. Here Bonaventure affirms that angels and men can belong to the same society, i.e., that of the Heavenly Jerusalem.

[8] "In societate autem considerantur duo, scilicet mutum auxilium et conformitas voluntatis." *Liber I S.,* d. 37, p. 1, dub. I, I, p. 650.

[9] "Et ideo possunt in eamdem societatem et ejusdem societatis ordinem convenire, cum major sit unitas voluntatum quam facierum et plus facit ad unitatem pacis et societatis et ordinis conservandam." *Liber II S.,* d. 9, a. 1, q. 5, ad 1, II, p. 251.

[10] *Ibid.,* d. 1, p. 1, a. 2, q. 1, f. 5, p. 26.

divine law" and that without such conformity it is impossible to maintain peace and arrive at the desired end.[11] Such a uniformity of operation should, furthermore, lead to mutual aid.

In comparing society to the human body the Seraphic Doctor demands that the various members of society should mutually aid each other as do the different members of the same material body.[12] The necessity for mutual aid is drawn out very clearly when the Franciscan Doctor discusses the conjugal and domestic societies. He shows that the cooperation of husband and wife is necessary both for the propagation of the offspring and for the proper management of the home.[13] This necessity is again brought into evidence when he speaks of the three classes of men in society—farmers, soldiers, and monks—and states that the farmers are to provide the food from which they and the others are to eat; that the soldiers are to defend the monks and the farmers; and that the monks are to pray for the others and feed them with the milk of preaching.[14]

Hence, it is obvious that for the saintly Doctor society is not a simple herding of humans, but a perfect union in which the constituents have a oneness of nature, of purpose, and of activity. In short, our author requires a perfect and complete union of wills in the pursuit of a common purpose. This moral union, resulting from conformity of purpose or will and of operation rather than from conformity of nature, is, indeed, the formal cause of society.

To render such a union of free beings permanent, strong, and energetic, there must be, besides the identity of end that attracts all and the conformity of operation, a bond which ties together the various members of the social body, a power which regulates their activity and rules over them, viz., authority. Society

---

[11] *In Hex.*, coll. I, n. 2, V, p. 329. Confer above, footnotes 1–2.

[12] "Debet etiam in unum convenire fratrum operatio per mutuam subventionem, sicut faciunt membra unius corporis ad invicem . . ." *In Joannem*, c. 17, coll. 61, n. 4, VI, p. 609. Confer *De Perf. Evan.*, q. 4, a. 1, ad 6, V, p. 182; *Liber IV S.*, d. 24, p. 1, a. 2, q. 1, ad 1, IV, p. 615; *De Donis*, coll. III, n. 13, V, p. 471.

[13] *Liber II S.*, d. 20, a. 1, q. 1, conc., II, p. 478; *Ibid.*, d. 38, a. 2, q. 2, conc., p. 893.

[14] *Op. XI, Apologia Pauperum*, c. xii, n. 14, VIII, p. 321; *De Perf. Evan.*, q. 2, a. 3, f. 12, V, p. 159.

postulates authority as an essential property, for unless someone be over all, directing all to strive earnestly for the common end and good, no society can long hold together.[15] Although authority flows from the essence of society, it is not, however, a constituent principle thereof. It is the necessary means required to direct and govern the group and to oblige the members to cooperate for the common good.[16] In a word, authority is needed to preserve society—primarily by promoting and fostering right order, which leads to harmony, peace, and the actual attainment of the end of society.

C. The Efficient Cause

The unity demanded of the various social entities is effected by a free act of the human will. Accordingly, the will appears as the efficient cause of society. This fact is seen most clearly in the conjugal society, which, as Bonaventure points out, is established by the free consent of both contracting parties.[17] At the same time, we must bear in mind that we are not referring to a completely independent will, but to a will acting in conformity with rational nature and right reason.

Nature, unlike the will, is an instrument moving itself not according to its own pleasure, but according to the form given it by the Creator.[18] Therefore, if man is, as we have seen, of his very nature a social entity,[19] human nature necessarily calls for a life in society—a life in company with his fellows. However, since God so rules the works of His hands that the creatures must act in conformity with the demands of their nature, and since man, in addition to being of a certain nature, is also a free agent—the lord and master of his own actions—then man must will this life in society. We distinguish, as a result, two factors,

---

[15] ". . . sine uno capite nulla respublica stare bene potest." *Op. XVI, Exp. Super Reg. Fr. Min.*, c. viii, n. 2, VIII, p. 427. Confer *Ibid.*, intro., n. 2, p. 392; *Liber IV S.*, d. 24, p. 2, a. 2, q. 1, f. 4, IV, pp. 629–630.

[16] *De Perf. Evan.*, q. 4, a. 1, V, pp. 179ss; *Liber II S.*, d. 44, a. 2, q. 2, ad 4, II, p. 1009; *Liber IV S.*, d. 24, p. 1, a. 2, q. 1, conc., ad 1–3, IV, pp. 614–615.

[17] *Liber IV S.*, d. 27, IV, pp. 647ss.

[18] *Brev.*, p. 3, c. 10, V, p. 239.

[19] Confer above, pp. 102ss.

each of which must be kept in mind when we seek to determine the efficient cause of society, namely: (a) the social nature imprinted upon man by his Maker, and (b) man's free will. From these two factors we may conclude that the efficient cause of society is man's free will acting in conformity with his rational and social nature, deliberately executing the divine plan imprinted on his created nature.

D. The Final Cause

To act with purpose—i.e., always in view of a desirable end to be attained and enjoyed—is an essential characteristic of the rational agent. Consequently, it is logical here to inquire into the final cause that prompts man to establish society. Each society is brought into being for the attainment of a particular end; its objective is to direct the operations of the various cooperating entities in such a manner that the oneness of purpose—the common good of the society—may be realized. Thus, for example, the end of the conjugal society is the procreating of another man for God, a future inhabitant of the eternal home.[20] This end is usually termed the proximate or immediate end of society.

Our purpose, however, is to attempt to determine the final end of society in general, or, better still, of social order—according to the mind of St. Bonaventure. In the first place, it is necessary to note that, as we have seen, all that is ordered proceeds as such from God, Who is the Source of all order.[21] Hence, the social order also proceeds from God, inasmuch as it is order. Moreover, all that exists, exists for the glory of God.[22] Therefore, all society must, in some manner, have God's glory as its ultimate and final end.

Besides, since happiness is the ultimate end of all man's actions, the goal towards which the rational soul naturally aspires,[23]

---

[20] ". . . matrimonium est ad procreandum prolem ad cultum Dei . . ." *Liber IV S.,* d. 34, a. 1, q. 2, conc., IV, p. 769.

[21] *Liber II S.,* d. 36, a. 3; q. 2, conc., II, p. 855. Confer above, c. 3, a. 2, s. 1.

[22] Confer above, pp. 34–35.

[23] ". . . finis ultimus omnis operationis rationalis est beatitudo perfecta

we may properly conclude that the end, or purpose, of society consists in enabling man to attain to his perfect and true happiness. However, since nothing finite nor any multiplication of finite goods can fully satisfy man's appetites, he can find true and perfect happiness only in the possession and fruition of the Supreme Good, God.[24] This is man's final end; consequently, its actual attainment by him must be the final end of all society also. For this reason, St. Bonaventure tells us that it is the duty of those constituted in authority to lead their subjects to the eternal life.[25]

This point can be more fully and readily understood when we recall that man is a *person* and, therefore, above all things created—ordered immediately to God as to his sole end.[26] As a person, man is not for society, but society is for man. Society is but a means for the person who, born to perceive God and immediately ordered to Him, cannot find rest and fruition except in God.[27] Accordingly, the final end of society is to aid man attain to eternal felicity in union with God, by providing him with the material, intellectual, and moral elements whereby he may the more efficaciously live a virtuous life and thus arrive at his final reward.

SECTION 3. THE STRUCTURE OF SOCIETY

As, for the actual structure of society, St. Bonaventure conceives it to be like an organism, a living body, in which all the members depend on one another and mutually aid one another in the common purpose of vital development. Referring to the law of charity, he remarks that just as the eye sees both for

---

. . . omnis anima rationalis naturaliter appetit beatitudinem . . ." *Liber II S.,* d. 19, a. 1, q. 1, ff. 5–6, II, p. 459.

[24] Confer above, pp. 62ss.

[25] ". . . finis autem officii regiminis est commissos sibi ad vitam aeternam dirigere . . ." *De Sex Alis.,* c. v, n. 4, VIII, p. 141.

[26] *Liber II S.,* d. 3, p. 1, a. 2, q. 2, conc., II, p. 106. Confer above, pp. 60ss.

[27] ". . . nata est anima ad percipiendum bonum infinitum, quod Deus est, ideo in eo solo debet quiescere et eo frui." *Liber I S.,* d. 1, a. 3, q. 2, conc., I, p. 41,

itself and the foot and the foot carries both itself and the eye, so should the various members of a society mutually aid one another.[28]   This quality of mutual interdependence and assistance our author stresses most emphatically in his teaching concerning the Church, the Mystical Body of Christ.[29]

Furthermore, in his scrutiny of corporeal life the Franciscan Doctor notices a certain unity on the one hand, and on the other hand a certain gradation of faculties and acts which contributes to the conservation and perfection of the entire organism. Indeed, the perfection of the living body requires a definite organization by means of which the different members are distinguished, ordered, and subjected to one another.[30]   Accordingly, the social organism, so closely paralleling the human body, in which there is a primacy of the principal parts—a hierarchy, in which the lower is subjected to the higher and influenced thereby—must also be hierarchically constituted.   In it must be found principal parts which influence and non-principal parts which are influenced.[31]   Besides unity, there must exist in society, for its conservation and perfection, a diversity of dignities and offices, according to which one member is subject to the other and governed by it.[32]   As all the members of the living organism are subject and obey the one principal member, so, too, the various

---

[28] ". . . lex caritatis facit in membris corporalibus et concivibus civitatis, quod unum membrum supplet indigentiam alterius—ut patet, quia oculus videt viam sibi et pedi, et pes fert se ipsum et oculum, et in civibus terrenae civitatis similiter contingit . . ." *Liber II S.,* d. 1, p. 2, a. 2, q. 2, conc., II, p. 46.

[29] Confer above, ft. 12.

[30] *Liber III S.,* d. 34, p. 1, a. 2, q. 3, ad 2, III, p. 750.

[31] " Sicut in corpore humano quaedam sunt membra principalia, aliis influentia et quaedam non principalia et influentiam ab aliis recipientia; sic in corpore Christi mystico, quod est Ecclesia . . ." *S. de Sanctis, De S. Mathia Ap.,* s. ii, IX, p. 517.

[32] ". . . sicut ad perfectionem corporis vivi requiritur aequalitas complexionis, in qua omnia membra conformantur, et multiformitas organizationis, in qua membra distinguuntur et ordinantur et secundum variam influentiam alia aliis praeponuntur, sic intelligendum est circa corpus Christi mysticum." *De Perf. Evan.,* q. 4, a. 1, ad 6, V, p. 182.

members of the social body should be subject and obedient to the one head.[33]

The necessity of one supreme head in society is another point that is stressed by our author, who writes: " Without one head no state can securely stand." [34] In addition, since this one ruler alone cannot efficaciously provide for all the needs of all the subjects, govern the whole of the social structure, and guard against all the dangers to the common good, right order, according to the thought of our saint, calls for the establishment of intermediate or inferior officials. Their power is limited (the supreme head alone possesses the fullness of power), and, though placed in positions of authority and influencing those subject to them, they are, in turn, subject to the supreme ruler, from whom they receive their limited power and by whom they themselves are influenced.[35]

This concept of a supreme head, minor officials, and subjects coincides with the three classes—*sacra plebs, sacri consules,* and *sacri principes*—that St. Bonaventure recognizes in that part of the ecclesiastical hierarchy which he terms the *ordo laicorum*.[36] Indeed, this gradation of powers, together with the fact that the princes influence the minor officials and through them the people, brings us into the very heart of Bonaventure's teaching on hierarchy.

---

[33] ". . . sic est in corpore materiali, quod omnia membra subjiciuntur et obtemperant uni membro principali, scilicet capiti; ergo sic erit in corpore spirituali, quod omnia membra spiritualia uni debent subjici tanquam capiti principali." *Ibid.,* a. 3, f. 15, p. 192.

[34] ". . . sine uno capite nulla respublica stare bene potest." *Op. XVI, Exp. Super Reg. Fr. Min.,* c. viii, n. 2, VIII, p. 427.

[35] *Liber IV S.,* d. 19, a. 3, q. 1, conc., and ad 6, IV, pp. 508–509; *De Perf. Evan.,* q. 4, a. 3, ad 13, V, p. 197; *Op. XIV, Quare Fratres Minores Praedicent et Confessiones Audiant,* nn. 2–4, VIII, p. 375.

St. Bonaventure is particularly concerned with the structure of the Church. However, he also alludes to the necessity of minor officials for right order in the civil society. " Item, videmus in curia regis terreni, quod ad hoc, quod sit sufficienter ordinata, ministri superiores indigent inferioribus, qui obediunt et subserviunt, et majores indigent minoribus . . ." *Liber IV S.,* d. 24, p. 2, a. 2, q. 1, f. 4, IV, pp. 629–630.

[36] " In ordine laicorum est triplex ordo, scilicet sacrorum plebium, sacrorum consulum, sacrorum principum." *In Hex.,* coll. XXII, n. 18, V, p. 440.

SECTION 4. HIERARCHY AND HIERARCHIES

We cannot treat of society without referring to hierarchy, for, as our author notes, all order—and, consequently, all social order—must be hierarchically constituted by command of the natural law.[37]   In point of fact, this concept plays a most important role in the writings of the Seraphic Doctor, even dominating his whole thought.   We find traces of this doctrine in his teaching regarding the creation and the universal order, in which God is the center and the various creatures gather around Him in gradated spheres.[38]   We encounter it again in the Blessed Trinity, in the hierarchy of the divine processions.[39]   Among the angels, too, there is a hierarchy of perfection—of knowledge, acts, and communications.[40]   We see it once more when our saintly author discusses the hierarchical ordering of the internal faculties of the human soul.[41]   Finally, we arrive at what the Seraphic Doctor terms the ecclesiastical hierarchy.[42]

A. The Nature of Hierarchy

It is not our purpose here to attempt to determine the exact nature of hierarchy according to the mind of St. Bonaventure, as that is indeed a complicated question, requiring separate and profound study.   We must, therefore, be satisfied to declare simply that whether we speak of God, angels, Church, or men, hierarchy means an ordered power, sacred in nature and belonging to a rational being, by virtue of which a superior being legitimately dominates the beings subjected to him.[43]   We should

[37] *De Perf. Evan.,* q. 4, a. 1, f. 7, V, p. 180.

[38] *Liber II S.,* d. 1, p. 1, a. 1, q. 1, ad 2, II, p. 17.   Confer above, c. 2, a. 1.

[39] *Liber II S.,* d. 9, praenotata, II, p. 238.

[40] *Ibid.,* pp. 240–241; *In Hex.,* coll. XXI, nn. 16ss, V, pp. 434ss.   Confer Gilson, *op. cit.,* pp. 254–257.

[41] *In Hex.,* coll. XXII, nn. 24ss, V, pp. 441ss.   Confer Gilson, *op. cit.,* pp. 426ss.

[42] *In Hex.,* coll. XXII, nn. 2–23, V, pp. 438–441.

[43] " Et sic patet ex praedictis definitionibus, quid sit hierarchia tam divina quam angelica; per quarum intellectum elicitur quaedam definitio magistralis, quae competit omni hierarchiae, licet non univoce, quae talis est: hierarchia est rerum sacrarum et rationabilium ordinata potestas, in subditis debitum retinens principatum." *Liber II S.,* d. 9, praenotata, II, p. 238.

also recall that all that enters into a hierarchical order—save the first term which gives all and receives nothing and the last term which receives all and gives nothing—is placed between the higher influence which it receives and the lower degrees on which its own influence is exercised.[44] This influence of the superior upon the inferior is threefold, namely: purification, illumination, and perfection.[45] Hierarchy, therefore, implies concurrence of entities, actions, and influences—entities placed one above the other, with each receiving influence from the one above it and imparting influence to the one below it.

B. *The Divine Hierarchy*

The Franciscan Doctor speaks of three main types of hierarchies: *supercaelestis* or divine, *caelestis* or angelical, and *subcaelestis* or human, i.e., ecclesiastical.[46] In the divine hierarchy we have most perfect order and beauty because of the highest unity and equality of the three Divine Persons—unity in trinity and trinity in unity.[47] Since the angelical and human hierarchies imitate the supreme hierarchy *only* inasmuch as they can, perfect order and beauty in the angelical and human hierarchies cannot reside in unity and equality, but in a certain diversity and in a proportional gradation of many.[48] The reason is that creatures, unlike the Divine Persons, do not possess the fullness of perfection.

C. *The Angelical Hierarchy*

The angelical hierarchy, according to St. Bonaventure, is divided into three hierarchies, each of which is subdivided into three orders. Thus we have the superior hierarchy (*suprema*),

---

[44] *In Hex.*, coll. XXI, n. 21, V, p. 435.

[45] *S. de B. V. M., De Assumtione B. V. M.*, s. i, IX, p. 689; *S. de Temp., De Trinitate*, IX, p. 354; *Liber IV S.*, d. 19, a. 3, q. 1, conc., IV, p. 508.

[46] *Liber II S.*, d. 9, praenotata, II, pp. 239–240; *S. de B. V. M., De Assumtione B. V. M.*, s. i, IX, p. 689.

[47] *Liber II S.*, d. 9, praenotata, II, p. 238. ". . . in suprema hierarchia propter summam perfectionem reperitur pulcritudo ex perfectissima aequalitate et similitudine parium . . ." *Ibid.*, a. 1, q. 8, conc., p. 255.

[48] *Ibid.*, ad 4, p. 256. Confer *Ibid.*, conc., pp. 255–256.

composed of three angelical choirs: the Seraphim, the Cherubim, and the Thrones; the intermediate hierarchy (*media*), made up of three angelical choirs: the Dominations, the Virtues, and the Powers; and the lower hierarchy (*infirma*), comprising three angelical choirs: the Principalities, the Archangels, and the Angels.[49]   In addition, our author speaks of a certain order (diversity and gradation) even in the angels belonging to the same choir.[50]   It appears, then, that no two angels, though they may belong to the same order, are perfectly identical.   Each individual angel possesses at least a certain nuance which differentiates it from all the others.   Accordingly, St. Bonaventure seems to affirm the existence of a perfectly proportional gradation, extending from the highest angel in the supreme angelical hierarchy to the lowest angel in the lower angelical hierarchy.

Commenting upon the angelical hierarchy, the Seraphic Doctor advances his doctrine of the influence—of purification, illumination, and perfection—which flows from the superior to the intermediate and from the intermediate to the inferior hierarchy. Furthermore, this influence, he remarks, descends to the human hierarchy from all three angelical hierarchies.[51]   This point must be kept in mind, for, says the holy Doctor, " the superiors are born to flow into (influence) the inferiors." [52]   In his study of the angelical hierarchies, moreover, Bonaventure notes that the harmony and concord existing among the angels of the different choirs is due to the fact that each angel remains in the place assigned to it in the hierarchical structure and generously communicates its own perfection to the one below it.[53]

---

[49] *In Hex.*, coll. XXI, nn. 16ss, V, pp. 434–436; *Liber II S.*, d. 9, praenotata, II, pp. 240–241; *S. de Sanctis, De S. Angelis*, s. i, IX, pp. 609ss.

[50] " Ideo et in eodem ordine ponenda est quaedam gradatio et quidem ordo, licet non sit tantus excessus, quantus reperitur in Angelis diversorum ordinum." *Liber II S.*, d. 9, a. 1, q. 8, conc., II, p. 256.

[51] *In Hex.*, coll. XXI, n. 21, V, p. 435; *Com. in Sap.*, prooemium, n. 9, VI, p. 109; *S. de B. V. M., De Assumtione B. V. M.*, s. i, IX, p. 689; *S. de Temp., De Trinitate*, IX, p. 354; *Liber IV S.*, d. 19, a. 3, q. 1, conc., IV, p. 508.

[52] ". . . superiora nata sunt influere in inferiora . . ." *Liber II S.*, d. 8, p. 2, a. 1, q. 3, conc., II, p. 228.

[53] " Ista concordia est in Angelis, quia nec superior Angelus ibi deprimit

The principles discovered in the angelical hierarchy should, in the mind of St. Bonaventure, prevail in the various human societies. Thus, e.g., the superiors in a human society are not to oppress their subjects, but to elevate them and to communicate to them those things with which they themselves have been blessed; the inferiors, avoiding all envy, are to perform the duty (role) assigned to them and thus promote the common good. In this manner society will be rightly ordered and blessed with harmony and concord.[54]

D. *The Ecclesiastical Hierarchy*

The Seraphic Doctor speaks of a third hierarchy, i.e., the human or ecclesiastical hierarchy, which, for him, is the Church, the Mystical Body of Christ. This hierarchy is likewise divided by our saintly author into three hierarchies, which correspond to the three angelical hierarchies. In considering the activities of the various members of the Church, the holy Doctor notices that certain men are active, that others are both active and contemplative, and that still others are pure contemplatives. Accordingly, he posits three orders in the ecclesiastical hierarchy —the *monastic,* which coincides with the order of contemplatives; the *clerical,* which corresponds to the order of prelates, who are both active and contemplative; and the *lay,* which coincides with the order of the actives.[55]

Taking his cue from the angelical hierarchy, St. Bonaventure tells us that the monastic order, which is as the *suprema* angelical hierarchy, contains a threefold order—those elevated to the state of *ecstasy,* corresponding to the Seraphim;[56] the *speculatives,*

---

inferiorem, nec inferior ibi invidet superiori. . . . Angeli superiores tam benigna condescensione condescendunt inferioribus, quod omnia eis communicant, omnes revelationes sibi factas. . . . Ita debet esse in hominibus, ut esset concordia et benevolentia inter eos." *S. de Sanctis, De S. Angelis,* s. v, IX, p. 628.

[54] *Ibidem.*

[55] *In Hex.,* coll. XXII, nn. 16–17, V, p. 440. St. Bonaventure has other divisions of the ecclesiastical hierarchy. For a more complete study thereof confer *Ibid.,* nn. 2–16, pp. 438–440.

[56] *Ibid.,* nn. 22–23, pp. 440–441. Bonaventure places St. Francis of Assisi

corresponding to the Cherubim;[57] and the *suppliants,* corresponding to the Thrones.[58] The clerical order, like the *media* angelical hierarchy, is again divided into three orders—the *pontifical,* corresponding to the Dominations; the *sacerdotal,* corresponding to the Virtues; and the *ministerial,* corresponding to the Powers.[59] In the lay order, which is similar to the *infirma* angelical hierarchy, Bonaventure likewise recognizes a threefold order—the *sacri principes* or rulers, corresponding to the Principalities; the *sacri consules* or inferior officials, corresponding to the Archangels; and the *sacra plebs* or people, corresponding to the Angels.[60]

At the very summit of the ecclesiastical hierarchy there must be, according to the teaching of our saintly author, one in whom is vested the supremacy of power and authority. This demand, he tells us, is evoked by the fact that a hierarchy cannot exist unless there be one at the very summit of the hierarchy to whom all the others must be subservient and obedient.[61] St. Bonaventure is most insistent on this point, expressly teaching that, although men may be bound to obedience by many and varied

---

in this order, which, according to his manner of thinking, is the highest order in the ecclesiastical hierarchy.

[57] *Ibid.,* n. 21, p. 440. These are engaged in speculation or the study of the Sacred Scriptures, which cannot be grasped except by pure souls. The Friars Preachers and the Friars Minor belong to this order, the second highest in the Church. The Seraphic Doctor distinguishes between these two religious orders. The Preachers, in his thought, "principaliter intendunt speculationi, a quo etiam nomen acceperunt, et postea unctioni." The Minors, "principaliter unctioni et postea speculationi."

[58] *Ibid.,* n. 20, p. 440. These are entirely devoted to prayer and divine praise except when they are occupied in manual labor for their own support as well as that of others. Amongst these Bonaventure places: "Cisterciensis, Praemonstratensis, Cathusiensis, Grandimontensis, Canonici regulares." The main difference between these and the Friars seems to be the fact that the Friars are mendicants, whereas the others are not.

[59] *Ibid.,* n. 19, p. 440.

[60] *Ibid.,* n. 18, p. 440.

[61] "Item, Ecclesia est una hierarchia: ergo debet habere unum praecipuum et summum hierarcham, cum ab unitate principis descendere debeat unitas principatus; sed uni et summo hierarchae ab omnibus obediendum est . . ." *De Perf. Evan.,* q. 4, a. 3, f. 17, V, p. 192.

ties, according to the diversity of their grades, offices, and powers, nevertheless there must be one in the ecclesiastical hierarchy, the Supreme Pontiff, who possesses the fullness of power and authority and to whom all the others are subject.[62] This oneness of supreme ruler in the Church, the saintly Franciscan writes, is demanded by justice, the oneness of the Church, and her efficaciousness.[63]

In the ecclesiastical, or universal human, hierarchy, St. Bonaventure recognizes two sections—the one referring to civil or lay authority, and the other referring to ecclesiastical or clerical authority.[64] The first section, the civil or lay authority, comprises the third order of the human hierarchy and concerns itself with the terrestrial and the temporal, i.e., with the goods of nature and the fortunes of private individuals and of the commonwealth as a whole.[65] The other section, viz., the clerical or ecclesiastical authority, includes both the first and second orders of the human hierarchy (i.e., the monastic and clerical orders) and concerns itself with the spiritual.

The structure of the universal human hierarchy is rendered still clearer when we recall to mind the three goods required for the conservation and right order of the Church Militant. These are: the *bonum inferius,* or the corporeal or material good; the *bonum exterius,* or the civil administrative good; and the *bonum interius,* or the spiritual good. Bonaventure recognizes a corresponding threefold work or activity required to

---

[62] "Licet diversi homines pluribus ligaminibus ad subjectionem obedientiae diversis sint astricti, secundum diversitatem graduum, officiorum et potestatum; tamen haec varietas ad unum reduci debet summum et primum Antistitem, in quo principaliter residet universalis omnium principatus; et non solum ad ipsum Christum, sed etiam jure divino ad ejus Vicarium . . ." *Ibid.,* conc., p. 193.

[63] *Ibidem.*

[64] ". . . Ecclesia constituitur ex duplici pariete, scilicet laicali et clericali; sed in pariete laicali est ordo, utpote imperator, rex, dux, comes, tribunus, centurio et decurio, omnia haec ordinem dicunt: si ergo Ecclesia militat militia spirituali, videtur quod et ipsa debeat esse ut castrorum acies ordinata." *Liber IV S.,* d. 24, p. 1, a. 2, q. 1, f. 3, IV, p. 614.

[65] ". . . in laicis, in quibus ordo attenditur quantum ad potestatem terrenam, quae respicit bona naturae vel fortunae specialis personae vel reipublicae . . ." *Ibid.,* q. 2, ad 3, p. 617.

provide for these goods and for the resultant conservation and well-being of the ecclesiastical hierarchy—viz., manual, administrative or civil, and spiritual activity.[66]   The manual and administrative works are the concern of the *infirma* hierarchy (the lay or active order), while the spiritual activity belongs to the *media* and *suprema* hierarchies.

More to the point, the *sacra plebs* is to engage in manual labor, which is productive of the material and corporeal good.   Their work or activity is necessary for the production and provision of food, clothing, homes, and the instruments needed for the various artisans and arts.[67]   The civil good is the concern of the two remaining orders of the lower hierarchy (*sacri consules* and *sacri principes*), who are to govern, defend, protect, and assist.   They are to promote the external good—to uphold order, justice, and peace.[68]   Finally, the internal or spiritual good is the concern of the intermediate and superior hierarchies.   The prelates (those comprising the intermediate hierarchy) are to correct the erring, to instruct the faithful in things divine, to dispense the sacraments, and to distribute the divinely given gifts, both spiritual and material.[69]   The contemplatives (members of the

[66] ". . . notandum est, quod regimen reipublicae in Ecclesia attenditur circa tria, scilicet quantum ad bonum inferius, quod est corporale; quantum ad bonum exterius, quod est civile; et quantum ad bonum interius, quod est spirituale.   Et secundum hoc triplex genus operis est necessarium ad regimen reipublicae et Ecclesiae militantis, scilicet opus artificiale, quod et manuale dicitur . . . opus civile et opus spirituale." *De Perf. Evan.*, q. 2, a. 3, conc., V, p. 161.

[67] "Opus manuale sive corporale dico, quod est necessarium ad praeparanda alimenta, vestimenta, habitacula et diversorum opificum et artium instrumenta." *Ibidem*.

[68] "Opus civile dico, quod est ipsorum praesidum gubernantium, militum defendentium, mercatorum negotiantium et famulorum ministrantium." *Ibidem*.

[69] "Opus spirituale dico, quod consistit in disseminando divina verba, in decantando divina cantica, in dispensando Sacramenta et in distribuendo bona sibi divinitus data, sive terrena, sive spiritualia." *De Perf. Evan.*, q. 2, a. 3, conc., V, p. 161.

"Ministrare vero debent praelati tripliciter, ut respondeant mediae hierarchiae in caelo, scilicet in correctionibus censurae. . . . In eruditionibus doctrinae. . . . In subventionibus spiritualis et corporalis indigentiae . . ." *S. de Temp., Dom. IV Adventus*, s. xii, IX, p. 85.

superior hierarchy), on the other hand, are to devote their lives to prayer, the chanting of the divine praises, sacred studies, and the contemplation of the Eternal.[70]

This thought is further strengthened by Bonaventure's three classes of men—*agricultores,* who through manual labor provide the social body with the *bonum inferius;* the *defensores,* who through administrative activity provide society with protection and promote order and harmony, the *bonum exterius;* and the *orantes,* who supply men with their spiritual needs and provide for the *bonum interius* of the social organism.[71] In this connection the Bonaventurian insistence upon interdependence and mutual aid is vividly apparent.

Accordingly, the picture of social living painted by the Seraphic Doctor is one in which each individual has a role to fulfill, a role that is never totally and solely personal. Each role, whether that of the lowest manual laborer or that of the most exalted contemplative, redounds to the good of all the members of the social whole. Should the individual fail in the fulfillment of the role assigned to him, the good of all is threatened. For example, should the farmer refuse to plow, neither those engaged in fostering the external good nor those whose duty it is to provide the others with spiritual goods would have the wherewithal to provide for their material needs. Both would then be unable to perform their respective offices and to provide for the continued good and success of the rest. Bonaventure, therefore, demands a society of friends and mutual abettors, a society in which all individual egotism is excluded. His plan is for a true unity whereby each member of the social organism may find support, consolation, and protection.[72] His aim is a society in which all aid each other so that all may ultimately attain to their final end—union with God.

---

[70] " Ministrare vero debent contemplativi tripliciter, ut respondeant hierarchiae supremae, scil., in devotionibus gratie. . . . In laudibus reverentiae. . . . In oblationibus et ardoribus excellentiae . . ." *Ibidem.* Confer *In Hex.,* coll. XXII, nn. 20–23, V, pp. 440–441.

[71] *De Perf. Evan.,* q. 2, a. 3, f. 12, V, p. 159; *Op. XI, Apologia Pauperum,* c. xii, n. 14, VIII, p. 321.

[72] *Com. in Sap.,* c. iv, vv. 9–12, VI, pp. 39–40; *In Joannem,* c. 17, coll. 61, nn. 3–5, VI, p. 609.

The Seraphic Doctor is actually referring to the Church Militant—the city of God here on earth—and not to the brotherhood of nations as such. Nevertheless, the ecclesiastical hierarchy, embracing all classes of men from all nations and races, does bring to mind the human family and the commonwealth of nations. That St. Bonaventure does teach the unity of the human race, the brotherhood of all men, and the fact of a universal human family cannot be denied. For instance, insisting upon the love that each man should have for his neighbor, the saintly follower of St. Francis remarks: " To commend this love God willed that all men be born of one father, Adam; be redeemed by the same Blood; and rewarded with the same reward." [73] These words recall the teachings of Pope Pius XII, who stresses the unity of all mankind in his encyclical " *Summi Pontificatus.*" [74]

As we have seen, the ecclesiastical hierarchy, according to Bonaventurian thought, is composed of two sections; one refers to the lay or civil authority, the other relates to the clerical or ecclesiastical authority.[75]   St. Bonaventure affirms that there is one universal hierarchy covering man's twofold aspect—viz., his spiritual nature, out of which arises the need of a spiritual society; and his material nature, which makes necessary a civil society to regulate the material or temporal affairs of man. These two sections of the ecclesiastical hierarchy (clerical and lay) must work hand in hand for the betterment of all the members of the universal human hierarchy, so that all may be given those means—material, intellectual, and moral—wherewith each may pursue and attain his final and eternal end.

Each section is powerful in its own field; each enjoys a certain right; each has a certain duty to perform. Still, because the spiritual is above the material, the spiritual society, in the mind of our author, enjoys the greater power. Accordingly, he writes: " For the support of heaven (i.e., the universal Church), God

---

[73] " . . . ad commendandam hanc dilectionem voluit Deus, quod nasceremur ex uno patre Adam; quod redimeremur eodem sanguine, scilicet sanguine Domini nostri Jesu Christi; quod remuneraremur eadem mercede . . ." *Com. in Ev. Lucae,* c. x, n. 49, VII, p. 268.

[74] Nn. 30–38.

[75] Confer above, footnote 64.

fashioned two great lights; that is, He instituted two dignities—namely: pontifical authority and regal power. However, that which presides over the days, i.e., things spiritual, is greater; that which presides over the nights, i.e., things carnal, is lower; so that from the difference that exists between the moon and the sun may be known the difference that exists between kings and pontiffs." [76]

ARTICLE II. MARRIAGE, OR THE CONJUGAL SOCIETY

By nature man tends towards the preservation not only of his individual and personal life, but also of the human race as a whole. St. Bonaventure tells us that there is innate in man a natural desire for the continuance of his being. [77] In conjunction with this instinct for the preservation of human life in the individual as well as in the species, arising out of the very law of nature, [78] there has been implanted in man generative power, given to him for the conservation of the human race. [79]

However, though the natural law compels man, as it were, to propagate and thus to conserve human life, man is unable of

---

[76] " Ad firmamentum caeli, id est universalis Ecclesiae, fecit Deus duo luminaria magna, id est, duas instituit dignitates, quae sunt pontificalis auctoritas regalisque potestas. Sed illa quae praeest diebus, id est spiritualibus, major est; quae autem noctibus, id est carnalibus, minor, ut, quanta est inter lunam et solem, tanta inter reges et Pontifices differentia cognoscatur." *Op. XI, Apologia Pauperum,* c. xi, n. 10, VIII, p. 313.

Indeed, the Seraphic Doctor seems to assert that the Supreme Pontiff enjoys supreme authority on earth in both temporal and spiritual matters. Confer *De Perf. Evan.,* q. 4, a. 3, ad 8, V, p. 196; *Ibid.,* q. 2, a. 2, conc., p. 155; *Liber IV S.,* d. 37, dub. IV, IV, p. 812.

For the relations of Church and State confer Legowicz, *op. cit.,* pp. 232–250.

[77] " Est naturaliter insertus homini amor sui esse continui . . ." *De Perf. Evan.,* q. 2, a. 3, ad 1, V, p. 162.

[78] " Item, ratione videtur: quia matrimonium ordinatum erat ad conservationem speciei quantum ad generativam, et esus lignorum ordinatus erat ad conservationem individui quantum ad nutritivam . . . sed esus cadebat sub praecepto; ergo et coitus." *Liber IV S.,* d. 26, a. 1, q. 3, f. 3, IV, p. 664.

[79] ". . . virum et mulierem debere conjungi propter prolis generationem, quia ad hoc data est vis generativa . . ." *Ibid.,* d. 33, a. 1, q. 1, f. 4, p. 747. Confer *Liber II S.,* d. 20, a. 1, q. 1, conc., II, p. 478,

himself and by himself alone to comply with this law of nature.[80] He has need of a helper—a helper like himself, yet different because complementary; he needs the assistance of a woman, who, the Seraphic Doctor states, was made for propagation, was brought into being after the creation of the first man, and was given to him as a helpmate.[81] Man seeks to enter into a union with this helper, and by virtue of the assistance gained in this union he is enabled to comply with the law that calls for the continuance of his being. This union of male and female, commanded by the natural law, is marriage.[82]

SECTION 1. THE DEFINITION OF MARRIAGE

In the teaching of our saintly author, marriage is *essentialiter* a union.[83] The Seraphic Doctor defines marriage as *the marital union of man and woman living together in undivided partnership.*[84] This definition, he tells us, contains the four causes of marriage—the formal cause, or the marital union; the efficient cause, or man and woman inasmuch as they consent; the material cause, or man and woman inasmuch as they are legitimate persons; and the final cause, or their undivided partnership (*bonum sacramenti*) which, he states, is the principal good of marriage.[85]

---

[80] " Et quia nec vir per se, nec mulier per se suffecisset ad generandum; ideo per commixtionem fieret conjunctio unius ad alterum, et mutuum sibi praeberent auxilium in procreatione prolis ad multiplicandum genus humanum." *Ibidem.* Cf. *Liber IV S.,* d. 26, a. 1, q. 1, conc., IV, p. 662.

[81] ". . . mulier propter procreationem liberorum facta est; unde facta est in adjutorium viri . . ." *Ibid.,* d. 27, a. 1, q. 2, conc., p. 678. Confer *Ibid.,* f. 4, p. 677.

[82] ". . . a dictamine scilicet naturae, ut vir cubet cum muliere ad conservationem ipsius naturae . . ." *Ibid.,* d. 31, a. 1, q. 2, conc., p. 719.

[83] ". . . matrimonium dicitur essentialiter et secundum genus suum conjunctio." *Ibid.,* d. 27, a. 1, q. 1, conc., p. 676.

[84] " Matrimonium est viri et mulieris conjunctio maritalis, individuam vitae consuetudinem retinens." *Ibid.,* dub. 1, p. 684.

[85] " Posset tamen dici, quod notetur ibi quadruplex genus causae, scilicet *formalis,* in hoc quod dicitur: conjunctio maritalis; *efficiens,* in hoc quod dicitur: viri et mulieris, quae, in quantum consentiunt, se habent in ratione causae efficientis; *materialis,* in hoc quod dicitur: inter legitimas personas; *finalis,* in hoc quod dicitur: individuam vitae etc., ubi tangitur bonum sacramenti, quod est principale bonum matrimonii." *Ibidem.*

Accordingly, in the teaching of our author, matrimony is not simply the union of two souls or of two bodies, but the union of a whole man (body and soul) with a whole woman (body and soul).[86] Since it is the union of two rational beings of different sexes, marriage cannot exist, therefore, except among human persons.

Furthermore, marriage is a union that continues in effect even when the contracting parties are separated from each other either in affection or in body.[87] The marital union of man and woman, therefore, is not a mere mating process. The generative instinct, though common to brute and man alike, is to be governed in man by his rational faculties. Our saint points out that, although nature calls for the multiplication of human entities, nevertheless this multiplication must be brought about in an orderly and just manner, according to the dictates of right reason.[88] Thus, right reason calls for a stable, permanent union between man and wife.[89] Again, while nature requires that man be united with woman for the sake of conserving human life, right reason demands that only one man be united with only one woman.[90] Besides, despite the natural desire or appetite for the continuance

---

According to his teaching, the words "*legitimate persons*" are not needed in the definition of marriage. They are sometimes included for a clearer and deeper understanding. Confer *Ibidem.*

[86] " Ad illud quod quaeritur, utrum sit corporum, an animorum; dicendum, quod animorum in corporibus, quia est conjunctio ratione utentium et habentium sexus distinctos . . ." *Ibid.,* d. 27, a. 1, q. 1, ad 4–5, p. 676.

[87] ". . . illa autem conjunctio, quae respicit totum conjunctum et est matrimonium essentialiter, non est affectio animorum, vel approximatio corporum, sed quoddam vinculum obligatorium, quod non perimitur, sive affectu, sive corpore separentur." *Ibidem.*

[88] " Ad illud quod objicitur, quod est ad multiplicationem talis actus etc.; dicendum, quod etsi natura dictet, prolem esse multiplicandam, tamen dictat: debite et ordinate, et ita quod nulli fiat injuria . . ." *Ibid.,* d. 33, a. 1, q. 2, ad 4, p. 750.

[89] Confer above, ft. 87.

[90] ". . . a dictamine scilicet naturae, ut vir cubet cum muliere ad conservationem ipsius naturae, et sic bonum prolis; a dictamine rationis rectae, ut vir cum sua et non cum alia cubet muliere, et sic bonum fidei . . ." *Liber IV S.,* d. 31, a. 1, q. 2, conc., IV, p. 719.

of his being, man remains free with regard to both the fulfillment of this command [91] and the choice of a partner.[92]

In point of fact, then, the Seraphic Doctor regards marriage as a true social union. This thought is patent when we recall that he expressly terms the nuptial state a society.[93] Indeed, he defines matrimony not as the consent to cohabitation or carnal copulation, but as the consent to live together in conjugal society.[94] The social nature of the matrimonial tie becomes even more manifest in the light of the twofold love that our author distinguishes as necessary to marriage. He speaks of a *conjugal* love required for the procreation of the offspring and of a *social* love needed to permit the espoused to live together in amity.[95] The social aspect is again stressed by Bonaventure's affirmation that the principal good of marriage is undivided partnership—the undivided community of life and the mutual development and perfection of husband and wife.[96]

It would be worth while to note here that in the mind of our saint matrimony and its use are a *bonum*.[97] Since marriage is a *bonum in se,* he argues, no one (not otherwise legitimately impeded) can be forbidden to enter the marital state.[98] All men have an equal right to matrimony; all men are free to marry or not to marry.[99] Accordingly, he teaches that slaves have every

---

[91] *De Perf. Evan.,* q. 3, a. 2, ad 4, V, p. 174.

[92] ". . . quamvis Dominus praeciperet contractionem matrimonii cum aliqua, tamen, utrum cum hac quis contraheret, vel cum alia, reliquit in mere libertate contrahentis." *Liber IV S.,* d. 26, a. 1, q. 3, ad 4, IV, p. 665.

[93] *Ibid.,* d. 32, dub. 1, p. 742; *Ibid.,* d. 31, dub. 5, p. 713; *Liber II S.,* d. 18, a. 1, q. 1, conc., II, p. 432.

[94] *Liber IV S.,* d. 28, a. 1, q. 6, IV, pp. 695–696; *Ibid.,* d. 30, dub. V, p. 713; *Ibid.,* d. 26, a. 2, q. 3, pp. 669–670; *Ibid.,* d. 29, a. 1, q. 2, f. 3, p. 701.

[95] ". . . sponsus et sponsa se diligunt. Nam diligunt se amore sociali ad convivendum; diligunt se ulterius amore conjugali ad prolem procreandam . . ." *Liber I S.,* d. 10, a. 2, q. 1, conc., I, p. 201. Confer *Liber IV S.,* d. 37, a. 2, q. 2, f. 3, IV, p. 808.

[96] *Ibid.,* d. 27, dub. 1, p. 684.

[97] This point will be considered in detail when we come to an examination of Bonaventure's teaching concerning the goods of marriage.

[98] "Quia ergo matrimonium bonum est, nullus ab eo prohibetur, nullus repellitur . . ." *De Perf. Evan.,* q. 3, a. 2, conc., V, p. 172.

[99] *Liber IV S.,* d. 29, a. 1, q. 3, conc., IV, p. 703.—Bonaventure is here

right to marry and can contract matrimony even when their masters forbid them.[100]   However, because this good, through the Fall of man, is united with that which diminishes its honesty, utility, and spiritual " jucunditas," no one can be *obliged* to marry.[101]

We may ask how anyone can teach that man is free not to marry when the natural law commands the conservation of the human race through the marital union of man and woman. Bonaventure replies to this objection by pointing out that the law of nature calling for the conservation of the human species does not oblige except in common.   It is obligatory only upon mankind as a whole, not upon the individual.   It does not oblige any particular person as long as there is another who fulfills this dictate of nature.[102]

---

concerned with the power of the father over the son. He asserts that the father cannot command his son to marry, nor can he command that he marry a certain party, unless there be some special and serious reason that warrants it.

[100] *Ibid.,* d. 36, a. 1, q. 1, conc., p. 792.

[101] ". . . quia vero annexum habet aliquid, quod et minuit honestatem et utilitatem et spiritualem jucunditatem; hinc est, quod nullus ad ipsum arctatur invitus, quia potius ab ipso abstinere sive continere suadetur, tam a Domino, quam ab ipso Apostolo . . ." *De Perf. Evan.,* q. 3, a. 2, conc., V, pp. 172–173.

[102] ". . . quod praeceptum naturae est duplex: quoddam, quod respicit statum communem; quoddam, quod respicit statum singularis personae. Primum non ligat aliquem per se et determinate, quamdiu est alius, qui illud mandatum suppleat vel possit implere. Et quoniam multi sint, qui generationi carnali operam dant, quantum sufficit naturae; praecepto illi non repugnat in singulari personae servatio continentiae. Praeceptum enim illud non descendit ad aliquam personam determinate, nisi in casu, in quo natura non possit subsistere, nisi persona illa generationi operam daret . . ." *Ibid.,* ad 4, p. 174. Confer *Ibid.,* q. 2, a. 3, ad 3, p. 162.

Moreover, he writes, certain precepts of nature (e.g. that God is to be loved) oblige *simpliciter;* others (v.g. that all things are to be possessed in common) oblige at certain times. The precept of using marriage, since it is a natural precept of the second type, obliges the individual only at certain times, i.e., when the continued existence of human life is in danger. Confer *Liber IV S.,* d. 26, a. 1, q. 3, conc., IV, p. 665.

SECTION 2.   THE MATERIAL CAUSE OF MARRIAGE

Since matrimony is the union of two rational beings of different sexes and since woman was made to be man's helper—similar in some respects, different in others—it must follow that man and woman, who are the material cause of marriage, are of different yet complementary natures.   This distinction of the sexes, Bonaventure asserts, was brought into being for the purpose of generation.[103]   However, it is not purely physiological —it transcends the biological order and extends into the psychological sphere.   Human personality, in other words, manifests itself differently—both physiologically and psychologically—in each sex.   Man, our author tells us, is predominantly active, whereas woman is predominantly passive.[104]   The masculine personality is characterized by strength, virility, and stability; the feminine personality by weakness, gentleness, and tenderness.[105] Accordingly, in marriage these two different physiological and psychological natures are to supply each other with what is lacking in their respective make-up, to complement each other in both the physical and psychical order.[106]

Nevertheless, despite their differences, man and woman, because they are both man—i.e., members of the human race—enjoy a strict equality.   Bonaventure insists that the expression *"vir occasionatus,"* as applied to the female sex, must be put aside, that woman is not an abnormality.[107]   Sex, he affirms, does not differentiate the species.   Both men and women are humans, endowed with the same rational nature, enjoying all the essential attributes of human nature.[108]

---

[103] ". . . distinctio sexuum non est nisi propter generationem . . ." *Liber II S.,* d. 20, a. 1, q. 1, f. 3, II, p. 477.

[104] *Brev.,* p. 6, c. 13, V, pp. 279–280; *Liber III S.,* d. 12, a. 3, q. 1, conc., p. 271.

[105] *Liber II S.,* d. 18, a. 1, q. 1, conc., II, pp. 432–433; and ad 7–9, p. 434.

[106] "Vir enim et mulier secundum sexuum proprietatem et naturam sic facti sunt, ut invicem conjungerentur, et ex hoc unus in altero quietaretur et unus ab alio sustentaretur." *Ibid.,* conc., p. 432.   Confer *Ibid.,* d. 20, a. 1, q. 1, conc., p. 478.

[107] *Ibid.,* q. 6, ad 1, p. 487.   ". . . generatio tamen mulieris nec est praeter naturam nec contra naturam, sed secundum naturam."

[108] "Item, sexus non variat speciem, ergo vir et mulier sunt ejusdem

However, notwithstanding this equality of human nature, the Seraphic Doctor does not fail to note that the male possesses a certain superiority over the female. He grants to man a definite priority over woman, inasmuch as it was from the rib of Adam that the first woman was made.[109] Furthermore, our author teaches, man possesses by nature a certain perfection and leadership, or preeminence over woman.[110] In his mind, the female and the male are likened to the inferior and the superior parts of reason respectively. Accordingly, he says, just as the inferior part of reason is to remain subject to the superior reason, so, too, is the female to remain submissive to the male.[111] Because of the superiority of man over woman, Bonaventure concludes that in accordance with right order man is to occupy the place of authority in the marital society.[112] It is not in the nature of woman to rule, he tells us, since she was created to be of aid to man, and not vice versa.[113] Hence, it is the duty of the woman to remain subject to her husband, to be a good spouse, to aid and abet him.

This superiority on the part of the man and subordination on the part of the woman do not entail any degradation of the weaker sex. Indeed, the Seraphic Doctor points out, woman was made to be the *socia,* the associate or the companion of her husband, not his slave.[114] Although man is to be the superior,

---

speciei . . ." *Ibid.,* d. 16, a. 2, q. 2, f. 3, p. 403. Confer the whole question, pp. 403–404.

[109] " Tunc autem magis congruebat, mulierem educi de viro, ut ostenderetur, quod vir est caput mulieris, et quod non vir propter mulierem, sed mulier propter virum . . ." *Ibid.,* d. 18, a. 1, q. 1, ad 3, p. 433.

[110] " Excellit enim sexus virilis muliebrem et quantum ad dignitatem in principiando, et quantum ad virtutem in agendo, et quantum ad auctoritatem in praesidendo." *Liber III S.,* d. 12, a. 3, q. 1, conc., III, p. 271.

[111] *Liber II S.,* d. 18, a. 1, q. 1, conc., II, p. 433; *Ibid.,* d. 16, a. 2, q. 2, ad 1–2, p. 404.

[112] " Nam secundum rectum ordinem non mulier viro, sed vir praeficitur mulieri tamquam caput corpori . . ." *Liber III S.,* d. 12, a. 3, q. 1, conc., III, p. 271.

[113] ". . . mulier propter procreationem liberorum facta est; unde facta est in adjutorium viri . . ." *Liber IV S.,* d. 27, a. 1, q. 2, conc., IV, p. 678. Confer above, footnote 109.

[114] *Liber II S.,* d. 44, a. 2, q. 2, ad 1, II, p. 1008.

nevertheless, as Bonaventure expressly notes, this superiority of man over woman refers only to those acts that have special reference to the masculine sex—namely, the rule of the home and the like.[115] In all other things, husband and wife are equal. Theirs is a mutual society. Their obligations are equal; equal, too, are their rights.[116]

SECTION 3. THE EFFICIENT CAUSE OF MARRIAGE

In order to understand the efficient cause of marriage, we must posit a threefold distinction:—i.e., (1) marriage as an institution, (2) marriage *in fieri* (the contract, or constitutive act of matrimony), and (3) marriage *in facto esse* (the state of marriage, or the marital society).

Distinguishing between the marital contract itself and the institution of marriage as such, St. Bonaventure tells us that the Creator has founded marriage.[117] God is, therefore, the efficient cause of the institution of matrimony. The marital contract, on the other hand, must have the contracting, or consenting, parties for its efficient cause—they are the ones who consent and who thereby bring the contract into being.

In addition, the Seraphic Doctor distinguishes between the contract and the state of marriage, i.e., between the mutual consent or contract (*matrimonium in fieri*) and the marital society or *"vinculum"* resulting from this contract (*matrimonium in facto esse*).[118] He discovers two elements in matrimony: (a) a *permanent* element, i.e., the *vinculum* or the indivisible union of lives, the permanent bond by which the spouses are bound to observe undivided fidelity to each other; and (b) a *transitory* element, i.e., the expression of consent, or the contract itself,

---

[115] "Ad illud ergo quod dicitur, quod vir est superior; dicendum, quod illud intelligitur quantum ad illos actus, qui respiciunt sexum virilem specialiter, scilicet quantum ad regimen domus et consimilium." *Liber IV S.,* d. 32, dub. I, IV, p. 742.

[116] *Liber II S.,* d. 18, a. 1, q. 1, conc., II, p. 432; *Liber IV S.,* d. 33, a. 1, q. 2, f. 2, IV, p. 749; *Ibid.,* conc., p. 750; *Ibid.,* q. 1, f. 3, p. 747; *Ibid.,* d. 32, dub. I, p. 742; *Ibid.,* d. 27, a. 1, q. 2, ad 3, p. 678.

[117] *Ibid.,* d. 26, a. 1, q. 2., conc., p. 664.

[118] *Ibid.,* d. 27, a. 1, q. 1, conc., p. 676.

which gives rise to the marital society.[119]   Accordingly, the contract, or the free consent of both parties to enter the marital society, is the introductory cause. It is the efficient cause of marriage in the sense that it brings the marital bond into being—causes it to be. The *vinculum,* or the indivisible union of lives, is that which is brought into being.[120]

However, once the "vinculum" or marital society is established through the mutual consent of the contracting parties, the permanence of the union, as St. Bonaventure writes, does not depend upon the consent, but upon the Eternal, Who instituted marriage as the insoluble union of man and wife.[121]   This thought recalls to mind the words of Pope Pius XI:

> "Although matrimony is of its very nature of Divine institution, the human will too enters into it and performs a most noble part. For each individual marriage, inasmuch as it is a conjugal union of a particular man and woman, arises only from the free consent of each of the spouses; and this free act of the will, by which each party hands over and accepts those rights proper to the state of marriage, is so necessary to constitute true marriage that it cannot be supplied by any human power. This freedom, however, regards only the point whether the contracting parties really wish to enter upon matrimony or to marry this particular person; but the nature of matrimony is entirely independent of the

---

[119] ". . . sic in matrimonium est aliquid permanens, et hoc est vinculum, per quod ligatur vir et mulier, quantumcumque exterius separentur; et est aliquid transiens, sicut conjunctio primo facta per verbum exterius, vel per exteriorem actum . . ." *Ibidem.*

[120] "Et per hoc patet responsio ad illud de consensu: quia non est tota causa matrimonii . . . sed ulterius est ibi divina institutio. . . . Dicendum igitur, quod est causa introducens tantum, et introducens et conservans. Quando dicitur, quod si detruitur causa, et effectus; verum est de conservante, non autem est verum de introducente tantum; consensus vinculum illud introducit, non conservat . . ." *Ibid.,* d. 27, a. 3, q. 1, ad 3, p. 682. Confer *Ibid.,* a. 2, q. 1, ad 2-3, p. 679; *Ibid.,* d. 22, a. 1, q. 1, ad 3, p. 576.

[121] "In matrimonio namque duo sunt: et mutua obligatio et obligationis mutuae indissolubilitas; et quamvis primum sit hominis, secundum est instituentis . . ." *Ibid.,* d. 26, a. 1, q. 2, ad 4, p. 664.

"Est ergo consensus causa, ut matrimonium fiat, non ut permaneat." *Ibid.,* d. 27, a. 2, q. 1, ad 2-3, p. 679. Confer *Ibid.,* a. 3, q. 1, ad. 1-3, p. 682.

free will of man, so that if one has once contracted matrimony he is thereby subject to its Divinely made laws and its essential properties." [122]

The Seraphic Doctor, therefore, distinguishes between the cause that simply brings marriage into being (the consent) and the cause that is both efficient and preservative (divine institution).[123] He teaches that the marital union—the *vinculum*—has a twofold efficient cause: (a) a first cause, God; and (b) a proximate cause, the human pact, or the agreement of the contracting parties. Although the proximate efficient cause of marriage, consent is not, however, its entire cause. The full efficient cause of marriage is the consent of both parties, together with the institution of marriage by God.[124]

Accordingly, if we consider the institution of marriage alone, God is the efficient cause. If, on the other hand, we refer to the marital contract alone, the contracting or consenting parties are its efficient cause. If, finally, we consider the marital society as such, i.e., the resulting bond which unites one to the other, then both God and the consent of the contracting parties are its efficient cause.

St. Bonaventure teaches that this consent should be full and absolute,[125] freely given [126] by both parties [127] for all time.[128] It should be expressed externally [129] in words indicative of the

---

[122] *Casti Connubi.*

[123] Confer above, ft. 120, 121.

[124] ". . . sic matrimonium uno modo comprehendit vinculum et exterius signum, et sic matrimonium est consensus expressus, non ejus effectus; alio modo, prout stat pro vinculo interiori. Hujusmodi autem vinculum habet causam primam, et habet causam proximam; prima est divina institutio, proxima est humana pactio, quae est in convenientia consensuum duorum, scilicet maris et feminae. Et ideo dicendum, quod consensus est causa matrimonii, sed non tota, immo cum institutione divina; consensus autem non alterius, sed utriusque personae." *Liber IV S.,* d. 27, a. 2, q. 1, conc., IV, p. 679.

[125] *Ibid.,* d. 29, dub. I, p. 704; *Ibid.,* d. 28, a. 1, q. 2, pp. 690–691.

[126] *Ibid.,* d. 29, a. 1, pp. 699–704.

[127] *Ibid.,* q. 2, pp. 701–702.

[128] *Ibid.,* d. 28, a. 1, q. 2, pp. 690–691.

[129] *Ibid.,* q. 4, pp. 692–693.

present, not of the future;[130] and the outward expression must be accompanied by sincere internal consent.[131]

It is imperative to note here that the consent necessary for the essence of marriage is not the consent to mere cohabitation or carnal copulation, but the consent to conjugal society.[132] According to our author, carnal copulation is not necessary for the integrity of marriage.[133] The consent that constitutes marriage, he tells us, is the consent by which power over each other's body is exchanged and can be expressed in the words: I accept you as my husband or wife, as the case may be.[134]

SECTION 4. THE FORMAL CAUSE OF MARRIAGE

The formal element of marriage is the *union* of two human entities, one male and the other female, for, as our author writes, matrimony is essentially a union.[135] It is the union of two sexes, i.e., of two persons of different sexes—both of whom are required for the conservation of the human race.[136] It is also, as we have seen, the joining of two diverse psychological natures. This is so, Bonaventure adds, because each is to supply the other with what is lacking in his or her make-up; each is to complement the other.[137]

---

[130] *Ibid.*, q. 1, pp. 688–689.

[131] *Ibid.*, d. 27, a. 2, q. 2, pp. 679–681.

[132] *Ibid.*, d. 28, a. 1, q. 6, f. 1, p. 695; *Ibid.*, d. 30, dub. V, p. 713.

[133] *Ibid.*, d. 26, a. 2, q. 3, pp. 669–670.

[134] " Et propterea dicendum, quod consensus, qui matrimonium facit, est consensus in mutuam suorum corporum potestatem; et hoc sonant verba, cum dicunt: accipio te in meum, vel in meam; et sic consensit Beata Virgo et Joseph.—Sed notandum est, quod aliter datur potestas corporis in contractione matrimonii, aliter in consummatione. In contractione ita datur uni, ut non possit, illo vivente, dari alii; ita etiam datur illi, ut jus habeat petendi, et necesse sit reddere petenti, nisi moriatur mundo per votum castitatis solemne et ingressum in religionem. . . . In matrimonii autem consummatione omnino transfertur potestas, ita quod nec voto privato nec solemni possit petenti debitum adversari." *Ibid.*, d. 28, a. 1, q. 6, conc., p. 696. Confer *Ibid.*, d. 29, a. 1, q. 2, f. 3, p. 701.

[135] ". . . matrimonium dicitur essentialiter et secuundum genus suum conjunctio." *Ibid.*, d. 27, a. 1, q. 1, conc., p. 676.

[136] *Ibid.*, ad 4, p. 676.

[137] Confer above, p. 138.

The formal cause of matrimony, in the teaching of the Seraphic Doctor, is the indivisible and permanent bond (the *vinculum*) which arises from the legitimate contracting of marriage. He affirms marriage to be *essentialiter* that certain obligatory bond which will not be destroyed or dissolved, even though the espoused be separated from each other in affection or in body.[138] His teaching in this regard is borne out by the fact that the *bonum* which pertains to the very essence of marriage is the *bonum sacramenti* (the inseparable union of husband and wife).[139]

Accordingly, the essence of marriage is not cohabitation or copulation, but that certain inseparable union of lives through which one spouse is bound to maintain undivided fidelity to the other. As a result of this union, the two contracting parties acquire over each other certain definite rights and are bound by certain definite obligations—both of which are permanent.[140] The obligations bind both parties; the rights belong to both; for, notwithstanding the fact that right order demands man to be superior and to have supremacy over the woman, both parties enjoy equal rights.[141]

This union of husband and wife, brought into being by the marital contract, possesses two characteristic notes which determine the specific nature of the marital union and differentiate it from every similar union—namely, stability and unity.

Regarding the stability of the matrimonial bond, Bonaventure affirms that the *vinculum* is indissoluble as long as both parties live.[142] In his mind, the indissolubility of marriage proceeds from its very institution, since God so established matrimony that both

---

[138] ". . . illa autem conjunctio, quae respicit totum conjunctum et est matrimonium essentialiter, non est affectio animorum, vel approximatio corporum, sed quoddam vinculum obligatorium, quod non perimitur, sive affectu, sive corpore separentur." *Liber IV S.,* d. 27, a. 1, q. 1, ad 4, p. 676.

[139] ". . . dicendum, quod unum est bonum principale et inseparabile, scilicet sacramentale vinculum . . ." *Ibid.,* d. 31, a. 1, q. 2, ad 4, pp. 719–720.

[140] *Liber II S.,* d. 18, a. 1, q. 1, conc., II, p. 432; *Liber IV S.,* d. 33, a. 1, q. 2, IV, pp. 749–750; *Ibid.,* q. 1, f. 3, p. 747; *Ibid.,* d. 27, a. 1, q. 2, ad 3, p. 678; *Ibid.,* conc., p. 678.

[141] *Ibid.,* d. 32, dub. I, p. 742.

[142] *Ibid.,* d. 27, a. 3, q. 1, pp. 681–682. For the indissolubility of *matrimonium ratum* but not *consummatum,* confer *Ibid.,* q. 2, pp. 683–684.

husband and wife are bound to each other as long as both of them live.[143]   Our author further deduces the indissolubility of marriage from the fact that an enduring union of husband and wife is a requisite for the proper education and development of the child.[144]

Regarding unity, our saint asserts that right reason requires man to be united with his wife and with no other.[145]   This unity, he tells us, is commanded by the natural law.   His teaching is that polygamy, much more polyandry, is contrary to the natural law accepted in the proper sense (right reason) and in the common sense (Law and Gospel).[146]   The main philosophical reason used by our author in condemning polygamy and polyandry, as well as union with any other besides the husband or wife, is based on the natural law, which demands that we do unto another as we want the other to do unto us and teaches that both husband and wife enjoy a perfect equality as regards the rights of the marital union.

Thus, Bonaventure argues, in accordance with right reason, man is set against the union of his wife with another.   However, if the natural law commands that we do unto others as we want others to do unto us and if both husband and wife enjoy identical marital rights, it follows that the husband himself may not perform that action which he detests in his wife.[147]   Further-

---

[143] ". . . sic Deus instituit, ut amplius non solvantur, dum vivunt." *Ibid.*, d. 27, a. 3, q. 1, ad 1–2, p. 682.   Confer *Ibid.*, d. 26, a. 1, q. 2, ad 4, p. 664.

[144] *Ibid.*, d. 33, a. 1, q. 1, f. 4, p. 747.—It may be noted that the arguments used by the Seraphic Doctor against polygamy can also be used in defense of the indissolubility of marriage.   His main arguments in this respect are the love and the fundamental equality that must exist between husband and wife.

[145] ". . . a dictamine rationis rectae, ut vir cum sua et non cum alia cubet muliere . . ." *Ibid.*, d. 31, a. 1, q. 2, conc., p. 719.

[146] *Ibid.*, d. 33, a. 1, qq. 1–2, pp. 747–751.   As to polyandry, confer *Ibid.*, q. 3, ad 2, p. 752.   In reference to the dispensation regarding polygamy in the Old Law, confer *Ibid.*, q. 3, pp. 751–752.

With regard to Bonaventure's teaching concerning natural law in the common, proper, and more proper sense, confer above, pp. 93ss.

[147] "Item, jus naturale dictat, quod homo quod sibi vult fieri faciat alii, et non faciat alii quod sibi non vult fieri; sed maritus secundum rectam rationem abominatur et odit, quod alius suam cognoscat uxorem; ergo etc."

more, the Seraphic Doctor appeals to the special love that should exist between husband and wife—a love which is not to be communicated to an outsider—and concludes that, because of marital love, the wife is to love no one but the husband, and the husband no one but the wife.[148]

SECTION 5.   THE FINAL CAUSE OF MARRIAGE

As we have seen before, matrimony is a *bonum in se;* consequently, no one (not otherwise legitimately impeded) can be deterred from embracing the marital state.[149] Following in the footsteps of St. Augustine, the Seraphic Doctor speaks of a threefold good in matrimony: *bonum prolis, bonum fidei,* and *bonum sacramenti.*[150] In his teaching, the good of offspring (*bonum prolis*) is the useful good (*bonum utile*) of marriage; the good of fidelity (*bonum fidei*) is its moral good (*bonum honestum*); the good of the sacrament (*bonum sacramenti*) is its delectable good (*bonum delectabile*).

A.   The Moral Good—The Good of Fidelity (Bonum Fidei)

The *bonum fidei* of marriage, as the editors of Quaracchi note, refers not to the theological virtue of faith, but to that part of

---

Ibid., d. 33, a. 1, q. 1, f. 6, p. 747. Confer *Ibid.,* q. 2, conc., p. 750. "Item, recta ratio dictat, quod vir et mulier in actu illo uniuntur et fiunt una caro, et quod actus ille est aequalitatis, quoniam similis in specie et natura; sed unio ac aequalitas non est nisi uxoris et viri, aliter non sunt aequales . . ." *Ibid.,* q. 1, f. 3, p. 747. Confer *Ibid.,* q. 2, f. 2, p. 749.

[148] "Et hoc patet experimento, eo quod in matrimonio est quidam amor singularis, in quo non communicat alienus; unde naturaliter omnis vir zelat uxorem quantum ad hoc, ut nullum diligat, ut diligit ipsum in actu illo; et omnis uxor similiter zelat virum quantum ad hoc: unde stante natura, nunquam fuisset ibi communitas, etiam si cetera essent communio." *Ibid.,* conc., p. 750.

[149] Confer above, p. 136.

[150] Augustine, *De Bono Conjugali,* c. 24, n. 32.—The Seraphic Doctor treats of the marital goods in the following places: *De Perf. Evan.,* q. 3, a. 2, conc., V, pp. 172–173; *Liber IV S.,* d. 31, a. 1, pp. 717–721; *Ibid.,* d. 26, a. 2, q. 2, conc., p. 668.

For further study, we refer the reader to Philotheus Böhner, O.F.M., "Die natürlichen Werte der Ehe nach dem hl. Bonaventura," *Franziskanische Studien,* XXIV (1937), pp. 1–17.

justice which is termed fidelity or loyalty.[151] It signifies the fidelity which husband and wife owe to each other; it means that the rights over each other's body belong solely to each other and are not to be granted to a third party.[152] Thus, the *bonum fidei* coincides, as St. Bonaventure remarks, with the dictate of right reason which commands that man be united with his wife and with no other.[153] In a word, it refers to the right use of marriage.[154]

In the teaching of our author the rightful use of the marital act is a *bonum*.[155] The intrinsic goodness of the marital act is apparent in view of the fact that without it the human race cannot be propagated. Since the propagation of the human race, which is both something good and something much to be desired, cannot take place except by generation, it follows that the act of generation must be itself good.[156] Indeed, although it is a carnal act, the Seraphic Doctor elevates the conjugal act to the sphere of spiritual honesty when it is performed in due manner and with the right intention.[157]

Furthermore, he says, the goodness of the conjugal act is so deeply rooted in nature itself that it is only because of the Fall, with its consequent corruption of man and of the sexual act, that another good, that of virginity, is placed above it. According to the teaching of the Seraphic Doctor, then, marriage and the use thereof is more perfect than virginity in the state of

---

[151] Confer Scholion on p. 718, volume IV.

[152] ". . . fides est, quod suam cognoscat et non aliam; hoc est bonum moris de se ordinatum et cadit in genere honesti." *Liber IV S.,* d. 31, a. 1, q. 1, conc., IV, p. 718.

[153] ". . . a dictamine rationis rectae, ut vir cum sua et non cum alia cubet muliere, et sic bonum fidei . . ." *Ibid.,* q. 2, conc., p. 719.

[154] ". . . ratione debiti usus est bonum fidei . . ." *Ibidem.*

[155] He expresses himself most clearly and forcefully on this point in his *De Perf. Evan.,* q. 3, a. 1, V, pp. 166–171. He here asserts that sexual intercourse in marriage is in agreement with the natural law, the written law, and the law of grace.

[156] *Ibid,* ad 7–10, p. 170; *Ibid.,* f. 13, p. 167.

[157] ". . . conjugium tantae virtutis est, quod carnale opus ad spiritualem honestatem reducit." *Ibid.,* ad 2–3, p. 169. Confer the conclusion, pp. 168–169.

original justice.¹⁵⁸   Indeed, in this state the use of marriage is
a command.¹⁵⁹   In fact, the use of marriage seems to be preferred
to virginity even in the state of fallen nature—when it is necessary for the preservation of the human race.¹⁶⁰

In the present state of affairs, however, perfect virginity is the
greater good and, therefore, is to be preferred to conjugal
purity.¹⁶¹   The main reason for the pre-eminence of virginity lies
in the fact that the marital act has been vitiated by the Fall of
man.   In the Fall, Bonaventure explains, the sexual act was
vitiated, not *ratione sui,* but by reason of the *libido* that has been
annexed to it ¹⁶²—a *libido* which engulfs reason and renders man
entirely carnal.¹⁶³   Nevertheless, the use of marriage, when performed in a just manner, with the right intention, and by the
proper parties, remains an act of pure virtue.¹⁶⁴

B.   The Useful Good—The Good of Offspring (Bonum Prolis)

The *bonum prolis,* or the good of offspring, signifies the begetting, education, and up-bringing of children; it is, our author
asserts, the useful good (*bonum conferens,* or *utile*) of mar-

---

¹⁵⁸ *Liber IV S.,* d. 26, a. 1, q. 3, ad 2, IV, p. 665.

¹⁵⁹ ". . . cum secundum statum primum multiplicatio corporalis esset con-
juncta spirituali, videtur, quod omnes tenebantur . . ." *Ibid.,* f. 4, p. 664.
Confer *Ibid.,* conc., p. 665; *Liber II S.,* d. 22, II, pp. 477–489.

¹⁶⁰ *De Perf. Evan.,* q. 3, a. 2, ad 4, V, p. 174; *Ibid.,* q. 2, a. 3, ad 3,
p. 162; *Liber IV S.,* d. 26, a. 1, q. 3, conc., IV, p. 665; *Ibid.,* ad 2, p. 665;
Ibid., f. 4, p. 664.

¹⁶¹ *Ibid.,* d. 33, a. 2, q. 2, pp. 754–755.—For a study of Bonaventure's
teaching concerning virginity and *vidualis pudicitia,* confer *De Perf. Evan.,*
q. 3, aa. 2–3, V, pp. 171–179.

¹⁶² ". . . in generatione prolis attendendum, quod duo concurrunt, scilicet
conjugalis actus et libido, et ad invicem distinguuntur; quia, si homo
stetisset, actus conjugii esset absque libidine; peccatum igitur originale non
consequitur conjugii actum ratione sui, sed ratione annexae libidinis; et
ideo ex hoc non sequitur, quod ipse sit malus, sed quod libido sit mala."
Ibid., q. 3, a. 1, ad 7, p. 170.

¹⁶³ *Liber IV S.,* d. 31, a. 2, q. 1, conc., IV, pp. 722–723; *Ibid.,* d. 26, a. 2,
q. 2, conc., p. 668.

¹⁶⁴ For further clarification of the teaching of the Seraphic Doctor concerning the use of the marital act, confer *De Perf. Evan.,* q. 3, a. 1, V,
pp. 166–171; *Liber IV S.,* d. 31, a. 2, IV, pp. 721–726.

riage.[165] By stressing the *bonum prolis,* the useful good which
is to be sought in matrimony, Bonaventure states, man is able
to avoid the *inordinatio* of concupiscence, a result of the Fall, by
which he seeks only the gratification of his sensual appetites in
the sexual act.[166] Accordingly, the good of offspring elevates the
marital union above the sphere of sensuality and renders it a
truly useful union.[167]

That the good of offspring plays an important role in Bonaventurian teaching cannot be denied. Man, he tells us, desires
the continuance of his being.[168] This instinct of self-preserva-
tion proceeds from nature, which commands that man be united
with another, in order that he may be able, by virtue of the aid
received in that union, to comply with the law demanding the
preservation of the human race.[169]

However, the good of offspring does not consist only in the
begetting of children. They must be provided for, educated,
watched over, and given opportunity for development. For this
reason, the *bonum prolis* comprises the generation of children,
their education, and their up-bringing.[170] Of greater importance
is the fact that the *bonum prolis* is not simply the generating of
an heir or the propagating of another man or the begetting of
another citizen of this earthly city, but the bringing into the
world of another man for God.[171] Our author is most emphatic
on this point. In his defense of virginity he tells us that the
marital state peoples the earth, but the state of perfect virginity

---

[165] *Ibid.,* d. 31, a. 1, q. 1, conc., pp. 717–718.

[166] *Ibid.,* d. 26, a. 2, q. 2, conc., p. 668; *Ibid.,* d. 31, a. 1, q. 2, conc., p. 719.

[167] *Ibidem.*

[168] "Est naturaliter insertus homini amor sui esse continui . . ." *De
Perf. Evan.,* q. 2, a. 3, ad 1, V, p. 162.

[169] Confer above, pp. 133–134.

[170] *Liber IV S.,* d. 33, a. 1, q. 1, f. 4, IV, p. 747.

[171] ". . . (matrimonium) institutum est ad procreandam prolem ad cultum
divinum." *Ibid.,* d. 31, dub. I, p. 727. "Utilitas autem matrimonii, quae
consistit in procreatione filiorum ad Dei cultum . . ." *De Perf. Evan.,* q.
3, a. 2, conc., V, p. 172. Confer *Liber II S.,* d. 20, a. 1, q. 1, conc., II,
p. 478; *Ibid.,* ad 3, p. 478; *Ibid.,* d. 18, a. 2, q. 1, ad 3, p. 447; *Liber IV S.,*
d. 26, a. 1, q. 3, conc., IV, p. 665; *Ibid.,* d. 30, dub. VI, p. 713.

peoples the Eternal City and, consequently, is to be preferred.[172] This divine aspect must be borne in mind—generation not simply to increase the number of men, but generation to increase the *number of the elect,* the inhabitants of the Eternal Home. Therefore, the good of offspring is the desire for a child in order to educate him in religion, to lead him to God, and to enable him to attain to his ultimate end—union with God.

C. The Delectable Good—The Good of the Sacrament (*Bonum Sacramenti*)

The *bonum sacramenti,* as the editors of Quaracchi testify, pertains not to marriage elevated to the dignity of a sacrament, but to the indissolubility of the matrimonial bond which unites husband and wife permanently.[173] It signifies that inseparable union which is of such a nature that man is to leave his father and mother and cleave to his wife in such a manner that both may in truth become two in one flesh. This, our author affirms, is the delectable good (*bonum delectabile*) of marriage.[174]

This good refers, first of all, to that unique and permanent bond that unites the espoused to each other—the bond which the Seraphic Doctor discerns in the fact that one sex was produced

---

[172] "Ad illud quod objicitur, quod omne repugnans communi utilitati est vituperandum; dicendum, quod utilitas spiritualis est praeferenda carnali, et caelestis terrenae, et caelestis superponenda est terrenae, tanquam perpetua temporali, et sicut finis praeponendus est his quae sunt ad finem. Quia igitur haec continentia—licet videatur facere ad diminutionem hominum in civitate terrena—quia facit ad accelerationem numeri electorum, plus utilitati communi consonant, quam repugnet, maxime cum plus abundet in terrenis numerus virorum carnalium quam spiritualium, ex quibus repleri valeat paradisus." *De Perf. Evan.,* q. 3, a. 2, ad 6, V, p. 174. Confer *Ibid.,* a. 3, ad 11, p. 179.

[173] Confer Scholion on p. 718, volume IV.

[174] "Bonum vero Sacramenti cadit in genere delectabilis, quia tanta est ibi unio, ut relinquat homo patrem et matrem, et sint duo in carne una; unde praecipitur viris, ut uxores diligant sicut corpora sua." *Liber IV S.,* d. 31, a. 1, q. 1, conc., IV, p. 718.

This *bonum*—the inseparable union—enables man to exclude the ennui (*fastidium*) of concupiscence which causes man to tire of one wife and seek another. Confer *Ibid.,* d. 26, a. 2, q. 2, conc., p. 668; *Ibid.,* d. 31, a. 1, q. 2, conc., p. 719.

from the other.[175]   Accordingly, it relates to that indivisible community of lives through which the spouses acquire certain definite and equal rights over each other and by which each is bound to maintain individual and lifelong fidelity to the other.[176] In a word, it connotes that lifelong society which is brought into being by the free mutual consent of the contracting parties as they give themselves to each other.[177]

In this *bonum*, then, our attention is focused upon the fact that marriage is a society, a love-society. This point is stressed by the Seraphic Doctor. Because matrimony entails servitude of the body, he observes, no one can be obliged to marry, but does so only through his own free will. For this reason, there must be mutual love between the espoused.[178] This thought is again expressed by our author in that section of his writings where he refers to the special *quietatio* that the spouses find in each other.[179]

Accordingly, it must be apparent that the love-society plays a prominent role in Bonaventurian thought. However, this love, it may be remarked, is not mere physical attraction—corporeal

---

[175] "Quia igitur forti vinculo et singulari mulier conjungitur viro et e converso, ideo unus sexus productus est de altero." *Liber II S.*, d. 18, a. 1, q. 1, conc., II, p. 432.

[176] Confer above, p. 144.

[177] Confer above, pp. 140–143.

[178] ". . . sed in matrimonio, ubi est servitus corporis, et debet esse mutuus amor, decrevit Deus, ut nullus possit nec debeat nisi propria voluntate obligari." *Liber IV S.*, d. 36, a. 2, q. 2, ad 2, IV, p. 797.

[179] "Vir enim et mulier secundum suorum sexuum proprietatem et naturam sic facti sunt, ut invicem conjungerentur, et ex hoc unus in altero quietaretur et unus ab altero sustentaretur." *Liber II S.*, d. 18, a. 1, q. 1, conc., II, p. 432.

"Est enim ibi quoddam mirabile, quia homo invenit in muliere aliquam complacentiam, quam nunquam posset in alia invenire . . ." *Liber IV S.*, d. 36, a. 2, q. 2, ad 2, IV, p. 797. Confer *Ibid.*, d. 33, a. 1, q. 2, conc., p. 750.

This point is better understood if we bear in mind that the essence of *quietatio* is fruition, i.e., that love-union between the one enjoying and the one enjoyed. "Dicendum, quod fruitio de sui generali ratione dicit amoris unionem, scilicet fruibilis cum fruente." *Liber I S.*, d. 1, dub. XII, I, p. 44. Confer *Ibid.*, a. 2, pp. 35ss.

or natural love—but, as our author avers, a social love—a human and, therefore, spiritual love—whereby the two are united and enabled to live together in amity.[180]

A further point that derives from the consideration of the indivisible marital society is the fact that the spouses find in this union, into which they enter freely, mutual aid and mutual complement. This fact appears most manifest when we consider how husband and wife aid and complement each other in the fulfillment of the instinct implanted within them—the continuance of their being—and of the natural law which commands the preservation of the human race. Moreover, as we have seen,[181] the distinction of sexes, which transcends the biological order, extends into the psychological sphere, husband and wife complementing each other from every angle. In Bonaventure's teaching, the wife, predominantly weak and passive, finds strength and support in her husband. On the other hand the husband, predominantly active, virile, and aggressive, finds repose (*quietatio*) in his wife. His natural severity and sternness are moderated by the innate tenderness and gentleness of his wife.[182]

Therefore, the *bonum sacramenti*, according to the Franciscan Doctor, is that indivisible community of lives into which the espoused, motivated by love for each other, enter freely, in order that they may be of aid to each other in the attainment of perfection in both the corporeal and super-corporeal sphere.

D. The Primary End of Marriage

Discussing the relative importance of the three goods of matrimony, our author teaches that the good of the sacrament is the chief of the marriage goods. Inseparability of common life, he

---

[180] *Liber IV S.,* d. 37, a. 2, q. 2, f. 3, IV, p. 808; *Liber I S.,* d. 10, a. 2, q. 1, conc., I, p. 201.

[181] Confer above, p. 138.

[182] " Vir enim et mulier secundum suorum sexuum proprietatem et naturam sic facti sunt, ut invicem conjungerentur, et ex hoc unus in altero quietaretur et una ab altero sustentaretur." *Liber II S.,* d. 18, a. 1, q. 1, conc., II, p. 432.

". . . vir mulieri confert robur, et mulier per viri consortium vigoratur, vir autem per mulieris consortium emollitur . . ." *Ibid.,* ad 7–9, p. 434.

tells us, is absolutely necessary, as it pertains to the very essence of marriage. Consequently, marriage cannot exist without it.[183]

With regard to the other goods (fidelity and offspring), the Seraphic Doctor explains that in one way they are needed for the very *being* of marriage and in another way they are needed solely for the *well-being* of matrimony.[184] To understand this point, we must distinguish between the *use* of marriage and the contract of marriage. If we consider the use of marriage alone, then matrimony can exist (does exist, in fact) without these goods. In point of fact, even their opposites, as daily experience points out, do not destroy the being of marriage.[185] If, on the other hand, we consider the marital contract itself, then marriage can exist without these two goods. Thus, e.g., one who is sterile, who cannot have children, can contract marriage. Should the contract itself, however, contain anything that is positively contrary to either of these goods (e.g., the intention of procuring sterility or of giving the wife over to prostitution), then there is no matrimonial contract.[186] Hence, these two goods as such do not pertain to the very essence of marriage; their absence opposes the well-being, not the being of matrimony.[187]

---

[183] ". . . unum, scilicet Sacramentum, est de necessitate matrimonii." *Liber IV S.,* d. 31, a. 1, q. 3, conc., IV, p. 720.

[184] " Sed alia duo bona quodam modo sunt de esse, quodam modo de bene esse." *Ibidem.*

[185] " Si enim loquamur quantum ad matrimonii usum, sic sunt de bene esse, quoniam usus matrimonii absque his esse potest, sicut tota die est; et non solum est absque his, sed etiam cum suis oppositis. Unde sterilitas et abortus procuratio et fidei fractio non dissolvunt matrimoniale vinculum contractum." *Ibid.,* pp. 720–721.

[186] " Si autem loquamur quantum ad matrimonii contractum, qui est per matrimonialem consensum; sic potest esse contractus absque his duobus bonis, ut puta in sterilibus et in continentibus, sed tamen non est contra haec. Tunc autem est consensus contra haec, quando sub tali pacto consentitur, ut prolis sterilitas procuretur, vel uxor alii prostituatur; tunc enim non est consensus vel pactio matrimonii . . ." *Ibid.,* p. 721.

[187] " Sed carentia sive absentia horum duorum non repugnat: quia fides venit ex recto matrimonii usu; et quia possunt homines abuti ipso, ideo potest deesse fides. Similiter proles venit ex fructu ventris; et quia steriles possunt esse vel natura, vel arte: ideo matrimonium hoc bono potest carere." *Ibidem,*

Accordingly, says St. Bonaventure, the indivisible society of husband and wife is the principal benefit of marriage and is inseparable from it, whereas the other goods are benefits annexed to it.[188]   Indeed, this first good stands so high in his estimation that it towers over the *bonum prolis,* for, he observes, even if she is fruitless, man cannot, without violating the rights of his wife, put her aside and take unto himself a second wife as long as she lives.[189]

Can we conclude, therefore, that the inseparable union of husband and wife is, in Bonaventure's mind, the primary end of marriage?   Moreover, does the teaching of the Seraphic Doctor agree with the more recent evaluation of the ends of marriage?[190]   That he does agree to a certain extent with the

---

[188] " Ad illud quod objicitur, quod superfluunt, quia unius unus finis; dicendum, quod unum est bonum principale et inseparabile, scilicet sacramentale vinculum; et alia sunt huic annexa, et nihil impedit, quod aliquid habeat unum principalem finem et plures utilitates adjunctas." *Ibid.,* q. 2, ad 4, pp. 719–720.

[189] ". . . dicendum, quod etsi natura dictet, prolem esse multiplicandam, tamen dictat: debite et ordinate, et ita quod nulli fiat injuria; et ideo magis cessandum esse a generatione prolis, quam injuriam fieri alicui; et ideo nec uxorem aliam duci." *Ibid.,* d. 33, a. 1, q. 2, ad 4, p. 750.

[190] It is not our purpose to set forth the more recent interpretation of the ends of marriage, since space limits us.   It is enough to note that "this new interpretation of the ends of marriage would have us withdraw the ofttimes exaggerated emphasis on the procreation and education of children, as the principal end of marriage, and, while not depreciating this purpose of marriage, they [the advocates of this new interpretation] would direct more attention to the perfecting of mutual conjugal love, and the mutual development of the personality of husband and wife, which would find its concrete expression in the child." Anthony L. Ostheimer, *The Family, A Thomistic Study in Social Philosophy,* The Catholic University of America, Washington, D. C., 1939, Philosophical Studies, vol. 50, p. 41.
For further study on this point we refer the reader to Ostheimer, *op. cit.,* pp. 37–54; Dietrich von Hildebrand, *Die Metaphysik der Gemeinschaft* (München, 1930); *Reinheit und Jungfräulichkeit* (München, Kösel-Pustet, 1927), English translation: *In Defense of Purity* (New York, Longmans Green, 1931); Herbert Doms, *Vom Sinn und Zweck der Ehe* (Breslau, Ostdeutsche Verlagsanstalt, 1935), English translation: *The Meaning of Marriage* (New York, Sheed & Ward, 1939); Jacques Leclercq, *Marriage and the Family, A Study in Social Philosophy* (New York & Cincinnati,

modern trend concerning the evaluation of the ends of matrimony seems to be recognized.[191] This fact appears from his insistence upon the indissoluble life-partnership of the spouses, the social aspect of marriage, the social love that the spouses should bear for each other, and the mutual aid they are to exchange.[192]

At the same time, however, the Seraphic Doctor affirms that the distinction of the sexes came into being for the purpose of generation.[193] Marriage was instituted for procreation—to increase the number of the elect.[194]

Both points are stressed by our author—the birth into the world of another man for God and the indissoluble life-partnership of the espoused. This life-long union of husband and wife is for him the principal good of marriage—that good without which there would be no marriage. Since it coincides with the *vinculum*—the inseparable bond—this good, then, is the *formal cause* of marriage. On the other hand, the offspring—man for God—is the reason *why* marriage was instituted by the Creator. Accordingly, we are convinced that Bonaventure means the *good of offspring* to be accepted as the primary purpose of marriage.

Article III.   The Family, or the Domestic Society

The mutual consent to carry on life in common and the concomitant exchange of rights give rise, as we have seen, to a true social order between two married persons. This conjugal society leads, in turn, to the founding of another social order—the domestic society, or family, which comes into being with the appearance of the child, the *bonum conferens* of the marital union. Thereupon, a parental-filial relationship is added to the

---

Frederick Pustet, 1942) (second edition) (translation from the French by Thomas R. Hanley).

[191] Ostheimer, *op. cit.,* p. 52; Doms, *op. cit.* (English edition), pp. xvi-xvii.

[192] Confer above, pp. 143–146.

[193] ". . . distinctio sexuum non est nisi propter generationem . . ." *Liber II S.,* d. 20, a. 1, q. 1, f. 3, II, p. 477.

[194] ". . . (matrimonium) institutum est ad procreandam prolem ad cultum divinum." *Liber IV S.,* d. 31, dub. I, IV, p. 727.

husband-wife relationship, and the familial society is born as the natural extension and complement of the conjugal society. Accordingly, through marriage, which binds the husband and wife in an enduring union, and the birth of the child resulting therefrom, there is brought into existence the domestic social order which comprises both the husband-wife and the parental-filial relationships.[195] As is apparent, the family is a thoroughly natural society and has its external manifestation in the range of parental operations that have to do with the procreation, education, and preservation of the children; it concerns the good of the child, who later must himself take an active part in the common life of humanity.

SECTION 1. PARENTAL AUTHORITY

The Seraphic Doctor conceives parental authority as the power of cause over effect, like the power of an author over those ideas which he has conceived and brought into existence.[196] Parental authority has its origin in the fact that the children have proceeded from the parents, that the child is the result of the procreative act by which both parents have contributed to its being.[197] The child, having received something from both parents, is *of* its parents.[198] Therefore, the superiority of the parents— due to them because they are the author and the efficient cause of their children—is inherent in the very nature of parenthood.[199]

---

[195] Most medieval scholars acknowledged the existence of three types of relationships, and, consequently, societies in the familiar or domestic society: (a) relationship of husband and wife, or conjugal society; (b) relationship of parents and children, or parental society; and (c) relationship of master and servants, or servile society. However, our purpose in the present article is to consider solely the parental-filial relationship.

[196] ". . . auctor dicit foecunditatem et plenitudinem respectu procedentium ab ipso . . ." *Liber I S.,* d. 13, dub. IV, I, p. 240.

[197] *Liber II ·S.,* d. 20, a. 1, q. 2, conc., II, p. 479.

[198] *Liber III S.,* d. 4, a. 1, q. 2, conc., III, p. 101; *Ibid.,* d. 8, a. 2, q. 3, conc., p. 196; *Liber IV S.,* d. 27, a. 1, q. 2, conc., IV, p. 678; *Ibid.,* d. 36, a. 1, q. 3, conc., pp. 794–795.

[199] "Prima superioritas competit ipsi naturae ratione sui. . . . Prima superioritati debetur obedientia filialis . . . lex naturalis dictat obedientiam filialem, sive secundum statum naturae lapsae, sive secundum statum naturae

Needless to say, then, to deny them parental authority is to deny their right of parenthood.

Though both parents enjoy authority over their offspring,[200] nevertheless the husband and father is considered the head of the household. Because of the passive element in her character, the mother, says Bonaventure, exercises her authority in submission to that of the father. Indeed, as we saw above, the Seraphic Doctor grants man a certain priority, perfection, superiority, and preeminence over woman.[201] In accord with right reason, he asserts, man must occupy the place of authority.[202] This superiority of the husband over the wife, he adds, refers in a most special manner to the rule of the home.[203]

Accordingly, Bonaventure attributes to the male parent, above all, the titles of generator, educator, and provider or benefactor of the children.[204] This supremacy of the paternal rule is due to the fact that the father, as Bonaventure teaches, is the more active principle of generation and plays the more noble role in the procreative act.[205] Although this reason is not wholly sound, since modern biology refutes this opinion, we cannot, nevertheless, deny man the supremacy of authority in the home. The saintly Franciscan, we must bear in mind, advances other reasons to establish his stand. Thus, he affirms that man should pre-

---

institutae . . ." *De Perf. Evan.*, q. 4, a. 1, conc., V, p. 181. Confer *Liber II S.*, d. 44, a. 2, q. 2, II, pp. 1007–1009.

· 200 "... jus naturale dictat quod conveniant vir et mulier in tali actu ad generationem prolis, quae utrique succedat et cui communiter praesint, et illa utrique aequaliter subsit." *Liber IV S.*, d. 33, a. 1, q. 1, conc., IV, p. 748.

201 Confer above, pp. 139–140.

202 "Nam secundum rectum ordinem non mulier viro, sed vir praeficitur mulieri tamquam caput corpori . . ." *Liber III S.*, d. 12, a. 3, q. 1, conc., III, p. 271.

203 "... vir est superior . . . quantum ad illos actus, qui respiciunt sexum virilem specialiter, scilicet quantum ad regimen domus et consimilium." *Liber IV S.*, d. 32, dub. I, IV, p. 742.

204 *Decem Praeceptis*, coll. V, n. 4, V, p. 523.

205 "... principale principium propagationis residet penes virum . . ." *Liber II S.*, d. 22, dub. I, II, p. 527. Confer *Ibid.*, d. 20, a. 1, q. 2, conc., p. 479.

side, because: (a) he is of a more stable nature;[206] and (b) he excels the woman;[207] and (c) she was made to be his help-mate, not he hers.[208]

In ascribing the supremacy of domestic authority to the father, the Seraphic Doctor does not, however, exclude the authority of the mother.   While the father, as head of the family, takes precedence, the authority of the mother, though inferior to that of the father, still remains.   Indeed, as he points out, the wife, the mother of the family, is not the *domina,* nor the *ancilla,* but the *socia,* viz., the companion of her husband.[209]   As his companion, she tends towards the same end as her associate and remains faithful to him in misfortune as well as success; as his helpmate, she aids him in the care of the household and upholds him at all times.   The mother, loving her home, becomes the associate and the helper of the father, the defender of the children, and the guarantee of peace in the domestic order.[210]

In point of fact, as the saintly son of St. Francis expresses it, the father and mother together are to constitute one sole domestic authority; the concursus and mutual aid of both, imperative for the generation of the child, are required also for the right order of the home.[211]   Therefore, there must be concord and harmony between the father and the mother of the family—in their commands and activity; otherwise, there will be in the home none of the peace and right order which are commanded by the natural law.[212]

---

[206] ". . . sexus virilis est stabilior per naturam et debet regere feminam . . ." *Liber IV S.,* d. 35, dub. II, IV, p. 789.

[207] *Liber III S.,* d. 12, a. 3, q. 1, conc., III, p. 271.

[208] ". . . mulierem educi de viro, ut ostenderetur, quod vir caput est mulieris, et quod non vir propter mulierem, sed mulier propter virum . . ." *Liber II S.,* d. 18, a. 1, q. 1, ad 3, II, p. 433.

[209] ". . . ut viri videretur esse socia, non domina, vel ancilla." *Ibid.,* d. 44, a. 2, q. 2, ad 1, p. 1008.

[210] *S. de Temp., Dom. I p. Pent.,* s. ii, IX, p. 350.

[211] ". . . ex concursu patris familias et matris familias ad disponendum regimen domus reultat una potestas, ita quod altera non sufficeret." *Liber II S.,* d. 25, p. 1, a. 1, q. 3, conc., II, p. 599.

". . . tota dispositio familiae pendet ex consensu patrisfamilias et matris-familias . . ." *Ibid.,* d. 38, a. 2, q. 2, conc., p. 893.   Confer above, ft. 80.

[212] ". . . jus naturae dictat pacem inter domesticos, sed pax in domo est

Another point worth noting with regard to parental authority is that it is, by no means, of an absolute character. This fact becomes apparent when we bear in mind, as will be noted elsewhere,[213] that this type of superiority is of such a nature that it does not entail servitude on the part of the inferior.[214] The teaching of the Seraphic Doctor appears again in his insistence that the parents may not unduly interfere with the child's inborn right to select his own state of life after he has arrived at the age when he is capable of making a prudent choice. Thus, he declares, the father cannot compel his son to marry, since the son is free to marry or not to marry.[215] Nor can he compel his son to marry a particular individual, unless there be a reasonable cause.[216] Furthermore, the parents cannot command anything that is contrary to the child's conscience and eternal salvation. Should they presume to do so, the child is not obliged to obey; in fact, he is obliged not to obey.[217] Moreover, parental authority becomes less comprehensive in scope proportionately as the child becomes more capable of taking care of himself. It ceases when the child has attained his majority, especially when he leaves the household.[218] Should the child, however, even after attaining majority, remain under the family roof and in the family circle, he is still subject in some degree to the father, who is always the head of the household.[219]

The teaching of the Seraphic Doctor in this regard seems to be as follows. The child is bound to obey only in those things

---

'ordinata imperandi obediendique concordia' . . ." *De Perf. Evan.*, q. 4, a. 1, f. 5, V, pp. 179–180.

[213] Confer infra, pp. 184ss.

[214] *Liber II S.*, d. 44, a. 2, q. 2, conc., II, p. 1008.

[215] *Liber IV S.*, d. 29, a. 1, q. 3, conc., IV, p. 703; *Ibid.*, f. 1, p. 702; *De Perf. Evan.*, q. 3, a. 2, conc., V, pp. 172–173.

[216] *Liber IV S.*, d. 29, a. 1, q. 3, conc., IV, p. 703.

[217] *Decem Praeceptis*, coll. V, n. 10, V, p. 524.

[218] " Sed filii naturales nec semper cohabitant nec semper cum parentibus habent bona indivisa, immo cum emancipantur, patrem relinquunt; et hinc est, quod non manet illud vinculum." *Liber IV S.*, d. 42, a. 2, q. 3, conc., IV, p. 876.

[219] "Obligamur ad obediendum parentibus, quamdiu utimur ipsorum bonis . . ." *Decem Praeceptis*, coll. V, p. 10, V, p. 524.

which pertain to the rule of the household and to paternal honor (*honorificentia paterna*). In other respects, he tells us, the father can counsel, but not command.[220] Thus, we discover the purpose and, also, the limit of parental authority—domestic right order and the common good of the family. The paternal rule is to direct the various members of the family in order to insure right order, peace, and harmony within the family circle.

SECTION 2. DUTIES OF THE PARENTS

Having brought another man into existence together, both parents have the obligation to preserve and protect this new life. Therefore, the Seraphic Doctor declares, the parents are not only to generate children, but also to provide for their needs and cares.[221] Indeed, the father is to provide for the material needs of the whole family.[222] The child, on his part, has the right to demand of his parents the satisfying of his needs and the supplying of vital necessities. Moreover, since the child has received his existence from the substance of the father and mother, it is just that he should be the heir to those goods which have been acquired by the parents and which represent to a certain extent their being and their labor. Accordingly, St. Bonaventure asserts that the father is to leave his earthly goods to his children.[223]

What is more, the parents must provide not only for the

---

[220] ". . . de obedientia respectu patris, dicendum, quod . . . intelligitur solum quantum ad ea quae sunt de paterna honorificentia, et quantum ad ea quae spectant ad regimen familiae. Si autem quantum ad alia intelligatur, consilium est, non praeceptum . . ." *Liber IV S.*, d. 29, a. 1, q. 3, ad 2, IV, p. 703.

[221] ". . . ergo cum judicet, virum et mulierem debere conjungi propter prolis generationem, quia ad hoc data est vis generativa; judicatur, eos ex hoc simul convenire ad prolis educationem . . ." *Liber IV S.*, d. 33, a. 1, q. 1, f. 4, IV, p. 747.—Confer *Ibid.*, d. 42, a. 2, q. 1, conc., p. 874; *Ibid.*, f. 3, p. 873.

[222] "Paterfamilias non abscondit frumenta, nec permittit, mori fame familiam suam . . ." *S. de Sanctis, De S. Nicolao*, IX, p. 478. Confer *S. de Temp., Dom. VI p. Pent.*, s. i, IX, p. 379.

[223] ". . . ipsius est filio legare bona sua . . ." *Decem Praeceptis*, coll. V, n. 4, V, p. 523. ". . . sicut patris est generare filium, ita et fovere et hereditatem relinquere . . ." *Liber IV S.*, d. 42, a. 2, q. 1, f. 3, IV, p. 873.

material needs of their offspring, but also for their education. The Seraphic Doctor demands that the parents educate their children.[224] Indeed, he uses this—the demand that both parents cooperate in the education of their child—as one of his proofs for the unity and stability of the matrimonial union.[225] Most of all, the saintly Franciscan Doctor stresses the moral education of the children. It is the duty of parents to lead their children to God—to the first Beginning and the last End of all life. Religious thoughts must be instilled into the young minds. He asks, therefore, that the mother be inspired by the Cross of Salvation in attempting to form her child's character, so that the life of Christ may fill the thoughts of her child and excite his love.[226] He requires, furthermore, that parents watch over the moral development of their young, leading them to the inculcation of good habits and the acquisition of virtues. This they should do especially during the children's infancy and youth, as the vices as well as the virtues acquired in youth usually remain throughout life.[227] Since man lives for God, argues St. Bonaventure, the task of parents in education is to make their offspring just and upright men of God—just as the purpose in generation is the propagation not simply of men, but of citizens of Heaven.[228]

SECTION 3. FILIAL OBLIGATIONS

As was briefly pointed out, the parent is not only the generator, but also the provider and educator of his offspring. In respect to his child the parent fills the role of originator, of ruler, and of benefactor. The Seraphic Doctor uncovers in this threefold relation of parent to child a threefold honor that the child must render to his parents: namely, (a) the honor of reverence, because they are his generators; (b) the honor of obedience, because they rule the domestic society; and (c) the honor of beneficence,

---

[224] ". . . pater habens filium, ipsum generat, ipsum instruit et nutrit . . ." *Decem Praeceptis,* coll. V, n. 4, V, p. 523.

[225] *Liber IV S.,* d. 33, a. 1, q. 1, f. 4, IV, p. 747.

[226] *Vitis Mystica,* c. 18, n. 1, VIII, p. 183.

[227] *S. de Sanctis, De SS. Ap. Petro et Paulo,* s. ii, IX, pp. 551–552.

[228] Confer above, p. 149.

because they are his benefactors.[229] Therefore, there are certain filial obligations which the child must perform. Some of these are of a permanent nature, while others are only temporary.

Among the permanent filial obligations is the one that commands the children to love their parents. This obligation, Bonaventure indicates, is a command of the natural law.[230] The love that man must have for his parents, our author teaches, must surpass that love that man bears for his own offspring. Even though nature, through the medium of natural love, inclines man to his own children more than to his parents, nevertheless our parents are to be loved more than our children. The reason for this, he tells us, is man's greater dependence upon his parents— the dependence of effect upon cause, which is greater than the dependence of the cause upon effect—and the fact that man has received greater benefits from his father and mother.[231]

Another permanent filial obligation is that which commands the children to honor, respect, and revere their parents.[232] This obligation, again, is commanded by the natural law.[233] Bonaventure declares the parents are to be honored and reverenced above all

---

[229] " Intellige secundum litteralem intelligentiam, quod pater nominat personam generantis, personam instruentis et personam educantis, quia pater, habens filium, ipsum generat, ipsum instruit et nutrit, et ipsius est filio legare bona sua; et secundum haec tria pater respectu filii tenet rationem originis, rationem regiminis et rationem benefactoris. Et secundum hoc debetur patri triplex honor: honor reverentiae, honor obedientiae et honor beneficentiae. Primo, dico, patri, in quantum tenet rationem originis, debetur honor reverentiae. . . . Secundo ratione regiminis debetur patri honor obedientiae. . . . Tertio debetur patri honor beneficentiae, quia tenet rationem benefactoris . . ." *Decem Praeceptis,* coll. V, nn. 4–5, V, p. 523.

[230] *De Perf. Evan.,* q. 4, a. 1, f. 1, V, p. 179.

[231] ". . . principiatum plus pendet a principio quam e converso; sed ubi est major dependentia, ibi est major inclinatio; et ubi major inclinatio, ibi major amoris conversio: cum ergo habens patrem et filium ad patrem comparatur sicut principiatum ad principium, ad filium vero sicut principium ad principiatum; videtur, quod secundum regulam amoris magis debet converti ad patrem quam ad filium." *Liber III S.,* d. 29, a. 1, q. 4, f. 4, III, p. 646. Confer *Ibid.,* f. 3.

[232] ". . . cum aliis personis debeamus beneficentiam, parentibus nostris non tantum debemus beneficentiam, sed etiam honoris reverentiam . . ." *Ibid.,* d. 37, dub. IV, p. 833.

[228] Confer above, p. 149.

other men.[234] Here, in addition, we meet with the obligation that the child has of coming to the aid and support of his parents if they should be in need.[235]

Subjection to parents and, consequently, obedience to parental authority—another filial obligation—are commanded of the child by the natural law, says St. Bonaventure.[236] This obedience, he notes, must be of a filial, not of a servile nature.[237] It is a filial obligation that is only temporary in nature. He tells us that the child must obey his parents, as they rule the household.[238] Accordingly, as he expresses it, the child is bound to obey his parents as long as he uses their goods, i.e., as long as he remains under the family roof.[239] Therefore, the obligation of obedience to parents ceases when the child, upon reaching his majority, leaves the household.[240] Furthermore, the child is not obliged to obey when the parents overstep the bounds of their authority, e.g., when they attempt to interfere with the child's inherent right to

---

[234] ". . . pater est honorandus specialiter prae aliis hominibus . . ." *Liber IV S.*, d. 42, a. 1, q. 1, f. 4, IV, p. 869.

[235] *Ibid.*, d. 33, a. 1, q. 1, f. 4, p. 747.

[236] "Pietas enim naturalis dictat, parentes esse honorandos; sed honor parentum est in exhibitione reverentiae, exhibitio autem reverentiae est obtemperando et obediendo: ergo . . ." *De Perf. Evan.*, q. 4, a. 1, f. 1, V, p. 179. Confer *Ibid*, f. 2.

[237] "Dicitur enim alter alteri esse superior aut quantum ad originem naturae, aut quantum ad dominium potentiae seu praesidentiae, aut quantum ad regimen providentiae. Prima superioritas competit ipsi naturae ratione sui, quia 'natura est vis insita rebus ex similibus similia procreans.' . . . Primae superioritati debetur obedientia filialis. . . . Hinc est igitur, quod lex naturalis dictat obedientiam filialem, sive secundum statum naturae lapsae, sive secundum statum naturae institutae." *Ibid.*, conc., p. 181.

[238] ". . . ratione regiminis debetur patri honor obedientiae . . ." *Decem Praeceptis*, coll. V, n. 5, V, p. 523.

[239] "Obligamur ad obediendum parentibus, quamdiu utimur ipsorum bonis; et debemus eis obtemperare in exercitatione actuum virtuosorum sive salubrium, in dispensatione temporalium et in subministratione obsequiorum; quid debemus vivere secundum consilium ipsorum et expendere secundum ipsorum imperium et quando, exigunt, subministrare obsequium." *Ibid.*, n. 10, p. 524.

[240] *Liber IV S.*, d. 42, a. 2, q. 3, conc., IV, p. 876. Confer above, footnote 218.

select freely his own state of life.[241] Nor is he bound to obey when they, unmindful of the superior authority of the Eternal, presume to command something that is contrary to God's law and the salvation of the child's immortal soul.[242]

The various filial obligations, finally, can be viewed as rooted in the virtue of filial piety—a part of the cardinal virtue of justice.[243] The obligation of children to filial piety, Bonaventure adds, is an obligation founded on the natural law.[244]

ARTICLE IV. THE STATE, OR THE CIVIL SOCIETY

As we peruse the writings of the Seraphic Doctor in search of his idea of the Civil Society, the most striking fact we perceive in this regard is that he treats of the state *ex professo* on only *one* occasion—if we exclude his short mention of it in the *Collationes in Hexaemeron* (in which, however, he is really concerned with what he terms the *justitiae morales*) and in the *Commentary on the Sentences* (in which he refers to the power of man over man).[245] Still, by recalling to mind the various points already brought out in our consideration of society in general and by taking into consideration the various incidental remarks he utters concerning the State, we can reconstruct a fair picture of his thought concerning civil society. Our attention in the present article will be centered about three main themes: the structure, end, and origin of the civil society.

---

[241] *Liber IV S.*, d. 29, a. 1, q. 3, IV, pp. 702–703.

[242] " Si tamen parentes aliquid velint, dicant, vel imperent, quod sit contra profectum nostrae salutis, non est ipsis in talibus pietas exhibenda. . . . Vult Dominus, quod ex affectu paterno non dimittat homo facere quod pertinet ad salutem suam." *Decem Praeceptis,* coll. V, n. 10, V, p. 524.

[243] Confer infra, pp. 250–251.

[244] " Secundum autem quod (pietas) ordinat ad parentes, adhuc etiam non tenet rationem doni, sed potius est species justitiae-virtutis, pro eo quod ad hoc ordinatur secundum regulam naturalis juris et secundum obligationem necessitatis." *Liber III S.*, d. 35, a. 1, q. 6, conc., III, pp. 785–786.

[245] *In Hex.*, coll. V, nn. 14–20, V, pp. 356–357; *Liber II S.*, d. 44, aa. 2ss, II, pp. 1005ss. The question of authority is also dealt with in *De Perf. Evan.*, q. 4, a. 1, v, pp. 179ss.

SECTION 1. STRUCTURE OF THE CIVIL SOCIETY

A. *Hierarchical Construction*

From what has already been said concerning society in general, it appears that, according to the thought of the Seraphic Doctor, the State must be hierarchically constituted.[246] As we have seen, our author recognizes three distinct orders or hierarchies—monastic, clerical, and lay—forming what he calls the ecclesiastical hierarchy.[247] In addition, the lay order, which coincides with the lay or civil section of the universal human hierarchy and can, consequently, be identified with the civil society or State, is itself hierarchically constituted. The saintly son of St. Francis distinguishes in the lay order three distinct orders or grades. These are: the *sacri principes.*, i.e., the princes or rulers of the State; the *sacri consules,* i.e., the minor officials, or, as Bonaventure expresses it, the "ministers of the ministering"; and the *sacra plebs,* i.e., the common citizenry.[248]

In the mind of our author, then, the State must be hierarchically constituted. Civil society appears as an organism in which there is a certain unity derived from oneness of nature, will, and operation;[249] and a diversity or gradation of powers, all of which contribute to the well-being of the social whole.[250] Mindful of what has been said concerning the nature of hierarchy (viz., that the superiors are to exert influence upon the inferiors),[251] we assume that the head (*princeps*) of the civil society is to direct the people (*sacra plebs*) to whom he is as the father, through the medium of his ministers and counsellors (*sacri consules*).

The interrelation and interdependence of the various grades of

---

[246] Confer above, pp. 121ss.

[247] Confer above, pp. 127ss.

[248] "In ordine laicorum est triplex ordo, scilicet sacrarum plebium, sacrorum consulum, sacrorum principum." *In Hex.,* coll., XXII, n. 18, V, p. 440.

". . . ministri ministrantium . . ." *Liber IV S.,* d. 24, p. 2, a. 2, q. 1, f. 4, IV, p. 630.

[249] Confer above, pp. 121ss.

[250] *Liber IV S.,* d. 24, p. 1, a. 2, q. 1, ad 1, IV, p. 615; *De Perf. Evan.,* q. 4, a. 1, ad 6, V, p. 182.

[251] Confer above, p. 125.

civil society are of the greatest importance, according to Bonaventure. One part of the civil society so vitally affects the other
that the goodness or evil of one grade necessarily affects the others
and, as a result, the whole social body.[252] Indeed, so intimate is
the interrelation of the three grades of civil society that Bonaventure does not hesitate to place the blame for a bad administration upon the people and, on the other hand, to impute the evils
of the subjects upon the head of the State.[253]

From the foregoing it is clear that the Seraphic Doctor requires
in every civil society one in whom is vested the supremacy of
power and authority. For example, in commenting upon the Rule
of the Friars Minor, he refers to the Minister General to whom all
Friars must be subservient and draws the pointed parallel that
without a leader no State can stand securely.[254] This oneness of
supreme head, he notes, is required by justice and the common
good, because without it dire consequences would ensue. If there
were no supreme judge to whom the final decision in all cases
might be referred, no quarrel would be terminated. Without a
supreme leader the republic would be divided against itself [255]
and destroyed, since "every kingdom divided against itself will
perish."[256] Such oneness of supremacy in the civil society is also
patent from the fact that nature requires hierarchical constitution

---

[252] "Boni enim principes habent bonos consiliarios. Et boni principes et
boni consules habent bonas plebes, quia erudiunt illas. Econtra mali principes habent malos consiliarios, et per consequens male instruunt plebes.
Malae plebes eligunt malos principes." *In Hex.*, coll. XXII, n. 18, V, p.
440.

[253] *Liber IV S.*, d. 14, dub. XIII, IV, p. 344.

[254] ". . . sine uno capite nulla respublica stare bene potest." *Exp. Super
Reg. Fr. Min.*, c. viii, n. 2, VIII, p. 427.

[255] "Civilis etiam justitia requirit, quod unus sit principalis judex, a quo
fiat causarum finalis decisio; unus etiam principalis dux et rector, a quo
fiat juris latio, ne pro divisione capitum schisma et devisio in corpore
reipublicae oriatur; et paribus contradicentibus judicibus, si nullus sit judex
supremus, numquam litigium terminetur." *De Perf. Evan.*, q. 4, a. 3, conc.,
V, p. 194.

[256] "Omne regnum in se ipsum divisum desolabitur . . ." *Com. in Ev.
Lucae*, c. xi, n. 44, VII, p. 291. St. Bonaventure's source is the *Gospel of
St. Luke*, c. xi, v. 17.

in all order.[257] However, an order cannot be hierarchically constituted unless there be one to whom all others must be subservient and obedient.[258] Consequently, in order that civil society may be hierarchically constituted (and it must be hierarchically constituted, as nature demands this of all order) there must be one in the civil society who is vested with the fullness of authority.

The same doctrine may be deduced from Bonaventure's writing on the necessity of one supreme head in the Church. As we have seen, he is very profuse on this point, arguing that the oneness of sovereign authority is postulated by justice, by the oneness of the Church herself, and by the unity that must prevail in the universal ecclesiastical society. Because of this oneness of sovereign authority, he affirms, the Church becomes more permanent, her influence grows more powerful, and she acquires greater preeminence and esteem.[259] The selfsame teaching and reasoning can be applied to the civil society by parallel.

While calling for oneness of sovereign, however, our author does not fail to recognize the fact that no one individual can of himself cope with the vast task of governing the civil community—efficaciously providing for all the needs and cares of his various subjects, supplying the manifold necessities of the State, or detecting the multiple dangers that may arise and guarding against them. Accordingly, St. Bonaventure demands the establishment of intermediate officials, who, remaining subject and obedient to the one sovereign prince, aid him in managing the civil organism, in promoting the *bonum exterius,* and in providing for the common good. The institution of the minor officials, our author adds, is demanded by right order, i.e., so that the State may be rightly ordered.[260]

---

[257] ". . . jus naturae dictat ordinem hierarchicum . . ." *De Perf. Evan.,* q. 4, a. 1, f. 7, V, p. 180.

[258] ". . . Ecclesia est una hierarchia: ergo debet habere unum praecipuum et summum hierarcham, cum ab unitate principis descendere debeat unitas principatus; sed uni et summo hierarchae ab omnibus obediendum est . . ." *Ibid.,* a. 3, f. 17, p. 192.

[259] *Ibid.,* conc., pp. 193–198.

[260] *Liber IV S.,* d. 24, p. 2, a. 2, q. 1, f. 4, IV, pp. 669–670; *Ibid.,* d. 19, a. 3, q. 1, conc. and ad 6, pp. 508–509; *De Perf. Evan.,* q. 4, a. 3, ad 13, V, p. 197.

B. *Constitutional or Mitigated Monarchy*

Insisting upon a oneness of supreme ruler in the civil society, the Seraphic Doctor necessarily favors a governmental organization that is monarchical in character. However, we would distort the teaching of our author, were we to affirm that he prefers a monarchy, pure and simple. He seems to hold that the people have a good deal to say with regard to who is to govern them.

We may uphold our stand from the fact that the saintly son of St. Francis does not hesitate to place the blame upon the people when the State is badly administered.[261] Why should he blame the people if not because they have some choice in the matter of who is to rule? The argument becomes clearer when we bear in mind that our author is openly opposed to succession of power— to that form of government in which the administration becomes the right of a certain family. Thus, speaking of the *norma praesidendi* (i.e., the relations that should exist between the ruler and his subjects), our saint avers that societies which are ruled by leaders who have been designated through heredity are generally governed badly; this type of ruler, he says, administers society according to his personal interests and not the common good. On the other hand, he argues, those societies which are governed by rulers *elected* by the people are far better regulated.[262] To show his point he appeals to the history of the Roman people and remarks that the Roman Empire was well-governed when the Romans elected their rulers, whereas such was no longer the case when their rulers were designated by heredity.[263]

Accordingly, the Franciscan Doctor favors elected leadership, as being more conducive to a well-regulated society and to the promotion of the common good. This doctrine is deserving of special attention and emphasis. Basing his conception of the civil society on the example of the Church (such is our opinion), Bonaventure demands a governmental structure which is both

---

[261] ". . . punitus est populus . . . propter connexionem populi ad principem . . ." *Liber IV S.,* d. 14, dub. XIII, IV, p. 344.

[262] *In Hex.,* coll. V, n. 19, V, p. 357.

[263] "Unde quamdiu Romani illos qui praeessent, elegerunt, sapientissimos elegerunt; et tunc bene gubernata est respublica; sed postquam ad successionem venerunt, totum fuit destructum." *Ibidem.*

monarchical and constitutional in its administration—a government in which the prince who is to rule over all is elected to office through the will of the people.

C. No Absolute Authority

The Seraphic Doctor has not failed to emphasize the fact that civil authority is by no means absolute. In the first place, the authority of the civil order, inasmuch as it is authority, proceeds from God, from Whom is all authority.[264] Coming as it does from God and being merely given to the ruler, his authority, then, can by no means be absolute in its origin. Wherefore, the saintly Franciscan recalls the words that Christ addressed to Pilate: "Thou wouldst have no power at all over me were it not given thee from above." [265]

The non-absolute character of civil authority is also seen in the fact that it has been given to the ruler for a definite purpose—to provide for the utility of those living together in society by conserving right order and thus enabling men to live together in harmony and peace.[266] Hence, the ruler is not free to administer. the affairs of the state according to his own personal pleasure or for the sake of his own private gain. Rather, as ruler, he is bound to foster orderly living, so that the common good of all may be promoted. The ruler who fails in this respect is, according to the Seraphic Doctor, a *tyrant*.[267]

This point of our author's doctrine becomes more apparent when he champions the right of the people to overthrow the sovereign who abuses the power given to him. If, says St. Bonaventure, right order is not preserved, but perverted and

---

[264] *Liber II S.,* d. 44, a. 2, q. 1, II, pp. 1005ss. Confer art. 1 of the following chapter in which the question of authority will be considered in detail.

[265] *Gospel of St. John,* c. 19, v. 11; *Liber II S.,* d. 44, a. 2, q. 1, f. 1, II, p. 1005.

[266] *Ibid.,* q. 2, ad 4, p. 1009. Confer the article on authority.

[267] ". . . princeps non debet suam utilitatem quaerere, sed reipublicae. Philosophus dicit (*Ethics,* lib. viii, c. 10), quod differt tyrannus et princeps: tyrannus quaerit propriam utilitatem . . . princeps autem communem utilitatem intendit." *In Hex.,* coll. V, n. 19, V, p. 357.

destroyed, then justice (*juris rectitudo*) acknowledges that the ruler who has brought about such a state of affairs deserves to lose his authority and power.[268] There are those who object that what comes from God cannot be taken away and that, therefore, the authority of the civil ruler, which comes from God, cannot be taken away. The Seraphic Doctor answers that the objection is true only when that which is given by God is given in an absolute manner. Such, however, is not the case with regard to the authority invested in the ruler. This, he says, has been given in such a manner that it can be taken from the ruler should the law of justice so demand. Instituting a comparison between the authority bestowed on the ruler and the life granted to man, St. Bonaventure notes that although God gave life to the criminal, nevertheless, because the law of justice so commands, the judge may justly take it away from him. The same, he states, is true of the authority given to the ruler; according to the rectitude of law, he who abuses the power bestowed on him merits to have it taken from him.[269] In our author's mind, therefore, not only those who usurp authority, but also those who exercise their lawful authority unjustly, deserve to be deposed.[270]

This teaching can be deduced again from the fact that while affirming subjects must be obedient to their rulers the Seraphic Doctor reminds us that this obligation ceases in things which are against God, against conscience, and against right reason. " Christians," he writes, " are bound to obey their earthly lords— not, however, in all things, but only in those things that are not

---

[268] *Liber II S.*, d. 44, a. 2, q. 1, ad 5, II, p. 1006.

[269] " Ad illud quod objicitur, quod nihil quod est a Deo datum, est auferendum; dicendum, quod illud verum est, si Deus simpliciter ei dedit; si autem solum ad tempus datum est, sicut Dominus voluit dare, ita etiam voluit per ministerium humanum auferre. Hoc autem cognoscimus, quod Deus velit, quando videmus, ordinem justitiae sic exigere. Deus enim dedit vitam latroni, et tamen judex juste illam aufert ei, exigente hoc mandato justitiae, quo dicitur: Maleficum non patieris vivere. Sic etiam intelligendum est se habere in potestate nostra et principum, quia secundum juris rectitudinem tam dominium quam potestatis privilegium meretur amittere qui concessa sibi abutitur potestate." *Ibidem.*

[270] *Com. in Ecc.*, c. x, v. 7, q., conc., and ad 3, VI, p. 82.

against God."[271] Nor is this the only limitation, for he adds that they are bound to obey only in those things that are reasonably ordered, such as tributes, taxes, and the like.[272]

Thus, it is apparent that those constituted in authority, themselves bound by the eternal law, cannot command whatever they please. In fact, should they command anything that is against God, then, as our author affirms, the subjects, besides not being bound, are actually forbidden to obey.[273] Indeed, the ruler who commands something against the Eternal is abusing the power given to him and therefore deserves to have it taken away from him.[274]

Finally, the non-absolute character of the State and civil power is again obvious in the fact that the constituent elements of the civil organism are persons. The person, as we have seen, is above all things created—ordered immediately to God, as to its sole end; and society is for man—a means whereby he may the more efficaciously attain God—and not man for society.[275] It must follow, then, that those constituted in authority are not to command or do anything that is detrimental to man's exalted dignity as a person or to uphold the State as the end of man.

From these considerations it is easy to see that our author calls for a civil society that is organically and hierarchically constituted. He envisions a society in which we have a gradation of powers—*sacra plebs, sacri consules,* and *sacri principes.* He wants a society in which the various grades work hand in hand

---

[271] " Christiani terrenis dominis sunt obligati, non tamen in omnibus, sed solum in his quae non sunt contra Deum . . ." *Liber II S:,* d. 44, a. 3, q. 1, conc., II, p. 1010.

[272] " Et ideo concedendum est, quod Christiani sunt terrenis dominis obligati, non tamen in omnibus, sed in his solum, quae non sunt contra Deum; nec in his omnibus, sed in his quae secundum rectam consuetudinem rationabiliter statuta sunt, sicut tributa et vectigalia et consimilia." *Ibid.,* p. 1001.

[273] ". . . tali justum est subesse in his quae spectant ad justitiam; sed in his quae contra Deum sunt, non debet homo subesse . . ." *Com. in Ecc.,* c. x, v. 7, q., conc., VI, p. 82.

[274] ". . . et 'quia privilegium meretur amittere qui concessa sibi abutitur potestate,' etsi juste ingressus fuerit; tamen justum est, eum amoveri." *Ibidem.*

[275] Confer above, p. 121.

for the promotion of the common good. Moreover, St. Bonaventure insists that the supremacy of civil authority is to be vested in one individual, who is to act as the head of the State; that the leader is to be elected by the people; and that his power is to be, by no means, absolute. Therefore, he demands a government in which the needs and desires of the people are taken into consideration and respected; an administration in which there reigns among the various grades perfect uniformity of nature, purpose, and operation;[276] a government that is monarchial yet constitutional—in a word, a mitigated monarchy.

SECTION 2.   THE END OF THE STATE

Treating of the authority of rulers and of the purpose or end of their power, the Seraphic Doctor cites the words of St. Paul to Timothy.[277] The Apostle tells Timothy to pray for princes, so that under their control and guidance men may enjoy order, peace, and tranquillity.[278] Therefore, reasons St. Bonaventure, it is the duty and purpose of those constituted in authority to promote the utility of the living, to foster peaceful and harmonious relations among men, and to protect right order.[279] The end of the State, therefore, is apparent.

First of all, because the civil organism is essentially terrestrial and temporal, its purpose is to establish right order in the temporal sphere and thereby to provide for the common material welfare of all the individuals as such and of the society as a whole.[280] It is for this reason—the preservation of right order—that St. Bonaventure gives the rector of civil society coercive power— *potestas coercendi subditos.*[281] For, after all, if an individual member of society can, by the abuse of his free will, disturb and

---

276 Confer above, pp. 117ss.

277 *Liber II S.,* d. 44, a. 3, q. 1, ad 4, II, pp. 1011–1012.

278 *First Epistle of St. Paul to Timothy,* c. ii, v. 2.

279 *Liber II S.,* d. 44, a. 2, q. 2, conc., II, p. 1008; *Ibid.,* ad 4, p. 1009.

280 ". . . in laicis . . . ordo attenditur quantum ad potestatem terrenam, quae respicit bona naturae vel fortunae specialis personae vel reipublicae . . ." *Liber IV S.,* d. 24, p. 1, a. 2, q. 2, ad 3, IV, p. 617; *Ibid.,* d. 40, a. 1, q. 3, conc., p. 852.

281 *Liber II S.,* d. 44, a. 2, q. 2, conc., II, p. 1008; *Ibid.,* ad 4, p. 1009.

pervert the order which the rector of the society is seeking to establish and preserve, it is only just that the latter should have the power to prevail upon this individual and constrain him to the observance of right order, so as not to place the common good of all in jeopardy.[282] It is the common good of all that Bonaventure stresses. This being the end of society, it is the duty of the civil authority to foster it. In fact, the same rule— seek the common good—is to govern the activities of both the ruled and the ruling.[283]

The purpose of the civil society becomes even more manifest when we stop to consider Bonaventure's insistence on the political virtues—the virtues needed to promote the common good of all.[284] The influence of these virtues in the social field is indeed great, for they foster harmonious social relations. As a matter of fact, it is only through these virtues or through men imbued with these virtues that we can arrive at the various conditions necessary for harmonious living, true peace, and right order. Hence, the saintly Doctor tells us:

> " Through the medium of these virtues good men are enabled to support the commonwealth and defend the cities; to revere parents, love children, and esteem neighbors; to provide for the welfare and well-being of the citizens; to protect fellow-citizens by considerate

---

[282] " . . . decet rectorem in subditis servare debitum ordinem: si ergo homo per libertatem suae voluntatis poterat inordinari, opportunum et convenientissimum fuit, ipsum ad rectum ordinem astringi." *Liber III S.,* d. 37, a. 1, q. 1, f. 2, III, p. 813. Confer *Liber II S.,* d. 44, a. 2, q. 2, ad 4, II, p. 1009.

[283] " Tertia est norma praesidendi, id est qualiter princeps ad populum debet se habere, et e converso. Et haec emanat a veritate prima; quia populus debet assistere punienti et vindicanti; princeps non debet suam utilitatem quaerere, sed reipublicae." *In Hex.,* coll. V, n. 19, V, p. 357. Confer Tinivella, *op. cit.,* p. 183.

[284] The virtues referred to, of course, are the cardinal virtues—prudence, fortitude, temperance, and justice—to which has been assigned the task of rendering man rightly ordered for a life in common with his fellows. (*Liber III S.,* d. 33, dub. V, III, p. 730.) The Franciscan Doctor discusses them in detail, in so far as they affect political life, and goes on to enumerate the various auxiliary virtues that proceed from them. (*In Hex.,* coll. VI, n. 29, V, p. 364.)

foresight and to become united with them through just liberality; to make others mindful of them through the conferring of benefits upon them." [285]

Needless to say, a society based on these virtues would be conducive to the greatest possible joy here on earth—true peace, real tranquillity, perfect harmony, concord, and order.

However, as the Seraphic Doctor never considers man without seeing in him his last end, God, it is necessarily Bonaventure's teaching that all societies in general, as their ultimate and final purpose, must enable man to follow his supreme destiny. So, too, for this reason, with civil society. St. Bonaventure is explicit on this point, stating that it is the duty of those constituted in authority to lead their subjects to eternal life.[286] That the civil society must promote the eternal welfare of man is apparent also from the *ritus colendi*, which the holy Doctor advances as the first of the moral justices to be inculcated by the political laws.[287] Consequently, if the State is to provide that the *ritus colendi* be observed, we must conclude that the purpose of the civil society is not simply the common temporal welfare; the State must also foster the common spiritual well-being. This it must do not only by allowing the individuals to honor and reverence their Creator, but also by *demanding* that this " sacrifice of praise " be offered by supplying those things necessary for it, and, what is more, by punishing those who refuse to revere their God.[288]

SECTION 3.   ORIGIN OF THE STATE

An attempt to determine the thought of our author concerning

---

[285] "His boni viri reipublicae consulunt, urbes tuentur; his parentes venerantur, liberos amant, proximos diligunt; his civium salutem gubernant; his socios circumspecta providentia protegunt, justa liberalitate devincunt, hisque 'sui memores alios fecere merendo.'" *Ibid.,* n. 28, p. 364.

[286] ". . . finis autem officii regiminis est commissos sibi ad vitam aeternam dirigere et ad similia virtutum merita fideliter promovere." *De Sex Alis.,* c. v, n. 4, VIII, p. 141.

[287] *In Hex.,* coll. V, n. 14, V, p. 356.

[288] "Sacrificium autem laudis in corde naturale judicatorium dictat, et est de dictamine naturae; et in hoc consenserunt omnes veri philosophi. Unde dicit ille, quod 'qui dubitat, utrum parentes honorandi sunt, et Deus venerandus, poena dignus est.'" *Ibid.,* n. 17, pp. 356–357.

the origin or the efficient cause of civil society is not without its difficulties. First of all, the saintly Franciscan has not, as far as we have been able to discover, taken this question into consideration—i.e., he has not done so explicitly and directly. Furthermore, his teaching is rendered confused by the writings of certain authors, chief among whom is Zeiller.[289]

Arguing from Bonaventure's doctrine that the *potestas coercendi subditos* is natural only to the state of fallen nature—that it did not exist in the state of original justice and would not have come into existence if man had not fallen from his pristine innocence— Zeiller concludes that the state, according to the teaching of the Seraphic Doctor, is a result of the condition of sin.[290]

The conclusion of Zeiller is not licit. It would have been licit only if the coercive power were an essential constitutive element of civil society in the sense that the State could not exist without it. Let us recall that we must distinguish between the origin of the State and the origin of civil authority. They are two entirely distinct questions, which must be kept distinct in order to grasp a full understanding of either or both. Again, a second distinction must be kept in mind—viz., on the one hand coercive power, which alone is proper to the state of sin, and on the other hand those kinds of authority which existed before the Fall.[291]

In concluding that the State is proper only to sinful man because the *potestas coercendi subditos* exists solely in the state of fallen nature, Zeiller failed in both respects. He did not, first of all, keep the two distinct questions—origin of civil society and origin of civil authority—distinct. Secondly, in his concentration upon the *potestas coercendi subditos* (which, though proper only to the state of fallen nature, is after all but *one* type of authority of man over man), Zeiller overlooked the fact that in Bonaventure's teaching a certain authority of man over man would always have existed among men considered as wayfarers (*in statu viae*),

---

[289] Zeiller, J., *L'idee de l'Etat dans saint Thomas d'Aquin.* Paris, Alcan, 1910.

[290] *Op. cit.,* pp. 70, 123, 125.

[291] This will be dealt with in detail in the first article of the following chapter.

whether in the state of original justice or in the state of original sin.[292]

The teaching of the Seraphic Doctor demands in every type of created order some kind of authority and submission—a demand made by nature itself. His insistence upon this point appears in the various places in which he refers to the need of a hierarchically constituted order in which the inferior must be subject to the superior. We find this point stated most forcefully and explicitly in his *Q. D. De Perfectione Evangelica,* where he shows that the submission of man to man is not contrary to natural law, but is actually demanded by it.[293] Some kind of authority, therefore, is demanded in all orders, hierarchies, or societies—irrespective of the status of man. That this authority, however, is of a coercive nature, so that the ruled become in actuality servants or slaves and the ruler becomes a lord and master, is due to the fallen and corrupt nature of man.[294]

Accordingly, contrary to the teaching of Zeiller, who denies at least implicitly that the origin of civil society, in the mind of the Seraphic Doctor, is based on human nature, we insist with St. Bonaventure that the institution of the political order, far from being attributed exclusively to fallen nature, proceeds from man's own social nature and answers to a command of the natural law.[295]

As we saw when we considered society in general, the efficient cause of all society is the free will of man acting in accordance with the social nature given to him by the Eternal Maker.[296] Thus, we may again rightly conclude that the State is brought into

---

[292] " Dum durat mundus, Angeli Angelis, homines hominibus, praeerunt ad utilitatem viventium; sed omnibus collectis, jam omnis praelatio cessabit, quia necessaria non erit." *De Perf. Evan.,* q. 4, a. 1, conc., V, p. 181. Confer the whole of this article and *Liber II S.,* d. 44, a. 2, q. 2, II, pp. 1007ss.

[293] Q. 4, a. 1, V, pp. 179–183.

[294] *Liber II S.,* d. 44, a. 2, q. 2, II, pp. 1007ss; *De Perf. Evan.,* q. 4, a. 1, V, pp. 179ss. Confer article 1 of the following chapter.

[295] Legowicz, though he appears a little hesitant, brings this forth in opposition to Zeiller. He does so by appealing to the fact that St. Bonaventure teaches that man is by nature a social entity. Confer *op. cit.,* pp. 207–217.

[296] Confer above, pp. 119–120,

being by man's free will acting in conformity with his rational and social nature. Since it is inborn in the very nature of man that he live in society, civil society cannot be an institution demanded by the sin of the first man, but it is a natural institution. It is natural in the sense that it is not simply according to nature, but from nature; for it is human nature, or, better still, God, the Author of human nature, Who commands man to live in society. The origin of the State, therefore, is to be sought in man's social nature and in God, the Author of human nature.

CHAPTER V

SOCIAL FORCES AND INSTITUTIONS

Our purpose in this fifth and final chapter is to explain, as concisely as we can, the teaching of the holy Franciscan Doctor with reference to authority, wealth, and the virtues—i.e., the manner in which these factors and institutions influence the social life of man.

Article I. Authority

SECTION 1. THE DIVINE ORIGIN OF AUTHORITY

First and foremost in the mind of our author is the divine origin of authority. In order to have a true understanding of his teaching, we must, together with the Seraphic Doctor, distinguish between the virtue of power, or authority in itself, and the person in whom this authority resides, or the manner in which authority is acquired and used.[1] Accordingly, there are three points that must be kept distinct: (a) authority in itself, i.e., inasmuch as it is authority; (b) the manner of acquiring authority; and (c) the manner of exercising it. In itself, authority is always good and from God. The acquisition and exercise of authority, on the other hand, may be evil and only permitted by God.[2]

Our author next mentions three ways in which authority may be acquired; namely, by justice, by cunning, and by violence.[3] If we consider authority which has been justly acquired—i.e., *ex*

---

[1] " Illud autem, per quod praesidet, dupliciter potest dici: uno modo dicitur ipsa virtus, per quam quis praevalet alteri, et haec virtus absque dubio a Deo est; alio modo illud, per quod praesidet, dictur modus deveniendi vel permanendi ad hanc virtutis excellentiam . . ." *Liber II S.*, d. 44, a. 2, q. 1, conc., II, p. 1005.

[2] *Ibid.*, pp. 1005–1006.

[3] " Nam quidam praesunt aliis ex justitia, quidam ex astutia, et quidam ex violentia." *Ibid.*, p. 1005.

justitia—there is, then, no doubt concerning its divine origin, both in regard to the one who possesses it and in regard to those over whom this authority is exercised.[4] Apropos of authority acquired by astuteness, violence, or any other unjust means, the question becomes slightly complicated. A distinction must be made; we must consider such authority from the viewpoint of the one over whom it is exercised and from the viewpoint of the one who exercises it. Considered from the viewpoint of the subjects, it is just—because it is either for the trial of the good or for the punishment of the wicked; thus, we can say that it comes from God, *a Deo faciente et ordinante*. Considered from the viewpoint of the ruler, who has unjustly acquired it, however, such authority is necessarily unjust and is only permitted by God—after the manner in which He permits sin in the world.[5]

For this reason we can hold with St. Bonaventure, that all authority, inasmuch as it is authority and in so far as the subjects are concerned, is just and comes from God. On the other hand, the manner of acquiring authority—i.e., authority considered in the ruler—can be either just or unjust. If it is just, it comes from God; if unjust, it is simply permitted by God. Therefore, although the possession of authority may be unjust on the part of the ruler, it is never so *in se* or with reference to the ruled. Hence our conclusion with the Seraphic Doctor, that all authority, without exception, has in some way or other its origin in God.[6]

---

[4] "Quando autem praeest aliquis aliis per justitiam, tunc illa potestas dominandi, simpliciter loquendo, a Deo est et respectu praesidentis et respectu subjacentium." *Ibidem.*

[5] "Quando autem praeest aliquis per astutiam, vel per violentiam, tunc dicendum est, quod talis potestas et habet comparari ad voluntatem praesidentis, et habet comparari ad meritum subjacentis. In comparatione ad meritum subjacentis talis praesidentia justa est, quia aut est ad bonorum probationem, aut ad malorum punitionem. Si autem comparetur ad voluntatem praesidentis; sic injusta est. Et primo quidem modo dicitur esse a Deo faciente et ordinante. . . . Secundo autem modo, scilicet in comparatione ad voluntatem praesidentis, sic dicitur esse a Deo permissive, non autem approbatorie . . ." *Ibid.*, p. 1006.

[6] "Concedendum est igitur, quod omnis potestas praesidendi secundum id quod est, et etiam respectu ejus super quem est, justa est et a Deo est. . . . Concedendum est nihilominus, quod modus deveniendi ad hanc praesidentiam

The saintly Franciscan takes up the position of unjust rulers in his *Commentary on Ecclesiastes*. Here he distinguishes between three types of unjust rulers. We have on the one hand the ruler who is unjust in himself—i.e., who lives an immoral life—but has attained to his office in a lawful manner and justly exercises it. Such a one, our author notes, can lawfully rule, and the subjects may licitly obey him and should.[7] In this connection he affirms that it is not an evil to society to have in places of authority evil men who rule well.[8]

In the second place, there are those who have unjustly usurped their authority and exercise it in an unjust manner. These, he tells us, cannot lawfully preside; nor should man be subject and obedient to them.[9]

In the third place are those who, having acquired their positions of authority in a lawful manner, administer this power in an unjust manner—harming the good and promoting the evil. With regard to these, Bonaventure teaches that it is just to be subject to them in what is lawful; in those things, however, that are not lawful no man may obey them.[10] Here we find the

---

in comparatione ad voluntatem praesidentis potest esse justus et injustus; et secundum quod justus est, a Deo est, secundum quod injustus est, a Deo non est. Quia vero numquam est ita injustus ex una parte, quin sit justus ex altera; ideo de nulla potestate praesidendi dici potest, quod non procedat a Deo." *Ibidem.*

[7] " Respondeo : dicendum, quod malus vel injustus praelatus est sub triplici differentia. Quidam est injustus in se, tamen juste ingreditur et juste exsequitur; et talis juste praeesse potest . . . et justum est tali subesse." *Com. in Ecc.,* c. x, v. 7, q., conc., VI, p. 82.

[8] ". . . dicendum, quod malos, qui bene regunt, praeesse, non est malum reipublicae . . ." *Ibidem.*
Faced with the objection that for the ignorant to preside over the wise and the evil over the good is against right order, the Seraphic Doctor answers that while a certain disorder does appear, nevertheless behind such apparent disorder is concealed the beautiful order of the Eternal whereby the good are tried and the evil punished. *Liber II S.,* d. 44, a. 2, q. 1, ad 3, II, p. 1006.

[9] " Est et alius, qui injuste ingreditur et exsequitur; et talis non potest juste praeesse, nec tali debet homo subesse." *Com. in Ecc.,* c. x, v. 7, q., conc., VI, p. 82.

[10] " Est et alius, qui injustus est, sed tamen juste ingreditur, sed injuste exsequitur, quia affligit bonos et promovet malos; tali justum est subesse

Seraphic Doctor distinguishing between the power that the ruler has received from God and the exercise of this power by the ruler. Since the ruler has authority from God, he is to be obeyed. Because he exercises this power unjustly, he can, on the other hand, be removed.[11] Accordingly, St. Bonaventure teaches that this type of ruler may be deprived of his authority, even though he has attained it in a lawful manner, for he who abuses the power committed to him deserves to lose it.[12]

SECTION 2. THE NECESSITY OF AUTHORITY AND SUBMISSION

As we seek to penetrate the thought of the Seraphic Doctor in regard to the necessity for authority and the submission thereto, we must first of all recall that, according to his teaching, certain commands of the natural law refer to all states of human existence. These are the absolute commands of the natural law. An example of this sort of command is the one which demands that honour be rendered to God. Other commands of the natural law, however, refer only to a certain state of human existence. These may be termed relative precepts of the natural law—relative to a certain condition of man. Thus, for example, that everything must be possessed in common is a command of the natural law which refers to man in the state of original justice; whereas, that things should be possessed privately is a command of the natural law which concerns the state of fallen nature.[13]

---

in his quae spectant ad justitiam; sed in his quae contra Deum sunt, non debet homo subesse . . ." *Ibidem.*

Here again—in the fact that those who rule badly are in places of authority—we find the Divine plan concealed behind apparent disorder. Confer *Ibidem* and *Liber II S.,* d. 44, a. 2, q. 1, ad 3, II, p. 1006.

11 ". . . talem potestatem habuit a Deo, sed exsecutionem a se; potestatem habuit juste, sed exsequitur injuste: et ideo quamdiu a Deo habet potestatem, est obediendum; sed quia injuste exsequitur, ut non habeat, est laborandum." *Com. in Ecc.,* c. x, v. 7, q., ad 3, VI, p. 82.

12 ". . . et 'quia privilegium meretur amittere qui concessa sibi abutitur potestate,' etsi juste ingressus fuerit; tamen justum est, eum amoveri." *Ibid.,* conc., p. 82.

13 ". . . quaedam sunt de dictamine naturae simpliciter; quaedam de dictamine naturae secundum statum naturae institutae; quaedam de dictamine

We meet this dual role of the natural law again in Bonaventure's teaching concerning the authority that one man possesses over another. First, the natural law commands in a certain manner that there must be a certain gradation in all states of human existence and a resultant certain superiority and inferiority among humans. Second, the natural law calls for a different type of superiority and inferiority dependent upon the different conditions of human existence. Therefore, the present section will be divided into two parts; the first is concerned with the general command of the natural law, and the second with the various kinds of authority and submission demanded by the various conditions of human nature.

A. The General Precept of Authority and Submission

As we have seen, the Seraphic Doctor demands that all order—consequently, also society—must be hierarchically constituted.[14] This requisite, he tells us, arises out of the natural law.[15] Hierarchy, however, demands a certain gradation of powers, offices, and dignities in the social organism—in other words, it postulates social gradation and inequality. In so doing, hierarchy also makes imperative the submission of the inferior to the superior. Therefore, Bonaventure concludes, in demanding a hierarchically constituted order, natural law demands the subjection of the inferior to the superior.[16] Thus, as our author remarks, in

---

naturae secundum statum naturae lapsae. Deum esse honorandum, dictat natura secundum omnem statum; omnia esse communia, dictat secundum statum naturae institutae; aliquid esse proprium, dictat secundum statum naturae lapsae ad removendas contentiones et lites." *Liber II S.*, d. 44, a. 2, q. 2, ad 4, II, p. 1009. Confer *De Perf. Evan.*, q. 4, a. 1, conc., V, p. 181.

[14] Confer above, pp. 106–110; 121–133; 165–167.

[15] *De Perf. Evan.*, q. 4, a. 1, f. 7, V, p. 180.

[16] ". . . jus naturae dictat ordinem hierarchicum, qui descendit a summa hierarchia per angelicam usque ad humanam; sed ordini hierarchico consonat, quod inferior superiori obtemperat; ergo . . ." *Ibidem.*

". . . jus naturale dictat, gradum esse servandum, 'quia, si essent omnia aequalia, non essent omnia'; ubi autem gradus, ibi est superioritas et inferioritas; sed si inferius non subjaceat superiori, non servatur gradus: ergo . . ." *Ibid.*, f. 6, p. 180.

commanding submission and obedience to the superior the natural law, as must appear, also commands a certain superiority, authority, or precedence.[17]

We find this teaching stated most clearly and forcefully in his *Q. D. De Perfectione Evangelica*.[18] In this treatise St. Bonaventure, defending the religious life and the vow of obedience against the *murmurantes* of the time (*modo speciali*, William of Saint-Amour),[19] shows that the subjection of man to man is not against the natural law, but that this same natural law actually demands the inferior to be subject to the superior.[20] This requirement is, according to the thought of our author, in perfect accord with man's rational nature; for, as right reason demands the subordination of the lower faculties to the higher in the individual man, it must likewise ordain the subordination of the inferiors to the superiors in the social life.[21]

The arguments employed by the saintly Doctor to prove his point are many and various. Natural law, he tells us, calls for order, which is the disposition whereby each thing attains to its proper place. Consequently, if it is of the nature of the superior to preside and of the inferior to be submissive and obedient, then the natural law which demands order likewise commands the obedient submission of the inferior to the superior.[22] He comes to the same conclusion from the natural injunction placed upon man, viz., that he live in peace and harmony. This condi-

---

[17] ". . . dicendum, quod sicut lex naturae dictat subjectionem, sic et praelationem. Sicut enim dictat, quod quis debet subjici alteri ad obedientiam; sic dictat, quod alter debet praefici alteri per providentiam." *Ibid.*, ad 8, p. 182.

[18] Q. 4, a. 1, V, pp. 179ss.

[19] Confer the Prologomena to vol. V, pp. vi–viii, where the editors of Quaracchi prove that this "*quaestio disputata*" was written against William of Saint-Amour.

[20] ". . . lex naturalis, quae manat a lege aeterna, naturaliter dictat, quod inferior superiori obediendo subjaceat . . ." *De Perf. Evan.*, q. 4, a. 1, conc., V, p. 181.

[21] ". . . de dictamine juris naturalis est, quod homo totus obediat rationi rectae in se: ergo pari ratione jus naturae dictat, quod minus peritus et ignorans obediendo subjaceat magis perito et scienti: ergo videtur, quod homo obtemperet homini, consonum esse juri naturali." *Ibid.*, f. 10, p. 180.

[22] *Ibid.*, f. 4, p. 179. Confer *Ibid.*, conc., p. 181.

tion, however, cannot obtain without submission to authority, since peace is the ordered harmony of command and obedience. Accordingly, the natural law, in commanding peace and harmony also commands submission to authority.[23] Moreover, the law of nature requires that honor, respect, and obedience be rendered to parents.[24] As our saint points out in his *Collationes De Decem Praeceptis*, all persons vested with authority bear the title of father.[25] Therefore, this injunction of the natural law is to be extended to the obedience and reverence due to all those lawfully constituted in places of authority.

There can be no doubt concerning our author's thought. In his teaching, the natural law, which proceeds from the eternal law, naturally dictates (in a certain general manner) that the inferiors be submissive and obedient to the superiors.[26] As long as the world remains, he tells us, angels will preside over angels and men will preside over men. The reason for this, he avers, is the "*utility of the living.*"[27] Furthermore, this obedience and submission, he adds, is in agreement not only with the natural law, but also with the written law and the law of grace,[28] which, as we have seen, are nothing else but more explicit and more perfect determinations of the natural law.[29]

B. Different Types of Authority and Submission, Corresponding to the Different Conditions of Man

The Seraphic Doctor, we have learned, teaches that the natural law in a general manner directs men to be submissive and obedient to their superiors. This submission and obedience, he points out, is prescribed in different ways according to the different types of superiority and inferiority that correspond to the different states of man.[30] From a study of our saintly author's

---

[23] *Ibid.*, f. 5, pp. 179–180; *Ibid.*, a. 2, conc., p. 185.

[24] *Ibid.*, a. 1, ff. 1–2, p. 179.

[25] Coll. V, nn. 11–13, V, p. 524.

[26] Confer above, ft. 20.

[27] ". . . 'Dum durat mundus, Angeli Angelis, homines hominibus praeerunt ad utilitatem viventium . . .'" *De Perf. Evan.*, q. 4, a. 1, conc., V, p. 181.

[28] *Ibid.*, pp. 181ss.

[29] Confer above, pp. 95–96.

[30] " . . . lex naturalis, quae manat a lege aeterna, naturaliter dictat, quod

writings we have come to the conclusion that he advocates two kinds of authority of man over man, which we have termed: (a) *the power of precedence;* and (b) the *potestas coercendi subditos,* i.e., *coercive power.*[31]

According to Bonaventurian teaching, the power of precedence, in virtue of which the inferior is bound to render filial obedience,[32] is proper to the *status viae*[33] and is postulated by the natural law in the state of original justice, the state of original sin, and the state of repaired nature.[34] In other words, this type of superiority, decreed by natural law, will continue as long as the world remains—as long as man leads a terrestrial life. Under this kind of superiority the Seraphic Doctor includes: (a) the authority of father over son;[35] (b) that of husband over wife;[36]

---

inferior superiori obediendo subjaceat; et hoc quidem dictat in generalitate quadam, diversimode tamen, secundum quod superioritatis et inferioritatis reperire contingit differentia diversas." *De Perf. Evan.,* q. 4, a. 1, conc., V, p. 181.

[31] *Ibid.,* a. 1, pp. 179ss.; *Liber II S.,* d. 44, a. 2, q. 2, conc., II, p. 1008.

The Seraphic Doctor, it is true, speaks of a third type of authority of man over man—the rule of providence, or jurisdictional power—in his *De Perf. Evan.* (q. 4, a. 1, conc., V, p. 181). However, we are of the opinion that this type of authority can be reduced to the power of precedence. In fact, it is nothing more than the power of precedence in reference to the present status of man (status naturae reparatae). Our opinion is strengthened by the fact that he does not make mention of this type of authority in his *Liber II S.,* d. 44, a. 2, q. 1, conc., II, p. 1008.

Legowicz, *op. cit.,* p. 211, ft. 727, is of the same opinion.

The other "potestas" referred to in *Liber II S.,* d. 44, a. 2, q. 1, conc., II, p. 1008 is the power that man wields over irrational creatures and, consequently, does not pertain to our present study.

[32] *De Perf. Evan.,* q. 4, a. 1, conc., V, p. 181.

[33] *Ibidem; Liber II S.,* d. 44, a. 2, q. 2, conc., II, p. 1008.

[34] "... potestas dominandi sive praesidendi dicit excellentiam potestatis in imperando ei qui est capax rationis et praecepti ... competit statui viae, sive pro statu naturae institutae, sive pro statu naturae lapsae. Si enim homo stetisset, et vir posset imperare uxori, et pater potuisset imperare filio. Et hoc reperitur etiam in Angelis, quamdiu sunt administratorii spiritus, quia ex illa parte aliquo modo sunt in statu viae. Haec tamen praesidentia non manebit in gloria ..." *Ibidem.* Confer *De Perf. Evan.,* q. 4, a. 1, conc., V, p. 181.

[35] Cf. above, ft. 34; *Liber II S.,* d. 9, a. 1, q. 6, conc., II, p. 252.

[36] Cf. above, ft. 34.

(c) that of one angel over the other;[37] (d) that of one demon over the other;[38] and (e) the authority that one man would have exercised over the other had the state of innocence remained in effect.[39]

For perfect precedence St. Bonaventure requires that the one who presides: (a) excel those over whom he presides; (b) influence them in some manner; and (c) command them, i.e., enjoin upon them certain things that are to be done.[40] However, there is one point especially with reference to this authority that must be borne in mind, i.e., that it does not make the superior the lord and master of the inferior; nor, on the other hand, does it render the inferior the servant of the superior. Thus, when referring to the authority of husband over wife, Bonaventure cautions that although the wife is to be subject to her husband, nevertheless she was created to be his companion, not his servant. Indeed, while the husband is called the head of the woman, he is not her lord in such a manner that she becomes his slave.[41] The same teaching is again propounded by our author when he considers the authority of one angel over the other. He tells us that although one angel presides over the other and has authority to command something of the lower angels, yet the inferior angel is never said to be the servant of the other superior angels.[42]

---

[37] Cf. above, ft. 34; *De Perf. Evan.*, q. 4, a. 2, f. 13, V, p. 185; *Liber II S.*, d. 9, a. 1, q. 6, conc., and ad 3, II, p. 252; *Ibid.*, q. 8, conc., and ad 4, pp. 255–256.

[38] *Ibid.*, d. 6, a. 3, q. 2, conc., p. 169; *Ibid.*, ad 2.

[39] "Nisi enim essent hujusmodi dominia coercentia malos, propter corruptionem, quae est in natura, unus alterum opprimeret, et communiter homines vivere non possent. Non sic autem esset, si homo permansisset in statu innocentiae; quilibet enim in gradu et statu suo maneret." *Ibid.*, d. 44, a. 2, q. 2, ad 4, p. 1009.

[40] "Ad rationem autem perfectae praelationis ista tria concurrunt, ut qui praefertur natus sit, eum cui praefertur, excedere et in ipsum aliquo modo influere et eidem praesidere." *Ibid.*, d. 9, a. 1, q. 6, conc., II, p. 252.

[41] "Nam etsi mulier sit viro quodam modo inferior ratione infirmioris sexus, nihilominus, quia non est creata, ut esset ei in adjutorium ut famula, sed ut socia; hinc est, quod quamvis dicatur caput ejus, non tamen dicitur dominus, quia ipsa non est ancilla ipsius." *Ibid.*, d. 44, a. 2, q. 2, ad 1, p. 1008.

[42] "Ad illud quod objicitur, quod praelatio est in Angelis; jam patet

Existing even before the Fall and continuing in force as long as man leads a terrestrial life, this power of precedence, therefore, dictated by nature, prescribes a certain submission and obedience, but neither renders the superior the lord and master of his subordinates nor enslaves the inferiors. It requires that he who presides should be more noble and of greater excellence than the one over whom he prescribes—e.g., the father as regards the son, the husband with regard to the wife, and the superior angels in regard to the inferior angels. Furthermore, in line with Bonaventure's hierarchical teaching, the superiors are to aid their charges—purifying, illumining, and perfecting them. The subordinates, on the other hand, remaining in the grades assigned to them and refraining from all envy, are to perform their various duties willingly, freely, and gladly.[43] In short, this authority calls for perfect and free order—an order in which there is no coercion, no force; an order in which the superior does not oppress, but elevates his charges; an order in which the inferior gladly and freely performs the role assigned to him.

The other authority referred to by our author is coercive power, i.e., the power of coercing subjects. This kind of authority entails a certain limitation of freedom; to it corresponds *dominion* on the part of the superior and *servitude* on the part of the inferior.[44] According to St. Bonaventure coercive power exists as a punishment for sin, because the servitude which corresponds to this type of power is actually the result of original sin.[45]

---

responsio, quia, quamvis unus praesideat alteri et imperet alteri et auctoritatem habeat super alterum imperandi ei aliquid, quod pertinet ad officium ministerii, tamen unus Angelus non dicitur servus alterius Angeli . . ." *Ibid.*, ad 2, p. 1008.

[43] *S. de Sanctis, De S. Angelis,* s. v, IX, pp. 628ss. Confer above, pp. 126–127.

[44] " Tertio modo potestas dominandi dicitur potestas coercendi subditos; et haec potestas dicit quandam arctationem libertatis; et talis potestas dominandi proprie dicitur dominium, cui respondet servitus." *Liber II S.,* d. 44, a. 2, q. 2, conc., II, p. 1008.

[45] " Tertio vero modo potestas dominandi in homine est solum secundum statum naturae lapsae; inest enim ei secundum culpae punitionem, non secundum naturae institutionem, et hoc, quia servitus sibi correspondens, secundum quod dicunt sancti, est poena peccati." *Ibidem.*

Accordingly, this type of authority, to which servile obedience must be given, is proper solely to the state of fallen nature. In this state, then, it is prescribed by the natural law.[46]

Coercive power and servile obedience, therefore, are decreed by the natural law, not *simpliciter*, but for the state of original sin. For this reason, this kind of authority, according to Bonaventurian doctrine, is not in opposition to the universal and absolute dictate of the natural law, but is contrary to that dictate of natural law which refers to the state of original justice and is preceptive in virtue of the natural law which refers to the state of fallen nature.[47]

---

[46] *De Perf. Evan.*, q. 4, a. 1, conc., V, p. 181.

At this point it would be well to note once again that, in the teaching of our author, not all authority of man over man is due to the Fall. Hence, faced with the objection that no one need be subject and obedient to another, since all men are created free and equal and man possesses dominion over irrational creatures alone and not over his fellows, St. Bonaventure replies that this freedom and equality do not exclude all subjection and obedience, but only enforced servitude, which did not exist in the state of original justice and would not have existed if sin had not come to disease man's nature. (*Ibid.*, ad 1-3, p. 182.)

At first sight, Bonaventure's teaching, as contained in his *Q. D. De Perfectione Evangelica*, does not seem to agree with that contained in his *Commentary on the Sentences* (d. 44, a. 2, q. 2, II, pp. 1007ss.). In the latter work he observes: freedom is in man by nature; but the power of lordship is destructive of freedom; therefore lordship would seem to be not from nature (*Ibid.*, f. 3, p. 1007). (Basing his interpretation of the Seraphic Doctor's doctrine on this passage of the *Commentary on the Sentences*, Bede Jarrett, *Social Theories of the Middle Ages*, The Newman Book Shop, Westminster, Maryland, 1942, pp. 9-11, seems to assert that all authority of man over man, except that of father over son, and of husband over wife, is due to sin, which, as we have seen, is not the case.) However, there is no difficulty. We must remember that Bonaventure here is concerned not with all types of authority of man over man, but only with coercive power, which is to a certain extent destructive of freedom and which is, consequently, due to man's fallen condition. Accordingly, the editors of Quaracchi note (Scholion, n. 2, p. 1007) that when the Seraphic Doctor holds the authority of man over man to be due to the fallen nature of man and to be commanded by the natural law for the state of original sin alone, he has reference solely to coercive power.

[47] " Cum ergo dicitur, quod potestas dominandi est contra jus naturae, hoc non intelligitur quantum ad universale dictamen naturae, sed quantum ad

According to the Seraphic Doctor, then, coercive power, which would not have been needed if man had not fallen, is necessary in the present state of affairs. Because of man's Fall and his subsequent proneness to deviate from the path of righteousness and oppress his fellows, thus disturbing right order and harmonious social living, this coercive power must be vested in the ruler, in order to keep in check the evil tendencies of his subjects.[48] Therefore, Bede Jarrett has concluded: "Authority is lawful, because the evil are to be constrained." [49] However, this need, i.e., of restraining evil, is not, as Bede Jarrett would have us understand, the real reason for such authority. The subjection of the evil is but a means, a necessary step; whereas, the end of coercive power is the utility of the living, the promotion of harmonious social living, the conservation of right order.[50]

SECTION 3.   QUALITIES AND DUTIES OF THOSE CONSTITUTED IN AUTHORITY

In speaking of civil society, as we have seen, the Seraphic Doctor rejects the transmission of power from father to son and seems to prefer that governmental make-up in which the ruler is chosen by the people.[51] With this thought in mind, we come to

---

dictamen naturae alicujus status determinati, in quo quidem non esset subjectio servitutis, nec praelatio potestatis." *Liber II S.,* d. 44, a. 2, q. 1, ad 4, II, p. 1006.

[48] "Unde ita moriuntur Christiani sicut et alii, et propter pronitatem ad malum et concupiscentias militantes in membris, ex quibus consurgunt bella et lites, ita indigent regi terreno principe, sicut et aliae gentes—et ideo non solum secundum humanam institutionem, sed etiam secundum divinam dispensationem inter Christianos sunt reges et principes, domini et servi . . ." *Ibid.,* a. 3, p. 1, conc., p. 1001.

"Nisi enim essent hujusmodi dominia coercentia malos, propter corruptionem, quae est in natura, unus alterum opprimeret, et communiter homines vivere non possent. . . . Et sic patet, quod illa ratio non concludit, quod servitus vel dominium respiciat naturam institutam, sed solum quod respicit naturam lapsam, ubi ordo habet perturbari et potest per dominium conservari." *Ibid.,* a. 2, q. 2, ad 4, p. 1009. Confer *Liber IV S.,* d. 24, p. 1, a. 2, q. 1, conc., IV, p. 614; *Com. in Ecc.,* c. viii, vv. 12-13, q. 1, VI, p. 69.

[49] *Op. cit.,* p. 10.

[50] Confer above, ft. 27, 48.

[51] Confer above, p. 168.

the questions: to whom should authority be given? what qualities must be present in those selected for positions of power? how should they act?

Confronted with the question as to who is to be chosen for a certain position, we must keep two things in mind: (a) the excellence of the office or dignity, and (b) the sufficient merit of the one who is selected. Accordingly, as St. Bonaventure expresses it, there are two questions that must be answered: *Who* is to be selected? to *What* is he to be appointed? The first question concerns those personal qualities of an appointee which can be reduced to a high moral standing or an irreproachable life. The second question, on the other hand, deals with those qualities which refer to the selectee's capability of administering this dignity in a worthy manner.[52]

Thoroughly recognizing the fact that the various grades of any social organism are interrelated and interdependent in such a way that they vitally influence one another—so much so, in fact, that the goodness or evil of one grade necessarily affects the others and, as a result, the whole social body[53]—St. Bonaventure avers: "As the ruler, so the ruled."[54] Mindful of this fact—that the ruled will be greatly influenced by those in authority, especially by their mode of action—he does not hesitate to exact of those in authority a high moral standing.[55] A superior cannot, he tells us, have an ordered family, unless he himself is ordered; nor chaste subordinates, unless he himself is chaste.[56] It is for this reason, then, that in discussing the political virtues—prudence, fortitude, temperance, and justice—Bonaven-

---

[52] ". . . in qua electione duo sunt attendenda, scilicet officium excellens et meritum sufficiens, id est, ad quod debet eligi et qualis debet eligi." *S. de S., De S. Mathia Apostolo,* s. i, IX, p. 516.

[53] Confer above, pp. 165–166.

[54] ". . . qualis princeps civitatis, talis et habitantes in ea." *De Donis,* coll. IV, n. 10, V, p. 475. Confer *Com. in Sap.,* prooemium, n. 9, VI, p. 109.

[55] "Officium vero praelationis sine culmine virtutis et meritis non est vera sublimatio, sed dejectio, non gloriosa excellentia, sed periculosa ruina . . ." *Op. XI, Apologia Pauperum,* c. iii, n. 22, VIII, p. 250.

[56] "Non potest aliquis habere ordinatam familiam, nisi ipse sit ordinatus. Si velit aliquis habere servientes castos; et ipse non erit castus, hoc non potest esse." *De Donis,* coll. IV, n. 10, V, p. 475.

ture charges those placed in authority to be governed by these.[57]

The point that the Seraphic Doctor stresses most, in this regard, is that he who is elected to a place of authority should be able to rule himself. Leaving no possible doubt in the minds of his readers, he expressly enjoins that man must learn to rule himself before he presumes to rule others.[58] Indeed, how can an individual presume to rule others if he has not the ability to rule his own person? It must be clear that no man can rightly govern his family, if he himself is not rightly governed; and no man can possibly govern the state, if he is not able to promote true peace and order in his own family circle.[59] As St. Bonaventure aptly phrases it, " He is king, who can rule himself." [60]

Furthermore, one who is elected to a position of authority should possess some knowledge of law-making and of the administration of society, since it goes without saying that an individual will not be able to foster harmony and establish right order unless he is well versed in the art of governing. St. Bonaventure is very emphatic on this point. Forcibly he laments the abuses of his day. He cites the fact that knowledge of navigation is required of him who pilots a ship, and yet none care about the knowledge of administration in him who pilots the state. In truth, he calls this state of affairs a *magna abominatio*.[61]

Above all else, our author writes, a superior must be well versed and must excel in those things which pertain to his office.[62] Besides the knowledge of law-making and administration, the saintly Doctor calls for a knowledge of those whom the superiors

---

[57] *In Hex.*, coll. VI, nn. 28–29, V, p. 364.

[58] " . . . vir bonus primum sui atque inde reipublicae rector efficitur . . ." *Ibid.*, n. 29, p. 364.

[59] " Non potest aliquis habere ordinatam familiam, nisi ipse sit ordinatus. . . . Similiter nisi homo bene regat familiam suam, non poterit bene regere civitatem, quia qualis princeps civitatis, tales et habitantes in ea." *De Donis*, coll. IV, n. 10, V, p. 475.

[60] " Rex est qui se regere potest . . ." *S. de B.V.M.*, *De Purificatione B.V.M.*, s. 1, IX, p. 637.

[61] " Tamen hodie magna abominatio est in his qui praesunt, quia in navi non ponitur rector, nisi habeat artem gubernandi; quomodo ergo in republica ponitur ille qui nescit regere? " *In Hex.*, coll. V, n. 19, V, p. 357.

[62] *Op. XI, Apologia Pauperum*, c. iii, n. 24, VIII, p. 251.

are to govern, since " no one can rule well those of whose nature he is ignorant." [63]

In conformity with his teaching on hierarchy—viz., that the superiors are to influence their subordinates by purifying, illumining, and perfecting them—we find our author likewise demanding wisdom in those who are appointed to rule. Through the medium of Boethius the Seraphic Doctor reverts to the teaching of Plato and asserts that the republic over which wise men (philosophers, or kings who philosophize) rule is well governed.[64]

Accordingly, when faced with the question as to who is to be raised to positions of authority, we may reply that he who is to be elected should, in truth, be superior to those over whom he presides. He should enjoy a high moral standing as well as wisdom, in order that he may wholesomely influence his subordinates. Again, he should be able to rule himself and should know how to rule others. Finally, he should excel in those qualities which are demanded by his office.

The most exhaustive treatise by the Seraphic Doctor on the qualities that should be present in a superior is contained in his *De Sex Alis Seraphim,* in which he considers the virtues that a religious superior should possess.[65] Six virtues, especially, are stressed by the saintly son of Francis of Assisi. They are: (a) zeal for justice, (b) pity or compassion, (c) patience, (d) edification or an exemplary life, (e) prudent discretion, and (f) devotion or piety. He writes:

> " Every religious who has to govern himself and to account for others at the judgment seat of God should

---

[63] ". . . nullus bene regit et gubernat ea quorum naturam ignorat . . ." *Liber II S.,* d. 23, a. 2, q. 1, f. 3, II, p. 537.

[64] " Reges admonet diligere sapientiam, sine qua regnare non possunt; tunc enim bene regitur respublica, cum philosophi regnant, et reges philosophantur." *Com. in Sap.,* c. vi, vv. 20–22, VI, p. 149. Confer *Ibid.,* proemium, n. 9, p. 109.—Bonaventure's source is Boethius, *De Consolatione Philosophiae,* lib. 1, prosa 4, n. 44, *P. L.* 63, 615–616. The original source, however, is the *Republic* of Plato.

[65] *Opusculum VIII,* VIII, pp. 131–151. For English translation confer *The Virtues of a Religious Superior,* being a translation from the Latin of Bonaventure's *De Sex Alis Seraphim,* by Fr. Sabinus Mollitor, O.F.M., Herder, St. Louis, 1921.

be adorned and carried upward by these wings, that he may be fervent in justice, compassionate towards others for God's sake, patient in adversity; that he may edify others by a good example, be circumspect in all things, and, above all, be intimately united with God through prayer." [66]

The *first wing* with which a superior should be equipped is *zeal for justice*, in virtue of which the superior cannot bear to see injustice perpetrated without protesting.[67] Inspired by zeal for justice, the superior should, as our author affirms, seek to promote good and extirpate evil, to relieve the oppressed and punish the oppressors.[68] First of all, he should see to it that his own actions are in conformity with justice, i.e., that he does not do or teach anything that is wrong.[69] Second, he should see that justice be observed by others—and this especially by not permitting evil to go unpunished.[70] The promotion of justice should be his continuous aim. Indeed, this fostering of right order is, as we have seen, the reason why man has been given power over his fellows.[71] Nothing should deter the superior from the attainment of this end. Bonaventure writes:

"He should not falter in his zeal through sloth, nor tire in his exertions, nor be deflected by counsels, nor foiled by cunning, nor carried away by friendship and

---

[66] "Quilibet etiam religiosus, qui se ipsum habet regere et de sui ipsius regimine rationem Deo est redditurus in extremo examine, his alis et pennis, quantum sibimet indiget, debet adornari et in superna sublevari, ut sit fervens in justitia, compatiens proximis propter Deum, patiens in adversis, bono exemplo alios aedificans, circumspectus in omnibus et super omnia Deo per orationis studium familiariter adhaerens . . ." *De Sex Alis,* c. vii, n. 15, VIII, pp. 150–151.

[67] "Prima ala rectoris animarum est zelus justitiae, qua non potest aliquid injustum sine cordis murmure in se et in aliis sustinere." *Ibid.,* c. 2, n. 1, p. 133.

[68] "Quoniam igitur de vestra praesumo industria, sollicitudine et zeli vivacitate, quod prompti sitis ad exstirpanda mala, promovenda bona, refovenda debilia et fortia confortanda . . ." *Op. XIX, Epistolae Officiales,* Ep. 1, n. 1, VIII, p. 468. Confer *Com. in Ev. Lucae,* c. xviii, n. 8, VII, p. 450.

[69] *De Sex Alis,* c. 2, n. 12, VIII, p. 135.

[70] *Ibidem.*

[71] Confer above, pp. 188–189.

flattery, nor terrified by threats, nor become discouraged on account of long standing abuses, but he should fulfill his duty." [72]

As the very basis of this zeal for justice the Seraphic Doctor assigns charity—love of God and of neighbour, which he teaches is " required above all of His (God's) representatives, who according to His Will, should be governed by love of justice and hatred of iniquity." [73]   Indeed, as our author affirms:

> " In proportion to the ardor with which you love God and the purity with which you desire the things that are God's, you grieve over the offences committed against Him. . . . And according to the depth of your love for the salvation of your neighbor, you will grieve over his ruin and the obstacles laid in his way toward heaven." [74]

A short examination of Bonaventure's ideas on punishment and correction is not out of place at this point. As we have noted, the Seraphic Doctor insists that faults should not be allowed to go unpunished.[75]   The superior who " fails to correct delinquents permits the growth of bad habits and the introduction of evil practices and allows those that have crept in to increase and spread." [76]   Therefore, he adds, " the sins of his subjects, which he could have and ought to have corrected, are imputed

---

[72] " Ostendat ergo bonus zelator, quantum diligat Deum, in eo quod beneplacitum ejus in se et in aliis promoveat nec ab hoc zelo mollescat per desidiam nec labore lassetur nec consiliis flectatur nec astutitiis circumveniatur nec amicitia nec blandimentis deliniatur nec minis terreatur nec per diuturnae pravae consuetudinis praescriptionem desperet, quin suum officium exsequatur." *De Sex Alis.,* c. 2, n. 17, VIII, p. 136.

[73] " Et licet haec caritas requiratur in omnibus amicis Dei, maxime tamen in vicariis Dei, qui secundum cor Dei moveri debent amore justitiae et odio iniquitatis . . ." *Ibid.,* n. 6, p. 134.

[74] " Quantum vero diligis Deum et quae Dei sunt purius desideras, tantum doles de offensa Dei. . . . Et quantum diligis salutem proximi, tantum affligeris de perditione ejus et nocumento profectus ejus." *Ibid.,* n. 5, p. 134.

[75] *Ibid.,* n. 12, p. 135.

[76] " . . . si non corrigit delinquentes, si permittit sub se vitia crescere, et consuetudines malas oriri, et jam exortas roborari et dilatari . . ." *Ibid.,* n. 15, p. 135.

to him."[77] Finally, punishment of transgressions is always productive of some good. What applies to the social order in a special manner is the fact that punishment of transgressions teaches others to beware lest they fall into similar faults.[78] Our saintly author bids superiors to have the utmost prudence when it comes to the problem of correction and punishment.[79] For some—those that are manageable—he asks gentle and mild correction; for others—those that are rebellious and obdurate—he commends strong measures.[80] For instance, those sinners who do not contaminate others and for whom there is hope of amendment should be punished, it is true. However, this punishment should be so imposed that the transgressor, while made to realize the gravity of his fault, will be treated with clemency.[81] When transgressions, on the other hand, are of a serious and public nature, when there is no hope of correction on account of obstinacy or an inveterate habit, when there is danger of infecting others and scandal—then " nothing remains to be done but to cast away the rotten egg and to cut off the putrid member lest sound organs become infected and corrupted."[82] Although Bonaventure here is principally concerned with religious, nevertheless he applies the same principle to the civil society. According to his teaching, piety and justice demand that the pestiferous members—obdurate sinners—be not allowed to remain and to corrupt the whole body of the social structure. When man has

---

[77] " . . . omnia peccata subditorum, quae poterat et debuerat correxisse et praecavisse, imputantur ei . . ." *Ibid.,* n. 16, p. 136.

[78] " Item, quia per hoc alii erudiuntur, ut caveant similia perpetrare . . ." *Ibid.,* n. 12, p. 135.

[79] *Ibid.,* c. 6, n. 3, p. 143.

[80] " . . . in moralibus duplex est modus corrigendi, unus per dulces monitiones, alter per asperas increpationes; et hoc secundum duo genera hominum, quia quidam sunt tractabiles et plicabiles, quidam duri et rebelles." *Liber IV S.,* d. 18, p. 2, a. 1, q. 1, conc., IV, p. 485.

[81] *De Sex Alis,* c. 2, n. 15, VIII, p. 135; *Ibid.,* c. 6, n. 8, p. 144.

[82] " Ubicumque ergo quatuor illa conveniunt, scilicet graviter, aperte peccare, et non esse spem correctionis propter obstinationem seu inveteratam mali consuetudinem, et alios infici per ejus exemplum, vel scandalizari, quia talia tolerantur; quid restat, nisi ut ovis morbida abjiciatur, et membrum putridum praecidatur, ne sana inde inficiantur et corrumpantur?" *Ibid.,* n. 10, p. 144.

a corroded tooth, he argues, it should be extracted lest it infect the others. The same, he affirms, is true with society.[83] Throughout his discussion of correction and punishment, however, we find the Seraphic Doctor insisting that the rigor of justice be tempered by clemency.[84] In rulers two things must go hand in hand—zeal for justice and mercy or compassion.[85] In fact, the ruler must act as the father and the *socius* of his subjects, not as their adversary.[86] Thus, although the saintly Doctor

---

[83] " Scitote, quod justi judices non debent parcere potestati malorum, quando inveniuntur pervertentes alios. Socii etiam debent talem expellere a sua societate. Bene scitis, quod quando aliquis homo habet dentem putridum in ore, nisi ejiciatur, corrumpit alios, sic malus socius bonos." *S. de S., De Nativitate S. J. Baptistae,* s. i, IX, p. 542. Confer *Op. XIX Epistolae Officiales,* Ep. ii, n. 4, VIII, p. 470.

Our author, it may be noted, is in favor of capital punishment. (*Liber IV S.,* d. 44, p. 2, a. 1, q. 1, conc., IV, p. 922.) He answers the objection that evil should be conquered by good, saying this principle does not refer to those constituted in authority. For, being ministers of the law, it is their duty to promote right order; consequently, when they punish or even kill, it is not they but the law that punishes and kills. (*Decem Praeceptis,* coll. VI, nn. 6–7, V, pp. 526–527; *Com. in Ev. Lucae,* c. iii, n. 34, VII, p. 78.) Of course, there must be a just cause. Furthermore, those who punish must do so not with the desire of vengeance, not because of hatred for the persons to be punished, but out of love for justice. (*Ibid.,* c. xviii, n. 8, VII, p. 450; *Decem Praeceptis,* coll. VI, nn. 6–7, V, p. 527.)

We may note at this point that in Bonaventurian teaching war is licit when it is waged: (a) by lawful authority; (b) by the proper parties (by this he wishes to exclude religious and clerics from the ranks of combatants); and (c) for a just cause—for the defense of the homeland, or of peace, or of faith—and, consequently, with a just intention, since, as he explains, war cannot be licitly waged for the glory of man or out of hated revenge. This teaching is contained in his *Commentary on the Gospel of St. Luke,* c. iii, n. 34, VII, p. 78. For a more complete treatise of Bonaventure's teaching concerning the liceity of war, confer Di Fonzo, P.L., O.F.M. Conv., " De Liceitate Belli, Quid Conseat S. Bonaventura," *Miscellanea Francescana,* 41, 1941, pp. 34–48.

[84] " . . . increpando per justitiam et sanando per clementiam. Debet autem esse rigor justitiae respectu culpae, sed dulcor clementiae respectu naturae." *Com. in Ev. Lucae,* c. ix, n. 81, VII, p. 242.

[85] " Ad perfectionem vero praelationis duo necessario requiruntur, scilicet zelus justitiae et affectus misericordiae; misericordia enim et veritas custodiunt regem." *Brev.,* p. v, c. vi, V, p. 259.

[86] " Non desaevit in subditum tanquam in adversarium, sed corripit

instructs that no crime go unpunished, nevertheless he asks for gentleness and compassion. Without gentleness, he points out, there is not correction, but destruction.[87] This consideration brings us to the *second wing* with which a superior should be equipped, viz., *pity* or *fraternal compassion.* With reference to this, Bonaventure writes:

"As the love of God inflames him (the religious superior) with zeal for justice, so fraternal love should imbue him with affection. For, if the rod is to be held over evil-doers, the staff is required for the support of the weak." [88]

This thought brings to mind what was already said when we considered Bonaventure's teaching on hierarchy, namely, that the superior is to influence, elevate, and aid the inferiors.[89] As in the angelical hierarchy, so, too, in the human hierarchy, the superiors are to condescend to the inferiors and communicate to them all that they themselves have received.[90] Thus, according to St. Bonaventure, the duty of the superior is not limited to merely promoting order and justice. Nay, he should defend the flock committed to his care; he should feed, nourish, and support those placed in his charge.[91] Indeed, the Bonaventurian teaching is that the superiors, servants of the others, are to

tanquam fratrem et socium . . ." *S. de S., De S. P. N. Francisco,* s. v, IX, p. 594. Confer *De Donis,* coll. IX, nn. 15–16, V, pp. 502–503.

[87] ". . . sine mansuetudine not fit correctio, sed destructio." *S. de S., De S. P. N. Francisco,* s. v, IX, p. 594.

[88] ". . . sicut eum caritas Dei ad zelum justitiae inflammat, ita fraterna dilectio ad pietatem informet. Nam etsi vitiis debetur virga feriens, sed infirmitati necessarius est baculus sustentans . . ." *De Sex Alis,* c. iii, n. 1, VIII, p. 136.

[89] Confer above, pp. 126–127.

[90] *De Donis,* coll. III, n. 14, V, p. 472; *Liber III S.,* d. 13, a. 2, q. 1, conc., III, p. 284; *Ibid.,* ad 2, p. 285; *Ibid.,* d. 1, a. 2, q. 2, ad 7, p. 27; *S. de T., Dom. II in Quadragesima,* s. 1, IX, p. 217; *S. de S., S. De S. Angelis,* s. v, IX, p. 628.

[91] ". . . ad bonum pastorem pertinet erga suum gregem habere sollicitudinem vigilantiae in custodiendo, deinde affectum benevolentiae in fovendo et nutriendo . . ." *S. de T., Dom. II p. Pascha,* s. i, IX, p. 294. Confer *Op. XIX, Epistolae Officiales,* Ep. 1, n. 1, VIII, p. 468.

minister to the inferiors and are not tó be ministered to by them.[92]
Hence, we find the Franciscan Doctor writing:

> "A good superior realizes that he is the father and not
> the task-master of his brethren, and he acts like a
> physician, not like a tyrant. He does not consider his
> subjects as beasts of burden or slaves, but as chil-
> dren . . ."[93]

Moreover, quoting from St. Bernard, he declares:

> "Learn to be towards your subjects like mothers, and
> not like masters; strive to be loved, rather than feared;
> and if severity is sometimes necessary, let it be paternal
> and not tyrannical. Show yourselves as mothers in lov-
> ing, as fathers in chastising. Be gentle, avoid harsh-
> ness; hang up the rod, and give the breasts. A mother's
> breasts should bulge with milk, not swell with fever.
> Why do you load your subjects down with your burdens
> when yóu ought to be bearing theirs?"[94]

Patience and forbearance, the superior's *third wing,* is necessary, St. Bonaventure says, on account of: (a) his manifold
duties, cares, and occupations; (b) the slow progress of his
subjects; and (c) the ingratitude of those for whom he labors.[95]
Impatience in a superior, according to his teaching, causes im-
pediments to the attainment of the good which he should promote,

---

[92] "Ministri tantum, quorum est ministrare et non ministrari . . ." *Op.
XVI, Exp. Super Reg. Fr. Min.,* c. iv, n. 22, VIII, p. 418. Confer *Ibid.,* c.
viii, n. 2, p. 427; *S. de T., Epiphania,* s. i, IX, p. 148.

[93] "Bonus autem praelatus agnoscit se fratrum suorum patrem, non
dominum, et exhibet se eis medicum, non tyrannum, nec reputat eos ut
jumenta sua vel servos emptionis, sed ut filios . . ." *De Sex Alis,* c. iii,
n. 4, VIII, p. 136.

[94] "Bernardus: 'Discite, subditorum matres vos esse debere, non dominos;
studete magis amari, quam metui; et si interdum severitate opus est, paterna
sit, non tyrannica. Matres fovendo, patres vos corripiendo exhibeatis.
Mansuescite, ponite feritatem; suspendite verbera, producite ubera; pectora
lacte pinguescant, non typho turgeant. Quid jugum vestrum super eos
aggravatis, quorum potius onera portare debetis?'" *Ibid.,* n. 9, p. 138.—St.
Bonaventure's source is St. Bernard's *Sermo XXIII in Canticum,* n. 2.

[95] *Ibid.,* c. iv, nn. 1–4, pp. 138–139.—Bonaventure also insists upon fortitude
in the superiors. Confer *De Donis,* coll. V, n. 14, V, p. 482.

renders him contemptible in the eyes of his subjects, provokes others to impatience, scandalizes others, gives rise to murmurings and complaints, makes him feared and disliked, repels timid souls, and engenders cowardice. Because of it the subjects dare not inform him of their needs, nor does anyone dare to correct the superiors in those matters in which he ought to be corrected.[96] Accordingly, our saintly author calls upon those constituted in authority to exercise forbearance, to cultivate calmness, and to treat each one with gentleness, deliberation, and kindness.[97]

As for the *fourth wing—exemplary life* or *edification*—he writes:

" A superior ought to be a model for his subjects and should teach by example as well as words, just as one who teaches geometry exhibits his demonstrations by figures to make himself more easily understood." [98]

Our author, it is true, is referring to religious superiors; nevertheless, certain of the points he advances in this regard can be usefully applied to all kinds of superiors. Thus, for example, his insistence that the superior be not too aloof;[99] that he be humble in his bearing;[100] and that he be honest and sincere;[101] that he refrain from that frivolity which savours of disrespect;[102] that he be not partial, especially in his external conduct;[103] and that he be not fickle in his counsels, " wishing now this, and now that, though there is no reason for the change." [104]

[96] *De Sex Alis,* c. iv, n. 5, VIII, p. 139.
[97] *Ibid.,* nn. 5–7, p. 139.
[98] " Ipse namque debet ceteris esse norma vivendi, ut quae docet verbis ostendat actionum figuris, sicut qui geometriam docet pingit in sabulo figurarum demonstrationes, ut quod dicit melius capiatur . . ." *Ibid.,* c. v, n. 1, p. 140.
[99] *Ibid.,* n. 2, pp. 140–141.
[100] *Ibid.,* n. 3, p. 141.
[101] *Ibid.,* n. 6, p. 141.
[102] *Ibidem.*
[103] *Ibid.,* n. 7, p. 141.
[104] " Item, si non sit levis in proposito et inconstans in consilio, ut quod jam placet mox displiceat; modo velit unum, modo contrarium, ubi rationabilis causa non apparet." *Ibid.,* n. 8, p. 141.

The point that is most noteworthy is Bonaventure's teaching that the superior should be affable, so that his subject may have easy access to him and may speak with confidence of his needs.[105] Here, again, we meet with the Seraphic Doctor's insistence that the superior " should seek to be loved rather than feared, for men more willingly obey one who is loved than one who is feared."[106] However, the saintly son of St. Francis does not fail to instruct that though a superior is to be loved rather than feared, yet this love should not degererate into that kind of familiarity which breeds contempt. The superior, he explains, ought to be feared by the insolent.[107] More to the point are his words: " Love itself is sweeter, as it were, when mixed with respect."[108]

That those in authority should be equipped with *prudence* as the *fifth wing* is most apparent in Bonaventure's thought. As we have seen, one cannot presume to rule others if he does not know how to rule himself.[109] Great prudence, he tells us, is required for the rule of self, still greater prudence for the rule of the family, and the greatest prudence for the rule of a society.[110] Thus, he writes:

" The superior is a guide for the flock committed to his care, and if he errs, the flock is confused and led astray. As the eye is the light of the body, so the shepherd is the light of the flock entrusted to him."[111]

According to the teaching of our author, the superior should be equipped with the following four abilities.

---

[105] *Ibid.,* n. 4, p. 141.

[106] ". . . studeat magis amari quam timeri, quia libentius obeditur ei qui diligitur, quam qui timetur." *Ibidem.*

[107] *Ibid.,* n. 6, p. 141.

[108] " Ipse amor aliquo modo suavior sentitur cum reverentia mixtus . . ." *Ibidem.*

[109] Confer above, p. 191.

[110] " Magna prudentia requiritur ad regimen sui, major ad regimen familiae, sed maxima circa regimen civitatis." *De Donis,* coll. IV, n. 10, V, p. .475.

[111] " Rector enim est dux gregis sibi commissi, et si ipse erraverit, grex in dispersione confusus interibit. Sicut oculus est lux totius corporis, ita pastor gregis commissi . . ." *De Sex Alis,* c. vi, n. 1, VIII, p. 142.

" The first of these is the ability to govern those committed to his care, so that his good subjects advance and persevere. The second is the ability to correct and amend those that have erred and sinned. The third is the ability to dispose of the business matters requiring his attention. The fourth is the ability to conduct himself prudently in all these things." [112]

In this regard, the superior should know how to observe the golden mean between rigor and laxity. This ability, he states, " requires considerable discretion in a superior." [113] But, as St. Bonaventure warns, since the superior cannot always please everybody,

> ". . . he will err less by permitting kindness to influence his conduct, because it renders him more amiable to his subjects and induces them to obey him more willingly and to have recourse to him with greater confidence in their troubles. . . . His power and authority causes his subjects to fear sufficiently; if to it he adds austere severity, he burdens the minds of his subjects." [114]

In this section Bonaventure also alludes to the fact that the ruler of a society should know the limits of his subordinates, since not all are blessed with the same capabilities, and should assign the various offices and duties accordingly.[115] His teaching is that the superiors should not impose upon their subjects burdens that exceed their strength.[116] Indeed, he cautions, the

---

[112] " Primum est, quomodo in statu debito commissos sibi gubernet, ut boni sui proficiant et persistant; secundum, quomodo lapsos et devios corrigat et emendet; tertium, quomodo exteriora negotia, quae requiruntur ab eo, congrue disponat; quartum, quomodo se in his custodiat et gerat." *Ibid.*, n. 3, p. 143.

[113] " In hoc indiget praelatus non modica discretione, ut sciat inter rigorem et remissionem medium tenere." *Ibid.*, n. 7, p. 144.

[114] ". . . minus tamen deviat, si ad benignitatis partem plus declinat, per quam redditur subditis magis amabilis, ob quam ei libentius obtemperant et audacius ad eum recurrunt, in quibus indigent . . . Ipsa enim potestatis auctoritas facit eum satis timendum subditis; et si huic jungitur austeritatis severitas, pavidis fit mentibus onerosa . . ." *Ibid.*, n. 17, p. 146.

[115] *Ibid.*, n. 4, p. 143.

[116] *Ibid.*, c. iii, n. 9, p. 137.

superior is to temper and moderate the rule of life in accordance with circumstances and necessities.[117]

Finally, the superior should exercise discretion concerning himself. The point that seems to be most important in this connection is the fact that our author calls upon those in authority to listen carefully to the advice of others and to seek it humbly.[118] He asks them to seek the advice of others, especially of the learned, and this for three reasons—namely:

> ". . . for the sake of enlightenment, to clear up doubtful matters; for the sake of authority, to give it greater force because the question was discussed with certain persons; and for the sake of peace, that no one may have reason for complaint." [119]

In reference to the *sixth* and last *wing* our author writes:

> " The sixth and last wing of the ecclesiastical Seraph, without which the others can accomplish nothing and which is, therefore, the most necessary of all, is *piety* or *devotion to God*. It incites zeal for justice, infuses loving compassion, strengthens patience, sets up an edifying example, and enlightens discretion." [120]

Although Bonaventure's words concern religious superiors in a most particular manner, they may, at the same time, apply to the superiors of a civil society, who should likewise exercise piety or devotion to God. Indeed, as we have seen, the first moral justice, upon which the whole structure of social existence is to be based, is the moral justice which commands that God be worshipped and adored.[121]

---

[117] He brings this forth in commenting upon the rule of the Friars Minor. Confer, *Exp. super Reg. Fr. Min.*, c. iv, n. 22, VIII, p. 419.

[118] *De Sex Alis,* c. vi, n. 18, VIII, p. 146.

[119] ". . . propter emendationem, ut discatur de quo dubitatur; propter auctoritatem, ut magis habeat vigoris quod per tales consultum fuerit, et propter pacem, ne habeant aliqui occasionem murmurandi . . ." *Ibid.,* n. 20, p. 147.

[120] " Sexta et ultima ala, sine qua reliquae perfici non valent, maxime est necessaria, ut sit devotus ad Deum, per quem zelus justitiae accenditur, pietas compassionis infunditur, patientia roboratur, exemplum bonum conditur, discretio clarificatur." *Ibid.,* c. vii, n. 1, p. 147.

[121] Confer above, pp. 27–28; 110–111.

As must appear from all that has been stated, the superiors have not been elevated to positions of authority for their own personal gain and good. Our saintly author is most emphatic on this point. It is this which distinguishes a true ruler from a tyrant, for the true ruler seeks the common good of the society as such, while the tyrant seeks his own individual and private gain.[122] Furthermore, in Bonaventurian thought, the superiors are placed in positions of authority to minister to others, to support them, and to serve them, not to be ministered to, supported, and served. In truth, they are the servants of the others. Accordingly, he who presides, influenced by the spirit of the highest charity, should preside usefully—for the common good.[123] In seeking the common good, those in authority are to promote the utility of the living, to foster peaceful and harmonious relations among men, and to protect right order in the social structure.

SECTION 4. DUTIES OF THE SUBJECTS

Since authority comes from God and since it is necessary for right order, then, authority must be respected and obeyed. In fact, as our author shows us, it is the natural law which exacts this obedience on the part of the inferiors.[124] Accordingly, the Seraphic Doctor commands the Christians to be subject to their rulers.[125] He points out, moreover, that if this obedience is not freely given, the one invested with authority has a right to force it. Thus, for instance, he tells us that it is the duty of the ruler to promote right order. If, however, an individual member of the society abuses his free will and thereby perverts the right order which the rector is trying to establish, the rector has the right to prevail upon this individual and to constrain him to the observance of right order.[126]

Still, this subjection is not to extend to each and every thing. Indeed, our author tells us that it is stupid to be subject to the

---

[122] *In Hex.*, coll. V, n. 19, V, p. 357.

[123] *De Perf. Evan.*, q. 4, a. 2, ad 12, V, p. 188.

[124] "Lex naturalis dictat in generalitate quadam, quod inferior superiori obediendo subjaceat . . ." *Ibid.*, a. 1, conc., p. 181.

[125] *Liber II S.*, d. 44, a. 3, q. 1, conc., II, p. 1011.

[126] *Liber III S.*, d. 37, a. 1, q. 1, f. 2, III, p. 313. Confer above, ft. 48.

will of another in all events, according to no law, no rule, no fixed norm.[127]   Again it is true that St. Bonaventure is here dealing chiefly with religious and the vow of obedience; nevertheless, his teaching holds good for all forms of authority and submission.   To the point, he teaches that in civil society the subjects are to obey their leaders only in those things that are not contrary to God or right reason.[128]

Besides obeying, the subjects are bound to respect and revere those placed in authority.[129]   The natural law, our author notes, decrees that parents are to be honored, revered, and obeyed.[130] However, he includes under the name of parents all those who are constituted in positions of authority.[131]   Therefore, he demands that reverence and honor be shown to *all* superiors.   This point is rendered clearer when we bear in mind that according to his teaching superiors are the representatives of God.[132]   For this reason, he calls upon the subjects to obey and honor their superiors as the vicars of God here on earth.[133]   In answer to the objection that God alone is to be honored, our author asserts that God can be honored both in His own nature and in His image.   The honor, therefore, that is rendered to superiors is paid them because of God and, consequently, is referred to God.[134]   Here, then, we discover the principal reason why—i.e.,

---

[127] " Ad illud quod objicitur, quod periculosum est committere se homini ignoto ex toto: dicendum, quod si quis committeret se, nulla lege, nulla norma, nulla regula praefixa, sed in omnem eventum, hoc absque dubio esset stultum . . ." *De Perf. Evan.,* q. 4, a. 2, ad 13, V, p. 188.

[128] *Liber II S.,* d. 44, a. 3, q. 1, conc., II, p. 1011.

[129] *Com. in Joannem,* c. xix, n. 2, VI, p. 490.

[130] *De Perf. Evan.,* q. 4, a. 1, ff. 1–3, V, p. 179.

[131] *Decem Praeceptis,* coll. V, nn. 4–13, V, pp. 523–524.

[132] *De Perf. Evan.,* q. 4, a. 1, ad 9, V, pp. 182–183; *De Sex Alis,* c. 2, n. 6, VIII, p. 134; *Op. XIII, Deter. Quaestionum,* pars ii, q. 22, VIII, p. 372.

[133] ". . . hortamur subditos praelatis suis in omnibus, quibus de jure tenentur, fideliter obedire et jura sua illis persolvere et sententias eorum juste latas reverenter observare et eos quasi Dei vicarios honorare . . ." *Ibidem.*

[134] " Ad illud quod objicitur, quod honor Dei debitus nulli alio est reddendus; dicendum, quod honor debetur Deo et in propria natura et in imagine sua; honor enim, qui exhibetur homini propter Deum, ad Deum refertur . . ." *De Perf. Evan.,* q. 4, a. 1, ad 9, V, pp. 182–183.

because they are the representatives of God—superiors are to be obeyed, honored, and reverenced.

Finally, the Franciscan Doctor calls upon the inferiors to aid the rulers in their governance of the social organism. Thus, in speaking of the *norma praesidendi*—i.e., the relations that must exist between the ruling and the ruled—our author openly states that it is the duty of the people not only to observe just laws, but even to see that they are observed by others, to assist the ruler in punishing transgressors.[135] Accordingly, the subjects are to aid the ruler in promoting the end of society—right order, peaceful and harmonious relations, and the common good. In fact, as we have previously stated, the same rule of seeking the common good is to regulate the activities of both the ruled and the rulers.[136]

ARTICLE II. WEALTH

It was previously stated that the Eternal Good, Who is the first principle and last end of all good, has brought into being three degrees of participated goods: the purely spiritual, the purely material, and, finally, the creature that is both material and spiritual—man.[137] Furthermore, we learned that man possesses a rational and immortal soul, made according to the image and likeness of the Eternal, in virtue of which he is capable of attaining to God and of participating in His Eternal Perfection; that he is a person, for which reason he is immediately ordered to God as to his sole end; that he is destined for an eternity of supreme happiness in union with Happiness Itself. We then came to the conclusion that nothing in the whole expanse of creation is more noble than man.[138]

It was also pointed out that as there is but one efficient cause from which all things proceed, so there is but one ultimate end towards which all things, whether rational or irrational, tend—the Glory of God. However, as we noted, the irrational creation has

---

[135] *In Hex.*, coll. V, n. 19, p. 357. Confer *Liber II S.*, d. 44, a. 3, q. 1, conc., II, p. 1011.
[136] Confer above, p. 29.
[137] Confer above, pp. 35–36.
[138] Confer above, pp. 45ss.

been given a secondary and subordinate end, i.e., it has been ordered to man as to its proximate end. Brought into existence for the sake of man, those creatures, we concluded, were placed at the disposal of man and subjected to him in order to minister to him and to provide him with the needs of his body and soul.[139]

SECTION 1.   PRIVATE OWNERSHIP

Since material things were brought into being and were so constituted by the Creator that from them man might be furnished with the necessities of life, it follows that man has a natural dominion over the goods of earth—natural to such an extent that it is proper to man in all conditions of life.[140] This fact—man's natural right to make use of the lower creation— coincides with both the nature of man and the nature of the material goods.[141] Mindful of the principle which holds the less perfect to exist for the sake of the more perfect, one must realize that the common dedication to the service and good of mankind is inscribed in the very nature of irrational being. Consequently, we are assured of two things: (a) that the earthly goods have been dedicated to the good of all men; and (b) that man possesses a natural dominion—a dominion of use—over these things, so that he can make use of them in order to satisfy the necessities of his life here on earth, and thus becomes, as it were, the lord and master of his possessions.[142]

---

[139] Confer above, p. 41.

[140] "Primo modo potestas dominandi communis est omni statui, videlicet statui naturae institutae et naturae lapsae et naturae glorificatae; et excellentiori modo fuit in statu naturae institutae, quam sit in statu naturae lapsae." *Liber II S.,* d. 44, a. 2, q. 2, conc., II p. 1008.

It may be noted that man's power over the things of earth is not absolute but rather in the nature of a Divine stewardship. Confer *Com. in Ev. Lucae,* c. xvi, n. 3, VII, pp. 403–404.

[141] "Prima namque communitas est, quae manat ex jure necessitatis naturae, qua fit, ut omnis res ad naturae sustentationem idonea, quantumcumque sit aliqui personae appropriata, illius fiat, qui ea indiget necessitate extrema. Et huic communitati renuntiare non est possible, pro eo quod manat ex jure naturaliter inserto homini, quia Dei est imago et creatura dignissima, propter quam sunt omnia mundana creata." *Apologia Pauperum,* c. x, n. 13, VIII, p. 309.

[142] "Largissime dominandi potestas dicitur respectu omnis rei, qua homo

The material goods, therefore, are to subserve to the good of mankind, and man, on the other hand, enjoys a natural dominion over these goods—a dominion which, as Bonaventure states, is so necessary to man that he cannot renounce it.[143] This common natural right of mankind to utilize the earth and its fruits, then, is the primitive right and law of nature.[144] It affirms nothing else but the common dedication of the material creation to the utility of mankind and the natural right which all men have to the use of the goods of earth.

There now arises the question: how are the goods of earth to be possessed—in common, or privately? In other words, whence comes the distinction of possessions, the individual appropriation of the material goods that were brought into being for the common good of all men? That the Seraphic Doctor affirms the lawfulness and necessity of private property in the present state of affairs, we can have no doubt. Indeed, our author says that in obeying the law of nature, which demands that he preserve his actually extant individual nature,[145] man must act in a rational manner—i.e., he is not to live from day to day, but must so organize his terrestrial existence that he provides for future needs. Furthermore, the very nature of paternity requires, as we have seen, that the father make provision for the nourishment and the care of his children.[146] Because of these and other duties imposed upon man by nature, the Seraphic Doctor explicitly states that man has a right to private property.[147]

In order to understand the doctrine of the Seraphic Doctor

---

potest ad libitum et votum suum uti: et hoc modo dicitur homo esse dominus possessionum suarum, sive mobilium, sive immobilium." *Liber II S.*, d. 44, a. 2, q. 2, conc., II, p. 1008.

[143] " Nam usus temporalium necessarius est vitae humanae. . . . Qui autem sic vellet temporalia abjicere, ut non vellet alimenta suscipere nec operimentum habere, non operaretur perfecte, sed stulte." *De Perf. Evan.*, q. 2, a. 1, ad 3, V, pp. 131–132. Confer *Apologia Pauperum*, c. vii, nn. 3–4, VIII, pp. 272–273; *Ibid.*, c. x, n. 13, p. 309; *Ibid.*, c. xi, n. 5, p. 312.

[144] Confer above, ft. 141.

[145] *De Perf. Evan.*, q. 2, a. 3, ad 1–2, V, p. 162; *Ibid.*, ad 3–4.

[146] Confer above, pp. 160–161.

[147] ". . . aliquis omnino liber est in possidendo temporalia . . ." *Liber IV S.*, d. 20, p. 2, a. 1, q. 3, ad 4, IV, p. 535.

with regard to private possessions, we must once again distinguish with him between two classes of precepts arising from the natural law. The first are the absolute precepts of nature, remaining immutably valid in all the states of human life; the second are the relative precepts, which can be changed according to the various conditions in which man finds himself.[148] Thus, the right to private property seems to arise from a relative precept of nature, since, according to St. Bonaventure, all things were common in the state of original justice and would have remained commonly possessed if man had not fallen into sin. In the present state of affairs, however, the division of possessions enjoined by the relative precept of nature is, because of the corruption of man, a necessity—it is needed to preclude quarrels and contentions.[149]

From what has been said, then, it clearly follows that in the mind of the Franciscan Doctor the common possession of material goods—or economic communism, if you wish—is not, strictly speaking, contrary to nature *in se*. Even in the present state of affairs, it is not only lawful, as Bonaventure points out, but even praiseworthy for certain groups to follow the communistic mode of life. He cites as an example the religious order to which he belonged.[150]

Indeed, the necessity for private property has arisen with the Fall of man—not that private property is a direct consequence or punishment of sin—for if man had remained in the state of

---

[148] " Ad illud quod objicitur, quod illud quod dicatur a natura habet durationem perpetuam; dicendum, quod illud est verum de eo quod natura dictat simpliciter, sed non est verum de eo quod natura dictat pro statu . . ." *De Perf. Evan.*, q. 4, a. 1, ad 7, V, p. 182. Confer *Liber IV S.*, d. 26, a. 1, q. 3, conc., IV, p. 665; *Liber II S.*, d. 44, a. 2, q. 2, ad 4, II, p. 1009.

[149] " Et secundum hoc quaedam sunt de dictamine naturae simpliciter; quaedam de dictamine naturae secundum statum naturae institutae; quaedam de dictamine naturae secundum statum naturae lapsae. Deum esse honorandum, dictat natura secundum omnem statum; omnia esse communia, dictat secundum statum naturae institutae; aliquid esse proprium, dictat secundum statum naturae lapsae ad removendas contentiones et lites." *Ibidem.*

[150] The Seraphic Doctor defends the mendicant orders against the "murmurantes" of his time. His main defense thereof is contained in *De Perf. Evan.*, V, pp. 117–198, and *Apologia Pauperum*, VIII, pp. 233–330,

original justice, then all things would have been commonly possessed.[151] As a consequence, we may rightly assert that for our saintly author the distinction of possessions, which is commanded by a relative precept of the natural law for the state of fallen nature and which appears as a determination of the indefinite and primary right which all men have to use the goods of earth, was brought into being because of the corruption of fallen man and for the sake of conserving peace and order.

SECTION 2. THE USE OF MATERIAL GOODS

The whole universe is the object of God's never-failing prodigality, but upon man in particular does He send an unceasing shower of benefits. Indeed, all the goods that man possesses, whatever they may be, have been bestowed on him by God as gifts, according to St. Bonaventure.[152] Our author classifies the infinite variety of divine blessings in hierarchical order according to their worth. At the summit of the pyramid are the gifts of grace; farther down are the gifts of nature—e.g., health and strength; and, finally, at the base are the goods of fortune—e.g., prosperity.[153]

The Seraphic Doctor, then, looks upon the material goods of earth as the least of the gifts showered upon man by his Eternal Maker.[154] It must be borne in mind, however, that for St. Bonaventure the goods of earth are essentially good [155] and can, consequently, be licitly, usefully, and even virtuously used and possessed.[156] The usefulness of earthly possessions must be

---

151 " Si enim homo non peccasset, nulla fuisset agrorum divisio, sed omnia communia." *In Hex.*, coll. XVIII, n. 7, V, p. 413. Confer *Exp. super Reg. Fr. Min.*, c. iv, n. 3, VIII, p. 413.

152 *Liber IV S.*, d. 33, dub. VI, IV, p. 764.

153 " . . . bona fortunae, quam naturae, quam etiam gratiae sunt dona Dei; sed fortunae minima, naturae media, sed gratiae optima. Inter dona naturae computatur salus et fortitudo; inter bona fortunae prosperitas et quies." *Com. in Ecc.*, c. v, q. 4, conc., VI, p. 49.

154 *Ibidem; Com. in Ev. Lucae.*, c. xvi, n. 17, VII, pp. 408–409; *Liber III S.*, d. 28, a. 1, q. 5, ad 1, III, p. 631.

155 " . . . omnia sunt bona essentialiter . . ." *Exp. super Reg. Fr. Min.*, c. vi, n. 17, VIII, p. 423.

156 " . . . licet ista temporalia contemnenda sint tanquam minima, tamen

apparent, for they provide in an adequate manner for the conservation of life and promote the development—both material and spiritual—of the human personality.[157] In fact, our saintly author considers their use so necessary to human existence that although he praises the evangelical virtue and vow of poverty which demands the renunciation of earthly possessions and the limited use of earthly things, he does not refrain from pronouncing a *fool* the individual who proposes to renounce, *in a total manner,* the use of the goods of earth.[158] Therefore, he asserts, man cannot renounce the inborn right that he, as the image of God, has to the use of the goods of earth.[159]

Nevertheless, though the material goods of earth are essentially good and can, for that reason, be licitly and fruitfully possessed, they cannot hope to satisfy the yearnings of man's heart.[160] Furthermore, the Seraphic Doctor looks upon riches as an occasion to sin, for they render man earth-bound,[161] separate the heart from God,[162] and are an incentive to cupidity—the root of all

---

fidelis horum dispensatio non debet contemni, quia et eadem est fidelitas in re magna et parva, et fidelis dispensatio rerum temporalium disponit ad fidelem dispensationem et custoditionem spiritualium et aeternorum . . ." *Com. in Ev. Lucae,* c. xvi, n. 17, VII, p. 409. Confer *De Perf. Evan.,* q. 2, a. 1, ad 3, V, p. 131; *S. de T., Dom. IV p. Pent.,* s. 1, IX, p. 374; *S. de S., De S. P. N. Francisco,* s. v, IX, p. 591.

[157] *Apologia Pauperum,* c. viii, n. 12, VIII, p. 290.

[158] " Nam usus temporalium necessarius est vitae humanae, qui tamen haberi potest absque dominio et proprietate, sicut patet in pauperibus, qui nihil proprietatis habent. . . . Esse igitur contentum usu tegumenti et alimenti est modus perfectae virtutis . . . Qui autem sic vellet temporalia abjicere, ut nec vellet alimenta suscipere nec operimentum habere, non operaretur perfecte, sed stulte." *De Perf. Evan.,* q. 2, a. 1, ad 3, V, pp. 131–132. *Apologia Pauperum,* c. xii, nn. 19–21, VIII, pp. 322–323.

[159] Confer above, ft. 141.

[160] ". . . tantae capacitatis es, quod nulla creatura infra Deum sufficit satiare tuum desiderium." *Soliloquium,* c. 1, n. 6, VIII, p. 31. Confer *Op. VI, De Perfectione Vitae ad Sorores,* c. v, n. 10, VIII, p. 120; *Com. in Ecc.,* prooemium, nn. 5, 7, VI, p. 4; *S. de T., Dom. II, p. Pent.,* s. 1, IX, pp. 407–408.

[161] *Com. in Ev. Lucae,* c. xii, nn. 24, 25, 28, VII, pp. 317–318; *Ibid.,* c. xiii, n. 24, p. 342; *Ibid.,* c. xiv, n. 42, p. 372; *Ibid.,* c. xviii, n. 44, p. 464; *S. de T., Dom. XIV p. Pent.,* s. 1, IX, pp. 407–408.

[162] *Com. in Ev. Lucae,* c. xviii, n. 44, VII, p. 464; *S. de T., Dom. IV p.*

evil.[163] It is for this reason, therefore, that Bonaventure is totally opposed to the accumulation of wealth—whose end is not the satisfaction of man's needs and whose result is inordinate love for temporal possessions. He condemns not riches in themselves, but the inordinate love of riches.[164] Here we see the Holy Doctor as the loyal follower and true son of the Seraphic Father, St. Francis of Assisi. Like the Poverello, he teaches that the heart of man must be detached from the love of material goods, that it is erroneous, nay iniquitous, so to focus our attention upon the temporal that it becomes the source of joy when wealth abounds and the cause of sorrow when it is lacking.[165]

As a result, the Seraphic Doctor condemns not the material goods themselves, but their unlawful use, or " dissipation." [166] For him, the goods of earth should lead man first of all to the Eternal and to things eternal; they should subserve him in the attainment of his ultimate end—union with God.[167] Indeed, as we have seen, Bonaventure teaches that the material creation, besides administering to man's bodily needs, should be of service to his soul—i.e., should offer him the means whereby he may ascend to the praise and love of the Eternal.[168] The material things of

---

Pent., s. 1, IX, p. 373; *S. de B.V.M., De Annuntiatione B.V.M.*, s. iv, IX, p. 676.

[163] ". . . radix omnium malorum est cupiditas . . ." *De Perf. Evan.*, q. 2, a. 1, conc., V, p. 129. Confer *Apologia Pauperum*, c. x, n. 15, VIII, p. 309; *S. de T., Dom. in Albis*, s. 1, IX, p. 289.

[164] ". . . divitiae non sunt in culpa, sed cupiditas divitiarum . . ." *De Perf. Evan.*, q. 2, a. 2, ad 8, V, p. 143. ". . . omnia sunt bona essentialiter, sed occasionaliter mala sunt ex humana infirmitate." *Exp. super Reg. Fr. Min.*, c. vi, n. 17, VIII, p. 423.

[165] ". . . nequitia autem est mundum istum diligere, et ea quae nascuntur et transeunt pro magno habere et ea concupiscere, et pro his laborare, ut acquirantur, et laetari, cum abundaverint, et timere, ne pereant, et contristari cum pereunt." *De Perf. Evan.*, q. 2, a. 1, conc., V, p. 129.

[166] St. Bonaventure terms the illegal use of material goods, a dissipation. Confer, *Com. in Ev. Lucae*, c. xvi, n. 3, VII, pp. 403–404.

[167] ". . . quia bona temporalia sunt, ut per haec acquirantur bona aeterna. Cum ergo haec temporalia sic habentur, quod propter illa aeterna perduntur; tunc absque dubio dissipantur." *Ibid.*, p. 404. ". . . corporale bonum non debet desiderari nisi propter spirituale . . ." *Ibid.*, c. xi, n. 8, p. 279.

[168] Confer above, pp. 40–41.

earth, consequently, do not constitute the end of human living. They are, in fact, nothing more than means to man's one true goal. Accordingly, to use the temporal goods in such a manner that they lead us away from the one true Good—the Eternal—is a dissipation of these goods.[169] Again, to elevate them so that they actually assume the role of an end is to disfigure the divine image that has been impressed upon man's soul and to degrade the human person, which, as a person, should be ordered to God, and to God alone.

Furthermore, our saintly author states, earthly possessions are dissipated when they are not distributed.[170] In other words, though man has individually appropriated the goods of earth, he must at the same time so use them that they are of service to all. Considering this point, the Seraphic Doctor likens the one blessed with the goods of earth to the sun. As the sun must shed its rays of light and warmth for the benefit of all, so should the individual who possesses an extra amount of earthly riches distribute his worldly goods in such a manner that they may be of benefit to others.[171] The basis for this teaching, without doubt, is the prime and universal purpose of material goods—their dedication to the good of humankind.

This principle of distribution—viz., that the goods of earth are dissipated unless distributed—first appears in the case of extreme necessity. Relative thereto, our author teaches that in

---

[169] Confer above, ft. 167.

[170] "Qui ergo haec temporalia sic expendiunt, quod non quaerunt in eis meritum salutis, sed solatium carnis, temporalia non dispensant ad modum boni villici, sed dissipant . . . Tunc autem haec temporalia bene dispensentur, quando in opera misericordiae distribuntur . . ." *Com. in Ev. Lucae,* c. xvi, n. 3, VII, p. 404. ". . . intelligitur . . . de divitiis, quae justo titulo possidentur; et tamen iniquitatem pariunt, nisi distribuantur . . . De his, inquam, divitiis debent fieri amici per largitionem eleemosynarum, quae manifestant pietatis affectum . . ." *Ibid.,* n. 14, p. 408. Confer *Com. in Ecc.,* c. v, q. 1, conc., and ad 1–2, VI, p. 47.

[171] "Exemplum de sole: si dedisset Dominus soli animam intellectivam et radios ad mundum illuminandum, et ipse clauderet radios suos, ne illuminaret mundum, propter quod Deus fecit illum; nonne esset dignus poena? Certe sic; ita dico tibi: si Dominus dedit tibi multa bona temporalia, quae tibi pro te et pro multis aliis sufficiunt; si claudis ea et includis et non elargiris aliis, certe dignus es poena . . ." *S. de S., De S. Nicolao,* IX, p. 475.

such cases it is licit for the person finding himself in extreme necessity to take that which is necessary, even though it has been appropriated by another. The foundation for this teaching is the fact that man has an inherent right to that which is needed for the preservation of his life.[172] This principle is again brought to bear in the case of a superfluity of material goods, in which case the possessor is morally bound to distribute his surplus goods for the benefit of the less fortunate. Those who have a superabundance of the riches of earth, the Seraphic Doctor expressly states, are bound not merely in charity, but in *justice*, to come to the aid of the needy.[173] More, he teaches that all superfluities *belong* to the poor and must be distributed among them.[174] We should note here that our author speaks of a twofold necessity, hence a twofold superfluity: (1) strict necessity, and (2) necessity conditioned upon the status of a person or the common life of a people or society.[175] The sharing of those goods which are superfluous in the first sense—i.e., which are not required for the preservation of nature (*respectu naturae*), but are needed by the person's status (*respectu personae*)—is a counsel; whereas the sharing of those goods which are superfluous in the second sense—i.e., which are not needed either *respectu naturae* or *respectu personae*—is a precept.[176] Nevertheless, St. Bonaventure reminds

---

[172] Confer above, ft. 141.

[173] ". . . dare eleemosynam indigenti hoc potest esse dupliciter: aut solum quia considerat indigentiam, et sic est pietatis; aut quia considerat indigentiam et debitum, quia sibi impositum, vel quia ipse debet, cum habet superfluum; et sic est pars justitiae . . ." *Liber IV S.*, d. 15, dub. v, IV, p. 378.

[174] ". . . omnes superfluitates divitum sunt una res publica pauperum." *Exp. super Reg. Fr. Min.*, c. vi, n. 23, VIII, p. 424. Confer *Com. in Ev. Lucae*, c. vi, nn. 72-73, VII, p. 155; *Ibid.*, c. xvi, n. 38, p. 416; *S. de S.*, *De S. Laurentio M.*, IX, p. 567; *Ibid.*, *De S. Bartholomaeo, Ap.*, p. 572.

[175] " Ad illud quod quaeritur de necessariis et superfluis, dicendum, quod necessarium dicitur dupliciter: vel secundum naturae arctitudinem, vel secundum communem usum vivendi." *Liber IV S.*, d. 15, p. 2, a. 2, q. 1, conc., IV, p. 371.

[176] ". . . superfluum . . . duplex est, scilicet respectu naturae, sed non personae; et hoc dare est perfectionis et consilii; superfluum autem naturae et personae, cum locus et tempus adest, et videt hominem indigentem, nisi

us that many things which today are looked upon as necessities would be considered superfluous, if we would recall the purpose of wealth—viz., to supply life's necessities.[177]

However, this distinction cannot satisfy the Seraphic Doctor fully. Accordingly, he reminds us that although *justice* commands the *haves* to come to the aid of the needy only when there is a superfluity in the true sense of the term, *piety* commands this at all times, i.e., whenever our fellowman is in need.[178] Thus, he calls upon those who have been blessed with the material goods of earth to step beyond the realms of justice and to enter into the realms of love, of mercy, and of liberality, for justice is oftentimes powerless and ineffective.[179]

Allied to this consideration is Bonaventure's condemnation of the practice of usury. For him, usury is the misappropriation of that which belongs to another.[180] To appreciate the teaching of our author, we must recall that he considers money an indestructible good.[181] Besides, money, in itself and of itself, does not produce fruit.[182] Indeed, Bonaventure tells us that money becomes fruitful only through the agency of man.[183] Now, in the actual lending of money the *dominium* is transferred from

---

reservet magis egenti, hoc dare est praeceptum . . ." *Com. in Ev. Lucae,* c. iii, n. 27, VII, p. 76.

[177] *Ibid.,* c. xx, n. 4, p. 521; *Liber IV S.,* d. 15, p. 2, a. 2, q. 1, conc., IV, p. 371.

[178] Confer above, ft. 174.

[179] ". . . intelligitur de divitiis quae justo titulo possidentur, et tamen iniquitatem pariunt nisi distribuantur . . . De his, inquam, divitiis debent fieri amici per largitionem eleemosynarum quae manifestant pietatis affectum . . . 'Qui habuerit substantiam hujus mundi et viderat fratrem suum necessitatem habere et clauserit viscera sua de eo, quomodo caritas Dei manet in illo?' . . . 'Perde pecuniam propter amicum et ne abscondas illam sub lapide in perditione . . .'" *Com. in Ev. Lucae.,* c. xvi, n. 14, VII, p. 408.

[180] ". . . in usuria est quaedam violentia et quaedam fraudulentia; fraudulentia in hoc, quod vendit homini rem suam." *Liber III S.,* d. 37, dub. vii, III, p. 835.

[181] ". . . pecunia, dum in usum vertitur, non consumitur nec deterioratur . . ." *Ibid.,* p. 836.

[182] ". . . pecunia quantum est de se, per seipsum non fructificat . . ." *Ibidem.*

[183] ". . . tota ratio utilitatis est ex parte utentis." *Com. in Ev. Lucae,* c. vi, n. 81, VII, p. 157.

one person to another, so that the one who receives the loan receives full power over the money and becomes the sole proprietor thereof.[184] Consequently, if this money produces fruit it is through the agency of the borrower who, with the transfer of the money, has received the power to use it. Hence, does not the lender, in demanding part of this fruit, exact something that *per se* belongs to the borrower, who has caused this money to fructify? [185]

Furthermore, the Seraphic Doctor presupposes that the one who borrows is poorer than the one who lends. Being poorer, he has enough difficulties to contend with in paying his debt. The lender, on the other hand, being richer, is already obliged to assist his needy brother. He should, therefore, be satisfied if the loan is repaid in full; nor should he demand recompensation for an act of beneficence to which he is already obligated.[186]

SECTION 3. THE COMMAND OF MANUAL LABOR

In the thought of the saintly son of St. Francis, labor is an essential of human life. It is a duty prescribed not by a mere dictate of some positive institution, but by a precept of the very nature of man—by a dictate of the natural law that obliges all men.[187] Accordingly, it is natural for man to labor, since each man is to put to fruitful use the powers and gifts that have been bestowed upon him.[188] Indeed, like the Seraphic Father, St. Bonaventure has no use whatsoever for " Brother Fly "—the parasite of human society. Therefore, he states that he who

---

[184] ". . . in mutatione pecuniae transfertur pecunia in dominium alienum." *Liber III S.,* d. 37, dub. vii, III, p. 836.

[185] " In mutuo meum fit tuum ; et si tu acquiras aliquid per industriam tuam ex illo mutuo, et ego aliquid de illo repeto, vendo tempus, quod est commune, et quod non est licitum vendere." *Decem Praeceptis,* coll. VI, n. 19, V, p. 528.

[186] " Tenetur enim unusquisque subvenire proximo in mutuo ex divino mandato ; dum ergo vendit ei illud quod tenetur ei facere, ipsum fraudat et decipit." *Liber III S.,* d. 37, dub. vii, III, p. 835.

[187] ". . . nullus homo debet esse sine labore in hac vita . . ." *De Perf. Evan.,* q. 2, a. 3, ad 1–2, V, p. 162. Confer *Exp. super Reg. Fr. Min.,* c. v, n. 4, VIII, p. 420.

[188] ". . . ut unusquisque data sibi gratia utatur . . ." *Ibid.,* n. 3.

will not work does not deserve to eat.[189] Unhesitatingly he asks that such individuals be excluded from charity and be severely punished by the civil authorities, because otherwise they deprive the truly needy of the charity which is rightly theirs.[190]

Although all men are obliged to labor and no one is to be idle, it does not follow, however, as Bonaventure remarks, that each individual man is obligated to *manual* labor.[191] In Bonaventure's teaching, manual labor is necessary and obligatory only if the end thereof—viz., the acquisition of the necessities of life, the abolition of idleness from which many evils arise, and the subjugation of man's carnal appetites to reason—cannot be attained by some other legitimate means.[192]

Two kinds of precepts are to be distinguished in the natural law—those that oblige all men individually (as the precept of divine cult), and those that bind the race as a whole (as the precept of propagation).[193] Like the dictate of propagation, the

---

[189] " De isto pane qui non laborat non manducet; qui vero laborat non indiget . . ." *In Joannem*, c. vi, coll. 26, n. 5, VI, p. 565.

[190] ". . . tales, qui laborare poterant et tunc circa nihil occupati erant et abundare volebant, proni erant ad maleficia et rapinas. Et ideo justo judicio rector reipublicae tales a mendicatione arcebat et poena gravissima puniebat." *De Perf. Evan.*, q. 2, a. 2, ad 13, V, p. 146.

[191] ". . . nullus homo debet esse sine labore in hac vita . . . sed ex hoc non sequitur, quod oportet occupari circa laborem manuum et maxime lucrativum." *Ibid.*, a. 3, ad 1–2, p. 162.

Manual labor in Bonaventurian teaching is extended to include all lawful activities by which man secures the necessities of life. *Ibid.*, conc., p. 161. Furthermore, our author classifies the mechanical arts—weaving, armor-making, agriculture, hunting, navigation, medicine, and the dramatic art—amongst the servile works. *Decem Praeceptis*, coll. IV, n. 9, V, p. 521. For further study of the Mechanical Arts, confer *De Reductione*, n. 2, V, pp. 319–320; Healy, *op. cit.*, pp. 81–88.

[192] ". . . dicendum, quod natura ad hoc non astringit nisi ratione periculi vitandi. Nam si ex lege naturae haec manaret obligatio, cuncti essent universaliter et aequaliter obligati; quod absurdissimum est. Ideo, si quis a natura astringitur, hoc non est nisi propter vitandum periculum; et hoc potest esse tripliciter: aut quia non potest sine labore vivere, aut quia non potest honeste vivere, aut quia non potest fructuose vivere; in primo periclitatur entitas, in secundo honestas, in tertio utilitas." *De Perf. Evan.*, q. 2, a. 3, ad 1–2, V, p. 162. Confer *Ibid.*, ad 5–7, pp. 162–163.

[193] Confer above, p. 137.

precept of manual labor binds the whole human race in common, but not every individual in the race, except in certain circumstances.[194] Furthermore, the binding force of manual labor is based upon the necessity of sustaining human life; accordingly, it has binding force only if man cannot otherwise provide himself with the necessities of life. Therefore, the matter of precept is the end, not the particular means—i.e., the securing of the necessities of life, not the manual labor itself. This particular means, manual labor, becomes a matter of precept only in the event that no other just means is available to attain that end.

Accordingly, Bonaventure writes that each individual is obliged to manual labor only when he cannot otherwise live, or honestly live, or fruitfully live.[195] Furthermore, in the teaching of our author, it is unreasonable to demand that all men be engaged in manual labor, since there are many other occupations—occupations of much greater import—that must be carried on if the fullness of the common human good is to be attained.[196] These other occupations may not produce new material values, but, after all, the material is not the full good of man and of society. For man, the material element of society, is composed of both the material and the spiritual creation. Accordingly, both man and society are in need of something more than mere material goods and values.

In fact, the Seraphic Doctor, as we have seen, teaches that the well-being of the social organism postulates a threefold good and, consequently, a threefold activity.[197] It demands corporeal, or material goods; civil, or administrative goods; and spiritual

---

[194] *De Perf. Evan.*, q. 2, a. 3, ad 3, V, p. 162.

[195] " Sic igitur astringitur necessario ad manualiter operandum pauper validus, si in tali articulo constitutus est, quod non potest aliter vivere, vel non potest honeste vivere, vel etiam non potest aliter vivere fructuose. Si autem aliter potest hoc periculum vitare aeque vel magis utiliter, astringi ad hoc non habet ex lege naturae." *Ibid.*, ad 1–2, p. 162.

[196] " His autem, qui maxime sunt idonei ad spiritualia opera praedicta, vel etiam ad civilia, et minime ad haec manualia, hujusmodi opera lucrativa et artificialia non sunt in praecepto, nec etiam in consilio; quia stultum esset, quod pro re modicae utilitatis commune bonum magnum incurreret detrimentum . . ." *Ibid.*, conc., pp. 161–162.

[197] Confer above, pp. 129–131.

goods.   Bonaventure recognizes as corresponding to this threefold good, a threefold work or activity that is needed to provide
for these goods and thereby to promote the true well-being of
the social body—viz., manual, administrative, and spiritual activity.[198] Indeed, this threefold good and its concomitant activity,
as our author states, are absolutely necessary for the well-being
of society.[199] Furthermore, not all men are equally fitted for
these various types of activity.   Some, he tells us, are more
equipped to promote the material goods; others, the administrative; and still others, the spiritual.[200]   Hence, he concludes that
it is absurd—absurd, since it would be detrimental to the common
good—to oblige all men to work with their hands.[201]

Because the various kinds of labor are necessary for the common well-being of man and society, it follows that not only those
engaged in manual labor, but also those engaged in civil and
spiritual activities contribute to the betterment of the human
race.   They devote their time, energy, and effort to the service
of their fellowmen and society, hence, a return—a return that
is *due* them—must be made to them by the social body, for he
who serves society should, in turn, be served by society.[202]

---

[198] "Ad cujus pleniorem evidentiam notandum est, quod regimen reipublicae in Ecclesia attenditur circa tria, scilicet quantum ad bonum inferius,
quod est corporale; quantum ad bonum exterius, quod est civile; et quantum
ad bonum interius, quod est spirituale.   Et secundum hoc triplex genus
operis est necessarium ad regimen reipublicae et Ecclesiae militantis, scilicet
opus artificiale, quod et manuale dicitur, . . . opus civile et opus spirituale."
De Perf. Evan., q. 2, a. 3, conc., V, p. 161.

[199] *Ibidem.*

[200] ". . . inter membra Christi sunt quaedam maxime idonea ad operationes
corporales et minime ad spirituales, quaedam e converso, quaedam medio
modo . . ." *Ibidem.*

[201] Confer above, ft. 196.

[202] "Sicut ergo qui intenti sunt operibus civilibus reipublicae ad opera
manualia per apostolicum praeceptum non intelliguntur astricti; sic nec hi
qui intenti sunt spiritualibus, maxime si redundent in aliorum salutem,
commodum et profectum." *De Perf. Evan.,* q. 2, a. 3, conc., V, p. 161.

". . . habere potestatem vivendi de alieno, hoc est tripliciter: vel secundum
legem justitiae, vel secundum legem clementiae; vel mixtim secundum
utramque.   Secundum legem justitiae habent illi qui habent auctoritatem
officii et operis onus; et tales possunt potestative petere et in judicium

Accordingly, St. Bonaventure holds that those who are devoted to the promotion of the civil and spiritual goods are entitled to receive the necessities of life from those who work with their hands.[203]

Bonaventure, therefore, speaks of three classes of men in society. They are: *agricultores,* who through manual labor provide the social body with the earthly goods, the necessities of life; the *defensores,* who through administrative activity provide society with protection and promote order and harmony; and the *orantes,* who supply men with their spiritual needs and provide for the spiritual good of the social organism.[204]   According to his teaching, then, each man has a role to fulfill, a role that is never totally and solely personal.   Each role, be it that of the lowest manual laborer or that of the most exalted contemplative, redounds to the good of all the members of the social whole.

Finally, with reference to the manner of working, Bonaventure, together with the Seraphic Father, prescribes that our labor should be directed to the glory of God—that men " should labor faithfully and devoutly, so that banishing idleness, the enemy of the soul, they do not extinguish the spirit of holy prayer and devotion, to which all temporal things should be subservient." [205]

---

trahere.—Secundum legem clementiae potestatem habent vivendi de alieno qui possunt sufficientem allegare miseriam, per quam digni sunt misericordia, ut pauperes infirmi.—Secundum utramque, vero habent illi qui opera faciunt apostolica, non tamen incedunt eum auctoritate dignitate sed cum humilitate paupertatis; et ideo digni sunt sustentari tanquam operarii et tanquam egeni." *Ibid.,* ad 9, p. 163.

203 In his teaching, as appears from the previous footnote, both the Mendicant Friars and the unfortunate—the poor who cannot work—are entitled to the aid of the faithful. In fact, Bonaventure refers to three types of mendicants: (a) the unfortunate, who beg from necessity; (b) the Mendicant Friars, who beg for superhuman motives; and (c) those who beg *ex vitiositate culpae.* Only this last type of begging is represensible; the other two have a right to our aid. *Ibid.,* a. 2, V, pp. 140ss.—The Seraphic Doctor also teaches that those striving after learning should be aided. *Ibid.,* p. 142.

204 Confer above, p. 131.

205 *Rule of the Friars Minor,* c. 5.   Confer *Exp. super Reg. Fr. Min.,* c. v, n. 1, VIII, p. 419.

ARTICLE III.   THE VIRTUES

The third and final social force to be considered is virtue. Accordingly, the scope of the present article is to submit to scrutiny St. Bonaventure's teaching concerning the various virtues and the influence they exert on the social order. This article will be divided into four sections; the first dealing with the nature of virtue in general and the various virtues mentioned by our saintly author; the second treating of the cardinal virtues; the third devoted to the virtue of justice and its allied virtues; and the fourth considering the supernatural virtue of charity.

SECTION 1.   NATURE AND KINDS OF VIRTUES

Man, as we know, is endowed with both existential and operative life—he not only exists, but also acts. However, since he is not a substance of immediate operation, man must be endowed with certain powers or faculties destined for action; these faculties must then be further determined by habits, or to be more explicit, by virtues.[206]

A.   The Definition of Virtue

As the Seraphic Doctor uses the term, *virtue* in its widest sense signifies the excellence or perfection of a thing. The very word is associated with the idea of power; for, as he writes, virtue, etymologically considered, signifies that which invigorates and raises to activity.[207] However, besides connoting power and activity, virtue also carries the idea of goodness.[208] In this instance we find virtue identified with the right or good use of the will.[209] Therefore, besides being a habit that facilitates the activity of the faculty in which it resides, virtue is also a *pondus*

---

[206] *Brev.*, p. 5, c. iv, V, p. 256; *Liber I S.*, d. 32, a. 2, q. 2, ad 4–5, I, p. 564; *Liber II S.*, d. 40, a. 1, q. 3, conc., II, p. 925; *Liber III S.*, d. 33, a. 1, III, pp. 712ss.

[207] ". . . virtus de ratione sui nominis dicit, quod ad agendum erigit et vigorat." *Ibid.*, d. 34, p. 1, a. 1, q. 1, conc., p. 738.

[208] In fact, virtue, our author notes, is a *bonum in se*—an ordering good, since it directs *ad bonum*. Cf. *Liber II S.*, d. 27, dub. 2, II, p. 670; *Apologia Pauperum*, c. i, n. 7, VIII, p. 238.

[209] "Virtus est bonus usus voluntatis . . ." *Liber II S.*, d. 27, dub. 2, II, p. 671.

inclining and moving man to the golden mean of right living.[210]
Thus, it appears that virtue is mostly concerned with the rectitude of life—with what is to be done.[211] Finally, virtue, in the
truest and most proper sense, according to the teaching of the
Franciscan Doctor, adds still another note, that of merit—of
leading man onward to his final and ultimate goal.[212]

The thought of the Seraphic Doctor can best be understood if,
together with him, we bear in mind that the term *virtue* can be
understood *communiter, proprie,* and *magis proprie.*

Commonly understood, he writes, virtue can be defined in a
twofold manner: (a) with reference to the act alone, and (b)
with reference to the act and the end. In the first instance,
"virtue is the ultimate of power"; in the second, "it is the
disposition of the perfect towards the best." Here, Bonaventure
further remarks, we find the two notions common to all virtues:
(a) the notion of completion of power—i.e., a certain aptness or
facility for acting, and (b) the notion of perfecting a thing in
view of its end—i.e., a disposition towards perfection. It is
under this grouping that we find both the natural, or a-moral,
and the moral virtues. Here also, then, are to be found the
purely intellectual virtues.[213]

Though these virtues confer a certain aptness or facility for
acting, they do not, on the other hand, determine the right use

---

[210] ". . . quaelibet virtus est quoddam pondus recte inclinans et movens ad
medium, circa quod habet consistere." *Liber III S.,* d. 33, a. 1, q. 2, ad 5,
III, p. 715.

[211] *Ibid.,* d. 26, a. 1, q. 1, ad 2–3, p. 557.—Another point to be borne in
mind is that, as Bonaventure states, virtues are essentially *boni usus* and
cannot be put to evil use. *Liber IV S.,* d. 9, a. 2, q. 2, ad 1, IV, p. 209.

[212] *Ibid.,* q. 1, conc., p. 214; *In Hex.,* coll. VII, n. 5, V, p. 366.

[213] "Dicendum, quod virtus accipitur communiter, proprie, et magis
proprie.—Secundum quod communiter accipitur, sic comprehendit virtutem
moralem et naturalem; et sic dupliciter habet definiri: aut in comparatione
ad actum, aut in comparatione ad actum et finem ultimum. Primo modo
definitur a Philosopho de *Caelo et Mundo,* cum dicit: 'Virtus est ultimum
potentiae de re.' Secundo modo definitur ab eodem in septimo *Physicorum:*
'Virtus est dispositio perfecti ad optimum.' Istae enim duo sunt notifica-
tiones virtutis in sua generalitate, prout comprehendit virtutem moralem et
naturalem." *Liber II S.,* d. 27, dub. 3, II, p. 671. As appears, Bonaventure's source is Aristotle.

of this activity; consequently, these virtues can be put to bad use. We thus come to virtue properly so called.

Properly understood, virtue can be considered both in relation to its act and in relation to its directive principle. Taken in relation to its act, virtue in the proper sense is defined as "a habit which perfects the worker and his work." [214] Relative to the directive principle, however, it is defined as "a voluntary habit consisting of a mean, this being determined by right reason, as the wise man would determine it." [215] Only the moral virtues —those virtues which not only confer an aptness towards a certain type of activity, but also determine the right use of this facility—are included under this grouping. [216]

Although virtue, understood in the *proper* sense, according to our author, can be predicated of the gratuitous virtues, nevertheless these latter are, strictly speaking, virtues in the *more proper* sense. This last kind of virtue can be examined under four aspects, viz., according to its fourfold cause. Thus, with relation to the final cause, virtue is defined as "right reason leading to its end"—the end in this case being the supernatural end of man. Relative to the material cause, or the subject it informs, virtue is defined as "*bona voluntas.*" When compared to its formal cause, i.e., its proper act or complement, it is defined as "the order of love or ordered love." Finally, when reference is made to the effective principle, virtue is defined as "a

---

[214] "Alio modo consideratur virtus proprie, prout comprehendit moralem tantum, extenditur tamen ad politicam et gratuitam. Et sic dupliciter habet considerari: aut per comparationem ad ipsum actum, aut per comparationem ad principium directivum. Si per comparationem ad actum, sic definitur a Philosopho in *Ethicis:* 'Virtus est habitus, qui perficit habentem et opus ejus bonum reddit.'" *Ibidem.* Cf. Aristotle, *Nicomachean Ethics,* b. 2, c. 5 (1106a23).

[215] "Per comparationem autem ad principium directivum sic definitur ab eodem Philosopho ibidem: 'Virtus est habitus voluntarius in medio consistens, recta ratione determinatus, prout sapiens determinabit.'" *Liber II S.,* d. 27, dub. 3, II, p. 671. Cf. Aristotle, *Nicomachean Ethics,* b. 2, c. 6 (1106b36–1107a2).

[216] In this category, then, are to be classified the naturally acquired moral virtues, or *consuetudinales,* as the Seraphic Doctor is wont to term them, and the political-cardinal virtues, which are, in fact, essentially *consuetudinales.* Cf. above, ft. 214; *Liber III S.,* d. 33, a. 1, q. 5, f. 1, III, p. 721.

good quality of the mind by which we live righteously, of which no one can make bad use, which God forms in us without us." [217] Under this heading are found the theological virtues and the gratuitous-cardinal virtues, i.e., the cardinal virtues informed by grace and charity.[218]

---

[217] " Tertio modo potest considerari virtus magis proprie, prout accipitur pro virtute gratuita; et sic quadrupliciter potest comparari, videlicet ad finem, ad subjectum, ad actum, et ad suum principium: secundum quadruplex genus causae, videlicet finalis, materialis, formalis et efficientis. In comparatione ad finem sic definitur ab Augustino in Soliloquiis: ' Virtus est ratio recta ad suum finem perveniens.' In comparatione vero ad subjectum, quod informat, quod est ipsa voluntas, sic definitur ab eodem de Civitate Dei: ' Virtus est bona voluntas.' In comparatione vero ad actum proprium, sive complementum sic datur illa de Moribus Ecclesiae: ' Virtus est ordo amoris sive amor ordinatus.' In comparatione vero ad suum principium effectivum datur illa quae ponitur a Magistro in littera: ' Virtus est bona qualitas mentis . . .' In qua definitione hoc quod dicitur qualitas mentis, ponitur pro genere, et subjunguntur tres differentiae. Per hoc quod dicitur: qua recte vivitur, separatur a bonis corporalibus. Per hoc quod dicitur: qua nemo male utitur, separatur a proprietatibus spiritualibus et naturalibus. Per hoc autem quod subjungitur: quam Deus in nobis sine nobis operatur, separatur a proprietatibus spiritualibus et consuetudinibus, quae etsi sint boni usus potentiarum animae, non sunt tamen per infusionem sed per acquisitionem." *Liber II S.*, d. 27, dub. 3, II, pp. 671–672.

[218] Only these are perfect virtues in the teaching of our author. The naturally acquired moral virtues are, in his thought, virtues in the proper sense—since they succeed in rectifying and invigorating man's faculties with reference to the acts of justice; since they adjust man's powers so that it may be easy for him to act in conformity with the laws of morality and to perform morally good acts; since they perfect the will and dispose our appetitive powers to act in accordance with right reason. (*Liber III S.*, d. 33, a. 1, q. 3, conc., III, p. 717.) Still, though they are undoubtedly perfections which enable man to order his life rightly, they do not of themselves render our activity meritorious; nor do they lead us to our true end. Accordingly, Bonaventure insists that the purely natural virtues alone cannot suffice.

What, then, is perfect and true virtue according to our author's mind? His answer is explicit. The true virtue is that which leads man to God, the source of all being, truth, and goodness, and which enables him to rest therein in certain eternity and perfect peace. (*In Hex.*, coll. VII, n. 5, V, p. 366.) The task that St. Bonaventure assigns to the true virtue is threefold: (a) to direct the soul on to its final end; (b) to rectify the *affectus* of the soul—fear, sorrow, joy, and hope—so that fear becomes holy, sorrow

B. *The Various Kinds of Virtues*

1. The Intellectual Virtues

The intellectual virtues, or *speculationes intellectuales,* as Bonaventure terms them, are the first set of virtues to command our attention. It is in his *Collationes in Hexaemeron* that we find our author's most complete treatment of these virtues.[219] Aristotle, especially the treatise on these virtues in the sixth book of the *Nicomachean Ethics,* is the source of Bonaventure's teaching.[220]

just, joy true, and hope certain; (c) to heal the diseases of the soul—infirmity, ignorance, malice, and concupiscence—which, affecting the cognitive, affective, and operative powers of man, spoil the whole soul. Without grace—i. e., aid from on high—he adds, man cannot accomplish this threefold task. (*Ibid.,* nn. 5–12, pp. 366–367.)

Bonaventure, therefore, adopts in the domain of action the self-same attitude that he set forth in the domain of knowledge. Aid must be received from on high; grace must come to elevate the natural virtues. Indeed, although the natural moral virtues themselves habilitate the powers of the soul, enabling man to perform morally good acts, they do not give any added power. (*Liber II S.,* d. 28, a. 2, q. 3, f. 1, II, p. 688.) Hence, there is need of another habit—grace—which, coming from above, not only ennobles the soul, but actually gives it an added power, moving it and elevating it above itself, onward to the Divine. (*Ibid.,* dub. 1, pp. 690–691.) The natural moral virtues are, in truth, perfections, but perfections which need to be further perfected both by grace and by charity. They must be perfected by grace, so that they may produce acts that are truly pleasing and acceptable in the sight of God; and by charity, in order that they may be rightly ordered and truly directed to the ultimate end of all human activity. (*Liber III S.,* d. 36, a. 1, q. 6, III, pp. 805–807.)

[219] Coll. V, nn. 12–13, V, p. 356.—Bonaventure touches upon this or that intellectual virtue in other sections of his writings, but nowhere else do we find an *ex professo* treatment of these. The reader is referred to *Liber III S.,* d. 23, a. 1, q. 1, ad 2, III, p. 472; *Ibid.,* d. 33, a. 1, q. 3, ad 5, p. 718; *Ibid.,* d. 34, p. 1, a. 2, q. 2, ad 2, p. 748; *Liber IV S.,* d. 18, p. 1, a. 3, q. 2, ad 4, IV, p. 481.

[220] Indeed, Tinivella, *op. cit.,* p. 178, writes: " concordantia ad particulares usque perducta dependentiam Collationes in Hexaemeron, a. 1. VI Ethicorum Aristotelis ostendit."

However, in his own treatment of these virtues, the Seraphic Doctor does not fail to add an original note. Thus, what have been proposed by Aristotle as pure fruits of our mind, Bonaventure refers to a higher source, to that First Principle whence comes every good gift. For, it is the light

Adhering to the doctrine of the Philosopher, St. Bonaventure mentions five intellectual virtues—science, art, prudence, wisdom, and understanding.[221] These virtues, he tells us, are necessary in order that the intellect may be able to operate rightly in its search for truth. To them has been given the task of perfecting the intellect so that it may elicit acts that are ordered to truth.[222] Their subject is the rational faculties of man—*rational* understood as opposed to affective.[223]

That these virtues influence the moral life of man, there can be no doubt. Indeed, in order that reason may not fail in the selection of the golden mean, it must be itself rectified by the intellectual virtues. Hence, we find the saintly Doctor concerned with these virtues when he comes to the science of Ethics; he numbers them among the illuminations of the light that is good.[224]

2. The *Consuetudinales,* or Moral Virtues

The task assigned to these moral virtues is the perfection of the rational affective or appetitive faculties, whether concupiscible or irascible. They are to teach man to depart from extremes and to adhere to the golden mean indicated by right reason.[225]

As was the case with the intellectual virtues, here again Aristotle is the source whence Bonaventure draws most heavily, if not exclusively.[226] In his treatment of these virtues the Fran-

---

from above—indeed, the second ray of the light that is good—that illumines the mind in reference to these *speculationes intellectuales.* Cf. *In Hex.,* coll. V, n. 12, V, p. 356; *Ibid.,* n. 1, p. 354.

[221] *Ibid.,* n. 12, p. 356.

[222] *Liber III S.,* d. 33, a. 1, q. 3, ad 5, III, p. 718.

[223] *Ibid.,* conc., p. 717; *In Hex.,* coll. VII, n. 13, V, p. 356.

[224] *Ibid.,* n. 13, p. 356; *Ibid.,* n. 1, p. 354.

[225] *Ibid.,* n. 2, p. 354.—The word *moral,* as applied to these virtues, comes from *ex more,* and signifies a certain custom, i.e., acquired by custom. (Cf. footnote 1 of the Editors of Quaracchi, II, p. 688.)

These virtues, Bonaventure tells us, are neither entirely from nature nor entirely from acquisition or custom—they are both innate and acquired. (*Liber II S.,* d. 39, a. 1, q. 2, conc., II, p. 902.)

[226] The most complete treatment of the moral virtues by our author is found in *In Hex.* (coll. V, nn. 2–11, V, pp. 354–356). Although he speaks of these in other sections of his writings, this seems to be the only place where he treats of them *ex professo.*

ciscan Doctor notes that Aristotle made mention of twelve *medietates:* (1) fortitude, (2) temperance, (3) liberality, (4) magnificence, (5) magnanimity, (6) *philotimia*, (7) gentleness (*mansuetudo*), (8) truthfulness, (9) *eutrapelia*, (10) friendship, (11) shamefacedness (*verecundia*), and (12) *nemesis.*[227] After enumerating these twelve, however, our author selects but six—viz., temperance, munificence, fortitude, gentleness, benignity, and magnanimity—since the exercise of these six is sufficient for the eradication of all vices.[228]

3. The Cardinal Virtues

The third set of virtues which we meet is the four cardinal virtues—prudence, temperance, fortitude, and justice. Since it is our intention to treat of these elsewhere at length, it will suffice for the present merely to mention the fact that these virtues provide man with the complete equipment of determinations necessary for the right ordering of his faculties. E.g., prudence governs his intellectual faculty; temperance, the concupiscible appetite; fortitude, the irascible appetite; and justice, all his extrinsic actions.[229]

His source is the *Nicomachean Ethics* of Aristotle, book 2, cc. 2, 4, 7. Confer Tinivella, *op. cit.,* p. 174, ft. 2–3.

[227] *In Hex.,* coll. V, n. 2, V, p. 354.

[228] *Ibid.,* nn. 2, 6, 9, 11, pp. 354–356.—Once again, St. Bonaventure does not fail to transfer and elevate to the order of grace what Aristotle has taught through the medium of unaided human reason. Thus, in his consideration of the virtue of temperance, for example, he comes to the defense of the religious, showing that the vow of poverty as well as the vow of chastity falls under the virtue of temperance. (*Ibid.,* nn. 4–5, pp. 354–355.) Moreover, he reprimands Aristotle on two points. In his treatment of benignity he extolls the love of enemies, in opposition to the Philosopher. (*Ibid.,* n. 9, p. 355.) Again, he asserts that the virtue of magnanimity does not consist in the desire for honors, unless the honors desired are eternal, and introduces the virtue of humility, which despises the apparently-great and appreciates those things which appear ignoble, but which are in reality noble. (*Ibid.,* n. 10, p. 355.) Finally, he reverts once more to the teaching that underlies all his writings, i.e., the subjection of reason to faith—demanding the submission of reason to faith in the study of virtues also. (*Ibid.,* n. 11, pp. 355–356.)

[229] *Liber III S.,* d. 33, a. 1, q. 4, conc., III, p. 720.

4. The Theological Virtues

Although the cardinal virtues supply man with the complete array of determinations necessary for the right ordering of his faculties and operations, nevertheless they do not suffice for the full and complete rectitude of man. In fact, the cardinal virtues, whether purely natural or elevated to the supernatural stage, are solely concerned with the "*ratio inferior.*" However, the complete and perfect rectitude of man demands that he, his soul, and his powers should be rectified according to its twofold aspect—the *inferior* and the *superior*. Hence, we must seek another set of virtues which are concerned with the *ratio superior* of man and which will enable him rightly to order his faculties under this new aspect.[230]

For this reason, we have three theological virtues—faith, hope, and charity—whose principal object is the Infinite considered as Infinite, e.g., the Eternal Good and the Eternal Truth.[231] In the theological virtues, contrary to the cardinal virtues, there is no excess of intensity. The reason for this is apparent. Their object is the Infinite, Who cannot be excessively believed in, relied upon, and loved or desired.[232]

These freely given and divinely infused virtues rectify the powers of the soul and order them directly to the Blessed Trinity in accordance with the prerogatives that are characteristic of the Three Divine Persons. Faith directs to the Sovereign Truth

---

[230] *Brev.*, p. 5, c. 4, V, p. 256.—Moreover, the cardinal virtues, political or gratuitous, are concerned only with those things that pertain to the end—i.e., with the means that lead to the end. (*Liber III S.*, d. 33, a. 1, q. 1, ad 3, III, p. 712.) All cardinal virtues, no matter what their dignity, have as their object the finite, the created. Indeed, such is their nature that they cannot be so elevated as to have God for their proper and immediate object without ceasing to be cardinal virtues. (*Ibid.*, q. 6, conc., p. 727; *Ibid.*, q. 3, conc., p. 717.) Consequently, in order that man may be rightly ordered with reference to both the creatures and the Creator, he must be blessed with virtues that have as their immediate and proper object the very end of the cardinal virtues, God, the supreme Good. (*Ibid.*, q. 4, ad 1, p. 721; *Ibid.*, d. 26, a. 1, q. 3, f. 2, p. 560.)

[231] ". . . objectum principale virtutis theologicae non est aliquid creatum, sed est bonum increatum sub conditionibus increatum, quae quidem sunt summa bonitas et summa veritas." *Ibid.*, d. 9, a. 2, q. 3, ad 6, pp. 218–219.

[232] *Ibid.*, d. 26, a. 1, q. 3, ad 1, p. 562.

by means of an act of assent; hope leads to the Supreme Reward by the sentiments of expectation and confidence that it inspires; and charity unites to the Infinite Goodness by desire and love.[233] Thus, the rational is clarified by the steadfastness of faith; the irascible is fortified by the security of hope; and the concupiscible is tempered by the sincerity of love.[234]

5. Further Ramifications of Grace

When sanctifying grace is infused into the soul, the latter is at once clothed with the three theological virtues, which give back to the soul the rectitude despoiled in it by sin.[235] The soul, then, receives all that is strictly necessary to bring it into right relation with God—but nothing more. Therefore, St. Bonaventure reminds us that these virtues are but the first out-pouring of grace. The faculties of the soul, rectified by the theological virtues, must be strengthened further in order to attain a higher perfection.

It is the *gifts* of the Holy Spirit which confer upon the soul's faculties this added energy. Their special task is to *set right* the faculties of the soul, to *fit* them for a higher state. They both liberate the soul from the bonds (*symptomata*) that would hold it back and fortify it with the resources needed for its actual advance.[236] However, there is still a third series of gratuitous habits which operate in the soul—the *beatitudes*.

---

[233] ". . . anima fertur recte in summam Trinitatem secundum tria appropriata tribus personis; ita quod fides dirigit in summe verum credendo et assentiendo, spes in summe arduum innitendo et exspectando, caritas in summe bonum desiderando et diligendo." *Brev.*, p. 5, c. 4, V, p. 256.

[234] ". . . quia ex fidei firmitate clarificatur rationalis, ex spei securitate fortificatur irascibilis, ex amoris sinceritate dulcoratur concupiscibilis." *S. de T., Feria Quinta in Coena Domini*, s. ii, IX, p. 252.

Moreover, through the medium of these virtues man is, in a way, rendered divine. (*Liber III S.*, d. 33, dub. 5, III, p. 730.) Indeed, when the spiritual faculties (memory, understanding, and will) have been directed to their proper object by the theological virtues, the soul becomes by that very fact *deiform,* and in it once more is readily perceived the image of God. (*De Donis*, coll. III, n. 5, V, p. 469.)

[235] *Liber III S.*, d. 34, p. 1, a. 1, q. 1, ad 5, III, pp. 738–739.

[236] *Ibidem.*

These perfect the powers of the soul and permit them to reach the maximum of their activity. Enabling the soul to act and to be acted upon in a perfect manner, the beatitudes lead the soul to its perfection.[237] In addition, the soul in which these habits are present and operative is blessed with a state of *quietude* and *delight*, i.e., a certain *spiritualis refectio* and the perception thereof. Thus, to the already mentioned ramifications of grace, our holy Doctor adds the *fructus* and *spirituales sensus*.[238]

SECTION 2. THE CARDINAL VIRTUES

A. The Cardinal-Political and the Cardinal-Gratuitous Virtues

In seeking to determine Bonaventure's thought concerning true and perfect virtue we learned that he was not fully satisfied with purely natural virtues. In order that they might enable man to perform acts that are meritorious and might lead him on to his final end, the naturally acquired virtues, we saw, had to be further perfected by the influence of both grace and charity.[239] Thereby we arrive at a division of the cardinal virtues—cardinal-political (the naturally acquired virtues) and cardinal-gratuitous (the virtues informed by grace and charity).[240]

Naturally, our attention must be focused upon the cardinal-political virtues, whose task is to render man rightly ordered for life among men—a life in common.[241] Although these

---

[237] *Ibid.*, conc., pp. 737–738.

[238] *Ibidem.*—These, as Bonaventure notes, are not new habits, but the perfect state (*fructus*) and use (*sensus*) of the preceding habits.

For a more thorough study of Bonaventure's teaching along these lines, we refer the reader to the scholarly work of Fr. Ephrem Longpré, "La Theologie Mystique de S. Bonaventure," *Archivum Franciscanum Historicum*, XIV (1921), Quaracchi, pp. 36–108. The point in consideration is contained on pages 44–54.

[239] Confer above, footnote 218.

[240] *Liber III S.*, d. 33, a. 1, q. 5, III, pp. 721–724.—The Seraphic Doctor, it must be known, also makes use of the Plotinian division of the cardinal virtues: *politicae, purgatoriae, animi jam purgati*, and *exemplatae*. (*In Hex.*, coll. VI, nn. 24–32, V, pp. 363–364.) Although Bonaventure makes use of this division, he does not, so it seems, make it his own. Confer Tinivella, *op. cit.*, p. 176, footnote 3.

[241] ". . . istae virtutes dicuntur politicae, quia reddunt hominem **bene**

virtues, which refer to man, the social animal, are concerned
with life in society, nevertheless their first influence must be felt
in man's private and personal life. Man must first be ordered
in reference to himself before he can be rightly ordered in reference to his neighbor. Only when man has become *right* in his
own personal life through the exercise of the virtues of prudence,
temperance, and fortitude, can he hope to become right in relation to his neighbor through the exercise of the virtue of justice.[242]

B. Why Are These Virtues Called Cardinal?

The virtues of prudence, fortitude, temperance, and justice
are called *cardinal* for several reasons, according to our author.
The first reason he advances is that they alone can open the
way and introduce the soul to the other virtues. His argument
proceeds as follows: virtue is concerned with the golden mean;
it is the duty of prudence to discover and select this mean, of
temperance to guard it, of justice to distribute it (i.e., to see to
it that this mean is observed in man's actions *ad extra*), and
of fortitude to defend it; therefore, if this golden mean, essential
in all the moral virtues, is discovered, guarded, distributed, and
defended by the four cardinal virtues, it obviously follows that
the cardinal virtues open the way to the other virtues—that they
alone can introduce the soul to all the other virtues.[243]

Again, he tells us that these virtues are called cardinal because
they are the principal ones, to which all the other moral virtues
are reducible. Thus, he writes, patience and various similar
virtues depend upon fortitude; humility and obedience can be

ordinatum ad vivendum inter homines . . ." *Liber III S.*, d. 33, dub. 5, III,
p. 730.

[242] *Ibid.*, a. 1, q. 4, conc., p. 720.

[243] "Philosophus dicit, quod 'virtus est medium duarum extremitatum,
secundum quod sapiens determinabit;' est enim in medietate consistens.
Virtus enim secundum Augustinum . . . non est aliud quam modus. Hunc
modum prudentia invenit, ut in omnibus non excedas, sed circa centrum
consistas. Unde prudentia auriga est virtutum. Unde dicit prudentia: ego
inveni modum; et temperantia custodit et dicit: et hoc volebam ego; justitia distribuit, ut non tantum velit sibi, sed et alteri; et quia postmodum
multiplices adversitates eveniunt, fortitudo defendit, ne perdatur modus."
Ibid., n. 12, p. 362.

reduced to justice; and so on for the rest of the virtues.[244] The same thought is expressed when he reasons thus: those virtues are the principal virtues in which every other one is integrated; now, the activity of virtue is fourfold—viz., to modify, to rectify, to order, and to stabilize; but temperance modifies, prudence rectifies, justice orders, and fortitude stabilizes. Ergo, these four are the principal (or cardinal) virtues.[245]

More properly, these virtues are called cardinal because they give direction to all our faculties of action and are, as it were, the four cardinal points of our moral universe—the four *cardines* of human activity by which the whole of human existence is governed.[246] Now, man possesses two faculties—knowing and willing—the right exercise of which constitutes the first and most important of his duties towards himself. Hence, man must have a virtue that regulates the exercise of his faculty of knowing (viz., *prudence*) and two virtues that regulate the two principal functions of his will (viz., *temperance*, by means of which he orders his desires, or the concupiscible part of his will; and *fortitude*, by means of which he orders his powers of attack and defense, or the irascible part of the will). Finally, man needs a virtue to direct his actions *ad extra* (i.e., his actions relating to his neighbor). This last is accomplished by the virtue of *justice*. Thus, the virtues of prudence, temperance, fortitude, and justice (i.e., the cardinal virtues) provide man with the full equipment of determinations necessary for the right ordering of his actions.[247]

---

[244] *Liber III S.,* d. 33, a. 1, q. 4, ad 4, III, p. 721.

[245] " Item, 'secundo dicuntur cardinales, quia secundum actus accipiuntur integrantes virtutes, qui sunt quatuor: modificare per appositionem circumstantiarum, rectificare—est enim recta ratio ducens in finem, consequens legibus—ordinare, stabilire. . . . Temperantia modificat, prudentia rectificat, justitia ordinat, fortitudo stabilit." *In Hex.,* coll. VI, n. 13, V, p. 362. Confer *Liber III S.,* d. 33, dub. V, III, p. 730.

[246] *In Hex.,* coll. VI, n. 14, V, pp. 362-363.

[247] " Cum enim virtus cardinalis dicatur, quia ordinat hominem circa ea quae sunt ad finem sive circa quid creatum; cum homo habeat comparari ad se ipsum et ad alterum, virtus cardinalis aut est regulativa actuum hominis respectu sui, aut respectu proximi. Si respectu sui: hoc potest esse tripliciter secundum actum principalem triplicis virtutis, videlicet

C. *How are the Cardinal Virtues Acquired?*

The acquisition of the cardinal virtues, as well as their dependent virtues, is radically an operation arising from nature. That is to say, these virtues are naturally acquired.[248] As proof of this, St. Bonaventure cites the fact that many men, though lacking the added light of revelation and the aid of grace, have actually acquired these virtues.[249]

Briefly, the teaching of our author as regards the birth of these virtues is as follows: they are both innate and acquired, neither entirely from nature, nor entirely from the frequent repetition of acts.[250] Man has, implanted within his soul, a certain innate rectitude of the will which confers upon him an aptitude, even if imperfect, for the accomplishment of good.[251]

---

rationalis, circa quam est prudentia, concupiscibilis, circa quam est temperantia, et irascibilis, circa quam fortitudo consistit.—Si vero ordinat ad alterum, sic est una virtus, quae quidem dicitur justitia, quia una est ratio, secundum quam ad alterum ordinat, videlicet ratio debiti." *Liber III S.,* d. 33, a. 1, q. 4, conc., III, p. 720.

Most properly, however, these virtues are called cardinal because they lead us to our eternal home. Here, without doubt, the Seraphic Doctor is referring to the cardinal-gratuitous virtues, which, then, are *the only true cardinal virtues.* Indeed, in this connection the saintly doctor, seeking to establish the difference between the *consuetudinales* and the cardinal virtues, asserts that only those virtues which lead man to his final end are cardinal virtues. Now, as we have seen, only the cardinal-gratuitous virtues, since they alone are perfected by grace and charity, are capable of leading man to his final end. Consequently, the appellation of cardinal, even though so used by our author, can be applied to the political virtues only in an improper manner. (*Ibid.,* dub. 5, p. 730. Confer Tinivella, *op. cit.,* pp. 175–176, especially footnote 3, on page 176.)

[248] As must appear, we are referring to the cardinal-political virtues, which are essentially *consuetudinales,* and to which all the *consuetudinales* can be reduced. "Eadem est virtus cardinalis et consuetudinalis secundum rem et essentiam; sed virtus consuetudinalis completum esse habet ab assuefactione . . ." *Liber III S.,* d. 33, a. 1, q. 5, f. 1, III, p. 721. Confer the whole question.

[249] *Ibid.,* f. 4, p. 722.

[250] ". . . virtutes consuetudinales nec sunt omnino a natura nec omnino ab acquisitione . . ." *Liber II S.,* d. 39, a. 1, q. 2, conc., II, p. 902.

[251] " A natura, inquam, sunt radicaliter, quia plantatam habemus in nostra natura rectitudinem, per quam apti sumus, licet imperfecte, ad opera virtutis

In addition, the germs of these virtues—i.e., germs from which the moral virtues can be developed—are also innate in man.[252] Considered at their very source, then, the cardinal-political virtues in us are no more than marks left upon our will to render it capable of good. Subsequent exercise develops these natural aptitudes. Through the medium of oft-repeated acts, therefore, the soul, already possessing an innate rectitude of the will and innate germs of these virtues, comes to the possession of the cardinal-political virtues themselves.[253]

D. The Virtue of Prudence

Though classified among the intellectual virtues residing in the intellect and considered as perfective of the rational (as opposed to the appetitive) powers of man, nevertheless prudence is not concerned with speculative truth as such, but with truth as the rule of action.[254] Dealing with human conduct—i.e., with the reasonable manner of acting—prudence, therefore, is a virtue which tells us what must be done and how it is to be done.

---

et honestatis; sed dum assuescimus, paulatim efficitur nobis facile quod prius erat difficile . . ." *Liber III S.,* d. 33, a. 1, q. 5, conc., III, p. 723.

[252] *Ibid.,* f. 5, p. 722.

[253] However, the Seraphic Doctor does not stop here. Indeed, he cannot. For, in his mind, virtue without grace is like knowledge without revelation—stunted. The aid of grace is necessary—the aid of grace by which the naturally acquired virtues are confirmed, fully developed, and brought to perfection. The true cardinal virtues, therefore, considered in their perfection, draw their being from two quite different sources—from human nature and custom on the one hand, and from grace and divine liberality on the other. Thus, the cardinal virtues, originating from nature, are led to a certain completion by subsequent exercise, to a greater completion by the infusion of grace and charity, but to perfect completeness by both grace and exercise. (*Ibid.,* conc., pp. 722-723; *Ibid.,* d. 36, a. 1, q. 6, conc., p. 806; *Liber II S.,* d. 27, a. 1, q. 2, conc., II, pp. 657-658.)

Moreover, grace is capable not only of perfecting and completing our natural virtues, but also of causing them to arise when their natural root alone exists and the habit of them is totally lacking. (*Liber III S.,* d. 23, a. 2, q. 5, conc., III, p. 498.)

[254] *Ibid.,* d. 35, a. 1, q. 2, conc., p. 776; *Ibid.,* d. 33, a. 1, q. 4, conc., p. 720; *Ibid.,* d. 39, a. 1, q. 2, ad 3, p. 864.

"For a good act is not good of itself unless it is done well, that is to say, done as it ought to be done." [255]

Cognizant of its importance in the moral order, the Seraphic Doctor ranks prudence first among the cardinal virtues and calls it the *auriga virtutum*. Moreover, he tells us that prudence should be preferred to all the other moral virtues, since knowledge of virtue precedes its exercise.[256] For, "as reason sees both for itself and for the other powers, so do prudence and faith perceive both for themselves and for the other virtues." [257] Consequently, prudence is, as it were, the *moderatrix* of the other virtues. This concept becomes apparent when we recall that it is the office of prudence to discover the golden mean—the constitutive element of the moral virtues.[258]

The task assigned to the virtue of prudence is that of directing man in the performance of morally good actions, i.e., actions which refer to the rectitude and honesty of life, according to the dictates of the natural law or of right reason.[259] Hence, the virtue of prudence is a habit which perfects the soul and inclines man to judge rightly in moral actions. As such, it enables man to choose what is to be chosen and to flee what is to be fled where the good of man is concerned.[260] Finally, in its regulation of the soul, prudence is concerned not only with what is licit, but also with what is fitting and expedient according to right reason.[261]

---

[255] "Nam nec bonum simpliciter bonum est, nisi bene fiat, id est sicut decet." *De Sex Alis,* c. 6, n. 2, VIII, p. 142.

[256] *In Hex.,* coll. VI, n. 12, V, p. 362.

[257] ". . . sicut ratio videt sibi et aliis potentiis, sic prudentia et fides discernunt sibi et aliis virtutibus." *Liber II S.,* d. 24, p. 1, a. 2, q. 1, ad 6, II, p. 562.

[258] *In Hex.,* coll. VI, n. 12, V, p. 362.

[259] "Quaedam autem est, quae consistit in intellectu sive ratione, in quantum inclinat affectum ad operationem; et haec fundata est super principia juris naturalis, quae ordinatur ad rectitudinem et honestatem vitae; et hujusmodi est scientia prudentiae-virtutis." *Liber III S.,* d. 35, a. 1, q. 2, conc., III, p. 776.

[260] *Ibid.,* d. 35, a. 1, q. 4, conc., p. 781.

[261] ". . . est consilium, quo erudimur ad discernendum, quid licet, quid decet, et quid expedit secundum judicium rationis rectae . . ." *De Domis,* coll. VII, n. 10, V, p. 491.—We may remark that prudence is concerned with all the details of life—regulative of all of man's thoughts, affections,

In order that man may be truly prudent, our author teaches, he must (a) judge rightly, (b) choose well, and (c) proceed promptly. St. Bonaventure at this point reverts to the Aristotelian teaching of a threefold requisite for the perfect virtue—namely, that the intellect must know what is to be done, that the will must will to do it, and that what is known and willed must be brought into being.[262] Therefore, the prudent man must not only judge rightly, but also select well. Indeed, the holy Doctor avers that the man who discerns correctly and does not choose aright actually condemns himself.[263] Moreover, having judged rightly and having chosen well, the prudent man must also see to it that his decision is promptly carried out.

The *integral* parts of the virtue of prudence (i.e., the parts needed for the perfect act of prudence) seem to be: memory, reason, understanding, circumspection, foresight, docility, and caution. Amongst the *subjective* parts (i.e., the species of prudence) we find: (a) the prudence by which we rule ourselves, or *monastic* prudence; and (b) the prudence which refers to the governing of others (*gubernatrix multitudinis*); this latter is: (i) *domestic* (*oeconomica*), (ii) *political*, and (iii) *military*. Included among the *potential* parts of prudence (i.e., virtues which have something in common with the principal virtue, but

---

and actions. (*In Hex.*, coll. VI, n. 29, V, p. 364.)—Moreover, the activity of prudence, as the Seraphic Doctor notes, is concerned with the past, the present, and the future. (*Ibid.*, n. 16, p. 363.) Although the highest act of prudence seems to consist in guarding against future pitfalls, this is actually the direct concern of but one part of prudence, i.e., foresight. However, all parts of prudence (e.g., memory, understanding, and foresight) are ordained to this end, that we learn from past experiences to better our future conduct. (*Liber III S.*, d. 33, dub. 2, III, pp. 728–729.)

262 " Triplex est operatio, scilicet discernere recta, eligere bona et prosequi expedite. . . . Non sufficit bonam voluntatem habere, nisi homo velit eam expedire in opere, a virtute intellectiva in affectivam et ab affectiva in operationem. Philosophus dicit, tria ad virtutem esse necessaria, scilicet ' scire, velle, et impermutabiliter operari.' " *De Donis*, coll. VII, n. 8, V, p. 490. Confer Aristotle, *Nicomachean Ethics*, lib. 2, c. 4.

263 ". . . . nam qui bene discernitet et male eligit se condemnat." *S. de S.*, *De S. Laurentio M.*, IX, p. 566.

which fall short of its full perfection in some respect) are: *eubulia, synesis,* and *gnome.*[264]

A point well worth keeping in mind is our author's insistence upon the fact that great prudence is required for the ruling of one's self; that still greater prudence is needed for the governing of a family, and that the greatest prudence of all is necessary for the governing of a city.[265]   In other words, St. Bonaventure insists that, before one seeks to govern a family, he must learn to rule himself and that he should first know how to keep his family rightly ordered before he attempts to govern the city or state.[266]

E. The Virtue of Temperance

Residing as it does in the concupiscible appetite of man, the virtue of temperance regulates his desires—his natural appetite for the pleasures of sense.[267]   The task assigned to this virtue is that of holding the middle course between pleasure and pain.[268]   In so doing, temperance is to perfect man's concupiscible appetite to such a degree that he may be enabled to observe the law of

---

[264] *In Hex.,* coll. VI, n. 29, V, p. 364; *Ibid.,* n. 16, p. 363; *De Donis,* coll. IV, n. 10, V, p. 475; *Liber III S.,* p. 728, footnote 6 of the Editors of Quaracchi.

[265] "Magna prudentia requiritur ad regimen sui, major ad regimen familiae, sed maxima circa regimen civitatis." *De Donis,* coll. IV, n. 10, V, p. 475.

[266] "Non potest aliquis habere ordinatam familiam, nisi ipse sit ordinatus. Si velit aliquis habere servientes castos; et ipse non erit castus, hoc non potest esse.   Similiter nisi homo bene regat familiam suam, non poterit bene regere civitatem, quia qualis princeps civitatis, tales et habitantes in ea." *Ibidem.*—This point of self-rule first, an important point, the Seraphic Doctor proposes again when he reminds his readers that the gift of counsel refers first and foremost to the rule of self, and then, if it should abound, to the direction of others. (*Liber III S.,* d. 35, a. 1, q. 4, f. 4, III, p. 780; *Ibid.,* conc., p. 781.)—For the role of prudence in superiors, confer *De Sex Alis,* c. 6, VIII, pp. 142–147.

[267] ". . . temperantia circa delectationes et tristitias . . ." *In Hex.,* coll. V, n. 2, V, p. 354.   Confer *Liber III S.,* d. 33, a. 1, q. 4, conc., III, p. 720.

[268] "Cujuslibet enim virtutis est medium tenere; sed hoc appropriatur temperantiae, quia maxime opportunum est circa delectationes medium custodire . . ." *Ibid.,* q. 2, ad 5, p. 715.

moderation and rightly to subjugate his sensual appetite to the rule of right reason in all things.[269] Accordingly, we see temperance as the rule of reason over the sensual life.[270] This virtue has for its material object the pleasures themselves, for its formal object, their conformity with the dictates of right reason. By means of this virtue we check the carnal vices—especially those of lust and gluttony—repress and restrain impure pleasures, kindle holy sentiments and desires, and regulate the entire man.[271]

The necessity of this virtue is stressed greatly by the Franciscan Doctor. In fact, he tells us that this virtue is urgently needed, since man is tempted by corporeal delights as soon as he is born. He is tempted first by the pleasure of the sense of taste, and later by the pleasures associated with the sense of touch. This contemporaneous passion for corporeal pleasures—contemporaneous, since it begins in early years and continues until old age—must be moderated by the virtue of temperance.[272]

According to our author, the virtue of temperance includes: sobriety, chastity, and modesty, or discipline.[273] Sobriety, to which is related the virtue of abstinence, has as its object the pleasures of the sense of taste. While sobriety dictates the moderate use of food and drink, abstinence goes a step further and imposes abstention from even the otherwise licit use of food and drink.[274] Chastity and similar virtues, on the other hand,

---

[269] " Temperantiae est nihil appetere poenitendum, in nullo legem moderationis excedere, sub jugum rationis cupiditatem domare." *In Hex.,* coll. VI, n. 29, V, p. 364.

[270] *Ibid.,* n. 16, p. 363.

[271] *Ibid.,* coll. V, n. 11, p. 356; *Liber III S.,* d. 33, dub. 4, III, p. 729; *S. de B. V. M., De Purificatione B. V. M.,* s. v, IX, p. 655.

[272] " Primo incipiendum est a temperantia. Haec necessaria est in primis; non enim statim homo tentatur a timore mortis, sed statim, quando natus est, delectationes secundum gustum; unde puer appetit dulce secundum gustum et postea delectabile secundum tactum, quando magnus est. Hanc passionem contemporaneam nobis, quae incipit in pueris et terminatur in senibus, oportet primo domare . . ." *In Hex.,* coll. V, n. 3, V, p. 354.

[273] " Partes ejus sunt sobrietas in gustu, castitas in tactu, modestia in ceteris sensibus; quam modestiam vocant theologi disciplinam." *Ibid.,* coll. VI, n. 15, p. 363.

[274] ". . . sobrietas est in moderato usu cibi, abstinentia vero dicit cessationem et a licito usu . . ." *De Perf. Evan.,* q. 3, a. 1, ad 15, V, p. 171.

have as their object the pleasures of the sense of touch. They command: (a) an honest and chaste use of the conjugal act, as in the virtue of *purity* (*pudicitia*); (b) a chaste abstaining from the conjugal act, as in the virtue of *continence;* and (c) a total and perpetual abstinence from every carnal pleasure and desire, as in the virtue of *virginity.*[275] Finally, modesty relates to the other senses of man. In point of fact, it is concerned with man's whole outward tenor and mode of living. Thus, St. Bonaventure writes:

> " True modesty consists in humility and piety of intellect, in meekness and paucity of words, in mildness and devoutness of manners, in discreetness and agreeableness of actions, in benignity and probity of exhortations and counsels." [276]

For him, the modest man is he who knows neither excess nor defect—he who exceeds in nothing.[277] In a word, modesty seems to be the very essence of the virtue of temperance.

F. The Virtue of Fortitude

Since the subject of fortitude is man's irascible appetite, the role assigned to this virtue is that of regulating man's powers of attack and defence.[278] Accordingly, fortitude is the virtue which strengthens the soul and enables it to bear with and triumph over sufferings, adversities, and difficulties, in accord-

---

[275] ". . . pudicitia dicit honestum et castum usum, continentia vero castam dicit cessationem ab usu . . ." *Ibidem.*—" In virginity we have the dedication of the integrity of the flesh to the Eternal by an inviolable proposal of perpetually restraining from every carnal pleasure and desire." (*Ibid.,* a. 3, conc., and ad 5, pp. 176–178.)

[276] "Vera autem modestia consistit in humilitate et pietate intellectuum. . . . In mititate et paucitate semonum. . . . In lenitate et religiositate morum. . . . In discretione et suavitate actionum. . . . In benignitate et probitate exhortationum et consiliorum . . ." *S. de T., Dom. III Adventus,* s. ix, IX, pp. 69–70.

[277] *Op. VII, De Regimine Animae,* n. 8, VIII, p. 130.—Modesty consists primarily in the heart and affection from which it redounds to our speech and body. (*S. de B. V. M., De Annuntiatione B. V. M.,* s. v., IX, p. 681.)

[278] *Liber III S.,* d. 33, a. 1, q. 4, conc., III, p. 720.

ance with the dictates of the natural law and for the sake of conserving justice and honesty of life.[279]   The golden mean between undue fear and recklessness is the road upon which it seeks to place man, rendering him neither pusillanimous or timid nor thoughtless or reckless, enabling him to endure difficulties and to be prepared to die in the attempt, should the circumstances warrant it.[280]   Raising man above the undue fear of danger, fortitude teaches him to fear nothing but the shameful and the disgraceful, to conduct himself manfully in both adversity and prosperity.[281]

The virtue of fortitude, or constancy, the Seraphic Doctor tells us, must be founded upon the virtue of *patience,* which is particularly needed in times of affliction and adversity, as it enables man to possess his soul and to have dominion over himself;[282] it must be aided and abetted by the virtue of *confidence,* which elevates and sustains man;[283] and it must be brought to

---

[279] " Fortitudo enim virtus ordinat ad sustinenda qualiacumque et quantumcumque tormenta, antequam bonum virtutis et honestatem derelinquat . . ." *Ibid.,* d. 35, a. 1, q. 5, ad 5, p. 784. Confer *Ibid.,* conc., p. 783; *Ibid.,* d. 33, dub. 3, p. 729; *Ibid.,* d. 26, a. 1, q. 3, ad 4, pp. 562–563; *Ibid.,* a. 2, q. 5, conc., pp. 579–580; *In Sapientiam,* c. 8, v. 7, VI, pp. 161–162.

[280] " Tertia medietas est fortitudo, quae est circa timores et audacias. Haec est necessaria homini, ut non sit pusillanimis, vel temerarius, sed sustineat terribilia et etiam mori sit paratus.   Aliqui enim cadunt in ignaviam et pusillanimitatem. . . . Fortitudo enim in anima est, non in carne." *In Hex.,* coll. V, n. 7, V, p. 355. Confer *Liber II S.,* d. 19, a. 1, q. 1, f. 4, II, p. 458.

[281] " Fortitudinis est animum supra periculi metum agere, nihilque nisi turpia timere, tolerare fortiter vel adversa, vel prospera." *In Hex.,* coll. VI, n. 29, V, p. 364.

[282] Patience, Bonaventure tells us, is the root and guardian of all virtues. It is the virtue via which man possesses his soul, and has dominion over himself; the virtue that rectifies the rational, tempers the irascible, modifies the concupiscible, and brings the exterior act to its consummation. *Com. in Ev. Lucae,* c. xxi, n. 27, VII, p. 530; *S. de T., Dom. II p. Pascha,* s. ii, IX, p. 299.

[283] Confidence, the Seraphic Doctor tells us, is to be placed not in one's self, but in God. *S. de B. V. M., S. de Annuntiatione B. V. M.,* s. vi, IX, p. 686; *Dom. II in Quad.,* s. i, IX, p. 217.

completion through the virtue of *perseverance,* which enables man to continue on to the very end.[284]

SECTION 3.   JUSTICE AND ITS ALLIED VIRTUES

Although the Seraphic Doctor refers to justice as the rectitude of the soul in refraining from evil and performing good, as the rectitude of rendering to another what is his due, as the rectitude of meting out punishments, and as the rectitude of rewarding each according to his merits—nevertheless, he seems to distinguish but two main species of justice: *general* justice on the one hand, and *special* (i.e., cardinal) justice on the other.[285]

A.   General Justice

As the general virtue, justice is nothing else but rectitude or righteousness—i.e., rectitude of the will, of the *affectus,* of the whole soul, of human life.[286]   Identified with the rectitude of the will and inculcating the performance of good and the avoidance of evil, general justice contains within itself all the other virtues, theological as well as cardinal, and is opposed by all the vices.[287]   Moreover, partaking of the rectitude of the soul,

---

[284] " In hac autem constantia probantur et approbantur milites Christi: hoc autem fit triplicis suffragantis virtutis adjutorio, scilicet per: Fundamentum patientiae. . . . Sustentamentum confidentiae. . . . Perseverantiae complementum . . ." *S. de S., de S. Laurentio M.,* IX, p. 569.

Perseverance, considered as the fixed and continued persistence of the will in prolonged sufferings, is a species of fortitude. It can also be considered as the firm proposal of continuance in good until the very end. As a firm proposal of continuance in good, it is a condition joined to each virtue. As a continuance in good until the very end, it is a state consequent upon all virtues. (*Liber III S.,* d. 36, a. 1, q. 1, ad 3, III, p. 793.)

At other times, Bonaventure tells us that fortitude must possess: "magnanimitatem in aggrediendo, virilitatem in prosequendo, longanimitatem in perseverando." (*S. de S., In Festo Om. Sanctorum,* s. ii, IX, p. 604.) For other allied virtues of fortitude, confer: *In Hex.,* coll. VI, n. 29, V, p. 364; *Liber IV S.,* d. 14, p. 1, a. 1, q. 3, conc., IV, p. 322; *S. de S., De S. Vincentio, M.,* IX, pp. 510ss.

[285] *Liber III S.,* d. 33, dub. 1, III, p. 728; *Liber IV S.,* d. 44, p. 2, a. 1, q. 1, conc., IV, pp. 921–922; *Ibid.,* d. 46, a. 1, q. 4, conc., p. 961.

[286] *In Hex.,* coll. XVIII, n. 18, V, p. 417; *Liber I S.,* d. 48, a. 1, q. 2, f. 4, I, p. 853; *Brev.,* p. 5, c. 4, V, p. 256.

[287] *Liber III S.,* d. 33, dub. 1, III, p. 728; *Ibid.,* a. 1, q. 2, ad 4, p. 715; *Ibid.,* d. 35, dub. 1, p. 787.

inducing man to do good and to avoid evil, and comprising all virtues and excluding all vices, the virtue of general justice, therefore, must have as its object the promotion and protection of right order. Indeed, it can be identified with the order of justice itself, which demands:

". . . that the Immutable Good be preferred to the mutable good, that the moral good be preferred to the useful good, that the Divine Will be preferred to our will, that the judgment of right reason preside over sensuality." [288]

Accordingly, this virtue—whose office is to foster rectitude of will, of soul, and of the entire human life; to inculcate the avoidance of evil and the performance of good; to promote and protect right order—must necessarily be of prime importance in the social life. Though general justice should first exert its influence in the individual's own private life, since it fosters the rectitude of the will, nevertheless, because it embraces all of man's relations—towards God, himself, his neighbor, and the irrational creation—it applies to the common good of humanity as a whole.[289]

The all-embracive influence of the virtue of general justice, as it appears in the writings of the Seraphic Doctor, cannot be exaggerated; for, being identified with the rectitude of human life, it is concerned with all our activities as rational agents. Accordingly, St. Bonaventure reduces all the precepts contained in the Decalogue to the one command of justice. Like most Scholastics, he divides the Ten Commandments into two laws of justice. The first, regulating man's relations with God, comprises the first three precepts of the Decalogue; the second, dealing with man's duties towards his neighbors, includes the last seven precepts.[290]

---

[288] "Est autem ordo justitiae, ut bonum incommutabile praeferatur bono commutabili, ut bonum honestum praeferatur utili, et voluntas Dei praeferatur voluntati propriae, ut judicium rectae rationis praesit sensualitati." *Brev.*, p. 3, c. 8, V, p. 237. Confer *Liber III S.*, d. 33, dub. 1, III, p. 728.

[289] *De Perf. Evan.*, q. 1, conc., V, p. 121; *Liber III S.*, d. 37, a. 2, q. 1, conc., III, p. 822; *Liber IV S.*, d. 31, a. 2, q. 1, conc., IV, p. 722.

[290] *Decem Praeceptis*, coll. I, n. 21, V, p. 510; *Liber III S.*, d. 37, a. 2, q. 1, conc., III, p. 822.

This virtue, according to the teaching of our author, requires that we be: *pious* in reference to God (i.e., prompt in obeying His law, zealous for His Honor and Glory); *chaste* and *sober* with ourselves (so regulating our powers and faculties that they will be rightly ordered); *just* in our relations with our neighbor (rendering him no harm, being solicitous for his eternal welfare); and *disciplined* in regard to the inferior creation.[291]

B. Special Justice, or the Cardinal Virtue of Justice

Considered as the special virtue, justice is a cardinal virtue distinct from all the others.[292] Unlike general justice, the cardinal virtue of justice is not simply the rectitude of the will, but the rectitude of the will *ordering to another*.[293] Moreover, unlike the other cardinal virtues, which are concerned with man compared to himself, which are regulative of his acts *respectu sui,* and which perfect the powers of the soul considered *in se,* special justice is regulative of human acts *ad extra* and concerns and governs man's relations with regard to his neighbor.[294]   This

---

[291] ". . . mortificatio cupiditatis mundanae perducit nos ad vitam perfectae justitiae . . . ut respectu nostri vivamus sobrie, respectu proximi vivamus juste, et respectu Dei vivamus pie . . ." *S. de T., Sabbato Sancto,* s. ii, IX, p. 270-271. "Ad justitiam ordinatam, per obedientiam ad superiores, per sociabilitatem ad pares, per castigationem ad inferiores." *Op. VII, De Regimine Animae,* n. 9, VIII, p. 130.

[292] ". . . justitia specialis est virtus cardinalis, distincta ab aliis . . ." *Liber III S.,* d. 35, dub. 1, III, p. 787.

[293] "Justitia vero specialis non est simpliciter rectitudo voluntatis, sed rectitudo voluntatis ordinans ad alterum . . ." *Ibid.,* d. 33, a. 1, q. 2, ad 4, p. 715.—However, the *alterum,* as contained in the teaching of the Seraphic Doctor, is not exclusively reserved to our fellow-man—the neighbor. Indeed, the *alterum* can also be both God, and the self-same individual, i.e., when he assumes the role of a double person, or is compared to himself as if to another. This takes place, e.g., when man accuses himself, in which case, the self-same individual is both the one accused and the one accusing; or, when man judges himself, in which case, he is both the judged and the one judged. (*Brev.,* p. 5, c. 4, V, p. 256.) Confer *Liber III S.,* d. 33, a. 1, q. 4, ad 4, III, p. 721; *De Perf. Evan.,* q. 1, conc., V, p. 121.

[294] "Nam prudentia rectificat rationalem, fortitudo irascibilem, temperantia concupiscibilem, justitia vero rectificat omnes has vires in comparatione ad alterum." *Brev.,* p. 5, c. 4, V, p. 256. "Si vero ordinet ad

ad-alterum motif is essential to the cardinal virtue of justice, which is to direct man in his relations with others. This justice, then, is *ad alterum ordinativa.*[295] Its task, as Bonaventure notes, is to rectify the will in such a manner that it may be able to render unto each what is his due.[296] Here, consequently, we meet with the second characteristic note of the cardinal virtue of justice, i.e., the notion of *debitum;* for, the one *ratio* according to which justice orders us to the other is the *ratio debiti.*[297] Thus, the cardinal virtue of justice is that rectitude ordering us to another in rendering to him what is his due.[298] Concerned, then, with what belongs to another, special justice is assigned the office of respecting the rights of others and of preserving them intact.[299] From this viewpoint we argue that the more sacred and more intimate these rights are, the greater our duty is to respect them and to preserve them intact.

Since the cardinal virtue of justice is the rectitude of the will, it appears that the will is the subject of justice. Hence, the Seraphic Doctor writes: " Justice is in the will as in its subject." [300] However, as the saintly Franciscan affirms, the cardinal virtue of justice encompasses the various powers of the soul, operating in the rational, concupiscible, and irascible powers of man and perfecting them.[301] This operation takes place

---

alterum, sic est una virtus, quae quidem dictur justitia, quia una est ratio secundum quam ad alterum ordinat, videlicet ratio debiti." *Liber III S.,* d. 33, a. 1, q. 4, conc., III, p. 720.

[295] ". . . virtus justitiae, quae est ad alterum ordinativa . . ." *Ibid.,* ad 2, p. 721.

[296] "Directio vero justitiae consistit in hoc, quod voluntas rectificatur in reddendo unicuique quod suum est . . ." *S. de Diversis, De Modo Vivendi,* IX, p. 724.

[297] Confer above, footnote 294.

[298] "Alio modo dicitur justitia rectitudo ordinans ad alterum in reddendo ei quod suum est; et sic est virtus cardinalis." *Liber III S.,* d. 33, dub. 1, III, p. 728.

[299] ". . . justitia, ad quam spectat unicuique tribuere jura sua." *Ibid.,* q. 4, conc., p. 720. Confer *Liber IV S.,* d. 14, p. 1, a. 2, q. 1, conc., IV, p. 325.

[300] ". . . justitia est in voluntate tanquam in subjecto . . ." *Liber II S.,* d. 41, a. 2, q. 2, f. 3, II, p. 951.

[301] *Brev.,* p. 5, c. 4, V, p. 256.

through the medium of the potential parts of justice. Some of them, as *truth*, pertain to the rational; others, as *liberality*, are concerned with the concupiscible; and still others, as *zealous anger* and *penance*, regulate the irascible powers of the soul. Nevertheless, there remains but one virtue of justice because of the one *ratio*—render to each his due—in which the potential parts of justice participate. In short, Bonaventure's teaching is as follows: since the *ratio debiti* can, through the habits that are reducible to justice, extend to the acts of all the powers of the soul, it follows that the cardinal virtue of justice encompasses all the powers of the soul. At the same time, however, it remains one because of the one *ratio*.[302]

St. Bonaventure does not speak—at least, as far as we have been able to discover—of the subjective parts of the cardinal virtue of justice. We do not find him employing the terms: *commutative, distributive,* and *legal* justice.[303]   Still, this fact

---

[302] " Et si objicias: quomodo potest esse habitus unus? dico, quod justitia cardinalis esse habitus unus dicitur, non sicut conclusio particularis dicitur habitus unus, sed sicut una totalis scientia dicitur unus habitus; ut grammatica, quae multos continet habitus particulares, et geometria; sic et justitia, obedientiam, humilitatem, poenitentiam, et largitatem et veritatem; et secundum istos habitus particulares potest esse in diversis potentiis. Nam veritas est in rationali, largitas in concupiscibili, poenitentia et humilitas in irascibili; uniuntur tamen omnes in unam rationem, quae est reddere unicuique jus suum; et ideo subeunt rationem unius virtutis cardinalis." *Liber IV S.,* d. 14, p. 1, a. 2, q. 1, conc., IV, p. 325.   Confer *Liber III S.,* d. 33, a. 1, q. 4, ad 2-4, III, p. 721.

[303] This may be due to the fact that Bonaventure does not treat of the virtue of justice at any great length. Indeed, his most complete treatment of this virtue is contained in the 33rd distinction of the third book of his *Commentary on the Sentences.* (III, pp. 711–731.) But, here, his teaching concerning justice is brought out in his treatment of the cardinal virtues, which virtues are treated *in globo.* This is also the case with his treatment of justice as contained in his *Collationes in Hexaemeron* (coll. VI, n. 18, V, p. 363; *Ibid.,* n. 29, p. 364), as well as his treatment of justice in the fourth book of the *Sentences* (d. 14, p. 1, IV, pp. 318–330), in which section, he is chiefly concerned with the virtue of penance.

In reference to the quasi-integral parts of justice, it may be stated, that general justice, as Bonaventure notes, is the rectitude of the will in avoiding evil and doing good. (*Liber III S.,* d. 33, dub. 1, III, p. 728.) Therefore, since the cardinal virtue of justice is the rectitude of the will

does not allow us to conclude that he was ignorant of these species of justice. On the contrary, we find certain remarks in his writings which lead us to believe that he was surely acquainted with the various subjective parts of the cardinal virtue of justice.[304]

In point of fact, the cardinal virtue of justice, commanding that the other be given his due, seems to coincide with commutative justice, especially when this *other* is restricted to the neighbor and when cardinal justice is considered as controlling the mutual relations between private individuals taken in their fundamental equality. Moreover, the second of Bonaventure's *justitiae morales*, the *forma convivendi*, actually touches upon commutative justice, for here is contained the precept that reads: do not unto others what you do not want others to do unto you.[305]

That the Seraphic Doctor was acquainted with distributive justice appears certain from that section of his writings in which he teaches that the diversity of rewards should correspond to the diversity of merits, i.e., that each should receive according to his merits.[306] Besides, he tells us that this kind of justice is

---

in reference to the *other*, we may conclude that its quasi-integral parts are: to do the good which is due to the neighbor, and avoid the evil which is hurtful to him. (Confer footnote 2 of the Editors of Quaracchi, III, p. 728.)

[304] In reference hereto, Legowicz, *op. cit.*, pp. 114–115, has had recourse, for the basis of his division of justice into commutative, distributive, and legal, to the following text of the holy Doctor: " Est enim justitiae triplex actus, scilicet rectificare, coordinare et compensare. Justitia namque nihil aliud est quam recta voluntas, ordinata et recompensativa, quia per ipsam 'redditur unicuique quod suum,' secundum quod competit rectitudini juris et ordinis dignitati." (*De Perf. Evan.*, q. 4, a. 2, conc., V, p. 185.) Legowicz, then, identifies *rectificare* with legal justice, *coordinare* with commutative justice, and *compensare* with distributive justice. However, this interpretation of the Bonaventurean text is stretching matters a little too far. Furthermore, we must bear in mind that St. Bonaventure is, at this point, concerned with a special type of justice—*justitia abundans*— which consists in the perfect service of God by souls striving after perfection in the religious life.

[305] *In Hex.*, coll. V, n. 18, V, p. 357.

[306] " Necessarium est etiam ad servandum ordinem justitiae, ut unicuique reddatur secundum merita sua . . ." *Liber IV S.*, d. 44, p. 2, a. 1, q. 1, conc., IV, pp. 921–922. Confer *Ibid.*, d. 46, a. 1, q. 4, ad 3, p. 961.

incumbent in a most particular manner on the head of the society, whose duty it is to punish and reward according to the
deserts of the various individuals.[307] Nor is our Doctor ignorant
of vindicative justice, for he demands the punishment of crimes
and calls "the rectitude in meting out punishments" justice
accepted in the more proper sense.[308]

Finally, his *norma praesidendi,* the third of his moral justices,
seems to coincide with what is understood as legal justice. In
his teaching on the *norma praesidendi* St. Bonaventure sets forth
the duties of the citizens (viz., that they must be submissive to
the laws established for the common good and give aid to the
ruler in seeing to the observance of these laws) and mentions
also the duties of those in power (viz., that they seek not their
own private, utility, but the common good of the whole social
structure).[309]

Since the virtue of justice prescribes that each be given his
just due, we cannot exaggerate the important role that it plays
in the social order. Indeed, because it enjoins respect for the
rights of the various individual members of the social organism,
justice is therefore needed not only for the perfection of society,
but for its very existence. Without it, the fullness of the human
person—the rights natural to him as man and the dignity proper
to him as the image of God—would be denied. Without it, men
would become mere means for the advancement and aggrandizement of others and would, as a result, be degraded below the
human level. We perceive, then, why the Seraphic Doctor insists that the *norma praesidendi* (which regulates the respective
duties of citizens and rulers) cannot be observed unless the
forma convivendi (which demands that we do not unto others
what we do not want others to do unto us and requires, con-

---

[307] "Sextum medium est justitiae judiciali recompensatione. . . . Hoc
considerat jurista sive politicus, ut fiat retributio secundum merita." *In
Hex.,* coll. I, n. 34, V, p. 335.

[308] "Tertio modo dicitur justitia magis proprie, secundum quod dicit
rectitudinem in reddendo ei quod est poenae; et accipitur ibi justitia pro
severitate." *Liber III S.,* d. 33, dub. 1, III, p. 728. Confer *Liber IV S.,*
d. 44, p. 2, a. 1, q. 1, conc., IV, pp. 921–922.

[309] *In Hex.,* coll. V, n. 19, V, p. 357.

sequently, that each be given his due and right) is first put into force. In other words, there can be no hope of obtaining harmonious social relations if the rights of the individuals—sacred and innate—are not respected.

The teaching of the Franciscan Doctor does not stop here. He further asserts the impossibility of observing the *forma convivendi* unless the *ritus colendi* (which imposes the worship of God) is also first put into practice.[310] Without the reverence due to the Supreme Being it is impossible to attain not only to harmonious social relations, but also to justice towards one's fellow man. In fact, as our author testifies, the divine cult and honor is the beginning of the whole edifice of justice.[311] Therefore, the very existence of harmonious social relations postulates that both the rights of God and those of man are to be respected and preserved.

C. The Allied Virtues of Justice

Among the many allied virtues of justice mentioned by the Seraphic Doctor are the following: piety, religion, *latria*, obedience, reverence, penance, zealous anger, humility, truth, equity, fidelity, gentleness, clemency, benignity, meekness, innocence, benevolence, liberality, and mercy.[312] Since it would be out of place to consider each of these virtues individually, we shall attempt to touch only upon the more important in our considera-

---

[310] " Ad censuram judicandi non pervenitur nisi per normam praesidendi; nec ad normam praesidendi nisi per formam convivendi; nec ad istam nisi per primam." *Ibid.,* n. 14, p. 356. Confer *Ibid.,* nn. 14–19, pp. 356–357.

[311] " Nam justitiae est 'reddere unicuique quod suum est,' tam Deo, quam sibi, quam proximo. Deo autem principaliter debetur honor et reverentia; et ad hoc redendum praecipue disponit humilitas. . . . Quoniam ergo initium totius justitiae est cultus et honor divinus . . ." *De Perf. Evan.,* q. 1, conc., V, p. 121.

[312] *Liber III S.,* d. 9, a. 2, q. 3, conc., III, pp. 217–218; *Ibid.,* q. 4, ad 2, p. 220; *Ibid.,* d. 35, a. 1, q. 6, conc., pp. 785–786; *Liber IV S.,* d. 14, p. 1, a. 1, q. 1, conc., IV, pp. 318–319; *Ibid.,* q. 3, conc., p. 322; *Ibid.,* a. 2, q. 1, conc., p. 325; Brev., p. 5, c. 4, V, p. 256; *In Hex.,* coll. VI, n. 18, V, p. 363; *Com. in Ev. Lucae,* c. vi, n. 76, VII, p. 156; *S. de S., De S. Domenico,* IX, p. 565.

tion of the fourfold acceptance of *piety* found in the writings of our author.

First of all, the Seraphic Doctor speaks of piety towards God, in which case it is identified with the cult of the Divine and embraces, among others, the virtues of religion, *latria,* and *theosebia.* Then, he refers to piety towards parents, which is identified with man's obligations towards his parents and towards those constituted in authority. Again, he writes of piety towards the neighbor, in which case we have: (a) the virtue of mercy, and (b) the gift of piety.[313]

1. *Ad Deum*

Man must, in the first place, be benevolent towards God, worshiping Him as the One by Whom, according to Whose Image, and for Whom he was created.[314] *Religion,* inclining the will to give to God the worship due to Him because of His supreme excellence, is the allied virtue of justice whereby man is enabled to venerate the Supreme Being.[315] That man must honor and revere his God, affirms Bonaventure, is a command of the natural law.[316] In referring to the cult due to the Eternal, the Seraphic Doctor speaks of *theosebia,* or *eusebia,* and *latria. Theosebia,* concerned with the internal acts of divine cult, relates to the activity of the theological virtues.[317] *Latria,* on the other hand, an allied virtue of justice and a species of religion, is concerned with the external cult due to God. It considers God as the one to Whom the cult is due; the external worship, as that which is due; and the *ratio debiti,* as the reason for manifesting this worship, i.e., because

---

[313] *Liber III S.,* d. 35, a. 1, q. 6, conc., III, pp. 785–786; *Ibid.,* ad 1–4, p. 786; *Ibid.,* d. 9, a. 2, q. 1, ad 3, p. 214.

[314] *Liber III S.,* d. 35, a. 1, q. 6, ad 1–4, III, p. 786.

[315] "Rursus, quia species justitiae, secundum quam ordinatur ad venerandam naturam superiorem, est ipsa religio . . ." *Ibid.,* d. 9, a. 2, q. 3, conc., p. 217. "Religio est virtus, qua colitur ille qui est superioris naturae . . ." *Ibid.,* f. 1, p. 217.

[316] "Deum esse honorandum, dictat natura secundum omnem statum . . ." *Liber II S.,* d. 44, a. 2, q. 2, ad 4, II, p. 1009. Confer *Com. in Ev. Lucae,* c. xii, n. 84, VII, pp. 334–335.

[317] ". . . theosebia dicit cultum interiorem, qui proprie spectat ad virtutes theologicas . . ." *Liber III S.,* d. 9, a. 2, q. 3, conc., III, p. 218.

it is due to God.[318] It is concerned with the offerings of sacrifice—*sacrificium immolationis*—to God, a sacrifice due to God
and to Him alone.[319]

The virtue of *obedience,* another allied virtue of justice, enables
man to obey God. It considers God as the one Who must be
obeyed and the divine command as that which must be obeyed.[320]
Moreover, this virtue enables man to obey not only God, but
also those who take the place of God in this life, i.e., those constituted in authority.[321]

Another allied virtue of justice which is in some manner joined
to the service due to God is the virtue of *penance,* which enables
man to detest his personal sins and to amend his life.[322] It is
concerned with man's own sins against God, because of which
he is deserving of punishment.[323] It considers not so much the
sin that is detested, but the sinning subject against whom it rises

---

[318] ". . . latria non solum est in genere virtutis tanquam in genere remoto,
sed in genere virtutis cardinalis tanquam in genere subalterno; in genere
vero justitiae, sicut in genere propinquo; in genere vero religionis, sicut in
genere proximo." *Ibid.,* p. 217. ". . . ipsa latria respicit Deum, ut cui
honor exhibendus est; respicit etiam cultum exteriorem exhibendum;
respicit etiam rationem exhibendi, videlicet rationem.debiti; et haec est quasi
ratio formalis ipsius . . ." *Ibid.,* ad 6, pp. 218–219.

[319] *Ibid.,* q. 2, ad 3, p. 216; *Decem Praeceptis,* coll. II, n. 17, V, p. 513.—
Dulia, in contradistinction to *latria,* is concerned with the honor and reverence due and paid to the rational creatures. Confer *Liber III S.,* d. 9, a. 2,
q. 4, conc., III, p. 220; *Decem Praeceptis,* coll. III, n. 12, V, p. 517.

[320] ". . . obedientia, qua quis obedit Deo, respicit ipsum Deum, ut cui
obediendum est, ipsum autem mandatum et ejus obligationem respicit sicut
illud quod implendum est . . ." *Liber III S.,* d. 9, a. 2, q. 3, ad 6, III,
p. 218.

[321] ". . . obedientia non solum dicit servitutem debitam ipsi Deo, sed
etiam servitutem his qui sunt loco Dei . . ." *Ibid.,* q. 2, ad 3, p. 216.

[322] ". . . poenitentiae actus est detestari culpam sive peccatum, quia Dei
offensivam, et hoc in reconciliationem sive emendam. Et quia haec ratio
est ipsius justitiae, dico, quod poenitentia est virtus cardinalis, contenta sub
justitia." *Liber IV S.,* d. 14, p. 1, a. 1, q. 3, conc., IV, p. 322.

[323] ". . . poenitentia specialis virtus, quia respicit sub ratione mali proprii
a se contra Deum perpetrati, prout homo ex hoc dignus est puniri." *Ibid.,*
q. 2, conc., p. 321.

up and whom it punishes: not so much the fault, but the amends that must be made.[324]

Disposing man to acknowledge the supremacy of the Eternal and making it possible for him to render to God the honor, reverence, and obedience due Him, is the virtue of *humility,* which, according to the teaching of our author, is also allied to justice.[325] This virtue is the very essence of Christian perfection, for it is the gateway of wisdom, the corner-stone of justice, and the dwelling place of grace.[326] It leads to wisdom, because it teaches the nothingness of man and the sublime greatness of God.[327] It is the corner-stone of justice, because it enables man to render to each his due, especially that reverence and honor belonging to God, which, as Bonaventure expresses it, is "the beginning of justice." [328] It is the dwelling place of grace, because the grace of the Eternal Spirit reposes only in those souls which are humble.[329]

2. *Ad Parentes*

In the second place, piety calls for benevolence towards those who mirror the Eternal Father and from whom man has re-

---

[324] " Nam poenitentia non tantum respicit vitium, quod abominatur, quantum subjectum peccati, contra quod insurgit et quod insurgendo punit; et non tam respicit culpam sive offensam, quam etiam emendam . . ." *Ibid.,* a. 2, q. 1, conc., p. 325.

[325] *Liber III S.,* d. 33, a. 1, q. 4, ad 4, III, p. 721.

[326] ". . . est notandum, quod summa totius christianae perfectionis in humilitate consistit . . ." *De Perf. Evan.,* q. 1, conc., V, p. 120. " Est enim humilitas ostium sapientiae, fundamentum justitiae et habitaculum gratiae." *Ibidem.*

[327] *Ibid.,* pp. 120–121.

[328] " Est etiam fundamentum justitiae. Nam justitia est ' reddere unicuique quod suum est,' tam Deo, quam sibi, quam proximo. Deo autem principaliter debetur honor et reverentia; et hoc reddendum praecipue disponit humilitas. . . . Quoniam ergo initium totius justitiae est cultus et honor divinus, et hic exhibetur Deo ab humilibus; hinc est, quod totius justitiae radix et fundamentum est humilitas." *Ibid.,* p. 121.

[329] *Ibidem.*—Humility, which is the root, foundation, and guardian of all the virtues, empowers us not only to honor and revere God, but also to bear with our fellow-men and to acknowledge our very nothingness. (*Com. in Ev. Lucae,* c. xvii, n. 19, VII, p. 432; *Op. VI, De Perfectione Vitae ad Sorores,* c. 2, n. 7, VIII, p. 112.)

ceived his existence. This type of piety, our Doctor tells us, is commanded by the natural law.[330] To them (i.e., parents) must be rendered not only the *beneficence* due to all men, but *honor, reverence,* and *obedience.*[331] Indeed, as St. Bonaventure teaches, parents are to be honored above all humans, but never above God.[332] Reference may also be made, at this point, to the honor, reverence, and obedience due to those constituted in authority. These latter, he asserts, are to be considered in the same light as parents, because of their position.[333]

3. *Ad Proximum*

Relative to the neighbor, piety assumes the role of mercy, which virtue, together with gentleness, benignity, benevolence, and the like, is to govern man's conduct in reference to his fellow men.

The virtue of *gentleness* (*mansuetudo*) plays an important part in the thought of our author. In fact, he considers it a virtue truly proper to man, who, he tells us, is gentle by nature.[334] Gentleness, whose purpose is to render man social and companionable, stands in opposition to rage and fury.[335] However, it does not exclude all anger, but only that anger which is unjust and unbecoming. Accordingly, the Seraphic Doctor teaches that the individual who remains unmoved over the sin of his neighbor is not truly gentle.[336] For just and zealous anger, itself an allied

---

[330] *Liber III S.,* d. 35, a. 1, q. 6, conc., III, pp. 785–786; *Ibid.,* ad 1–4, p. 786.

[331] "... cum aliis personis debeamus beneficentiam, parentibus nostris non tantum debemus beneficentiam, sed etiam honoris reverentiam ..." *Ibid.,* d. 37, dub. 4, p. 833. Confer *Decem Praeceptis,* coll. V, pp. 522–525.

[332] *Liber IV S.,* d. 42, a. 1, q. 1, f. 4, IV, p. 869; *Decem Praeceptis,* coll. V, n. 10, V, p. 524.

[333] *Ibid.,* nn. 11–13, p. 524.

[334] "Hanc, dico, habuit per lenitatem clementiae, quae est nobilissima pars justitiae et maxime competit homini, quia ejus proprie proprium est, secundum Philosophum, 'esse mansuetum natura,' et ab hac humanitas, id est benignitas ..." *S. de S., De S. Domenico,* IX, p. 565.—Bonaventure's source, as the Editors of Quaracchi note (IX, p. 565, footnote 2) is the *Laws* of Plato and the *De Animalium Historia* of Aristotle.

[335] *In Hex.,* coll. XVIII, n. 29, V, p. 419; *Ibid.,* coll. V, n. 8, p. 355.

[336] "Tamen aliquando putas hominem mansuetum, qui tacet, alio peccante; hoc non est mansuetudo." *Ibidem.*

virtue of justice, demands that we detest every sin in our neighbor.[337]   In this case, however, in order that it may be truly just
and zealous, anger must be directed against the crime committed,
not the person perpetrating it.[338]

From the virtue of gentleness, Bonaventure asserts, is derived
the virtue of humaneness, or *benignity*.[339]   This virtue, also called
friendship, excludes all malice and habilitates the soul for benevolence, tolerance, and internal joy.[340]

In his treatment on benignity the Seraphic Doctor brings out a
teaching which is of importance in the social field, viz., that in
the granting of favors, dignities, and the like we must take into
consideration the manner in which they will be used.   Should
they accrue to the detriment of the individual or of the community, then benignity demands that they should not be given
to him, even if he is our friend, but, instead, that they be given
to one who will make good use of them, even if he is our enemy.
Accordingly, the virtue of benignity concerns the true good of
the individual and of the commonwealth and forbids that which
injures either.[341]   Furthermore, to be truly benign one must be
ready to sacrifice his own private good.   The Seraphic Doctor
tells us that this virtue was unknown in his day and age, because
men were ruled by malice and were too attached to the private
good.[342]

---

[337] ". . . ira per zelum, quae detestatur omne peccatum in proximo est
specialis virtus, quia respicit illud sub ratione digni poena . . ." *Liber IV
S.*, d. 14, p. 1, a. 1, q. 2, conc., IV, p. 321.

[338] "Debet autem esse rigor justitiae respectu culpae, sed dulcor clementiae
respectu naturae." *Com. in Ev. Lucae*, c. ix, n. 81, VII, p. 242.

[339] Confer above, footnote 334.

[340] "Tertio sequitur benignitas, quae est quidam dulcor animae, excludens
omnem nequitiam et habilitans ipsam animam ad benevolentiam, tolerantiam
et internam laetitiam." *Op. 1, De Triplici Via*, c. i, n. 9, VIII, p. 5.—
"Quinta medietas est benignitas, sive nemesis, sive amicitia, quae nihil
habet malignitatis, sed homo vult bonum alii homini . . ." *In Hex.*, coll.
V, n. 9, V, p. 355.
Allied to benignity is the virtue of innocence, whose law commands that
we do not unto others what we do not want others to do unto us. *S. de
T., In Ascensione Domini*, s. viii, IX, p. 325.

[341] *In Hex.*, coll. V, n. 9, V, p. 355.

[342] "Mundus hodie ignorat istam benignitatem; unde totus mundus in
maligno positus est, quia homo non diligit nisi bonum privatum." *Ibidem,*

Consequent upon benignity and allied to it is the virtue of *benevolence*, which not only excludes all malice, but empowers man to shower benefits and kindness upon all. Its law dictates that we do unto others as we would want others to do unto us.[343] The virtue of benevolence is principally opposed to the vice of envy, which Bonaventure terms the *fera passima,* the cruelest of wild beasts.[344]

Finally, we come to the virtue of *mercy,* which is concerned with our duty towards the neighbor who is in need. It is contained in that law of piety which commands that the weak be supported by the strong.[345] This virtue of mercy, acting in conformity with the dictate of the natural law and the rule of prudence, considers: (a) the need and misfortune of the neighbor, (b) the conformity of nature in the neighbor.[346] Mercy, however, must be in conformity with the laws of justice; otherwise it would be a vice, not a virtue.[347] Thus, for example, to show mercy to one who would, in turn, injure or corrupt the other members of the social body, is not an act of virtue.[348]

---

[343] "Ad perfectionem etiam benevolentiae exigitur, quod homo benefaciat in omnibus; unde et subditur: Et prout vultis, ut vobis faciant homines, et vos facite illis similiter." *Com. in Ev. Lucae,* c. vi, n. 72, VII, p. 156.

[344] *S. de T., Dom. III p. Pent.,* s. 1, IX, p. 367.

[345] "Item, lex pietatis, hoc exigit, ut sustentetur indigens a potente . . ." *Liber II S.,* d. 11, a. 1, q. 1, f. 4, II, p. 277. Confer *S. de B. V. M., De Annuntiatione B. V. M.,* s. vi, IX, p. 685; *Liber III S.,* d. 33, dub. 1, III, p. 728.

[346] ". . . misericordia-virtus respicit conformitatem in natura et necessitatem in indigentia sive miseria . . ." *Liber III S.,* d. 35, a. 1, q. 6, conc., III, p. 786. ". . . misericordia conformatur dictamini juris naturalis et secundum regulam prudentiae . . ." *Ibid.,* ad 1–4, p. 786.

[347] ". . . pietas misericordiae sine veritate justitiae est potius vitium quam virtus." *S. de T., Dom. in Palmis,* s. i, IX, p. 243.

[348] ". . . pietatis simul et justitiae lex exposcit; ne, dum crudeli misericordia uni membro putrido parcitur, in totius corporis sospitatem putrens corruptio diffundatur." *Op. XIX, Epistolae Officiales,* Ep. II, n. 4, VIII, p. 470. Confer *Op. XIII, Determinationes Quaestionum,* pars 1, q. 14, VIII, p. 346.

The Seraphic Doctor teaches that the inordinate love of private good is the cause of unmercifulness. (*Com. in Ev. Lucae,* c. xvi, n. 35, VII, p. 415.)

To complete the picture presented by our author, we have the *gift of*

D. *The Tenor of Justice in Bonaventure's Teaching*

In conformity with the command to render to each his due, the virtue of justice, as has been mentioned, so rectifies the soul that man is enabled to reverence and obey his superiors, to be benevolent to his equals, and to condescend mercifully to the aid of his inferiors.[349]

Hence, the Seraphic Doctor cannot be satisfied with that state of affairs in which the rule of strict, cold, and severe commutative justice governs the activities of the various social entities. Indeed, the characteristic note of justice, in the teaching of the saintly Franciscan, is not severity, but friendship, companionship, and agreeableness (*suavitas*).[350] Accordingly, he tells us that justice attains its utmost perfection in clemency, gentleness, and humaneness.[351] Only that justice which is identified with the meting out of punishment should possess the note of severity.[352] Even here, room must be made for piety and mercy; for, in such cases, the rigor of justice, which refers to the fault committed, must be tempered by clemency, which refers to the nature of the sinner.[353] For Bonaventure, he who is excessively severe

piety which enables man to be benevolent to all because of the divine image impressed upon all men. Whilst mercy considers the conformity of nature, the gift of piety considers the image of God in man; while mercy acts in accordance with the rule of the natural law, piety acts in conformity with the rule of the divine law; and whilst mercy is in conformity with the rule of prudence, piety is in conformity with the rule of the gift of knowledge. (*Liber III S.*, d. 35, a. 1, q. 6, conc., and ad 1-4, III, pp. 785-786.)

[349] " Directio vero justitiae consistit in hoc, quod voluntas rectificatur in reddendo unicuique quod suum est, utpote superioribus subjectionem et reverentiam, paribus conformationem et benevolentiam, inferioribus condecensionem et providentiam . . ." *S. de Diversis, De Modo Vivendi,* IX, p. 724.

[350] " Item, in occidente suavitas justitiae, quae est in exhibitione pietatis— volunt enim leges, poenas mitigari; unde finis justitiae non est severitas, sed benignitas . . ." *In Hex.*, coll. VI, n. 18, V, p. 363. Confer *Ibid.*, n. 10, p. 362.

[351] Confer above, footnote 334.

[352] " Tertio modo dicitur justitia magis proprie, secundum quod dicit rectitudinem in reddendo id quod est poenae; et accipitur ibi justitia pro severitate." *Liber III S.*, d. 33, dub. 1, III, p. 728.

[353] ". . . increpando per justitiam et sanando per clementiam. Debet

is not truly just. In fact, he believes justice is not right and true unless it is tempered by mercy.[354]

This teaching of the Seraphic Doctor cannot but exert tremendous influence upon the social sphere. Hence, we find our author calling for a society of mutual succour, not competition; a society of friends, not rivals and strangers. His plea is for a society that is governed by friendship, benevolence, and mercy—a society in which each individual member comes to the aid of his fellow and supplies for the latter's deficiencies, whether they are along the economical, educational, or moral lines. Witness, for instance, his words:

> "As good dispensers of the divine gifts, each one is bound to administer to the other according to what he has received. This is done by aiding the needy, by teaching the ignorant, by correcting the delinquents, by bearing with the malicious, by comforting the afflicted, by elevating the fallen, by having compassion on all unfortunates, by showing peace and love to all men." [355]

Indeed, one may ask how the Seraphic Doctor could, with all his constant insistence upon the unity of mankind, the brotherhood of all men, the universal human hierarchy, and the Mystical Body of Christ, teach otherwise.

SECTION 4. THE VIRTUE OF CHARITY

As we have seen, the duty of justice is to order rightly the external relations of the different human individuals, so that each

---

autem esse rigor justitiae respectu culpae, sed dulcor clementiae respectu naturae." *Com. in Ev. Lucae*, c. ix, n. 81, VII, p. 242.

[354] "Et haec est recta descriptio voluntatis bonae, in qua consistit rectitudo justitiae, quae esse non potest sine dulcore misericordiae." *S. de Diversis, De Modo Vivendi*, IX, p. 724. Confer *Liber IV S.*, d. 46, a. 2, q. 4, conc., IV, p. 966; *S. de T., Dom in Palmis*, s. i, IX, p. 243.

[355] ". . . quoniam unusquisque gratiam, secundum quod accepit, in alterutrum debet administrare sicut boni dispensatores multiformis gratiae Dei. . . . Et hoc idem fit, cum indigentibus exhibetur subventio, ignorantibus eruditio, delinquentibus correptio, malignantibus supportatio, afflictis confortatio, cadentibus elevatio, ceteris miseris compassio et cunctis hominibus pax et dilectio . . ." *S. de Diversis, De Modo Vivendi*, IX, p. 724.

individual member of the social whole occupies that place which rightly belongs to him. It protects the rights of the individual by commanding that unto each must be given his just due. However, while justice effects a certain unity and orderliness, this unity is neither lasting nor perfect. For, considering only those things which *must* be done—viz., those things that man *owes* to his neighbor—justice may effect a certain external orderliness, a certain unity and oneness of bodies. It does not, however, bring about a true unity of souls. The result is that the various social entities, though rendering to each his due and respecting one another's rights, continue to be strangers to one another.

Something more than justice, then, is required. Hence, as has been noted, the Seraphic Doctor urges man to step beyond the realms of strict and severe commutative justice. It is his desire that man should be governed not solely by the debt of strict justice that he owes his neighbor, but also by that justice which denotes friendship and reaches its supreme heights in clemency, gentleness, humaneness, benignity, benevolence, and mercy.

According to Bonaventure's teaching, justice itself will deteriorate—its observance will become difficult—unless it is perfected by love.[356] As he tells us, love, and love alone, will enable us to render unto each his due.[357] For this reason, he envisions a society of friends, who are united as one not by an imposition from without, but by the bond of mutual love.[358] Therefore, love, with its unifying force, must be the crowning element of the social order.[359]

The love that the Seraphic Doctor has particular reference to is the theological virtue of charity—the virtue by means of which man loves God above all else because of Himself, and his neigh-

---

[356] " Nisi enim quia proximum suum diligat, non est facile, ut jus debitum sibi reddat." *Liber III S.,* d. 33, a. 1, q. 4, ad 3, III, p. 721.

[357] ". . . nemini quidquam debeatis, nisi ut invicem diligatis." *S. de Diversis, De Modo Vivendi,* IX, p. 724.

[358] *In Joannem,* c. xvii, coll. 61, nn. 4–5, VI, p. 609.

[359] ". . . amor . . . vis est unitiva . . . vis est transformativa . . . est vis liberaliter diffusiva." *Apologia Pauperum,* c. iv, n. 2, VIII, pp. 252–253. Confer *S. de T., Dom. XIV p. Pent.,* s. i, IX, p. 407; *Liber II S.,* d. 38, a. 1, q. 4, conc., II, pp. 888–889.

bor because of God.[360] For the saintly Franciscan Doctor, charity
is rightly ordered love, the only virtue which can rectify the
affectus of man, because it prescribes that the greater good (God)
must be preferred to the lesser good (creature).[361] Above all,
charity is for him the virtue which unites man to the Infinite
Good, the virtue which enables man to adhere to God entirely and
to love whatever he may love because of God.[362]

From what has been said, it must readily appear that the
principal object of the virtue of charity is the Supreme and
Eternal Good.[363] As St. Bonaventure tells us, charity has but
one *ratio movens*—namely, the Highest Good, which is most
lovable (*summe amabilis*) both as it is *in se* and as it is participated in by creatures.[364] The *Summum Bonum,* therefore,
is the principal object of the virtue of charity, which desires that
it (the *Summum Bonum*) should be possessed by God *essentialiter*
and in a participated manner by all those who have been made
to the image of God, and who are, consequently, capable of
God, i.e., capable of possessing Him and delighting in Him.[365]

---

360 "Caritas enim Deum facit diligi propter se et proximum propter
Deum . . ." *Liber III S.,* d. 27, a. 2, q. 4, conc., III, p. 610. Confer
Ibid., q. 6, conc., p. 614; *Op. I, De Triplici Via,* c. 2, n. 8, VIII, pp. 9–10.

361 ". . . caritatis est rectificare affectum; sed affectus non est rectus,
nisi praeponat majus bonum minori bono . . ." *Liber III S.,* d. 29, a. 1,
q. 1, f. 4, III, p. 638. Confer *Ibid.,* q. 2, f. 4, p. 641; *In Hex.,* coll. VII,
n. 14, V, p. 367; *Brev.,* p. 5, c. 8, V, pp. 261–262.

362 ". . . maxima caritas maxime desiderat uniri Deo et habere Deum."
Liber III S., d. 26, a. 1, q. 1, ad 5, III, p. 557. ". . . caritas omnino
adhaeret summae Bonitati et propter illam amat quidquid amat . . ." *Ibid.,*
d. 27, a. 1, q. 2, f. 1, p. 594. Confer *Brev.,* p. 5, c. 8, V, p. 261.

363 ". . . istud autem bonum, quod caritas optat, unum solum est, videlicet
bonum aeternum et bonum summum." *Liber III S.,* d. 27, a. 1, q. 2, conc.,
III, p. 594.

364 "Sed caritas nam solam habet rationem moventem, videlicet ipsam
Summam Bonitatem, quae cum sit summe amabilis, et prout est in se, et
prout participatur a creatura, utroque modo caritas eam amat, et sic habet
unam rationem motivam . . ." *Ibid.,* ad 4, p. 595.

365 "Per caritatem enim diligo summum bonum Deo et summum bonum
mihi, ita quod volo, quod Deus habeat summum bonum et sit summum
bonum per essentiam, mihi vero per participationem . . ." *Ibid.,* d. 29, a. 1,
q. 2, ad 4, p. 642. Confer *Ibid.,* d. 37, a. 1, q. 2, conc., and ad 1, pp.
594–595.

Accordingly, the formal and proper act of charity is to love the *Summum Bonum* and him who is capable thereof.[366]

Charity, then, tends first of all to God, because He is its principal object. Hence, Bonaventure tells us that the *inclinatio ad Deum* is the cause of the *inclinatio ad proximum*.[367] Again, he remarks: " One cannot come to the perfect love of his neighbor unless he first comes to the perfect love of God, because of Whom the neighbor, who is not lovable except on account of God, is loved." [368] It is because of God, therefore, that we are to love our fellow-man—because of the image of God that has been imprinted on him. For, our author states, the honor as well as the dishonor rendered to the image of God in man refers back to the prototype—the Eternal.[369] Therefore, the two commands of charity—love of God and love of neighbor—are so intimately interwoven that we cannot have the one without the other.

Accordingly, the *ratio* of charitable affection towards our fellows must be the image of the Creator in them.[370] From this point we may argue that if the image of God in man is the *ratio diligendi*, then charity embraces all men. Thus, the Seraphic

---

[366] *Ibid.*, d. 28, a. 1, q. 1, conc., p. 622.—In Bonaventure's teaching, there are four which are to be loved *ex caritate:* God, our souls, our neighbor, and our body. God, since He is the *Summum Bonum in se*, and, consequently, the *summe beatum* and the *summe beatificativum.* Our soul and the neighbor, since they are *idonea beatificari*, i.e., capable of being united to and delighting in Him. Our body, since it, too, through its union with the soul, is *beatificabile* with the spirit. (*Brev.*, p. 5, c. 8, V, pp. 261–262; *In Hex.*, coll. XVIII, n. 27, V, p. 418.)

[367] ". . . caritas prius inclinat ad Deum quam ad proximum, cum Deus sit objectum principalius et inclinatio respectu ipsius Dei sit causa inclinationis respectu proximi." *Liber III S.*, d. 27, a. 2, q. 4, conc., III, p. 610.

[368] " Ad hanc perfectam dilectionem proximi non pervenitur, nisi prius perveniatur ad perfectam dilectionem Dei, propter quem diligitur proximus, qui non est amabilis nisi propter Deum." *Op. I, De Triplici Via*, c. 2, n. 8, VIII, p. 10.

[369] ". . . quia homo est imago Dei, et honor et dehonoratio imaginis ad prototypum refertur; ideo, sicut ex caritate diligi debet homo in quantum imago, sic etiam et in ipsum peccari potest." *Liber IV S.*, d. 15, p. 2, a. 2, q. 4, ad 1, IV, p. 376.

[370] ". . . ratio diligendi proximum est imago . . ." *Liber III S.*, d. 29, a. 1, q. 5, ad 3, III, p. 649. Confer *Ibid.*, d. 28, a. 1, q. 1, ad 2, p. 623.

Doctor tells us that all men, inasmuch as they are men—images of God, capable of eternal beatitude—are to be loved *ex caritate*.[371] Consequently, the neighbor whom we must love as ourselves is each and every man, no matter what his sex, dignity, race, color, or creed.[372]

Nevertheless, while St. Bonaventure acknowledges that we must love all men, he does not fail at the same time to speak of a certain gradation in reference to the virtue of charity. The following is the order of love established by the Seraphic Doctor: (1) God; (2) ourselves, or what he terms the *bonum proprium;* (3) those to whom we are joined by ties of blood—in this section our saintly author speaks of an ascending grade (love of son for father) and a descending grade (love of father for son); (4) those to whom we are united by some tie other than the conformity of nature, as, e.g., members of the same household, friends, members of the same profession, fellow-citizens, etc.; (5) those who share with us a conformity of nature—strangers and enemies; and (6) our bodies.[373]

This much needed virtue of charity plays a very important role in the social life. In the first place, it rectifies the *affectus* and will of man; by placing the greater good above the lesser, it gives him a true sense of values.[374] It requires that God be preferred to the creature, that the glory and honor of the Eternal be placed before our own temporal good,[375] that the neighbor be loved more than any present utility,[376] and that the neighbor's eternal salvation be valued more than his temporal prosperity.[377]

---

[371] *Ibid.*, q. 3, conc., p. 627.

[372] ". . . nomine proximi intelligitur omnis homo cujuscumque sexus, cujuscumque dignitatis, cujuscumque virtutis." *Ibid.*, dub. II, p. 634. Confer *Com. in Ev. Lucae,* c. x, n. 49, VII, p. 268.

[373] *Liber III S.,* d. 29, dub. III, III, p. 653; *Ibid.,* a. 1, q. 3, pp. 643ss; *Ibid.,* d. 28, a. 1, q. 4, conc., p. 629; *Liber II S.,* d. 3, p. 2, a. 3, q. 2, conc., II, p. 128; *Liber IV S.,* d. 40, a. 1, q. 1, f. 2, IV, p. 847; *Brev.,* p. 5, c. 8, V, pp. 261–262; *In Hex.,* coll. XVIII, n. 27, V, p. 418.

[374] Confer above, footnote 361.

[375] *Liber I S.,* d. 17, p. 1, a. 1, q. 1, ad 9, I, p. 295; *Liber II S.,* d. 1, p. 2, a. 2, q. 1, ad 2, II, p. 44.

[376] *Com. in Ecc.,* c. iv, v. 56, q. 4, VI, p. 39.

[377] *De Sex Alis,* c. 2, n. 5, VIII, p. 133.

In the second place, it fosters and protects right order, since charity, as our Saint writes, is not simply a tie that binds, but also a *pondus* (weight) effecting perfect order. Like corporeal weight, which draws bodies to the center of gravity, charity draws man towards God by virtue of its tendency to the *Summum Bonum*, and towards his fellow-men because of the image of the Eternal that has been impressed upon them.[378]

Again, it is charity which promotes the practice of virtue and the observance of law. Hence, St. Bonaventure calls charity "the mother of virtues." [379] He writes: "If you have love, you will be the lover of virtue in yourself, in others, and in its fountainhead (God)." [380] He also terms charity "the guardian of the necessarily observe the law, whose end is charity.[382] Further-laws." [381] According to his teaching, whoever loves *good* will more, through the medium of charity all sense of constraint, force, servitude, and fear gives way to true liberty, for whoever has charity performs the good because of love and, therefore, does so freely.[383]

Above all, it is charity that produces a true and perfect oneness among the various members of society—that oneness which is the end of all social living.[384] For the entrance of charity into

---

[378] "Nec tantum est caritas vinculum ligans, sed etiam pondus inclinans; 'quod enim est pondus in corporibus, hoc est amor in spiritibus.'" *Liber III S.*, d. 29, a. 1, q. 1, conc., III, p. 639. Confer *Ibid.*, d. 31, a. 3, q. 1, ad 3, p. 690; *Ibid.*, d. 27, a. 2, q. 1, f. 4, p. 602; *Ibid.*, d. 36, a. 1, q. 6, pp. 805ss.

[379] ". . . caritas dicitur esse mater virtutum, non quia illas generat, sed quia illa fovet et nutrit . . ." *Ibid.*, d. 23, dub. 6, p. 506.

[380] ". . . Concupiscentia disciplinae parit dilectionem. Cura ergo disciplinae est dilectio. Si enim habes disciplinae dilectionem, eris amator virtutis in te et in aliis et in suo fonte." *In Hex.*, coll. II, n. 4, V, p. 337.

[381] "Dilectio autem custodia legum est." *Ibidem.*

[382] "Si enim diligis bonum, observas legem, quia finis praecepti est caritas de corde puro." *Ibidem.*

[383] "Disciplina autem non debet esse servilis, sed liberalis, ut diligat disciplinantem, ut ex amore faciat, non ex timore." *Ibidem.*

[384] ". . . totius hierarchiae finis et consummatio est unitiva dilectio." *Exp. Super Reg. Fr. Min.*, Intro., n. 2, VIII, p. 392.
". . . amor virtus est unitiva, ubi major est amor, ibi major est et pax et unitas et concordia." *S. de B. V. M., De Purificatione B. V. M.*, s. iv, IX, p. 653.

the social order makes it possible for man to sacrifice the *bonum proprium* in favor of the common good; it enables the different members to aid one another, to support one another's burdens, and to join forces in the promotion of the common good.[385] Stressing the conformity of nature and the unity of grace and eternal reward, the virtue of charity enables us to love our neighbor as ourselves.[386] Moreover, recalling to mind our common divine origin, redemption, and sanctification, this virtue teaches us that the human race is a universal family, in which all men are the adopted children of the Eternal Father, the brothers of Christ and His co-heirs.[387]

When all is said and done, if all men could be joined together by the indestructible bond of charity, then the economic and racial differences which pit man against man would fade away—for we would all form a sole terrestrial human hierarchy, one Mystical Body of Christ.[388] This social ideal—all men *actually* welded into the one Mystical Body of Christ by the virtue of charity, which automatically safeguards the rights of justice and fosters all the other social virtues—lies at the very root of our Seraphic Doctor's social thought. It is the guiding principle of his whole social outlook. It is his social Philosophy.

In Bonaventure's teaching, good is the principle of order and unity in the domain of will and operations, whereas evil is the principle of multiplicity and dispersion. (*Liber II S.,* d. 38, a. 1, q. 4, conc., II, pp. 888–889.)

[385] *Liber III S.,* d. 29, a. 1, q. 3, ad 1, III, p. 644; *Liber IV S.,* d. 20, p. 2, a. 1, q. 1, f. 3, IV, p. 530; *Liber II S.,* d. 1, p. 2, a. 2, q. 2, conc., II, p. 46.

[386] " Et vere debet diligere proximum quasi se ipsum propter conformitatem naturae . . . propter etiam unitatem gratiae . . . propter unitatem mercedis aeternae. . . . Ideo ad commendandam hanc dilectionem voluit Deus, quod nasceremur ex uno patre Adam; quod redimeremur eodem sanguine, scilicet sanguine Domini nostri Jesu Christi; quod remuneraremur eadem mercede . . ." *Com. in Ev. Lucae,* c. x, n. 49, VII, p. 268.

[387] *Liber III S.,* d. 10, a. 2, q. 2, III, pp. 235–237.

[388] *De Donis,* coll. III, n. 13, V, pp. 471–472; *Brev.,* p. 4, c. 5, V, p. 246.

CONCLUSION

Despite the fact that St. Bonaventure did not devote a single work, nor even a notable portion of a single work, to problems of social philosophy, a careful study of his writings clearly reveals that he has left us many pertinent thoughts relative to the manner in which man should live in society. Without presuming to arrange his social teaching into a systematic study, we have endeavored to marshal these social thoughts of the Seraphic Doctor in orderly and logical fashion. One thing now remains—to summarize briefly what appear to be the most salient features of his social doctrine.

One of the more important points of St. Bonaventure's teaching is his insistence that the virtue of justice is, on the one hand, necessary for the existence of harmonious social relations and, on the other hand, insufficient of itself to guarantee perfect social living.

Since the virtue of justice prescribes that each be given his just due, its role in the social order cannot be exaggerated. Indeed, because it enjoins respect for the rights of the various individual members of the social organism, justice is therefore required not only for the perfection of society, but also for its very existence. Without justice, the fullness of the human person—i.e., the rights natural to him as man and the dignity which is his as an image of God—would be denied. Without it, man would become a mere means for the advancement and aggrandizement of others and would, as a result, be degraded to below the human level.

In his insistence upon the command of justice—viz., let each one receive his just due—the Seraphic Doctor stresses a point that should be given serious consideration by those who have been blessed with the gift of authority, no matter what this authority may be. He insists that there can be no hope of establishing and preserving harmonious social relations unless the rights of the individuals—rights that are sacred and innate—are respected. Nor does he stop at this point. He adds logically that the rights of the individuals, in turn, cannot be rightfully respected unless God—the Author of all rights—be first rendered *His* due. Not only the perfection, therefore, but the very existence of society demands acceptance of the fact that rights exist—rights that are innate and inviolable, that must be respected and protected. These rights are: first and foremost, the rights of God; and second, the rights of His image, man.

In this way, then, the Seraphic Doctor prescribes one of the remedies sorely needed to cure the evils of our day and age— evils which are rooted in neglect and contempt of duties. Indeed, if we examine modern mentality, we find that men and nations place undue stress upon their own rights while forgetting, neglecting, or relegating to the background the rights of others and the duties to which these rights give rise. Men and nations, today, concern themselves solely with what they *can* do, not with what they *must* do—solely with what is *due* them, not with what they *owe* others. This, in truth, is the cankerous sore of present-day society. Because of their egotistical concentration upon themselves and what is due them, men and nations forget that they, in turn, have duties to perform—towards God, towards their fellow-men, towards other nations.

This cancer must be cured if harmonious social relations are to exist. However, the cure cannot come from imposition from without. It cannot derive from more laws and increased authority. If anything, it must come from within, from a realization of the full extent of the law of justice, which demands that not only one's own rights, but the rights of all be respected.

At the same time, the Seraphic Doctor is nevertheless not satisfied with a state of affairs in which the rule of strict, cold, severe commutative justice governs the activities of the various social entities. Indeed, the characteristic note of justice, in the teaching of the saintly Franciscan, is not severity, but friendship. He urges man, therefore, to step beyond the realm of heartless " *do ut des.*" It is his desire that man's social relations be governed not solely by the debt of strict justice that he owes his neighbor, but also by that justice which is tempered by friendship and which reaches its zenith in benignity, humaneness, benevolence, and mercy.

As a matter of fact, according to his teaching, stern justice must deteriorate if left to itself. Justice alone is insufficient. By protecting the rights of individuals in commanding that each be accorded his just due, by rightly ordering the external relations of the various human individuals so that each member of the social whole occupies the place which rightly belongs to him, justice effects, it is true, a certain unity and orderliness. This unity, however, is neither lasting nor perfect. Something else is required to render this unity lasting and perfect, i.e., love or charity.

Since he envisions a society of friends, united as one not by an imposition from without, but by the bond of mutual love, he demands, therefore, that the rule of justice be complemented by the virtue of charity. Hence, not justice alone—but justice aided, abetted, and elevated by charity—is, according to Bonaventurian thought, the perfect rule of social life.

This thought brings us face to face with still another striking feature of Bonaventure's social thought, i.e., his demand for harmony and mutual aid in society—his demand for a society of friends and mutual abettors.

The Seraphic Doctor is fully cognizant of the fact that selfishness leads to disorder and destruction. He is fully aware that harmonious social relations are impossible when the actions of men and nations are regulated by selfishness, by personal and national aggrandizement, by inordinate greed for more wealth and inordinate lust for more power. This vicious struggle for increased power and increased wealth, destroying as it does all hope of just and lasting peace, cannot but bring about contentions and lay the foundations for yet other world-wide holocausts of young, innocent lives in total, bloody warfare.

Accordingly, the picture of social living painted by the Seraphic Doctor is one in which each individual has a role to fulfill, a role that is never totally and solely personal—never egotistical. Each role, whether that of the lowest manual laborer or that of the most exalted contemplative, must redound not solely to the good of the individual concerned, but also to the good of all the members of the social whole. For every gift received from the One and Eternal Benefactor is endowed with a social character—it was created for the good of humanity as a whole. Consequently, these gifts are not to be restricted to the advantage and advancement of the recipients alone. On the contrary, they must be put to work. They must be used in such a manner as to be of service to all. Indeed, if these *bona* (be they economical, intellectual, or spiritual) are not communicated—if they are not used in such wise that their benefits extend throughout human society—they do not live up to the purpose of their creation.

The Seraphic Doctor, therefore, calls for a society of friends and mutual abettors, a society from which all individual egotism is excluded. His plea is for a true unity whereby each member of the community (whether marital, familial, civil, national, or international) may find support, consolation, and protection. His ideal is a society in which all (both individual men and individual nations) work hand in hand for the betterment of all the members of the Universal Human Hierarchy—a society in which all men of all nations may be provided with those means (material, intellectual, and moral) with which each man may the more efficaciously live a virtuous and truly human life here on earth and thereby attain to his final and eternal end.

However, what strikes our inquiring gaze most forcibly is the fact that the saintly Franciscan recognizes nothing but the real and the entire man. For him, man is a creature composed of body and soul, made to the image and likeness of the Eternal and destined to ultimate union with that Supreme Good in Whom alone he can find true rest and perfect fruition. For him, man, as a person, is lifted above material creation and rendered a responsible agent—subject to rights and duties, deserving of rewards and punishments. For him, man is a social being ordained to live in society, but never to become so much a part of society as to lose his own identity, for man as a person is immediately ordered to God as to his one and only end. Finally, for him, man, having fallen from the state of innocence, has been redeemed by Christ and elevated to the supernatural life.

Therefore, the saintly son of the Seraphic Father, St. Francis of Assisi, is never totally and solely concerned with the material, the temporal, or the earthly aspect of man as such. As the basis of all his writings there underlies his one main theme: the ordering of all things to God, the central Being whence they came—the *Reductio.* Thoroughly imbued with this Theo-centric thought, the outstanding characteristic of all his writings, the Franciscan Doctor refuses to center his attention on man as the inhabitant of earth alone, but invariably reverts to the concept of man as destined for heaven. Man's last end—his return to God—is always brought to the fore. This, then, is the reason why he demands that the two constituent parts of the universal terrestrial hierarchy—the civil and the ecclesiastical—must work hand in hand towards the attainment of the same end, i.e., the formation here on earth of a vestibule to the Heavenly Jerusalem, whence man, when called by his Divine Judge, may safely step into his celestial home of eternity.

BIBLIOGRAPHY

PRIMARY SOURCES

Bonaventure, St., *Doctoris Seraphici S. Bonaventurae S. R. E. Episcopi Cardinalis Opera Omnia* . . . edita studio et cura PP. Collegii S. Bonaventurae . . . anecdotis aucta, prologomenis, scholiis notisque illustrata, ad Claras Aquas (Quaracchi) ex typographia Collegii S. Bonaventurae, 1882–1902.

——, *Breviloquium*, V, pp. 201–291.

——, *Collationes De Decem Praeceptis*, V, pp. 507–532.

——, *Collationes De Septem Donis Spiritus Sancti*, V, pp. 457–503.

——, *Collationes in Evangelium S. Joannis*, VI, pp. 533–634.

——, *Collationes in Hexaemeron, sive Illuminationes Ecclesiae*, V, pp. 329–454.

——, *Commentaria in Quatuor Libros Sententiarum Magistri Petri Lombardi*, I–IV.

——, *Commentarius in Ecclesiasten*, VI, pp. 1–99.

——, *Commentarius in Evangelium S. Joannis*, VI, pp. 237–530.

——, *Commentarius in Evangelium S. Lucae*, VII, pp. 1–604.

——, *Commentarius in Librum Sapientiae*, VI, pp. 105–233.

——, *De Reductione Artium Ad Theologiam*, V, pp. 319–325.

——, *Itinerarium Mentis in Deum*, V, pp. 295–316.

——, *Op. XI, Apologia Pauperum contra Calumniatorem*, VIII, pp. 233–330.

——, *Op. VI, De Perfectione Vitae ad Sorores*, VIII, pp. 107–127.

——, *Op. VII, De Regimine Animae*, VIII, pp. 128–130.

——, *Op. VIII, De Sex Alis Seraphin*, VIII, pp. 131–151.

——, *Op. XIII, Determinationes Quaestionum Circa Regulam Fratrum Minorum*, VIII, pp. 337–374.

——, *Op. I, De Triplici Via. Alias, Incendium Amoris*, VIII, pp. 3–27.

——, *Op. XIX, Epistole Officiales*, VIII, pp. 468–474.

——, *Op. XVI, Expositio Super Regulam Fratrum Minorum*, VIII, pp. 391–437.

——, *Op. XXIII, Legenda Sancti Francisci*, VIII, pp. 504–564.

——, *Op. III, Lignum Vitae*, VIII, pp. 68–87.

——, *Op. XIV, Quare Fratres Minores Praedicent et Confessiones Audiant*, VIII, pp. 375–385.

——, *Op. II, Soliloquium De Quatuor Mentalibus Exercitiis*, VIII, pp. 28–67.

——, *Op. X, Vitis Mystica, seu Tractatus De Passione Domini*, VIII, pp. 159–229.

267

Bonaventure, St., *Quaestiones Disputatae De Mysterio Trinitatis*, V, pp. 45–115.

——, *Quaestiones Disputatae, De Perfectione Evangelica*, V, pp. 117–198.

——, *Quaestiones Disputatae, De Scientia Christi*, V, pp. 3–43.

——, *Sermones De Beata Virgine Maria*, IX, pp. 633–721.

——, *Sermones De Diversis*, IX, pp. 723–731.

——, *Sermones De Sanctis*, IX, pp. 463–631.

——, *Sermones de Tempore*, IX, pp. 23–461.

——, *Sermones Selecti De Rebus Theologicis*, V, pp. 535–579.

GENERAL WORKS

Aristotle, *Works of Aristotle* translated into English under the editorship of W. D. Ross, Oxford, Clarendon Press, 1931.

Augustine, St., *De Bono Conjugali, P.L.*, 40, 373–396.

——, *De Civitate Dei, P.L.*, 41, 13–804.

——, *De Diversis Quaestionibus LXXXIII, P.L.*, 40, 11–100.

Bernard, St., *Sermones in Cantica*, Sermo 23, *P.L.*, 183, 884–894.

——, *Sancti Bernardi Abbatis De Considerate Libri Quinque ad Eugenium Tertium, P.L.*, 182, 727–808.

Bissen, Jean Marie, O.F.M., *L'exemplarisme Divin selon Saint Bonaventure*, Paris, Librairie Philosophique, J. Vrin, 1929.

Boethius, *De Consolatione Philosophiae, P.L.*, 63, 547–870.

——, *Liber De Persona et Duabus Naturis contra Eutychen et Nestorium, P.L.*, 64, 1338–1354.

Bonnefoy, J., O.F.M., *Le Saint-Esprit et Ses Dons selon Saint Bonaventure*, Paris, Librairie Philosophique, J. Vrin, 1929.

Bozitković, G., O.F.M., *S. Bonaventurae Doctrina de Gratia et Libero Arbitrio*, Balneis Marianis, Egerland, 1919.

de Carvalho e Castro, Léonard, O.F.M., *Saint Bonaventure, le Docteur Franciscain*, Études de Théologie Historique, Paris, Beauchesne, 1923.

Casanova, Gabriele, O.F.M., *Cursus Philosophicus ad Mentem D. Bonaventurae et Scoti*, in 3 volumes, Madrid, Aquado, 1904.

Culhane, Daniel, *De Corpore Mystico Doctrina Seraphici*, Doctoral Dissertation, Seminarium Sanctae Mariae ad Lacum, Mundelein, Ill., 1934.

Dady, Mary Rachael, *The Theory of Knowledge of St. Bonaventure*, C. U. Dissertation (Philosophical Studies, volume LII), Washington, 1939.

De Wulf, Maurice, *History of Mediaeval Philosophy* (third English edition based on sixth French edition) translated by Ernest C. Messenger, London, Longmans, Green and Company, 1935, 1938.

Doms, Herbert, *Vom Sinn und Zweck der Ehe*, Breslau, Ostdeutsche Verlagsanstalt, 1935.

——, *The Meaning of Marriage*, translated by George Sayer, New York, Sheed and Ward, 1939.

Gemelli, Agostino, O.F.M., *The Franciscan Message to the World*, translated by H. L. Hughes, London, Burns, Oates and Washbourne, 1934.

Gilson, Étienne, *La Philosophie de Saint Bonaventure*, Paris, Librairie Philosophique, J. Vrin, 1924.

———, *The Philosophy of Saint Bonaventure*, translated by Dom Illtyd Trethowan and F. J. Sheed, New York, Sheed and Ward, 1938.

Gratian, *Decretum, P.L.,* 187, 1–1912.

Gregory the Great, St., *Sancti Gregori Magni Romani Pontificis Moralium Libri, sive Expositio in Librum B. Job, P.L.,* 75–76.

Healy, Emma Therese, *Saint Bonaventure's De Reductione Artium ad Theologiam*, (A Commentary with an Introduction and Translation), Doctorial Dissertation, St. Bonaventure College, St. Bonaventure, N. Y., 1939.

Hugh of St. Victor, *Eruditio Disdascalia, P.L.,* 176, 739–838.

———, *Expositio In Hierarchiam Caelestem S. Dionysii Areopagitae, P.L.,* 175, 923–1154.

Isidore of Seville, *Etymologiarum Libri XIII, P.L.,* 82, 74–727.

James, O.F.M. Cap., *The Franciscan Vision* (Translation of St. Bonaventure's Itinerarium Mentis in Deum, with an introduction), London, Burns, Oates and Washbourne, 1937.

Jarrett, Bede, O.P., *Social Theories of the Middle Ages, 1200–1500*, Westminster, Maryland, The Newman Book Shop, 1942.

Killeen, Sylvester M., O. Praem., *The Philosophy of Labor According to Thomas Aquinas*, C. U. Dissertation (Philosophical Studies, volume XLIX), Washington, 1939.

Leclercq, Jacques, *Marriage and the Family*, translated by Thomas R. Hanley, O.S.B., second edition, New York and Cincinnati, Frederick Pustet, 1942.

Legowicz, Hippolyte, J. L., O.F.M., *Essai sur la Philosophie Sociale du Docteur Séraphique*, Fribourg (Suisse), Galley and Cie, 1936.

McDonald, William J., *The Social Value of Property According to St. Thomas Aquinas*, C. U. Dissertation (Philosophical Studies, volume XLVIII), Washington, 1939.

Mollitor, Sabinus, O.F.M., *The Virtues of a Religious Superior* (being a translation of St. Bonaventure's De Sex Alis Seraphim), St. Louis, Herder, 1921.

Nölkensmeier, Christ, O.F.M., *Etische Grundfragen bei Bonaventura*, Forschungen zur Geschichte der Philosophie und der Pädagogik, Band V, Heft 2, Leipzig, 1932.

O'Donnell, Clement M., O.M.C., *The Psychology of St. Bonaventure and St. Thomas Aquinas*, C. U. Dissertation (Philosophical Studies, volume XXXVI), Washington, 1937.

O'Leary, Conrad John, O.F.M., *The Substantial Composition of Man According to Saint Bonaventure*, C. U. Dissertation (Philosophical Studies, volume XXII), Washington, 1931.

Ostheimer, Anthony L., *The Family, A Thomistic Study in Social Philos-*

ophy, C. U. Dissertation (Philosophical Studies, Volume L), Washington, 1939.

Plato, *The Dialogues of Plato,* Jowett trans., 2 vols., New York, Random House, 1937.

Pope, Leo XIII, *Quod Universa.*

Pope, Pius XI, *Casti Connubi.*

Pope, Pius XII, *Summi Pontificatus.*

Von Hildebrand, Dietrich, *Die Metaphysik der Gemeinschaft,* München, 1930.

——, *Reinheit und Jungfräulichkeit,* München, Kösel-Pustet, 1927. English translation: *In Defense of Purity,* New York, Longmans, Green, 1931.

Van Lieshout, *La Theorie Plotinienne de la Vertu,* Fribourg, 1926.

Zeiller, J., *L'idée de l'Etat dans saint Thomas d'Aquin,* Paris, Alcan, 1910.

PERIODIC LITERATURE

Böhner, Philotheus, O.F.M., "Die Natürlichen Werte der Ehe nach dem hl. Bonaventura," in *Franziskanische Studien,* Münster, XXIV (1937), pp. 1–17.

di Fonzo, Laurentius, O.F.M. Conv., "De Belli Liceitate Quid Ceonseat S. Bonaventura," in *Miscellanea Francescana,* XLI (1941), pp. 34–48, Rome, edita per cura della Pontificia Facoltà Teologica dei Frati Minori Conventuali di Roma, 1941.

Doucet, Victorinus, O.F.M., "De Naturali seu Innato Supernaturalis Beatitudinis Desiderio," in *Antonianum,* IV (1929), pp. 167–208, Rome, 1929.

Imle, F., "Die Gemeinschaftsidee in der Theologie des hl. Bonaventura," in *Franziskanische Studien,* XVII (1930), pp. 325–341, Münster, 1930.

——, "Sozialuntersciede und Sozialausgleich nach dem hl. Bonaventura" in *Franziskanische Studien,* XIX (1932), pp. 81–98, Münster, 1932.

Longprè, Ephrem, O.F.M., "Bonaventure, S." in *Dictionnaire D'histoire et de Géographie Ecclésiastique,* 740–788, edit. A. de Meyer et Et. Van Cauwenbergh, Paris, 1937.

——, "La theologie mystique de saint Bonaventure" in *Archivum Franciscanum Historicum,* XIV (1921), pp. 36–108, Quaracchi, 1921.

McAndrew, P. J., "Theory of Divine Illumination in St. Bonaventure," in *The New Scholasticism,* VI (1932), pp. 32–50, Washington, 1932.

Meier, Ludger, O.F.M., "Bonaventuras Selbstzeugnis über seinem Augustinismus," in *Franziskanische Studien,* XVII (1930), pp. 342–355, Münster, 1930.

Tinivella, Felicissimus, O.F.M., "De Impossibili Sapientiae Adeptione in Philosophia Pagana Juxta Collationes in Hexaemeron S. Bonaventurae," in *Antonianum,* XI (1936), pp. 27–50, 135–186, 277–318, Rome, 1936.

Van den Borne, Crescentius, O.F.M., "De Fontibus Commentarii S. Bonaventurae in Ecclesiasten," in *Archivum Francescanum Historicum,* X (1917), pp. 257–270, Quaracchi, 1917.

Wegemer, Ludger, O.F.M., "St. Bonaventure, the Seraphic Doctor. His Life and Works," in *Franciscan Studies,* II (1924), pp. 5–38, New York, Wagner, 1924.

INDEX